D1029548

CHILD SEXUAL ABUSE

Child Sexual Abuse

AN INTERDISCIPLINARY MANUAL FOR DIAGNOSIS, CASE MANAGEMENT, AND TREATMENT

Kathleen Coulborn Faller

New York   Columbia University Press

Columbia University Press
New York   Guildford, Surrey
Copyright © 1988 Columbia University Press
Printed in the United States of America

Chapter 9 was written by Mary Westhoff, M.D. and Mary Steinberg.
Dr. Westhoff is in private pediatric practice and Dr. Steinberg
is Assistant Professor of Pediatrics, Oregon Health Services
University in Portland, Oregon. She was formerly Clinical
Instructor of Pediatrics, University of Michigan.
Chapter 15 was written by Donald N. Duquette, Professor of Law,
University of Michigan.

Library of Congress Cataloging-in-Publication Data

Faller, Kathleen Coulborn.
Child sexual abuse.

Bibliography: p.
Includes index.
1. Sexually abused Children—Mental health.
2. Sexually abused children—Mental health services.
3. Child psychotherapy.   4. Child molesters—Rehabilitation. I. Title. [DNLM: 1. Child Abuse, Sexual—
psychology. 2. Interview, Psychological. 3. Psychotherapy. WA 320 F194c]
RJ507.S49F35 1987   616.85'83   87-15064
ISBN 9-231-064705

c 10 9 8 7 6 5 4 3 2

Clothbound Columbia University Press Editions are Smyth-sewn
and printed on permanent and durable acid-free paper

Book design by J.S. Roberts

Contents

Acknowledgments

Endeavors in the sexual abuse field can be very lonely even in an academic community that is dedicated to the social welfare of disadvantaged and stigmatized populations. Therefore, special thanks are due to those who have offered me encouragement in my work.

First I would like to acknowledge my debt to Rosemary Sarri who has always supported me in my work even though my approach and field are different from hers.

Second there are three colleagues who read chapters of this book at crucial points in its development and offered me both suggestions and much needed encouragement. They are Betty Blythe, Vivian Shapiro, and Diana Russell.

Third I would like to express my appreciation to both Dean Harold Johnson and Associate Dean Yeheskel Hasenfeld of the University of Michigan School of Social Work who thought this book was a worthwhile pursuit and urged me to finish it.

Fourth my family, Lincoln Faller and Helen Marie McIntosh Faller, deserve my sincere gratitude for tolerating the many hours I was absent from them working on this book in my study.

Fifth I must also thank my colleagues from IPCAN, especially Sue Smith, the project coordinator, with whom I often discussed cases, Judi Kleinman, our child psychiatrist, and Donald Duquette, who has written the legal chapter of this book. Mary Steinberg and Mary Westhoff, the two doctors who wrote the medical chapter, also deserve my sincere appreciation.

Sixth I wish to express my gratitude to the Columbia University Press, and particularly to Maureen McGrogan who was so enthusiastic about the manuscript.

CHILD SEXUAL ABUSE

PART I: THE CHARACTERISTICS OF CHILD SEXUAL ABUSE

CHAPTER ONE

The Parameters of the Problem
for Professionals

I. INTRODUCTION

That adults can be sexually attracted to and sexually active with children is both bewildering and overwhelming to many people in the helping professions. Yet in increasing and alarming numbers, situations of sexual abuse are being recognized and require intervention. Physicians in their private practices and in public medical facilities are being asked if a medical diagnosis of sexual abuse can be made. Law enforcement personnel are obliged to investigate sexual abuse as a crime. Child protection case workers are receiving growing numbers of referrals of cases where children are at risk from ongoing sexual abuse. Social workers in a variety of capacities must identify, diagnose, and treat current situations of sexual abuse. Mental health professionals of all kinds are seeing adults who were victims of sexual abuse as children and who are finally seeking treatment. Lawyers are being required to employ the juvenile court process to protect victims and to pursue prosecution of sexual offenders in the criminal court.

An additional challenge to the helping professions is that cases may not manifest themselves as sexual abuse but rather as other types of child dysfunction. A delinquent adolescent may be displaying anti-social behavior because of a longstanding sexually abusive home situation. A child brought to a physician for enuresis, encopresis, or sleep problems may be having such symptoms because of sexual abuse. Children who have difficulty concentrating or doing school work may be victims of sexual abuse. Drug and alcohol use, suicide attempts, and running away may all be sequelae of sexual abuse.

Moreover, other family problems or problems of other family members may be related to sexual abuse. Situations where a mother seeks treatment for frigidity or a couple complains of marital discord may both have sexual abuse as an underlying difficulty. A wife may seek assistance in handling her husband's substance abuse although she does not request help for the sexual abuse it precipitates. A woman may come with her children to a battered women's shelter when her husband is physically and sexually assaulting not only her but her children as well.

Yet helping professionals receive little training in sexual abuse. It is not ordinarily covered in the curricula of schools of social work, psychology graduate programs, medical schools, or law schools. Sexual abuse is a specialty area and requires knowledge beyond that found in most professional training programs.

The purpose of this book is to provide important and needed information to professionals who are likely to be confronted with child sexual abuse. Although the book is directed primarily to mental health professionals, the authors are accustomed to addressing an interdisciplinary audience that also includes doctors and nurses, law enforcement personnel, attorneys, and child welfare and court staff. The material in this book regarding assessment can greatly assist protective services workers, medical staff, and attorneys, as well as mental health professionals, in investigation techniques. In addition, chapters on intervention can alert those persons not directly involved in treatment but responsible for important case decisions about how to structure intervention, what the treatment issues are, and how to assess the effects of intervention. Moreover, there are chapters in this book that are written by physicians and an attorney, known for their expertise in child sexual abuse, which can serve as guidelines for the respective professions, as well as inform mental health professionals and others about medical and legal aspects of child sexual abuse.

Nevertheless, the main purpose of this book is to provide a comprehensive assessment, case management, treatment manual for mental health professionals who find themselves involved in cases of child sexual abuse.

II. THE PROFESSIONAL'S OWN FEELINGS ABOUT SEXUAL ABUSE

Sex and death are two taboo and emotionally laden topics in our society. Not everyone is suited to working with the dying, and not everyone is suited to working with the sexually traumatized. A prerequisite for professionals who intend to work in the area of sexual abuse is to deal with their own emotional reaction to cases. Feelings must be recognized, understood, and handled if the professional is to be successful in helping victims and others who are affected.

Many people are not comfortable with their own sexuality, nor with the sexuality of others. Professionals likely to be involved in child sexual abuse are not immune to these difficulties. A level of comfort about sex in general is necessary; otherwise, uneasiness about human sexuality will exacerbate the professional's emotional reactions to sexual abuse.

In addition, the professional working in this area must arrive at sufficient understanding of the problem and its complexities so that feelings do not cause inappropriate responses to allegations of sexual abuse. We have noted two opposing emotional reactions. One is avoiding, ignoring, superficially dispensing with, or disbelieving sexual abuse allegations. The other is one of extreme rage at the perpetrator. Neither of these responses is productive in dealing with sexual abuse.

Avoidance or disbelief usually reflects the fact that the professional cannot conceive of an adult having a sexual relationship with a child and therefore goes to extreme lengths to explain away the sexual abuse. This explaining away can have several manifestations. One is that "something else happened." The child misinterpreted a gesture as a sexual one or physical evidence was in fact caused by something else. Kim's experience in the example below is illustrative.

> EXAMPLE 1:   Kim, age 11, told her school counselor that her mother's boyfriend had been fondling her breasts, had touched her vulva, and had placed her hand upon his penis. She said his penis was hard when she touched it. When the boyfriend was interviewed by the police officer investigating the case, he told the officer that he wrestled with Kim and may have accidentally brushed against her breasts which he observed were just beginning to blossom. When the officer interviewed Kim, he asked about wrestling with her mother's boyfriend. He did not ask about the fondling, and Kim was too awed to bring it up. The officer concluded that the boyfriend had accidentally touched Kim's privates during wrestling and that she had misinterpreted this. The officer had a ten-year-old daughter with whom he wrestled.

In this case the police officer identified with the boyfriend and concluded that something other than sexual abuse had happened. The officer wrestled with his own daughter but did not sexually molest her. The boyfriend must be like him, and therefore could not sexually abuse a child.

A second way of explaining away an allegation is to redefine it as a fantasy or a dream. This happened in Sally's case.

EXAMPLE 2:   Sally, age 7, told her father, stepmother, a police officer, and her physician about incidents of fondling by her stepfather. She said on visits to her mother, who is a noncustodial parent, that her stepfather would fondle her vagina. He did this for so long that it hurt and at one point he stuck his finger inside her vagina. Her mother and two brothers would be outside when these things happened. They had occurred in both the living room and the bedroom.

Sally's father took her to a psychologist who questioned her intensely about whether this had really happened. Since she had told her father about the abuse at bedtime, the psychologist began to suggest to her it was actually a dream. He also told her that if her stepfather had really done this, it was a very bad thing and he would go to jail. Sally did not want her stepfather to go to jail. Her mother was about to have his baby. After about three hours with the psychologist, Sally changed her story and said what she had thought was real was a dream. Subsequently, her father sought an evaluation from an expert in sexual abuse. The first thing Sally told the expert was that she had seen a man doctor who was very confusing. When she told him something happened, he told her it was a dream. After evaluating Sally, the expert concluded that Sally had been sexually abused but the psychologist wanted to believe the abuse was a dream.

Children do fantasize and they do dream. However, a true allegation of sexual abuse can almost always be differentiated from a fantasy or dream by the explicitness of the assertion about what has taken place: the child can describe the context in which the sexual abuse occurred and the specific sexual acts. (See chapter 5 for further discussion of fantasies and how to differentiate a true allegation from fantasy).

Third, persons may try to explain the sexual abuse away by attempting to prove that the child is lying. An argument may be made that children lie and make up stories, or alternatively, that this particular child is well known as a liar. The case of Susan is illustrative.

EXAMPLE 3:   Mrs. Brown elicited and obtained the support of her 13-year-old daughter, Susan's, school counselor in her efforts to persuade professionals that Susan was lying when she said her mother's living-together-partner had been sexually abusing her for two years. The reasons the counselor gave for siding with the mother and disbelieving Susan were that she regularly lied to her mother about why she was late coming home from school and she faked sick sometimes so she could leave school and go home. The counselor added that Susan encouraged other children to skip class and smoked cigarettes. Thus, you couldn't believe anything she said. The counselor assisted the mother in setting up a mental health evaluation of Susan that was to lead to her commitment to residential treatment. The counselor believed that any child so disturbed as to make up a story about sexual abuse should be institutionalized. The evaluator concluded Susan had been sexually abused and that removal from the home to foster care, not residential treatment, was indicated.

Children do lie, but generally to protect themselves. Quite the opposite outcome is likely when a child asserts she has been sexually abused. She may arouse the wrath of the perpetrator and sometimes of her mother. Further, she may perceive professional responses to her reports as problematic rather than protective (for further discussion of situations when children lie, see chapter 5). Clearly it is devastating for the child victim to have professionals wrongly assert she is a liar.

On the other hand, as noted earlier, an allegation of sexual abuse may elicit quite the opposite response from professionals, that of rage. Rage may be focused on the offender and sometimes on the situation that is seen as allowing him to engage in sex with children, for example, a collusive mother or a society which supports male dominance. Rage often leads people to see punishment and retribution as the only legitimate way of responding to sexual abuse. Thus, all perpetrators should be criminally prosecuted and incarcerated for as long as possible, as was the reaction in the case cited below.

> EXAMPLE 4: Mr. H was left to care for his two stepdaughters, Sandy, 11, and Jane, 9, while their mother was in the hospital having a mastectomy. He was playing a game called roly-poly with them in which he rolled them up in a blanket and then they rolled down the hill in the backyard. He became sexually aroused during the game and had them rub his penis. Mr. H confessed to his wife and sought treatment. The therapist called the police. Mr. H also confessed to the police. He was then criminally prosecuted. He pled guilty because he did not want the children to have to testify. He was given a three-year sentence. The whole family was quite bitter. Mrs. H had to go on AFDC and continued to have medical problems. She had no one to help her with the children. The children felt responsible for their stepfather going to prison and both tried to say the sexual abuse had not occurred.

In this case anger is focused on the perpetrator. The anger may also come to be focused upon the non-perpetrating parent, "the collusive mother." Believing an assertion made by some professionals (e.g., Walters 1975; Sarles 1975) that mothers collude in the sexual abuse of their daughters, professionals may blame and punish the victim's mother for the sexual abuse. Professionals may confront the mother, insisting she confess to knowledge of the sexual abuse, remove the victim from her care even though the child is safe from the perpetrator, isolate the mother from the child, exclude her from decisions about what will happen to the child, and fail to inform her of other actions being taken on the case.

The example below illustrates this type of professional response to the mother.

EXAMPLE 5:   An allegation was made by Mrs. J's babysitter to Protective Services that her daughter, Jane, 4, was a victim of sexual abuse. The allegation was based upon the fact that Jane was observed rubbing her vulva and it was red. The babysitter did not share her concerns about Jane with Mrs. J. Protective Services interviewed Jane in the presence of the babysitter and concluded that the father was sexually abusing the child. An ex parte order for emergency placement was obtained and Jane was removed from the babysitter's home to the children's shelter.

The worker returned to inform the mother that Jane had been placed in care and why. The worker was very confronting with the mother regarding her role in the sexual abuse. Only then did the worker find out that the parents were separated and that the father saw the child only on weekends. The worker then wanted to know why the mother did not supervise these visits. The mother was bewildered and affronted by these statements and queries. She had never thought of her husband as sexually aberrant. He had recently left her for another woman, and she had no indication of his being sexually attracted to children.

Subsequent mental health examination failed to validate that Jane had been sexually abused, and subsequent medical evaluation revealed Jane had pinworms which cause redness and itching of the vulva.

In this instance, the concerns on the part of the babysitter and the Protective Services worker were legitimate, but the trauma to the child and her mother would have been minimized if the worker had not immediately assumed the mother was colluding in the sexual abuse.

Similarly, persons may feel that our society is to blame for sexual abuse because it allows child pornography, does not vigorously prosecute sex crimes, and is male dominant. In the example below some of these attitudes lead to responses that are not in the children's best interest.

EXAMPLE 6:   Roberta was the director of an advocacy group that assisted victims of sexual abuse. She herself had been a victim of physical and sexual abuse as a child. She was assisting Mrs. D and her two children, Laura, 7, and Jeanie, 3. Mrs. D and her husband were divorced and Mr. D had sexually abused the girls when he had them for a three-week visit during the summer. Mrs. D's goal was to get treatment for her ex-husband and to have supervised visits for the children. However, Roberta told her that she ought to seek criminal prosecution. She also told Mrs. D that visits with the father would be traumatic even if supervised.

Roberta had counseling sessions with Mrs. D, her children, Mrs. D's fiance, and Mrs. D's parents, who were very supportive of Mrs. D. She frequently blamed men in general for sexual abuse of the girls and would talk about the need for women to stick together and combat male domination. This ideology was incompatible with the views of the D family, who held rather traditional views of male and female roles, and made the men in the D family uncomfortable. Roberta persuaded Mrs. D not to present the children for visits with Mr. D, which had been court ordered and were to be supervised by the paternal grandmother. As a result, Mrs. D was found to be in contempt of court and was jailed for ten days. Mrs. D gave Roberta temporary custody of the children while she went to jail, and Roberta "went underground" with them, taking them to a victims' shelter in another state. This experience was very traumatic for the girls.

Upon their return, the court ordered an evaluation of the whole family. Among the findings from the evaluation were that both girls had been sexually abused by their father, but they also loved him and wished visits if he wouldn't "do the bad things." Mr. D was also found to be treatable.

In this case, Roberta's angry reactions were rooted in her childhood experience, but professionals who have not suffered such trauma may also have to struggle with strong emotions. Roberta's lack of mastery of her feelings caused insensitivity to the D family's needs and concerns.

While a reaction of rage to sexual abuse is very understandable, it may cloud the professional's judgment. It can trigger a response that is traumatic for the child because it fails to take into account the individual child's needs. For example, the child may love the perpetrator and suffer when he is punished. Or the child may be further damaged by a requirement of court testimony. Further, a vindictive reaction may not make distinctions between sexual offenders who can be helped and those who are not treatable.

One goal of this book is to assist professionals so that their emotional responses do not interfere with their ability to help children and families who are involved in child sexual abuse. Identifying common emotional responses to child sexual abuse is one way of achieving this goal. Another way this book will endeavor to address this problem is by providing the best information presently available regarding diagnosis, case management, and treatment of this very troubling problem. If professionals have data and guidelines which assist them in understanding why sexual abuse happens, what its effects are, and what treatment is effective, such knowledge is likely to temper the professional's emotional reactions to sexual abuse.

In addition, this book hopes to desensitize the professional. Many explicit case descriptions are included. While initially they may seem overwhelming to the uninitiated, there is a reason for including them: it is not to shock but to desensitize the reader. Further, if we cannot name the problem, read about it, listen to victims, and talk with them about what has happened, how can we ever expect to help them? As long as we are too uncomfortable to deal directly with exactly what happened to them, we are aloof, too distant to help the children and their families.

III. A VICTIM-CENTERED APPROACH

This book propounds a victim-centered approach as a philosophy for dealing with sexual abuse. What this means is that, as professionals handle cases, they must be ever mindful of what is in the victim's best interest and pursue that interest. The ultimate question must be what will help the child to be safe from future sexual abuse, to resolve feelings, and to function better. Other interests must take a subordinate position.

In pursuing best interest, professionals must ascertain what the victim's wishes are. In most cases they will coincide with best interest, but occasionally they will not, and then the professional should pursue best interest. For example, in one of our cases, an eight-year-old girl, who was being made to have intercourse with her stepfather, cried when told she was going to go into foster care. She said she would miss her cat, was afraid there would not be anyone to play with, and did not want to go to a different school. She was placed despite these feelings because she could not be protected at home. In fact, there were other children at the foster home to play with, and she was transported to her old school. However, she did not get to see her cat. The older the child, the more able she will be to make realistic and rational requests, and therefore the more weight should be given to her wishes.

There are implications of a victim-centered approach at all stages of intervention. First, when children must tell professionals about the sexual abuse, efforts should be made to minimize the number of times they must tell the story. For example, the interview could well be taped. Also, children should be protected from interrogation by persons likely to disbelieve them. Second, in considering whether or not there should be a medical exam, not only should the likelihood of findings be considered but also the impact of the examination upon the child. If the potential benefits of the physical do not outweigh its potential costs, the exam should not be pursued. Third, in deciding whether or not to place the child outside the home, both the possibility of subsequent sexual abuse and the potential pressure from and emotional abuse by family members need to be assessed. Further, in deciding about a placement, the child's attachments as well as safety should be important considerations. Fourth, primary determining factors regarding criminal prosecution of the perpetrator should be the child's wishes and the anticipated effect upon the child of testifying, not the child's ability to testify and whether or not there is a "good legal case." If the child must testify, every effort should be made to minimize the trauma (see chapter 15). Fifth, when the child is placed and visitation is arranged, whom the child wants to see should be the most important consideration in visitation arrangements and care should be taken to ensure that the child is not harassed by family members during visits. Sixth, in long-term planning, issues regarding reunification of the family should be resolved based upon the child's wishes and the parents' ability to provide a safe and nurturing environment. These are just some of the guidelines that result from a victim-centered approach.

The logical conclusion of this approach is that the author does not adhere to a rigid protocol regarding handling of sexual abuse cases. The police or the criminal court need not always be involved, and there will even be cases where the juvenile court is not used although it could be. Because coercive intervention is often quite damaging to the child, the minimum amount of court intervention needed to achieve the child's best interest should be the criterion for court involvement. Sometimes it will be in the child's (and society's) interest to have the perpetrator prosecuted to the full extent of the law. Other times it will not be. Similarly, we do not always advocate a family-centered approach and treatment for family members. Such a plan should be pursued when it seems likely that such intervention will be successful, return is in the child's best interest, and reunification is desired by the child.

IV. DEFINITIONS of SEXUAL ABUSE

Professionals vary in the definitions they use for sexual abuse. The definitions employed in this book will be ones that are oriented toward mental health issues in child sexual abuse and will focus on how the victim experiences the sexual behavior.

A. General Definition

Sexual abuse is any act occurring between people who are at different developmental stages which is for the sexual gratification of the person at the more advanced developmental stage. This definition assumes a dyadic relationship. However, it is possible to have more than two people involved in a sexually abusive encounter, both victims and perpetrators. Ordinarily the actors in sexual abuse are adults and children, but sometimes both victims and perpetrators are children. The perpetrator may be an adolescent and the victim a latency-aged or younger child. Alternatively, the victim may be the same age as the perpetrator but at an earlier developmental stage because of mental retardation.

Some professionals may challenge this definition, arguing that sexual abuse is not a sexual act, that other motivations underlie the behavior. It is true that sexual gratification is not the only dynamic involved in sexual abuse (or, for that matter, in other sexual interactions) but it does play a role, and it is the feature that distinguishes sexual abuse from other interactions between people at different developmental stages. The definition does not preclude the possibility that the victim also experiences some sexual arousal and pleasure.

Finally, this definition includes both interactions where there is physical contact between perpetrator and victim and those where there is none. Subcategories will be defined below.

B. Specific Types of Sexual Abuse

1. *Noncontact sexual abuse.* There are three types of sexual abuse where there is no physical touching.

a. *"Sexy talk"* includes statements the perpetrator makes to the child regarding the child's sexual attributes, what he or she would like to do to the child, and other sexual comments. Examples are the following: "I'd like to fuck you," or "I bet you'd be good in bed." One perpetrator in our sample said, "I like to eat your mother's pussy and I bet yours would taste even better."

b. *Exposure* includes the perpetrator's showing the victim his/her intimate parts (breasts, penis, vagina, anus) and/or masturbating in front of the victim. One father in our sample would wait until his 14-year-old stepdaughter was looking at him and then pull open his bathrobe, exposing his penis. He would do this in the morning when she was getting ready for school.

c. *Voyeurism* includes instances when the perpetrator either covertly or overtly observes the victim in a state of undress or in activities that provide the perpetrator with sexual gratification. These may include activities others do not regard as even remotely sexually stimulating, for example, observing an infant having her diaper changed or watching a child take a bath. Sometimes the perpetrator will request that the child disrobe. A living-together-partner in our sample took the bathroom door off so that he could watch the 11- and 13-year-old daughters in the family going to the toilet, entering and exiting the shower, and engaging in other private behavior.

2. *Sexual contact* includes any touching of the intimate body parts. These are the breasts, vagina, penis, buttocks, anus, and perineal area. The perpetrator may fondle the victim, he may induce the victim to touch him, or the victim and perpetrator may engage in mutual fondling or masturbation. The fondling can be either on top of or underneath the clothing if participants are dressed and would be directly on the skin if the participants are not clothed. *Frottage* is sexual contact in which the perpetrator gains sexual gratification from rubbing his intimate parts against the victim's body or clothing. One father in our sample would sit with his 11-year-old daughter between his legs while they watched television and rub his erect penis against her buttocks and back while both of them were clothed.

3. *Oral-genital sex* involves the perpetrator's licking, kissing, sucking or biting the child's genitals or inducing the child to orally copulate with him. The behavior may be *cunnilingus* (oral contact with the vagina), *fellatio* (oral contact with the penis), or *analingus* (oral contact with the anus). It can include mutual oral copulation although this is relatively uncommon in sexual abuse, probably because the discrepancy in size between victim and perpetrator makes such encounters physically difficult to execute. In our sample, most of the oral-genital contact was fellatio, with a male perpetrator inserting his penis in a child victim's mouth. A typical example from our cases is one with two victims, ages three and five, who reported their daddy made them "kiss his wiener" and then he "peed in our mouths."

4. *Interfemoral intercourse* is intercourse in which the perpetrator's penis is placed between the child victim's thighs. The terms "dry" and vulvar intercourse are also used for this act. The offender usually places his legs outside the child's legs to keep them together. The child may be on top of or underneath. There may be rubbing of the penis against the child's vulva, but there is no penetration. This technique is frequently employed with young victims where the vaginal opening is too small to permit penile entry or when the perpetrator fears injuring the victim. Sometimes the perpetrator employs this technique because he thinks it permits the victim to remain a virgin. With an older child, interfemoral intercourse may be employed to avoid the risk of pregnancy. A three-year-old girl in our sample reported to her mother that her step-

father "humped" her. Further inquiry ascertained that he would lie on top of her, placing his penis between her legs and with his legs outside hers. He would ejaculate into a towel he placed underneath her.

5. *Sexual penetration* is characterized by some intrusion into an orifice. Four types have been noted in sexual abuse.

a. *Digital penetration* involves placing fingers in the vagina or the anus or both. Occasionally fingers in the mouth may be sexual abuse. Usually the victim is penetrated by the perpetrator, but sometimes the perpetrator induces the victim to engage in penetration. In one of the author's cases, a mother would have her seven-year-old daughter lie on her (the mother's) stomach, with both of them naked, and there would be mutual digital penetration of vaginas. The daughter was also instructed to suck the mother's breasts. Digital penetration is a form of sexual abuse found frequently with young victims. Sometimes digital penetration is a prelude to genital or anal intercourse. The perpetrator stretches the vaginal or anal opening with one, two, or more fingers and at a later time performs genital or anal intercourse.

b. *Penetration with objects* is a less frequent type of sexual abuse. The perpetrator puts an instrument in one of the victim's orifices—vagina, anus, or occasionally the mouth (for example, a dildo in the mouth). The most frequent type is vaginal penetration. The objects involved are of a variety of types. In our sample they include electric vibrators and dildos, an enema, a ruler, a pair of scissors, crayons, a carrot, and a cucumber.

c. *Genital intercourse* involves the penis entering the vagina. Sometimes the penetration is partial because of the small size of the victim's vagina. There is usually a male perpetrator and female victim, but occasionally a female perpetrator may be involved in genital intercourse with a male victim. The victim in the latter type of situation is likely to be somewhat older, frequently an adolescent. In our sample, ejaculation occurred in about half of the cases of genital intercourse and it was usually in the victim's vagina. A case which typifies sexually abusive genital intercourse is one where the mother's boyfriend initiated genital intercourse when the victim was ten. She said each time he would try to get his penis farther in. The victim described these encounters as very painful. She would beg him to stop. He would always ejaculate in her vagina; however, he told her he could not get her pregnant because he had been in an accident. This pattern persisted for three years.

d. *Anal intercourse* occurs when the perpetrator's penis is placed in the victim's anus. This technique often occurs with male victims but it is also sometimes employed with female victims. In the latter instance, the perpetrator may be trying to avoid pregnancy. However, in other cases in our sample anal intercourse occurred with female victims when a host of other forms of sexual abuse were also present, or when the perpetrator was very angry at the victim. For example, in one of our cases an 11-year-old girl was beaten and subjected to vaginal and anal intercourse by her 15-year-old half-brother.

6. *Sexual exploitation* includes situations of sexual victimization where the person who is responsible for the exploitation may not have direct sexual contact with the child. Often this responsible person is involved for financial gain and not for sexual gratification. Two types of sexual exploitation will be described.

a. *Child pornography* involves taking pictures of children. These may be stills or movies or videotapes. They may be for the perpetrator's private use; he may trade the pornography, or he may sell it. Still shots may be used in pornographic magazines, where a story or description augments the effects of the pictures. The nature of the sexual gratification is different from that of other types of sexual abuse that have been described, in that it arises primarily from viewing material (and in some cases reading about the pictures) rather than from engaging in acts with children.

The behavior of children in the pornographic material can comprise any of the sexual acts between children and adults described thus far. It can also include children posing in a manner that might be perceived as seductive, or children engaging in normal behavior, such as taking a bath, which, for the observer, is sexually arousing. In addition, sexual activities between children or between children and adults may be staged and photographed as child pornography.

Children who are runaways or for other reasons vulnerable to exploitation may be used in child pornography by persons who produce it commercially. We also have several cases in our sample of parents who made pornographic pictures or movies of their children, including some recorded on home video equipment, and then sold these to commercial producers of child pornography.

b. *Child prostitution*. Both male and female children may become involved in prostitution. Regardless of the sex of the victim, the clients are almost always male. In the majority of cases we are aware of, the children are in late latency or adolescence. However, in one case there was a victim who was five and in another a victim of six. Children who are caught up in prostitution are often runaways. They have escaped from what they viewed as an untenable home situation and have become involved in prostitution to support themselves. One of the girls in our sample, age 14, ran away from home where she was being sexually abused by her stepfather and was taken in by a pimp who had her having sex with seven or eight men a day.

Children rarely "go into business for themselves." Usually an adult introduces them to this form of activity. Thus, a pimp takes the child in or the victim is persuaded by an adult that prostitution is a way to make money.

7. *Sexual abuse in combination with other abuse.* The sexual behaviors described above include most of the types of sexual abuse noted in the literature and found in our sample. However, there are many variations and combinations of these acts, and sexual abuse may be found in combination with other insults. For example, occasionally urination and defecation play a role. In some cases physical mistreatment is an integral part in the sexual abuse; in others drugs and alcohol are given to the victim. Also there are instances where the perpetrator obtains gratification from rather bizarre encounters. An illustration of such a situation from our experience is a case in which a stepfather got into bed between his ten-and eight-year-old stepdaughters. While he engaged in anal intercourse with the ten year old, he had the eight year old fondle his nipples and call out repeatedly, "Do it to her."

C. Differentiating Intrafamilial from Extrafamilial Sexual Abuse

Sexual abuse is further divided for the purposes of this book into two categories, *intrafamilial* and *extrafamilial*. The term family implies not only to the status of living in the same household but also being related so that cases involving extended family members outside the household are intrafamilial. Most cases of intrafamilial sexual abuse are incestuous, that is, situations where the perpetrator and victim are related by blood and legally are prohibited from marrying. However, stepfathers and living-together-partners are members of the family and often psychological parents to victims; sexual abuse involving adults in these roles is also intrafamilial sexual abuse. Other authors may use different terms to make this distinction between related and nonrelated sexual abuse, but there is general agreement that these two categories should be differentiated. Not only will the nature of the sexual abuse and the closeness of the relationship between victim and perpetrator differ for the two categories, but legal intervention may vary. For further discussion of differences between intra- and extrafamilial sexual abuse, see chapter 3.

V. THE FUNCTIONS OF SEXUAL ABUSE

If one accepts the contention that even dysfunctional behavior is functional, then what purpose does sexual abuse serve? There are four common functions: (1) an outlet for sexual feelings; (2) an expression of angry feelings; (3) an effort to express and receive affection; and (4) an opportunity to exert power. The extent to which any sexually abusive act is motivated by each of these four functions will vary from case to case.

Some professionals have argued that sexual abuse is not a sexual act (Groth 1981; Sgroi 1982). However, as already pointed out, the characteristic that differentiates sexual abuse from other adult-child interactions is that it is sexual. Those who see it as nonsexual argue that other motivations are also present and may even prevail, but this is also true of other sexual interactions. For example, when a married couple engages in sexual intercourse, ideally this should also be an opportunity to give and receive affection. Yet we do not define such intercourse as a "pseudosexual act." Moreover, there are numerous descriptions by perpetrators of sexual arousal preceding sexual abuse and statements by victims describing erect penises and ejaculation. Thus, at minimum sexual abuse is an expression of sexual feelings. (See also Finkelhor 1984).

The second function sexual abuse may serve is the expression of rage. The anger can be toward women in general, a particular woman, the victim, or other circumstances in the perpetrator's life. Groth and Birnbaum (1979) describe anger rape as one of the major types of rape, noting that the rapist is usually angry at someone other than the victim. When the victim is a child, the mother is often the cause of the anger. This may be because there are marital problems or because she has dissolved the marriage. Alternatively, the anger may be more primal and related to the perpetrator's uncaring relationship with his own mother when he was a child. Other circumstances in the perpetrator's life, including economic adversities, physical incapacities, and other personal disappointments, can lead to anger which is indirectly expressed as sexual abuse.

Thirdly, sexual abuse may be an attempt on the part of the perpetrator to give and receive nurturance or affection. Frequently sexual encounters will be preceded by appropriate physically affectionate behavior. For example, a father hugs and kisses his daughter while she is sitting on his lap but then becomes aroused and asks her to masturbate him. Sex and affection may be fused because the perpetrator has little experience in showing love other than with sex. The perpetrator may also be emotionally immature and thus feel at ease seeking care or sex from a child. In the latter type of case, the relationship between child and adult may be very intense and sometimes symbiotic.

Fourth, the expression of power or dominance may play a role in sexual abuse. The perpetrator chooses as a victim, a child, who by definition is weaker than the perpetrator and vulnerable to exploitation. Often he feels the need to exert such control because of his own sense of powerlessness in other situations. He may be a man who is under the control of others at work, is generally ineffectual in the world outside the family, has some disability, or has a dominant wife. Because he feels impotent in these arenas, he will strive for potency in encounters with the child.

VI. PREVALENCE AND INCIDENCE RATES

Sexual abuse is difficult human behavior to study. It is behavior that is taboo and usually enacted in secrecy. Both victims and offenders are loath to report occurrences. It is very likely that only a small percentage of cases come to professional attention. There are two major sources of data regarding prevalence and incidence: retrospective studies of adults concerning their experiences of victimization as children and cases reported annually to the child protection system which has a central data bank. Two recent retrospective studies have enormously enlightened professional understanding of the prevalence of sexual abuse, those of Finkelhor (1979) and of Russell (1983).

Finkelhor (1979; 1986) collected data from 796 students at six New England colleges and universities (530 females and 266 males). He inquired about their sexual experiences when they were children. His definition included noncontact sexual abuse as well as sexual contact. In his sample, 19.2 percent of women and 8.6 percent of men had been sexually abused as children. The perpetrator was more likely to be a relative in the case of female victims than in the case of male victims, where the perpetrator was more likely to be an acquaintance or stranger. The encounters with female victims were usually heterosexual (94%), whereas for males they were usually homosexual (84%). The mean age at onset was 10.2 for girls and 11.2 for boys. In 60 percent of the cases there was a single sexual encounter, and the sexual behavior was most often sexual contact or fondling. As a rule, males were less traumatized by the sexual abuse than females.

Finkelhor also collected data on incest, including child-child incestuous experiences, for example those between siblings, step-siblings, and cousins; 28 percent of female respondents and 23 percent of male respondents had such experiences, although not all of these situations were sexually abusive. Only 10 percent were cross-generational, and all of these occurred with female victims. The largest percentage of incestuous encounters occurred between siblings and between cousins.

In the other recent retrospective study, Russell (1983) interviewed 930 adult women in the San Francisco area, and found that 38 percent of the women had experienced sexually abusive contact as children. When noncontact sexual behaviors were included, 51–52 percent of the women had had such experiences. Unlike Finkelhor, Russell did not require that the perpetrator be five years older than the victim for an encounter to be defined as sexual abuse. This difference in definition probably in part accounted for Russell's higher reporting rates. Another possible reason for Russell's higher rates is that hers was a representative sample of the population whereas Finkelhor's was college students, which might be a less vulnerable group. (That is, since poor school performance is frequently found among victims of sexual abuse, it could be assumed that those persons who attend college are less likely to have been victims of sexual abuse).

Another interesting finding from Russell's (1984) research was the high incidence of stepfather abuse. While 2 percent of biological fathers were sexual abusers, 17 percent of stepfathers who played a significant paternal role were. When other stepfathers are included, 34.5 percent of stepfathers were abusers of their stepdaughters.

The major source of information about the incidence of sexual abuse is the data from the National Analysis of Official Child Neglect and Abuse Reporting (1977–1983). Data are collected annually on all types of child maltreatment, including sexual abuse. Although all 50 states participate in the data collection effort, the level of participation by locality may vary. Cases which are included in the National Analysis data are usually limited to those where a caretaker is either the perpetrator or has not been protective of a child who is sexually abused by someone else. An example of the latter might be a case where the mother's boyfriend is the abuser, and the mother has some knowledge of the sexual abuse but does not prevent his access to the victim. Thus only a small number of cases where the perpetrator resides outside the household are included in the National Analysis.

Data from the National Analysis show not only an increase in the number of all types of maltreatment reported—from 416,000 in 1976 (American Humane Association 1984), the first year data were collected, to 1.7 million in 1984 (American Humane Association, 1986)—but also an increase in the percentage of sexual abuse cases from 3 percent in 1976 to 13 percent in 1984. About half of the sexual abuse perpetrators in the 1984 sample were natural parents and 32 percent were step, foster, or adoptive parents.

Although recent National Analysis reports do not give the percentages of male vs. female victims of sexual abuse, other publications do (e.g., Herman 1981; Finkelhor 1984). Findings suggest that the vast majority of victims (between 75 and 95%) of reported cases are female.

VII. PLAN FOR THE BOOK

This book will attempt to give comprehensive guidelines for the clinician providing services to child sexual abuse cases. Chapter 1 has discussed the general purpose of the book, professional feelings about sexual abuse, definitions, functions and incidence rates. Chapter 2 will present statistical data on the clinical cases which form the basis of many of the observations and guidelines offered. The book has three additional parts, each consisting of two or more chapters. Part II includes material to assist the reader in understanding why sexual abuse occurs. Chapter 3 deals with the whole spectrum of sexual abuse cases, presenting three approaches to differential diagnosis: the closeness of the relationships between victim and perpetrator, the role relationship between victim and perpetrator, and perpetrator psychopathology. A typology of several abuse cases has been developed as a result of examining cases from these three standpoints. Chapter 4 discusses the causes of sexual abuse, focusing primarily on intrafamilial sexual abuse. These are conceptualized as prerequisite causes and contributing causes, the prerequisites being sexual feelings experienced by the perpetrator toward children, and a willingness to act upon these feelings, with contributing causes being divided into cultural, environmental, individual and family factors.

Part III addresses the assessment process in sexual abuse. It consists of five chapters, the first describing an overall approach to the evaluation, the three subsequent chapters discussing interviewing the victim, the alleged perpetrator, and the mother in order to determine the veracity of the allegation. The final chapter in this part, chapter 9, covers the medical assessment of sexual abuse.

Part IV addresses intervention in child sexual abuse. Chapter 10 provides guidelines for case management decisions; chapter 11 covers

treatment of the victim and describes issues and techniques that are pertinent to both intrafamilial and extrafamilial sexual abuse; chapters 12
through 14 discuss treatment issues and techniques which are of primary
relevance to intrafamilial sexual abuse. Chapter 12 articulates the general
goals and strategies for intervening in sexual abuse and improving family
functioning and individual treatment issues. Chapter 13 describes issues
and techniques for treatment of the mother-daughter dyad, the marital
dyad, and the father-daughter dyad. Chapter 14 discusses family and
group therapy. Finally, Chapter 15 deals with legal intervention in child
sexual abuse.

     Throughout the book, the author has employed the convention of
using the feminine pronoun when referring to victims and the masculine
pronoun when referring to sexual abusers. However, the reader should
not conclude that all victims are females or that all perpetrators are
males.

CHAPTER TWO

The Sample:
190 Victim-Perpetrator Dyads

I. INTRODUCTION

I have drawn extensively on a clinical population seen by myself and staff from the Interdisciplinary Project on Child Abuse and Neglect (IPCAN), in writing this book. It is important that readers also be familiarized with the case sample in order to critically evaluate the relevance of the material in the book to their own practice or situation as well as to judge the validity of the observations made in the book. The cases here presented themselves between 1978 and 1984, during which time about 200 cases were seen. Data on 148 cases and 190 victim-perpetrator dyads are available. Of the cases, 69 percent were referred by Child Protective Services, 2 percent by the courts, and 10 percent by other agencies, while 19 percent were self-referred by family members or victims. Cases came from counties throughout the state of Michigan, but the majority were from the most densely populated southeastern part of the state. Families were referred for the purposes of diagnosis, treatment planning, and treatment. In all except two cases, the victim was seen one or more times. In 45 percent of the cases, victim, nonabusing parent, and perpetrator were seen. In 35 percent the victim and nonabusing parent(s) were seen. The latter were usually cases where the perpetrator was not residing in the household. He might be evaluated by someone else or he might be interviewed by the police. In 20 percent of the cases the victim(s) only was seen. Some were cases where the victim was an adolescent and the offender was from outside the household. In many of the victim-only cases, the rest of the family had been scheduled to be seen and did not come for their appointments. In almost all cases the author had access to case materials from other agencies that had been involved, including child protective services, medical facilities, mental health agencies, courts, and law enforcement. Information was systematically gathered on demographic data, characteristics of the sexual abuse, family correlates commonly associated with sexual abuse, intervention strategies, and characteristics of caretakers and abusers associated with prognosis. Data will be presented below.

II. DEMOGRAPHIC DATA

The mean age for the victims at the time the cases were seen was 8.3 years, with the age distribution as found in table 2.1.

Table 2.1   Age distribution of victims at the time of case evaluation (N = 144)

1 yr	2 yr	3 yr	4 yr	5 yr	6 yr	7 yr	8 yr	9 yr
2.6%	4.2%	12.2%	12.7%	6.3%	8.5%	7.4%	4.8%	6.9%
10 yr	11 yr	12 yr	13 yr	14 yr	15 yr	16 yr	17 yr	18 yr
7.9%	3.2%	2.6%	3.2%	7.4%	3.2%	2.1%	1.6%	1.6%

These children are somewhat younger than those in other reported samples, probably because difficult cases with young children tend to be referred to a project such as IPCAN for diagnosis, while older, more articulate children do not need a special evaluation.

The mean age for mothers of victims was 31.4 years, the minimum being 19 and the maximum 51. The mean age for perpetrators was 34.1 years, the youngest being nine years, the oldest 75. The mean and distribution for maternal age is what one might expect, given the age range of the victims. That the spread of the perpetrators' ages is greater is a reflection of the fact that not all of them were parental figures. There are adolescents and older men in the perpetrator group. These groups are described in chapter 3.

Of the perpetrators, 92 percent were male; of the victims, 84 percent were female. This distribution is consistent with the findings of other analyses of reported cases. Ninety percent of perpetrators were white, 9.5 percent black. There was one sexual abuser who was American Indian. Similarly, 87.3 percent of victims were white, 7.9 percent were black, 2.6 percent were biracial, and 2.1 percent were American Indian. In almost all of the cases the victim and offender were of the same race. The racial distribution among cases is representative of that in the state of Michigan, the population of which is 88 percent white and 11 percent black (Andrews and Boger 1980).

The families in this sample were generally poor. There was a five-level variable for approximate income, and it was coded separately for victims' families and perpetrators. The findings are shown in table 2.2.

	1	2	3	4	5
Table 2.2 Income level for victims and perpetrators					
	$30,000 or more	$15,000-$29,999	$10,000-$14,999	$9,999 or less - empl. but receive food stamps, Medicaid, or other benefits	AFDC, GA unempl.
Perpetrators N = 140	8.2%	9.4%	33.5%	18.2%	30.6%
Victims N = 143	7.1%	8.2%	27.5%	18.1%	39.0%

The poverty status of these subjects is probably not a reflection of the fact that sexual abuse is a problem of the poor. Rather it is related to the fact that poor families where there is sexual abuse are more likely to be channelled into the public sector for intervention, while more affluent ones may never be reported or may seek services from the private sector, where child maltreatment is not readily reported. (Chapter 4 contains a further discussion of economic factors in child sexual abuse.) However, when these income levels are compared with those of all reported cases of maltreatment, the sexual abuse group is somewhat better off. For abuse and neglect cases in general, the proportion of families on public assistance is 45 to 50 percent (Michigan Protective Services Management Information System 1984; American Humane Association 1984).

The differences in distributions for perpetrators and victims and the slight tendency of victims to be poorer occur because sometimes victims and perpetrators live in separate households. Victims may receive public assistance, and the perpetrators are noncustodial fathers or friends of the mother who enjoy a higher socio-economic status than the victims.

Data were gathered on perpetrators' employment history. Adolescent perpetrators who were still in school were excluded from this analysis, and female perpetrators were not incorporated in this analysis because the significance of employment as an index of functioning for women is not as great as for men. The data were collapsed into a three-category code: (1) steady or regular worker; (2) works but has periods of unemployment; and (3) chronically unemployed or never worked.

More than half of the sample were regular workers. One-fourth had periods of employment and unemployment, and one-fifth were very marginal men who never worked or almost never worked (see table 2.3).

Table 2.3 Employment of perpetrators (N = 162)

1	2	3
Regular employment	Unemployment/ employment	Regular unemployment
53.7%	25.9%	20.4%

III. CHARACTERISTICS OF THE SEXUAL ABUSE

A. Multiple Victims and Multiple Perpetrators

In our sample, typically the offender had sexually abused more than one victim. In 59.2 percent of cases we were aware of two or more victims. In 16 of the single-victim cases there was only one child in the family. In another 11 there was only one female child. In the few cases where there was one female victim while other female children were available, the perpetrator was usually an adolescent residing outside the home. In the three cases where only one female child was victimized, other potential victims were available, and the perpetrator was in the household, the victims were all the oldest children. One was five and another was three years of age. Finally, it should be emphasized that it is quite possible that there are other victims of which we are not aware because of the secrecy that surrounds sexual abuse. The finding of multiple victims is inconsistent with the findings of some other researchers and clinicians (e.g., Herman and Hirschman 1980; DeVine, 1980; Kempe and Kempe 1984) who describe a syndrome in which the oldest daughter is the single victim and that child replaces the mother. For a further discussion of the dynamics of sexual abuse, see chapter 4.

In 17.5 percent of the cases, victims were sexually abused by more than one person. In some cases, this was by both mother and father, but more commonly they were victimized by more than one man. In one case nine different men had been sexually involved with the victim. The greater the number of men who had victimized the child, the more psychologically damaged she appeared. For a discussion of why children are multiply victimized, see chapter 11.

B. Age of Onset, Number of Sexual Encounters, and Time It Took the Victim to Tell

Data were gathered for approximate age of onset. The mean age at onset was 5.9 years, and the distribution for age groupings appears in table 2.4.

Table 2.4 Distribution for age at onset of sexual abuse (N = 115)

< 3	3-5	6-9	10-14	> 14
16.0%	37.0%	21.5%	23.8%	1.7%

Total, cols. 1 and 2: 53%

The age at onset for victims in this sample is quite young, with half being five or younger. They are much younger than those found in other studies where estimates are made that the mean victim age is about ten (Finkelhor 1979; Finkelhor 1986; Russell 1984).

The mean number of times a child was victimized by a given perpetrator was 23. In some cases the victim could readily identify the instances of sexual abuse, while in others the encounters were so numerous that the victim could only estimate. In such cases, we might ask the victim first how old she was when it first started and then about how many times a month or a week the abuse occurred, thereby obtaining an approximate number of sexual encounters. The distribution for number of times appears below in table 2.5.

Table 2.5 Distribution for the approximate number of times victims were sexually abused (N = 165)

1	2	3	4	5	6	7	8
12.6%	5.2%	6.3%	4.0%	12.6%	1.7%	1.1%	.6%
9	10	15	20	25	30	40	48
.6%	13.8%	3.4%	9.8%	.6%	5.2%	2.9%	.6%
50	60	80	90	98	99		
6.3%	.6%	1.7%	4.0%	1.1%	2.9%		

Data are widely distributed. The largest percentage of victims reported being abused ten times, followed by five times and one time and 20 times.

Data were also collected on the passage of time between the last incident of sexual abuse and the victim's telling someone about the maltreatment. The mean number of days was 94.9, with the shortest period of time being one day and the longest period being two years. A short period of time between the incident and the reporting was usually associated with a distant relationship between the victim and the perpetrator, whereas a longer period of time was associated with a close relationship between victim and perpetrator.

C. The Nature of the Sexual Abuse

Information was gathered on the nature of the sexual abuse itself: what type of sexual behavior was involved, the degree of coercion employed in the sexual encounter, whether the perpetrator admitted to the abuse, and the types of symptomatic behavior the child manifested after the sexual abuse.

The types of sexual abuse were collapsed into the nine categories described in chapter 1.

The mean number of types of sexual behavior per victim-perpetrator dyad was 3.18. The distribution of types of sexual abuse reported appears in table 2.6.

Table 2.6   Distributions of types of sexual abuse (N = 509)

1 Non-contact behavior	2 Sexual contact	3 Oral Sex	4 Inter-femoral	5 Anal	6 Digital
14.9%	41.2%	19.3%	1.8%	2.7%	1.8%

7 Genital	8 Child Pornography	9 Child Prostitution
15.7%	2.0%	1.0%

Sexual contact is the most prevalent type of abuse. This is followed by oral sex, and genital intercourse. Noncontact behaviors constitute 14.9 percent of the sexual acts. The less common forms of intrusion are anal, digital, and interfemoral penetration. These may be less common forms of sexual behavior in general. Pornography and prostitution are also found in only a small number of cases. However, such cases are likely to be dealt with by the police rather than by social agencies, and very few of our referrals came directly from the police.

The coding system for coercion was based upon an examination of the first 50 cases seen. There were eight possible levels of coercion which could be present in the sexual abuse. Table 2.7 displays those data.

Table 2.7 Degree of coercion employed in the sexual abuse (N = 190)

1	2	3	4	5	6	7	8
Forced, physical injury	Forced, no injury	Threat-ened with force	Other threats	Bribes, induce-ments	Seduc-tion	Mutual collab-oration	Victim initi-ated
16.1%	20.7%	8.8%	9.3%	16.6%	21.2%	7.3%	0.0%

Total, cols. 1-4: 54.9%

The eighth category, "victim initiated," was one into which none of the cases fit. In more than half the cases, some form of punitive coercion was employed, and in 16.1 percent of cases actual physical injury resulted. This indicates that the interaction with the perpetrator, quite apart from the meaning of the act and the feelings it engendered, was traumatic and unpleasant. The adult was threatening or forcing the child to engage in these behaviors. In cases where there was mutual collaboration, typically the child had a history of deprivation and prior sexual abuse, and cooperating in the sexual abuse was a way of receiving nurturance.

Another characteristic of the sexual abuse that was of interest was whether the perpetrator admitted to the sexual abuse, either to us, to law enforcement, to Protective Services, or to other persons involved. Admission was coded as a seven-category variable as found in table 2.8.

Table 2.8 Extent of admission to sexual abuse by perpetrators (N = 186)

1	2	3	4	5	6	7
Total confes-sion	Partial confes-sion	Indirect admis-sion	Denial	Vehement denial	Caught in act	Admitted after conviction
22.4%	5.3%	15.9%	32.7%	19.1%	4.3%	

Total, cols. 1-3: 43.6%
Total, cols. 4 and 5: 51.8%

A partial confession meant the perpetrator admitted to some of the sexual abuse but not everything other evidence validated. For example the offender might admit to fondling while denying intercourse, for which the criminal penalties are more severe. Indirect admission is a term used when the perpetrator implies the sexual abuse took place. For example, the perpetrator may say, "I do terrible things when I'm drunk and then I don't remember them the next day," or, "I could have rolled over and fondled her in my sleep, because I frequently have her sleeping with me." Alternatively, the perpetrator may say, "Well, I'll say I did it even though I didn't just so we can get on with treatment," or, "I'll admit to the petition so my daughter doesn't have to testify in court." These are all examples of indirect admission. For further discussion of admissions, see chapter 7, Interviewing the Alleged Perpetrator.

As can be seen, the cases are fairly evenly divided between perpetrators who made some kind of admission and those who denied the behavior. We had none who confessed as a result of being convicted in court; however most of the cases were seen before prosecution was completed.

Victims suffer in multiple ways from being sexually abused. A systematic effort was made to gather information about symptomatic behaviors commonly regarded as consequences of sexual abuse. These data were then collapsed into five categories. Sexual behavior includes such activities as excessive masturbation, initiating sexual interaction with other people, and sexual play with dolls or other toys. Sexual statements can consist of a child spontaneously saying, "Mr. Jones touches my peepee when I spend the night at their house," or demonstrating sexual knowledge beyond what one would expect for the child's developmental stage. Nonsexual behavior includes a range of problems such as sleep difficulties, enuresis, encopresis, problems in school, difficulties with peers, and suicidal behavior. Physical signs might consist of pregnancy, venereal disease, or physical injury as a result of sexual abuse. Delinquent behavior encompasses truancy, stealing, running away, aggressive behavior, incorrigibility, drug and alcohol use. The findings appear in table 2.9.

Table 2.9 Distribution of symptoms found among victims of sexual abuse (N = 416)

1	2	3	4	5
Sexual behavior	Sexual statements	Non-sexual behavior	Physical signs	Delinquent behavior
13.3%	39.3%	34.7%	10.1%	2.7%

The mean number of symptoms per victim was 2.6. As can be seen from the table, there was not much delinquent behavior. In contrast, a large percentage of reports were of sexual statements and the types of problems which were included under nonsexual behavior. Physical signs are about 10 percent and sexual behavior constitutes about 13 percent of the symptoms. In general, we found evidence of considerable damage to these children as a result of sexual abuse.

IV. RELATIONSHIPS BETWEEN PERPETRATORS AND VICTIMS

An important focus of this book is on how the relationship between the perpetrator and the victim affects the nature of the sexual abuse, the family's response to it, its impact upon the victim, and the type of intervention necessary. We collected data on the role relationship between perpetrator and victim, and we also developed a classification system to guide case management. The classification system cannot categorize all cases in the sample but does apply to most of them. Table 2.10 lists the percentages for the different role relationships found in our sample.

Table 2.10 Role relationship between perpetrator and victim (N = 187)

1	2	3	4	5	6
Biofather married to mother	Bio-father	Bio-mother	Step-father	Adopt. father	Grand-father
28.1%	7.6%	5.9%	17.3%	.5%	3.2%

7	8	9	10	11	12
Uncle	Mom's boy-friend	Dad's girl-friend	Close family friend	Brother	Stepbrother
4.3%	9.2%	1.5%	4.3%	1.6%	4.3%

13	14	15	16	17	18
Cousin	Baby-sitter	Teacher	Neighbor	Person known to child	Person known to family
1.1%	2.2%	1.1%	3.8%	2.2%	2.7%

In our sample, most of the perpetrators are paternal caretakers, biological fathers representing 35.7 percent, when those married to the mother are combined with those who are not. Next in frequency are stepfathers, and these are followed by mothers' boyfriends. Thus paternal caretakers constitute almost two-thirds of the perpetrators. Only 5.9 percent of perpetrators are mothers, and there were three fathers' girlfriends who were involved. Few of the perpetrators are unrelated people. However, this is probably not reflective of the true incidence rates among unrelated adults and children, but rather is an artifact of the source of cases. The vast majority of cases come from Departments of Social Services who have responsibility for sexual abuse cases only when the perpetrator is a caretaker or when the caretaker fails to protect the child. There are no strangers in our sample. (The child rape case described in chapter 3 comes from another therapist).

As noted above, cases were also coded based upon an eleven-category classification system developed for the purposes of case management. For an extensive discussion of the clinical characteristics of these casetypes, see chapter 3. The distribution of the cases by this system appears in table 2.11.

Table 2.11   Classification of sexual abuse cases (N = 180)

1	2	3	4	5	6
Biofather married to mother	Non-custodial parent	Single parent	Step-father LTP	Adolescent perpetrator	Old man perpetrator
18.0%	11.2%	4.5%	20.2%	9.0%	3.4%

7	8	9	10	11
Poly-incest-uous family	Retarded partici-pant(s)	Psychotic perpe-trator	Pedophile	Nonrelated perpetrator
18.5%	1.2%	1.2%	5.6%	8.4%

The largest percentage of cases fall into the stepfather-living-together-partner casetype, followed closely by the polyincestuous family and the biofather married to the mother (classical incest) case types. Noncustodial parent, adolescent perpetrator, and unrelated perpetrator cases are the next most numerous. Other types of sexual abuse appear in smaller percentages, among them single-parent cases, old men perpetrators, and pedophiles. Cases where the perpetrator is psychotic and those where participants are retarded constitute the smallest percentages in the sample.

V. CORRELATES OF SEXUAL ABUSE

There are certain individual and family characteristics which the clinical literature indicates are correlated with sexual abuse. Data were systematically collected on these variables. These correlates are discussed as contributing causes to sexual abuse in chapter 4.

A. Sexual Abuse in the Family of Origin

Sexual abuse in the family of origin is found with varying frequency in clinical populations of sexually abuse families. Our data on sexual abuse in family of origin are separated into mother abused, father abused, both parents abused, multiple sexually abusive relationships (both parents and others in families of origin), and none reported. Table 2.12 displays this information.

Table 2.12 Sexual abuse in the family of origin (N = 144)

Mother	Perpetrator	Both Parents	Multiple	None Reported
29.0%	17.2%	4.3%	8.1%	40.9%

In more than half the cases, sexual abuse was reported in the family of origin. Sometimes when there is an absence of report, it is because the family refused to discuss such material and occasionally the interviewer failed to cover it. When the latter happened, usually someone other than our staff was responsible for the parent interview(s). Thus it is safe to assume the percentages where sexual abuse was present are higher than actually reported. Our data suggest that sexual abuse of the mother only is the most commonly found, followed by perpetrator only. Moreover, when percentages for each parent are totaled, 41.4% of mothers have sexual abuse in their families of origin, as do 29.6% of perpetrators.

B. Chemical Dependency

Another problem commonly noted among sexual abusers is substance abuse. Data were collected on both alcohol and drug use. A three-category typology (table 2.13) for substance use was developed.

Table 2.13 Substance use (N = 188)

1 None	2 Moderate/social	3 Problem/addiction
11.6%	35.6%	52.7%

The moderate/social substance use category included those who drank occasionally as well as those who did so daily but in moderation (not enough to get drunk). The person was defined as having a substance problem or addiction based upon his statement, that of a significant other (including children), a social agency, or the evaluator that there was a substance abuse problem.

These data support clinical findings that drug and alcohol problems are experienced by large percentages (52.7%) of perpetrators of sexual abuse. Furthermore, these statistics are probably quite conservative because substance abusers tend to conceal their chemical dependency and lie when asked about it directly. For a discussion of how substance abuse data are gathered and the role of chemicals in sexual abuse, see chapters 4 and 7.

C. Other Intrafamilial Violence and Sexual Abuse

Data were collected on abuse and violence in addition to the sexual abuse against women and children. We were interested in instances of physical maltreatment (both abuse and neglect), spouse abuse, and other sexual abuse. Data were collapsed into five categories: (1) child abuse and neglect; (2) spouse abuse; (3) multiple forms of abuse (child, spouse, and/or sexual abuse); (4) other sexual abuse; and (5) none reported. With only 22.6 percent of perpetrators was there no evidence of other maltreatment. The distribution for types of maltreatment appears in table 2.14.

Table 2.14 Distribution for other maltreatment by perpetrators (N = 147)

1 CAN	2 Spouse	3 Multiple	4 Other sexual abuse	5 None report
16.9%7	5.8%	23.1%	31.6%	22.6%

These data indicate that in almost 80 percent of cases the reported sexual abuse is not the only victimization problem. Not only do many perpetrators sexually victimize more than one child, something discussed

earlier, but many of them also physically maltreat children, and almost
one-fourth engage in multiple forms of abuse. The reason for the small
percentage for spouse abuse is that it is usually found in combination
with other types of victimization. These data suggest this perpetrator
population appears to be quite aggressive within the family.

D. Marital Problems

Another common finding in the literature is the presence of
marital problems when there is sexual abuse. This can be sexual dysfunction and/or marital discord. A system for categorizing the marital or
significant other relationships was developed by examining the first 50
cases and includes the following categories: (1) no significant other; (2)
appropriate relationship with significant other; (3) perpetrator dominates significant other; (4) significant other dominates perpetrator; (5)
hostile relationship with significant other; (6) other. See chapter 4 for a
discussion of dominance in marriages where children are sexually
abused.

Data gathered regarding spousal relationships appear in table
2.15. Cases where the sexual abuser was female were not included in this
analysis. In cases where there was no significant other, the offenders
were either single parents, adolescents, or nonrelated perpetrators. Close
to one-fifth of the perpetrators appeared to have good relationships with
their partners. Perpetrators were much more likely to dominate than
were their spouses, and a surprisingly low percentage of couples were
judged to have had hostile marriages.

Table 2.15 Relationship of perpetrator with significant other (N = 148)

1	2	3	4	5	6
No signi-ficant other	Appropriate relationship	Perp. dominates	Non-perp. dominates	Hostile	Other
17%	18.2%	35.8%	4.7%	10%	14.0%

E. Sexual Abuse as Compulsive Behavior

We attempted to document in which cases the sexual abuse appeared to be an obsessional behavior. An obsessional pattern was defined as one where one or more of the following characteristics could be

identified: a ritualized sequence of events surrounding the sexual abuse; repetition of a particular sexual act or acts; multiple incidents very similar in nature, usually with different victims; and a reported absence of ability to control the behavior. Information was coded as a three-category variable and appears in table 2.16.

Table 2.16   Evidence of obsessional pattern in the sexual abuse (N = 110)

1	2	3
None	*Some*	*Definite*
34.9%	35.6%	29.5%

As table 2.16 indicates, there was a fairly even distribution of findings across the three categories. However, these figures may be an underestimate because frequently there was no admission of the sexual abuse by the perpetrator. In such instances we had to rely upon the victim's report and statements of others who had knowledge about the abuse. Many victims had considerable difficulty talking about their experiences, making it hard to discern whether the behavior was compulsive. The problems in assessing compulsion are reflected in the large percentage of cases being coded "some evidence, suggestive," as well as in the fact that the data were missing in 38 cases.

F.   Social Isolation

Social isolation is another factor found in the clinical literature to be associated with sexual abuse. We collected information on the victim's family's relationships with its informal network (friends, neighbors, and relatives) and with its formal network (social agencies, institutions, and helping professionals). The latter includes school personnel, mental health personnel, law enforcement, court staff, self-help groups, medical professionals, lawyers, etc. Coding systems for these two variables were based upon reviewing the clinical assessments of the first 50 cases. For the informal network, there was a five-category coding system as follows: (1) no informal supports; (2) few informal supports (1 person); (3) some informal supports (2-3 persons); (4) an appropriate number of informal supports (4 or more); and (5) too many/inappropriate informal supports. The final category was developed because in some cases the informal network was a source of trauma, was supportive or active in the sexual abuse, or encouraged the family to be uncooperative with intervention. Table 2.17 gives the distribution of ratings for informal supports.

Table 2.17 Distribution for informal supports (N = 133)

1	2	3	4	5
None	Few	Some	Appropriate number	Too many/ inappropriate
4.7%	38.5%	37.3%	17.2%	2.4%

These data do not support a hypothesis that sexually abusive families are totally isolated from informal supports. However, more than one-third have few supports, and another one-third only some supports. It may be that situations which are identified by an agency—as is the case with most of the families in our sample—are less isolated than those who are not so identified. In many instances, it is an extended family member or friend who makes the sexual abuse known to protective services or the court.

Agency involvement was coded as a five-category variable: (1) no agency supports/refuses services; (2) few agency supports/family hard to work with, usually one agency involved; (3) some agency supports/some good relationships, some bad, two or three agencies involved; (4) fair number of agency contacts, workable; and (5) optimal agency supports/appropriate use, cooperative. These data appear in table 2.18.

Table 2.18 Agency supports (N = 136)

1	2	3	4	5
None	Few	Some	Fair number	Optimal
4.7%	38.5%	37.3%	17.2%	2.4%

The findings are similar to those for informal supports. Although more than 40 percent of the cases had few or no agency supports, in general the sample cannot be described as totally isolated. However, a family defined as having few supports was one where only protective services was involved—the agency to which they were referred for child sexual abuse. Those who have some supports were usually involved with protective services and the courts. About one-fifth of the sample could be said to have adequate agency relationships.

VI. INTERVENTION

Data were collected on interventions recommended and/or carried out as a result of our involvement with families. (A study is now underway to ascertain the effects of these interventions.) In addition, information was gathered on court involvement.

Interventions were collapsed into seven categories: (1) none; (2) therapy; (3) concrete services; (4) court; (5) separation; (6) evaluation; and (7) visitation. Therapy included a range of treatment modalities—individual, group, and family, as well as lay therapy. Concrete services comprised such interventions as day care, homemakers, medical services, and financial assistance. Court referred to court involvement in addition to what might have already been undertaken prior to our intervention—usually criminal prosecution, termination of parental rights, or use of the circuit court to change visitation or custody orders in a divorce. Separation included interventions that would separate the victim from the family or the perpetrator from the family. Evaluation consisted of additional assessment of individuals or the family or assessment of family members not yet seen. Visitation was a category used for any recommendation or intervention directed at the contacts of family members with victims placed out of the home. Thus, it could include no visits, supervised visits only, and visitation daily without supervision.

A total of 397 interventions were coded for 190 victim-perpetrator dyads, or 2.1 interventions per case. The distribution of data regarding intervention appears in table 2.19.

Table 2.19   Distribution for interventions (N = 397)

1	2	3	4	5	6	7
		Concrete		Separ-	Evalu-	
None	Therapy	services	Court	ation	ation	Visitation
2.7%	37.2%	1.6%	24.1%	19.3%	6.7%	8.6%

In more than one-third of cases, some form of therapy was recommended or implemented. Given the nature of the problem discussed here, one might expect this percentage to have been higher. However, in many cases crisis work was done with the victim by IPCAN staff, and no further therapy was felt to be needed. This was particularly likely to be the recommendation if there was no close relationship between the perpetrator and victim. At the other end of the spectrum were cases so severe that criminal prosecution of the parents and termination of parental rights were sought. Often in such cases, the child was placed in a foster home where the environment itself was therapeutic and no treatment of the victim was recommended initially. In addition, as noted earlier, quite a number of victims were very young, and, for them, treatment might not be indicated, although therapy may be in order when the child becomes older.

The second most common intervention is court, followed by separation, visitation, and evaluation. In very few cases were any concrete services recommended. This is probably partly because the focus of our involvement was not on concrete services. However, it is also our experience—as well as that of others—that sexual abuse is not as closely tied as physical abuse and neglect to environmental stresses that might be alleviated by concrete services.

Information in addition to that included under interventions was gathered regarding court activity. This consisted of which court was involved and whether or not the child testified in court. Table 2.20 provides data on court involvement. Three different types of court involvement could be coded per case, but most were involved with only one court. Juvenile court means that legal intervention was sought to protect the child. Criminal court indicates that prosecution of the offender was pursued. In some cases, there was a divorce or legal separation, and in these, the circuit court might intervene to change custody, limit visitation, or order therapy.

Table 2.20   Court involvement (N = 200)

1	2	3	4
None	Juvenile	Criminal	Divorce
12.0%	48.5%	24.5%	15.0%

In only 12 percent of cases was there no court involvement; most of these cases were individuals or families who referred themselves to our project. Close to half of the reports were of juvenile court involvement. This is to be expected because the preponderance of cases were referred from departments of social services, which use the juvenile court as their arena for legal intervention. Nearly a fourth are of criminal court action. However, criminal conviction occurred in only about 10 percent of cases where warrants were issued. The low conviction rate is because sexual abuse cases are quite difficult to prove in court. They almost invariably require the victim's testimony and the standard of proof is quite high (see chapter 15). Finally, 15 percent of reports were of divorce court intervention, which sometimes occurred when the abuser was a noncustodial parent.

Data on child testimony appear in table 2.21. Child testimony was collapsed into a four-category variable: (1) no testimony; (2) juvenile court testimony; (3) criminal court testimony; and (4) spoke to the judge in chambers. Two types of child testimony per case could be coded; however only in three cases were children involved in more than one type of testimony.

Table 2.21 Child testimony (N = 155)

1	2	3	4
No testimony	Juvenile court	Criminal court	Spoke to judge
72.3%	9.0%	17.4%	1.3%

In almost three-fourths of cases, no child testimony occurred. If the child did testify, it was likely to be in the criminal court. In less than 10 percent of cases did the child testify in the juvenile court. It was also very rare for the child to talk to the judge in chambers—somewhat surprising because judges in Michigan are supposed to speak to the child in chambers in disputed custody cases.

VII. INDICATORS OF PROGNOSIS

Information was gathered systematically on certain variables which are judged by the author and others to be important indicators of prognosis. That is, there are certain areas of perpetrator functioning and certain areas of maternal functioning that are crucial in case planning, particularly in deciding whether the child should continue in the care of the parent(s) and whether the family and/or parents will respond to treatment. Variables for perpetrators and mothers are somewhat different. These predictors and their utility are dicussed extensively in chapters 7, 8, and 10.

Variables related to the perpetrator are his overall functioning, his superego functioning, and his relationship with the victim. Those variables important for the maternal caretaker (who is usually not a perpetrator) are overall functioning, her dependency, her protectiveness when she discovered the sexual abuse, and her relationship with the child. It was more difficult to develop reliable coding systems for these variables than for those discussed thus far because ratings depended heavily upon clinical judgments.

A. Perpetrator's Overall Functioning

The perpetrator's overall functioning is a composite variable and includes some factors which were also coded separately. It takes into account his education, employment, relationship with his children, relationship with spouse, mental illness, substance use, criminal activity, aggressive behavior, and other functioning. Each area was rated appropriate or inappropriate, and then the areas of appropriate and inappropriate behavior were summed, and the information was coded in a five-category Likert scale: (1) all areas of functioning appropriate (except sex); (2) many areas appropriate; (3) half and half; (4) many areas inappropriate; and (5) all areas inappropriate. The findings are displayed in table 2.22.

Table 2.22 Overall functioning of the perpetrator (N = 178)

1	2	3	4	5
All approp.	Many approp.	Half & half	Many inapprop.	All inapprop.
6.2%	9.0%	32.0%	33.1%	19.7%

Total, cols. 1 and 2: 15.2%
Total, cols. 4 and 5: 52.8%

As a group the perpetrators do not appear to be functioning particularly well. Only about 15 percent had all or many areas conflict-free. Almost one-third were half and half, and the remaining cases, more than half the sample, evidenced many or all areas with malfunction.

B. Perpetrator's Superego Functioning

Men who are sexual abusers are frequently described in the literature as psychopaths or as having gross superego deficits (Lukianowicz 1970; Justice and Justice 1981). Clinically, we tried to assess the extent to which the perpetrator accepted responsibility for and felt guilty about the sexual abuse, as well as the extent to which he might feel guilty about other transgressions. However, often when there were a lot of guilt feelings about the sexual abuse, the perpetrator staunchly denied having committed it. In such cases, we sometimes could rate his superego functioning based upon guilt feelings in other areas. Yet there were cases where the perpetrator had good superego functioning in most areas and lacunae in his superego regarding sexual functioning. Thus, coding superego functioning presented some difficulties. We used a five-category Likert scale to code superego functioning: (1) strong superego; (2) moderate superego; (3) somewhat impaired superego; (4) quite impaired superego; and (5) no superego, no apparent conscience. A person who is coded as a 5 would be a psychopath, and a person coded as a 4 would be severely character disordered. Data appear in table 2.23.

Table 2.23 Perpetrator superego functioning (N = 175)

1	2	3	4	5
Strong superego	Moderate superego	Somewhat impaired	Quite impaired	None
6.9%	16.0%	17.7%	37.1%	22.3%

Total, cols. 4 and 5: 59.4%

Our data support findings of others that persons who sexually abuse children have severe superego deficits, with more than half of them having quite impaired superegos or no apparent superegos.

C. Perpetrator's Affective Relationship with the Victim

Of interest was how appropriate the perpetrator's relationship was with the victim; the more appropriate, the better the prognosis for treatment and the more important to maintain that relationship for the child. As with social supports, the coding system was derived after reading clinical assessments of these relationships for 50 cases. The codes were then collapsed into a four-category variable: (1) close relationship, affectionate; (2) close sexual/symbiotic; (3) detached; and (4) hostile. Category 1 includes situations where the perpetrator appears to have appropriate concern, love, and caring for the child even though he has sexually abused her. Catgegory 2 consists of cases where the closeness is primarily sexual, and those where clinically the relationship might be described as fused or symbiotic. Detachment, category 3, may come about because the perpetrator does not have much contact with the child, or it may be a result of his inability to form intimate relationships. Cases where the perpetrator was unable to describe what the victim was like would fit here (see chapter 7). In situations coded as hostile, the perpetrator frequently was very angry at the victim for telling about the sexual abuse, blaming her for the family and personal disruption arising from public knowledge. In some cases, the hostility toward the child preceded the revelation of the sexual abuse, but in others it did not. Data regarding the perpetrator's relationship with the victim appear in table 2.24.

Table 2.24 Perpetrator's affective relationship with the victim (N = 169)

1 Appropriate	2 Sexual	3 Detached	4 Hostile
17.8%	30.2%	34.9%	17.2%

As can be seen from the table, less than one-fifth of the perpetrators evidenced appropriate caring for their victims, and for almost one-third, the closeness was abnormal. About one-third had detached relationships, and another fifth had hostile relationships.

D. Mother's Overall Functioning

In most cases, the mother was a nonoffending parent. Her overall functioning was assessed in a manner similar to that of the perpetrator. However, employment for mothers included housekeeping. These findings appear in table 2.25.

Table 2.25   Mother's overall functioning (N = 138)

1	2	3	4	5
All areas appropriate	Many areas appropriate	Half & half	Many areas inapprop.	All areas inapprop.
6.7%	20.8%	27.5%	18.0%	27.0%

Mothers appear to be somewhat better functioning than perpetrators. For example, although about equal percentages of mothers and perpetrators were rated category 1, higher percentages of mothers were coded as being appropriate in many areas of functioning. In addition, lower percentages of mothers were rated as having many areas of inappropriate functioning. However, about equal proportions of mothers and perpetrators were rated as having half appropriate and half inappropriate functioning and a larger percentage of mothers than offenders no areas of appropriate functioning.

E. Maternal Dependency

The extent to which the mother is a dependent person—and particularly the level of her dependence upon the perpetrator—is another important factor in case planning and treatment potential (see chapters 8 and 10). Several dimensions were explored clinically to determine the level of maternal dependency. These included her economic independence: whether she worked, had a skill, had worked in the past, or had her own public assistance check. In addition, whether she had ever lived on her own and whether she had a support system separate from the perpetrator were taken into account. In the case contacts, an effort was made to see the mother with her partner to determine how dominant she was in that relationship, and specifically to see whether she could disagree with him, could intervene on the children's behalf, and could see the children's interests as separate from and different from the perpetrator's. Dependence was rated on a four-point Likert scale: (1) very independent; (2) somewhat independent; (3) somewhat dependent; and (4) very dependent. Data are in table 2.26.

Table 2.26 Maternal independence/dependence (N = 139)

Very independent	Somewhat independent	Somewhat dependent	Very dependent
12.9%	19.4%	29.5%	38.1%

Total, cols. 1 and 2: 32.3%
Total, cols. 3 and 4: 67.6%

As can be seen from the table, about one-third are rated very or somewhat independent, whereas about two-thirds are rated somewhat or very dependent. Thus, taken as a whole, mothers of sexual abuse victims are a dependent lot.

F. Maternal Protectiveness

Another very important factor in predicting case outcome is how protective the mother's response was when she came to know about the sexual abuse (see chapter 10). Protective responses include calling Protective Services or the police, leaving the house with the children or making the perpetrator leave, initiating divorce proceedings, placing the child where the alleged perpetrator cannot have access, and insisting the perpetrator get treatment. Unprotective responses include disbelieving the child, blaming the child, and continuing to expose the child to risky situations after revelation of the sex abuse. Protectiveness was coded on a five-point Likert scale: (1) very protective; (2) somewhat protective; (3) first sided with the victim, then with the perpetrator; (4) somewhat unprotective; and (5) very unprotective. Information gathered from the victim, the mother, and others involved with the case was used to determine the rating. The mother's response sometimes changes over time, as indicated by category 3. The rating of protectiveness was based upon the mother's behavior from the time of discovery of the sexual abuse until our clinical evaluation of the family was complete. Table 2.27 indicates the distribution of maternal responses.

Table 2.27 Protectiveness of the mother's response (N = 147)

1	2	3	4	5
Very protective	Somewhat protective	Switched	Somewhat unprotective	Very unprotective
32.7%	14.3%	4.8%	19.7%	28.6%

Total, cols. 1 and 2: 47.0%
Total, cols. 3 and 4: 48.3%

The picture provided by the data is quite symmetrical. Close to one-third of the mothers were either very protective or very unprotective. Similarly about a fifth were somewhat protective and somewhat unprotective, respectively, and a small percentage of mothers could be identified as switching loyalties from daughter to perpetrator.

G. Mother's Affective Relationship With the Victim

The final important factor in terms of prognosis is the mother's relationship with the victim (see chapters 8 and 10). A four-point coding system for mother-victim relationship was based upon an examination of clinical data from the first 50 cases. It is somewhat different from the coding system developed for the perpetrator-victim relationship. The codes are as follows: (1) very warm, loving relationship; (2) somewhat warm, loving relationship; (3) somewhat cold, unloving relationship; and (4) very cold, unloving relationship. Data to determine the ratings were derived from a series of clinical questions asked of the victim, the mother, and others with direct knowledge of the mother-child relationship. Findings appear in table 2.28.

Table 2.28 Mother's affective relationship with victim (N = 147)

1	2	3	4
Very loving	Somewhat loving	Somewhat unloving	Very unloving
22.3%	36.0%	35.4%	6.3%

Total, cols. 1 and 2: 58.3%
Total, cols. 3 and 4: 41.7%

A small percentage of mothers had very unnurturing relationships with their victim-children, more than half had very loving or somewhat loving relationships with these children, and about one-third had somewhat unloving relationships. Thus, the data do not support uniform difficulties in the mother-child relationship often cited in the literature (Walters 1975; Benoist 1977; Sarles 1975). There is quite a lot of variability in these relationships, but the preponderance of mothers have adequate relationships with the victim.

VIII. SUMMARY

This clinical sample of 190 victim-perpetrator dyads is predominantly poor. More than 90 percent of the time the perpetrator is male and in over 80 percent of cases the victim is female. Multiple victimization by the perpetrator occurred in almost 60 percent of the cases, and in the majority of the single victim cases there was no other available victim or available female victim. Close to one-fifth of victims had been sexually abused by more than one person. Victims were young, more than half being five or under when the sexual abuse began. They tended to be victimized multiple times by the perpetrator, the mean being 23. There was a delay between the last incident of sexual abuse and telling, the average delay being about three months.

The sexual abuse included every possible sexual act, but close to half the instances were of fondling. In more than half of the cases some force and threats were employed, and in close to half the cases the perpetrator acknowledged or admitted the sexual abuse at some level. In general victims being seen for diagnosis and treatment had numerous symptoms that appeared to be related to the sexual abuse.

The perpetrators had a range of relationships with the victims, but almost two-thirds were paternal caretakers of the victim, most frequently being biological fathers, stepfathers, or mothers' boyfriends.

Data were collected on correlates of sexual abuse cited in the literature. In a little more than half the sample, sexual abuse in the family of origin was noted. The overwhelming majority of perpetrators used chemicals, and more than half were described as having a substance problem or addiction. More than three-fourths of the offenders were involved in some additional form of maltreatment, physical maltreatment of children, spouse abuse, and/or other sexual abuse. Some type of marital problem could be found in more than half the cases, although in only 10 percent of cases was there evidence of hostility between the perpetrator and the partner. In close to one-third of cases there was definitive evidence the sexual abuse represented an obsessional pattern.

With regard to intervention, therapy was the most common type of recommendation, constituting more than one-third of the cases. In all but 12 percent of cases there was some type of court intervention, but the child's testimony was the exception rather than the rule, occurring in only about one-fourth of the sample.

Information was collected on characteristics of perpetrators and mothers which are indicators of prognosis. In more than half of the cases, perpetrators have serious problems in overall functioning, and about half have serious superego deficits, indicators of poor prognosis. Moreover, about four-fifths of these adults evidenced significant problems in their relationships with the victims, over and above the sexual victimization. Mothers of victims are somewhat better functioning overall than perpetrators, but more than one-fourth have severe problems in functioning. About two-thirds appear to be dependent people, and more than half were not protective of victims once they discovered the sexual abuse, meaning prognosis is not good. Finally, however, a more hopeful sign: more than half of the mothers had nurturing relationships with their victim-children.

PART II: UNDERSTANDING CHILD SEXUAL ABUSE

CHAPTER THREE

Differential Diagnosis
of Sexual Abuse

I. INTRODUCTION

Much is yet to be learned about the etiology and dynamics of child sexual abuse. One reason for the current state of ignorance is that there are a number of types of sexual abuse. However, many writers fail to make distinctions and speak of sexual abuse or incest as if it were a single entity (e.g., Machotka et al. 1967; Holder, ed. 1980; Rush 1980). Clinical and research literature sometimes adds to this problem by failing to fully appreciate the limitations of the case base being employed. For example, often published results are based upon very small samples, fewer than a dozen cases (Kaufman et al. 1954; Lustig et al. 1965; Sarles 1975; Awad 1976; Gutheil and Avery 1977). Alternatively, subjects come from a setting which is selective: a prison, a court, or a hospital (Jason et al. 1982; Molnar and Cameron 1975; Spencer 1978; Weinberg 1955). Further, most studies are of reported cases, the major exceptions being the works of Russell (1983) and Finkelhor (1979) described in chapter 1, and the National Incidence Study (1981). Moreover, observations are made on samples of people seeking treatment (Meiselman 1978; Mayer 1983) or cases where there was sufficient evidence to adjudicate and court order treatment (Kroth 1977; Gottlieb 1983). In addition, some descriptions of the sexual abuse population are derived from samples in programs that serve only intrafamilial sexual abuse, others from persons in programs dealing solely with extrafamilial sexual abuse, and still others from programs addressing both types of cases. Thus characteristics of most clinical and research samples both bias and limit the conclusions drawn from them.

The descriptive data from the IPCAN sample in chapter 2 apprise the reader of the strengths and weaknesses of our sample. From this data base, from consultation on other cases, from discussions with other professionals working in the area of child sexual abuse, and from the sexual abuse literature, several approaches to classifying sexual abuse cases have been developed. It is readily acknowledged that this system of classification is imperfect. Yet it represents an important step in the field. The purpose of the classification is to guide professionals in what to expect with regard to the dynamics of different types of sexual abuse, how to proceed in case management, what modes of treatment to employ, and which cases have good and bad treatment prognoses.

This chapter will concern itself with both intrafamilial and extrafamilial sexual abuse cases. Three ways of organizing and classifying cases will be presented. First, the impact of the degree of intimacy in the relationship between the victim and perpetrator will be examined, and then a related factor—the role status of the perpetrator vis-a-vis the victim and the victim's family—will be explored. Finally, four types of cases that are defined by individual perpetrator pathology will be described.

II. THE CLOSENESS OF THE RELATIONSHIP BETWEEN THE PERPETRATOR AND VICTIM

The first factor which helps one to understand different types of sexual abuse is the closeness or intimacy of the relationship between victim and perpetrator. The closeness of that relationship is determined by the biological relationship between perpetrator and victim, their legal relationship, the relationship between the perpetrator and the victim's family, and the frequency of contact between victim and perpetrator. Incestuous relationships (those where there is a biological relationship between perpetrator and victim) are generally more intimate than relationships where there is no blood relationship. In addition, if the perpetrator is married to the child's mother, though not the child's father, or he is otherwise legally related, the relationship will be closer than if no such tie exists. If the perpetrator lives within the household, the relationship will usually be more intimate than if he resides outside. Similarly, if the abuser is someone the child sees daily or weekly, the relationship will be more intense than if the child sees the person rarely.

It is possible to conceptualize sexually abusive relationships along a continuum of closeness vs. distance. The two ends of this continuum would be classical incest in which the abuser is the biological father of the child married to the mother, and, at the distant end, the child rape situation where the perpetrator is a total stranger to the victim. Figure 3.1 provides a visual display of the continuum.

The degree of closeness in the relationship between perpetrator and victim tends to have an impact on a range of factors related to the sexual abuse. These are (1) how the sexual abuse evolves, (2) its duration, (3) its frequency, (4) whether or not force is used, (5) the child's reaction to the sexual abuse, (6) parental reaction upon discovery of the sexual abuse, (7) strategies necessary to protect the child, (8) the source of the psychological damage for the victim, and (9) the treatment necessary.

A. Classical Incest

Classical incest is found in marriages of long duration, where typically there are several children. The mother is a fairly dependent person (the most dependent mothers in our sample). The oldest female child is usually the first victim, and she may take on maternal household responsibilities as well as the sexual role with the father. The fathers vary in their functioning; however, in our sample, they tend to be domineering and have many areas of their lives where they do not function well. Our findings are consistent with those of others (e.g., Tormes 1968; Nakashima and Zakus 1977; Lukianowitz 1978). In classical incest, the interaction between the father and daughter begins as appropriate affectionate physical behavior that gradually becomes sexualized, with the father perhaps initiating caressing of the child's perineal area. In such cases this sexual behavior is likely to begin with the child during the oedipal stage (3–5 years), as was the case in about half of our classical incest cases, and evolves into progressively more intrusive sexual behavior, perhaps mutual masturbation, oral/genital sex, and sometimes eventually genital intercourse. The pattern evolves and persists over a period of years, and the sexual behavior may become quite frequent, as often as weekly. While the oldest female child is usually the first victim, it is common to find multiple female victims in the household. (See also Lukianowitz 1970).

Frequently the perpetrator is kind and gentle, so unlikely to use force. He may use bribes and special favors as rewards for cooperation, or psychological inducements such as "You have to give me this pleasure because your mother won't," and "If you don't do this, I'll have to leave the family."

Often the perpetrator employs various tactics to persuade the child not to tell anyone about the sexual abuse, and these are successful. It is not uncommon for years to pass between the onset of the sexual abuse and the child's telling (Herman and Hirschman 1980). The child may not tell until she reaches adolescence and is somewhat less under the control of her father and family. Often she speaks out at a point when

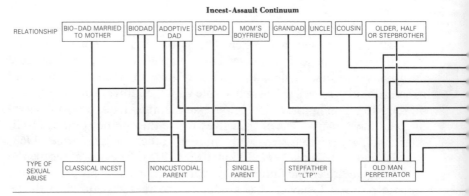

DIMENSIONS

1. Evolution of relationship
2. Frequency of sexual contact
3. Duration of relationship
4. Use of force
5. Child's response
6. Family's response
7. Psychological impact
8. Treatment

INCEST

1. Gradual evolution beginning with appropriate physical interaction.
2. As often as several times weekly.
3. May persist for years.
4. Force not likely to be used; other inducements.
5. Child does not tell; may after a period of time (years).
6. May not protect child, expel perpetrator, or seek help.
7. Damage more severe the more the child understands the meaning of the behavior. Damage occurs because perpetrator should be trusted, protective parent.
8. Family needs treatment; however, considerable variability in families.

FIGURE 3.1. Continuum of Intrafamilial–
Extrafamilial Sexual Abuse.

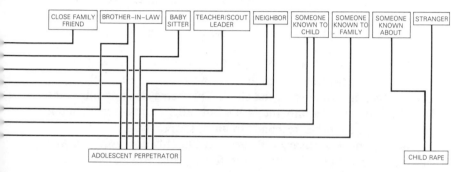

| CLOSE FAMILY FRIEND | BROTHER-IN-LAW | BABY SITTER | TEACHER/SCOUT LEADER | NEIGHBOR | SOMEONE KNOWN TO CHILD | SOMEONE KNOWN TO FAMILY | SOMEONE KNOWN ABOUT | STRANGER |

ADOLESCENT PERPETRATOR   CHILD RAPE

RELATIONSHIPS FALLING IN BETWEEN

1. Less abrupt beginning than in assault; more abrupt than in incest.

2. More frequent than in assault; less frequent than in incest; depending on access to child.

3. Lasts longer than assault; but not of the duration found in incest.

4. Force less likely to be used than in assault; more likely than in incest.

5. Child tells less readily than in assault; more readily than in incest.

6. Family more likely to protect than in incest; less likely than in assault, depends upon family's closeness to perpetrator.

7. Damage usually less severe than in either incest or assault.

8. Variability in prognosis and type of treatment appropriate; however, more treatable than in either classical incest or child rape cases.

ASSAULT

1. Abrupt evolution, no forewarning.

2. One incident.

3. Single encounter.

4. Force likely to be used.

5. Child tells parents immediately.

6. Parents respond appropriately; call police and take child to hospital; get treatment.

7. Protect child from risk situations; arrest perpetrator.

8. Trauma because use of force.

9. Child/family may not need treatment; treatment if traumatized. Perpetrator treated separately from child/family.

she is seeking to establish heterosexual peer relationships. Morever, if it is her mother from whom she seeks help, the response may not be protective and supportive. The mother may disbelieve the child or attempt to deal with and contain the problem within the family (Sarles 1975; Justice and Justice 1979). In our sample mothers in classical incest were the least protective group.

At the time of discovery, in order to protect the child from subsequent sexual abuse and psychological abuse by the family, it is usually necessary to separate the victim and perpetrator. This can mean the victim is placed out of the home, in foster care or with a relative, or it may be that the perpetrator leaves voluntarily, is arrested, or is court-ordered out. (Guidelines for which strategy to use to protect the child will be discussed in chapter 10.)

The psychological trauma from father-daughter incest arises in large part from the fact that a primary caretaker, and presumably a protector, is in fact an exploiter of the child. This betrayal undermines the child's ability to trust not only the father but other adults as well, and is compounded if the mother responds in an unsupportive manner.

The treatment necessary will vary considerably depending on who will constitute the child's family in the future, and will be dicussed in detail in later chapters. However, in no case should there be no treatment. In addition, if the child and some part or all of the family are to be reunited or remain together, family therapy as well as other modes of intervention will be necessary. The case described below is a typical classical incest family and contains most of the features discussed above.

EXAMPLE 1: The B family consists of two parents, Mr. B, age 36, and Mrs. B, age 36, who have been married for 17 years. They have three children: Brenda, 14, Colleen, 12, and Tommy, 10. Mr. B has a history of alcoholism and physically abusive behavior toward his children and, in the past, toward his wife. At present he is verbally and physically abusive toward the children and verbally abusive toward his wife. Formerly a salesman, he has been unemployed for the past two years. His wife works and they still receive some unemployment benefits. Mrs. B is described by her family and all those who encounter her as "a very sweet lady."

Brenda has been the longstanding target of sexual abuse by her father. She recalls the first incident when she was about four and her mother was away. Her father put his penis between her thighs from behind and "just left it there" for a few minutes. He was drunk at the time and she thought his penis was not fully erect.

As time went on, the sexual abuse would occur when he came into her room supposedly to say good night. Initially he would rub her vulva, putting his hand inside her pajama bottoms, but not inside her underpants which she wore to bed. Eventually, the abuse progressed to digital penetration. When Brenda was about ten, her father began having her masturbate him while he digitally penetrated her. When she was 12, he attempted cunnilingus. Brenda reports he was always drunk when he did these things and did not ever have a complete erection or ejaculate. For years Brenda did not tell her mother about the abuse because she did not think she would be believed.

Brenda finally told her mother at 13 when she became aware that her father was also sexually abusing Colleen. This was also a time Mr. B was particularly punitive with Brenda because he didn't like her friends. Initially Mrs. B did not believe Brenda, saying Brenda made up stories. Brenda then told her school counselor, who called Protective Services. With Protective Services involvement, Mrs. B found out about Colleen and left her husband, taking the three children. Mr. B then entered an alcohol treatment program and Mrs. B returned home. At the point of Mr. B's discharge, he insisted he be allowed to return home, saying he was cured of his alcoholism and that Brenda was a liar. He said maybe he did something to Colleen but he did not remember. Mrs. B wanted to give him another chance. Both girls, but particularly Brenda, felt betrayed and asked to be placed in foster care. This was done.

Brenda said she hated her father for what he had done to her life and would never marry. Colleen was angry but less vehement. Individual treatment was initiated for both girls and each parent, with the thought that, if sufficient progress were made, there would be a move toward marital therapy, treatment of mother and daughters as a group, and eventually family therapy.

Colleen asked to go home after two months in foster care. This was allowed with the provision that Mr. B move out. He agreed to do this but, in fact, he was continually harassing various family members, coming home when he was not supposed to be there, and being uncooperative with his therapist. He continued to refuse to admit responsibility for the sexual abuse of Brenda. After six months Mrs. B was strong enough to decide to divorce Mr. B. It took her four more months to file for divorce.

In the B case, we find the characteristic early onset and sexual abuse of ten years duration with the oldest child. The sexual abuse becomes progressively more intrusive with Brenda but does not culminate in intercourse, at least in part because Mr. B's drinking makes him unable to achieve a full erection. Brenda could recall specific encounters but did not know how frequently it happened. As is typical in classical incest, no force was used; however, no inducements were mentioned by Brenda. Brenda endured the sexual abuse for ten years, only telling out of concern for her sister.

Mrs. B is fairly typical of better functioning classical incest mothers. She was sufficiently dependent upon her husband that she stayed with him in a bad marriage for 17 years, allowed him back home after his hospitalization, and vacillated for a long time about divorce. Like many classical incest perpetrators, Mr. B evidenced dysfunctional behavior in a number of areas. Not only was he an alcoholic, but he had a history of unemployment and physical violence against his wife and children.

B. Stranger Child Rape

The situation of child rape by a stranger is in sharp contrast to classical incest. Although the perpetrator of child rape may sexually assault many children, in general there is a single sexual encounter with a given child at a particular point in time, rather than the multiple incidents over years with one child found in incest. Rather than a gradual evolution, there is no forewarning and the onset is abupt. A stranger suddenly grabs a child from his car or pulls a child into an alley. The sexual abuse itself is more likely to involve penetration than in incest and force is more often used. Therefore, injury is much more likely to result.

The child's reaction is usually quite different as well. The child is likely to report the incident right away to parents or other supportive persons. They, in turn, usually react appropriately by calling the police, taking the child to the doctor, and seeking mental health treatment if necessary. Protection is achieved usually by keeping the child within the safety of the family and home, rather than by separating the child from family, and if the perpetrator can be identified, his arrest will of course further protect the child.

The psychological trauma of stranger child rape is closely related to the use of force (Finkelhor 1979). If force is used, especially if there is physical injury, the child feels damaged, no longer whole, ruined. In some child rape cases, there will be no need for treatment. However, if the child exhibits emotional problems, if there was physical injury, or if the parents are not handling the situation well, treatment will be necessary. Generally, this will be individual therapy for the child. The caretakers may be a part of the therapy sessions but more to act as supportive persons or surrogate therapists (see chapter 11) than as recipients of treatment for themselves. Jean's experience, described below, illustrates most of the components of a stranger child rape situation.

> EXAMPLE 2: Jean, age 10, was walking home from school one day when a man of about 50 years, with sunglasses, and in a silver Mercedes, asked her if she needed a ride home. She said no, but the man grabbed her by the arm and pulled her into the car and drove away. She screamed at the

top of her lungs and the rapist pulled into a secluded lane, and ordered her to stop. He told her that she could have ten dollars if she cooperated. If she did not he would have to gag her. She screamed again, and he took off her underpants and stuffed them in her mouth. He took her into the back seat of the car. He then attempted to put his penis in her vagina. He did not have an erection, so he made Jean rub his penis and he achieved a partial erection. He attempted to penetrate her again, and she tried to get away. He got a full erection then. She reported that his attempts were very painful. He eventually gave up trying to penetrate her and put his penis between her thighs. Jean said this went on for a very long time, and the rapist was getting annoyed (apparently because he could not ejaculate). Eventually, he sat on her stomach and masturbated himself to orgasm. He ejaculated in her face.

A car turned into the lane and the rapist was distracted. Jean escaped from his car and ran toward the oncoming car. In the car were two black men. (Jean is white). Jean avoided the car and ran home. She immediately told her grandmother who babysat for her after school. Jean told her story to the police and her mother took her to the doctor. She had bruising on the thighs, redness in the vaginal area, and bruises on the face.

The rapist was caught. He had been out on bond pending trial on a rape charge involving a 14 year old. For a week Jean stayed home from school, and, when she did return, her grandmother came and picked her up after school.

Jean received four sessions of therapy. In the first session both parents were present and in the three subsequent sessions her mother was there. Concerns that Jean raised were whether she could ever get married now and why the man did that to her. She was also very frightened about being outside. In addition to the therapy, Jean had a follow-up visit to the doctor who told her that she was physically "OK." Her hymen was still intact, and the injuries were healed.

Jean's mother was also coached in how to respond to concerns Jean might raise and was alerted to the possibility Jean might need additional treatment in the future.

Jean's case fits the child rape situation in that there is one instance of violent sexual assault for which there is no forewarning. Suddenly the rapist grabbed Jean. Although he offered to pay Jean ten dollars, his major means of inducing compliance was the use of force. He grabbed her and pulled her into the car; he stuffed her underpants in her mouth, and he grabbed her and pulled her back into the car when she attempted to get away. She suffered physical injury as a result of the assault. As is typical of child rape, the first type of sexual behavior attempted was full genital intercourse. The rapist resorted to interfemoral intercourse and masturbation because he was unable to penetrate her vaginally. Consistent with the pattern in child rape, when Jean escaped and ran home, her immediate response was to tell her grandmother, and the family's response was appropriate.

C. Cases Which Fall Between Classical Incest and Stranger Rape

Cases falling between the two ends of this continuum will demonstrate a lot of variability in the dimensions described earlier. However, the frequency and duration of the sexual abuse will not be so great as in incest but will be greater than in stranger rape. The sexual relationship will usually have a less gradual evolution than in incest but will not generally be so abrupt as in stranger encounters. Force will more likely be used than in incest, but less likely than in stranger rape.

The response of the child will depend upon how close the child feels to the perpetrator, a delay in telling being more likely when there is an investment in this relationship. Similarly, parental response will vary depending upon how close the family is to the perpetrator, but a relative, such as a grandfather, is more likely to be protected than a nonrelative such as a storekeeper.

Measures necessary for protection will depend upon the perpetrator's access to the child and the family's ability and willingness to protect the child. If the perpetrator lives within the household, he or the child must usually be removed. If the parent continues to expose a child to the perpetrator, removal of the child should be considered. In one case in our sample, a mother continued to use as a babysitter a woman whose boyfriend had sexually molested her daughter. The mother worked and said there was no other babysitter close to her work. She added that besides she did not believe her daughter. Eventually this child was placed with her father.

Psychological trauma depends upon a variety of factors, the closeness of the relationship to the perpetrator, how the family has responded, and whether force was used. What is necessary in terms of treatment also will vary. If the perpetrator is someone the child has had little sexual contact with, is outside the home, and the family has responded in a supportive fashion, no treatment may be necessary for the victim and her family. However, either legal or mental health intervention or both will be indicated for the perpetrator. The case described below illustrates characteristics found in such cases.

> EXAMPLE 3: Yolanda is four-and-a-half and black. Her mother works full time, and her father, who is unemployed, is supposed to babysit for her, her two-year-old sister, and George, her ten-year-old brother. However,

particularly in the summertime, the father would take the children to his mother's and leave them. His mother, called Mother Jennings, is married to a man 15 years younger than she, Walter Jennings, who is a police officer. He is not Yolanda's father's father. Yolanda was sexually abused by Walter. She reported one incident to her brother, George, when it happened, hoping that George would tell her mother. On that occasion, Walter had taken Yolanda into the bathroom and made her fellate him while he sat on the edge of the tub and she knelt in front of him. He ejaculated, or, as she said, "snot came out of his thing and he made me swallow it." He told her not to tell anyone, but she told George. George did not tell anyone because he did not believe Yolanda. Two months after the incident, Yolanda told her mother. Her mother knew Yolanda's allegations were not made up when Yolanda talked about the "snot," and she immediately called Mother Jennings.

Mother Jennings did not believe Yolanda but said she would talk to her husband. Yolanda's mother then told Yolanda's father, who wanted to kill Walter. However, they agreed that Yolanda's father would get in touch with the FBI and that he should not take the children to his mother's anymore.

When her husband failed to follow through, Yolanda's mother called the FBI and there was a criminal investigation. During the investigation, Yolanda revealed an incident prior to the fellatio, in which Walter made her kneel naked in front of him while he masturbated himself. Yolanda also said she did not like Walter because he yelled at her and spanked her when she did not eat her vegetables, but she "liked his suit (uniform)." Criminal prosecution of Walter was unsuccessful because Yolanda was terrified during the court process and did not make a persuasive witness.

Both before and after the criminal prosecution, Yolanda wished she were dead. When the criminal prosecution was unsuccessful, Yolanda became convinced that Walter was going to kill her and her mother with his police revolver. Yolanda was also unwilling to go to school, partly because Walter's house was next door to the school. Yolanda received therapy, with her mother usually present, to deal with her suicidal feelings and her fears of Walter. The family was also helped to relocate. Yolanda's father was not involved in the treatment because he and his wife were in the process of getting a divorce. Individual sessions were provided to Yolanda's mother to help her deal with the sexual abuse, the failure of the criminal prosecution, pressures from the Jennings, and her divorce from her husband, who was a violent man and a drug user. Walter denied the sexual abuse, yet refused to take a lie detector test to corroborate his statements. Administrative procedures were taken against him within the police department and he was dismissed. Treatment was recommended for him but he did not follow through.

In the above case, with regard to frequency, duration, and evolution of the sexual abuse, we have a report of two incidents which occurred during one summer, the first being less intrusive than the second. There is no indication that the induction was gentle or gradual. Yolanda was told by Walter what to do, and, prior to the abuse, she reports some negative feelings toward Walter. She did not report the first incident when it happened, and with the occurrence of the second told neither her mother nor Mother Jennings, as one might expect in a stranger rape case, but rather her brother, with the hope that he would tell her mother. With regard to protection of Yolanda, her parents responded appropriately by no longer using Mother Jennings as a babysitter. Further, they sought criminal prosecution of Walter. The psycholgical trauma to Yolanda came in part from how she felt about herself after she had been abused, but it also was a result of the failure of criminal prosecution and threats by the Jennings family. Treatment in this case should have involved not only therapy for Yolanda and her mother, but also for Walter.

III. THE ROLE RELATIONSHIP BETWEEN PERPETRATOR AND VICTIM

A second but related way of differentiating sexual abuse cases is based upon the social role the perpetrator occupies for the victim (Biddle and Thomas 1966). Figure 3.1 specifies at the top some of the roles commonly filled by perpetrators. On the chart these persons are listed with proximate relationships at the left and more distant ones at the right.

From the study of our cases, we have identified some commonalities among cases where perpetrators have specific relationships with the child. We have identified five types of relationships where there are consistent patterns in the dynamics. We have also designated, based upon our experience, case management strategies for each type of case. The case types are stepfather—mother's boyfriend cases, noncustodial parent cases, single parent cases, old man perpetrator cases, and adolescent perpetrator cases. Each of these will be described and illustrated. While the factors with regard to the closeness of the relationship between victim and perpetrator are important in each of these types, there are also other significant characteristics. The emphasis of the discussion will be on the latter.

A. Stepfather—Mother's Boyfriend

Research and clinical experience suggest that the role relationship of stepfather or mother's boyfriend is one where the risk for sexual abuse is high (see chapter 2; Russell 1983; American Humane Association 1984). In our sample, cases classified as stepfather or mother's boyfriend perpetrator represent the largest subgroup in the sample.

While there are some differences in the boyfriend and the stepfather roles, there are enough commonalities to include them in a single type of sexual abuse. Often a man enters the household as a boyfriend and then becomes a stepfather. Cases where the boyfriend is not a living-together-partner (LTP) are different and are not included in this case-type.

In stepfather-LTP cases the incest taboo is attenuated or does not exist. In about half of our cases the sexual abuse began quite soon after the relationship with the mother was established. In such cases, the perpetrator often simultaneously courts mother and daughter, an observation also made by O'Brien (1986). Neither female is likely to be consciously aware of this process, but frequently it leads to a lot of tension and jealousy between mother and daughter. In other instances, we found the sexual abuse precipitated by some crisis in the perpetrator's life, such as loss of employment or a motorcycle accident.

One of the reasons the sexual relationship between stepfather and victim evolves so quickly in these cases is that the child may have been victimized by her own father or other men with whom the mother has had relationships. Often, examination of histories of previous men in the mother's life reveals a lot of dysfunction, and many times the current stepfather or boyfriend is better functioning than past men and the mother may be reluctant to leave him. However, in general, mothers, in stepfather-boyfriend cases can be differentiated from mothers in the classical incest family by their superior ability to extricate themselves from relationships with problematic men.

Children in our sample range from 3½ to 17 for this case type, and victims in stepfather-boyfriend cases tend to be somewhat older at onset than children in classical incest (mean age 7.4 years.) Moreover, generational boundaries may be even more blurred than in classical incest. Our experience is that frequently the perpetrator is younger than the mother. In one of our cases, the perpetrator, a stepfather, was 19, the mother 32, and the two victims 11 and 7. In another, the perpetrator, a living-together-partner, was 24, the mother 34, and the victims 17, 14, and 13. This age incongruity exacerbates the existing role confusion, which results from the perpetrator assuming a new status, parent, and from his concurrent courting of mother and daughter.

There are some guidelines for intervention. While there may be the possibility of maintaining and enhancing the relationship between the perpetrator and the mother, in many cases the mother will expel him from the household or will take the children and leave. When she does this, she should be supported. The mother and children then become the focus of treatment. However, in addition to a family therapy focus, there should be individual treatment for the mother, centering on her choices in men, and dyadic treatment for the mother and daughter. The case of the J's illustrates most of the components of stepfather-boyfriend cases.

EXAMPLE 4: Mrs. J married Mr. M at 16 to escape an abusive and punitive stepmother. She got pregnant in order to persuade her parents to allow her to get married. Soon after the marriage, Peggy, her first child, was born. Mr. M turned out to be a very abusive husband and father, although Mrs. J had no prior indication he would be. He also had a lot of paranoid thoughts, difficulties holding a job, and was obsessed with the thought his wife was cheating on him. Moreover, he drank excessively. Soon after Peggy was born, Mrs. J again became pregnant. Her husband doubted he was the father of the child. After the birth of their second child, Joan, Mrs. J went to work in a factory to support the family. One day, she discovered Joan, two, under a pillow and badly bruised when she returned from work. She attempted to take Joan to the hospital but her husband threatened to shoot Peggy with his shotgun if she left.

Afterward, Mrs. J hired a 13-year-old babysitter to watch the children while she worked. Her daughters could recall their father taking the babysitter into the back bedroom and teaching her about sex, but they could not recall being sexually abused themselves, only brutally physically abused. When Joan was four, a third child, Raymond, was born.

Their father was becoming more and more disturbed, being psychotic and drunk most of the time. Finally, one night while he was drunk and passed out, Mrs. J left with the children and went first to her father's house. He would let them stay only a short time. Therefore, Mrs. J took the children and left for a town in the South where she had relatives. She filed for a divorce. At this time the children were 12, 10, and 6.

While she was there she met Bruce J, whom she later married. At the time Mr. J was 24 and Mrs. J was 28. The children said at first they did not like Mr. J because they wanted their mom to marry someone else. But when Mr. J got a job, he bought them things. He also fixed up the house and made them do their chores. When he got mad, he only yelled and made them go to their room.

However, about a year after Mr. J married Mrs. J, he was in a motorcycle accident and his shoulder was badly dislocated. He lost his job and could not use his arm for six months. He grew bad tempered, and when he recovered sufficiently he started beating his wife and the children. He also sexually abused both girls. The first victim was Joan. He engaged in anal intercourse with her once. He told her that if she told he would go to jail and she did not tell. He had genital intercourse with Peggy five or six times.

Peggy told her mother, and her mother immediately took the three children and went to her sister's house. From there she called the police, and Mr. J was arrested the next day. Mrs. J then returned home, and she and her children participated in the criminal prosecution of Mr. J. Although Mrs. J was concerned about her husband's welfare and felt he would not get help in jail, she strongly asserted that she did not want him for a husband anymore.

Individual treatment was provided for Mrs. J to help her look at her own past and its relationship to her choices in men. Family therapy was provided to address feelings the whole family had about not only Mr. J and ensuing events, but also about Mr. M. There were also individual sessions for the girls, and their primary focus was on guilt feelings the children had because of their role in sending their stepfather to prison.

This case has most of the characteristics typical of stepfather case, although it lacks the level of animosity sometimes found between mother and daughter. This is so not only because Mrs. J was a nurturing and fairly adequate parent, but also because when Mr. J first entered the home, he did not court the female children. He became sexually involved with them only after he had suffered a major crisis, the disabling motorcycle accident.

B. Noncustodial Parent

Another case type which has emerged from our data with a distinct set of dynamics is sexual abuse by a noncustodial parent where there is a separation or divorce. We have had cases with both male and female perpetrators. As a rule, the sexual abuse occurs during visitation with the noncustodial parent. However, in our sample, we have one case where it occurred when the father was babysitting in the mother's home and another in which the perpetrator kidnapped the child and sexually abused her.

In only two cases was there evidence of an incestuous relationship before the separation. However, in all cases there were interactions between the child and parent prior to the demise of the marriage which might be viewed as precursors to sexual abuse. In several cases, the father experienced an erection while bathing with the child. In others, the perpetrator was observed by the nonabusive parent French-kissing or caressing the child in a sexual way. In a number of cases the abusive parent would sleep with the child when the other parent was absent. The children experiencing this type of sexual abuse were quite young, all except three being six years or under when the abuse began.

In all of the cases in our sample the abusing parent was not the instigator of, and in fact strongly resisted, the separation and divorce. Three factors seem to contribute to the risk of sexual abuse in this kind of case. The first is the loss of structure which had been present when the family was intact. The structure of family life may well have been what prevented the abuser from acting upon sexual feelings toward the children. In the unstructured situation of visitation, the perpetrator has unsupervised access to the children. Second, the offender is often devastated and lonely because of the loss of the spouse and turns to the child for emotional support, which leads to sexual interaction with the child. Third, the perpetrator frequently has a tremendous amount of anger toward the spouse who has precipitated the marital breakup. Some of the anger is expressed directly, but it is also expressed indirectly through the sexual abuse of the child. When revenge is a primary motivation, the sexual abuse may be forceful and result in physical injury to the victim.

The nonabusive parent's response to discovering the sexual abuse almost always is protective, although the initial reaction may be disbelief. In our sample this parent was also much more independent and autonomous than the nonabusive parents in the two types of intrafamilial sexual abuse already described.

Intervention in these cases usually begins by stopping visitation with the abusive parent or making visits supervised. This is done either in the court which has jurisdiction over the divorce or in the court which handles child protection cases.

The next step is treatment for the perpetrator, usually separate from the family. If visits have been stopped, they are resumed when the therapist thinks there has been sufficient progress in treatment, and these contacts are supervised. Resumption of unsupervised visits even after treatment has ended is generally not advisable. Usually, there is a grandmother or a new partner who can be present during visits. The reality is that many offenders never follow through on treatment and, in fact, lose interest in their children, as they establish other sexual relationships with adults. Treatment for the victim, usually in the presence of the custodial parent, is also indicated. The following example is a typical case of noncustodial parent abuse.

EXAMPLE 5: Mr. and Mrs. R separated when Mrs. R was pregnant with her second child because she could not tolerate her husband always "putting me down" and physically assaulting her. He also was pathologically jealous and imagined Mrs. R was having affairs. The precipitating event to the marital breakup was his knocking her down and kicking her in the stomach when she was pregnant. She went home to her family and he went home to his. Lee, their daughter, who was almost two, had weekend visits with her father. Although Mr. R's parents were around, Mr. R took primary care of Lee, took naps with her, and slept with her at night when she stayed over. Mr. R took no interest in his second daughter when she was born and refused to take her for visits.

When Lee was a little more than two, her mother noticed that she would return from visits with a red and sore vulva. She thought her ex-husband was not changing Lee when she wet her pants and instructed him to do so. However, the irritation continued and got worse after Lee was toilet trained. When Lee told her mom that her daddy hurt her pee-pee, Mrs. R called protective services. When evaluated, Lee showed with anatomically explicit dolls how her daddy would take off her night clothes and take off his pajamas and place his penis between her thighs, rub it against her vagina, and perhaps had attempted penetration. She said that he went "pee-pee," and it hurt her when he did this. He also would "rub my pee-pee and his pee-pee."

When the father was evaluated with the child, he engaged in an unusual amount of caressing and hugging of Lee which she resisted. He asserted he did not sexually abuse his daughter and that the allegation was cooked up by his wife. He said he would prove it by taking a polygraph. He took the polygraph and failed it.

Mrs. R recalled that before their separation her husband would always take baths with Lee. Ordinarily he kept a washcloth over his penis when he did this. One time she came into the bathroom and found that he had his penis uncovered and was letting Lee touch it. She immediately picked Lee up out of the tub, took her into her bedroom, and dried and dressed her. She never confronted her husband about this behavior.

When Mr. R was asked during the evaluation about his feelings about the divorce, he expressed bewilderment and a desire to reunite with Mrs. R. At the same time, he blamed Mrs. R for all the problems in the marriage and for leaving him.

Mrs. R received counseling primarily focused on how to handle Lee with regard to sexual abuse. Mr. R missed half of his individual therapy sessions during the first three months of treatment, and when he attended he refused to acknowledge that he had sexually abused Lee. He also harassed and threatened Mrs. R and violated the provision for supervised visits with their two daughters. Visitation was then terminated by the court.

Mr. R showed some signs of being sexually attracted to children when his marriage was intact, but serious sexual abuse does not seem to have started until after marital separation. He also displays other areas of dysfunction, for example, he is physically abusive of his wife. He projects blame, for instance blaming his ex-wife for the demise of the marriage. In this case, there is not a total loss of structure, but Mr. R's parents do not seem to have involved themselves much with Lee. Probably both a sense of loss and anger at his wife motivated the sexual abuse.

C. Single Parent

The primary characteristic that differentiates single-parent cases from the type of case just described is that the single parent is the custodial parent. However, the dynamics also differ. Both mothers and fathers are abusers in our sample. When mothers are the perpetrators, they are likely to be women who have never had a consistent partner. When fathers are the perpetrators, often the mother is dead, has deserted the family, or is not a fit custodian. The victim is usually the oldest child and sometimes the only child. He/she becomes a substitute for the absent parent in more spheres than the sexual one. Even more than in other types of intrafamilial sexual abuse, the victim is a parental child, caring for younger children, managing the household, and playing a role in financial decisions.

The sexual abuse appears to evolve in one of two distinct patterns. In cases where there has been a desertion, divorce, or death of a parent, the remaining parent and older child typically share their sad feelings, often not revealing these to younger children. The parental child may begin sleeping with the parent because either parent or child is upset and lonely at night. The sexual relationship develops from this sleeping arrangement. (See also Justice and Justice 1979:102-104). In other cases, the child appears first to have taken over the household management and child care roles of the absent parent, and then the remaining parent looks to the child to meet his/her sexual needs. In both types of cases, the sexual abuse evolves more gradually than with the noncustodial abusers. It also tends to be characterized by nurturance and affection and by the absence of force.

The family which fosters single-parent sexual abuse is often geographically or socially isolated. Thus, one reason the sexual abuse may occur is because the family has no ready access to adults to fulfill the roles assumed by the child. Moreover, because of this isolation, the sexual abuse may persist for years before coming to the attention of outside authorities. Further, for the victim, the benefits of the relationship with the perpetrator often outweigh the costs. Sometimes the child has no awareness that the sexual relationship with the parent is wrong. Others may conceal the sexual abuse and refuse to tell well intentioned outsiders, not only because the sexual abuse may be experienced as positive, but also because the offender is the only caring figure in the child's life, and the child is terrified of losing him. Lukianowicz (1978) in describing a case of this type notes that the child said she "did not mind," that she felt it "quite natural" for her father to have sex with her after her mother left him, and that she "knew he loved" her.

Intervention in cases of this kind is difficult and often heart-wrenching. It usually involves separation of the children from the parent. These children may not do well in foster care and may run back home. Placement with a relative may be a better solution than foster care and preferable to termination of parental rights because it allows maintenance of positive aspects of the perpetrator-child relationship. Unfortunately, the noncustodial parent, if available, may not be a good candidate for caretaker, as that parent's dysfunction may have led to custody with the abusing parent. Moreover, when it is a maternal caretaker who is the abuser, the children may have different fathers. It is usually inappropriate to separate the children in order to place them with their fathers.

Children should be provided treatment focusing primarily upon the meaning of the sexual behavior, appropriate and inappropriate interaction with adults, and self-protection. The abusive parent should also be provided treatment. However, without some change in family composition, that is, the bringing in of another adult into the household, reunification will be risky. Sometimes after two or three years, when the children have had an opportunity to profit from an alternative living situation, to benefit from treatment, and to become more independent of the perpetrator, reunification will be possible. The following case example illustrates some of the dilemmas of the single parent case.

EXAMPLE 6: Al, his younger brother, Brad, and their mother, Mrs. H, lived at the mercy of the boys' stepfather. The boys had different fathers and Mrs. H had been married to neither of them. Their stepfather had been in the Korean War and was supposed to be mentally disabled because of it. He was described by Al as a drug addict from all the pills the VA gave him and a mean bastard. He beat the boys daily and their mother about once a week. Al and his mother tried to get the stepfather to go to treatment but he refused. Mrs. H went into therapy to help her deal with her abusive husband. Al said when he was about ten, he and his mother "put our heads together and figured out how to get away" from the stepfather. They left town and moved across the state. Mrs. H got a job as a secretary for the police department, and Al "more or less became the man of the household." He bought the groceries, cooked supper, babysat for his younger brother, and gave advice to his mother when she had difficulties with the police officers who made passes at her. When he was 14, he obtained a job delivering milk before he went to school in the morning.

Al and his mother would stay up late at night having long talks in which his mother would hold his hand and give him hugs and kisses. When it was time to go to bed she often would suggest that Al come to bed with her so he would not wake his brother up.

By the age of 13, Al was having sexual intercourse with his mother regularly. When Al was 15, his brother, who was 11, walked in on Al and Mrs. H. Although he was told not to tell, he told his best friend, Robert. Robert told his father who was a detective and worked with Mrs. H. Instead of making it a police matter, the detective called protective services, and they interviewed both boys at school. Initially, Al denied anything was taking place but later admitted it. Al said he knew it was not really right but he did not care. He also said he thought his mother was very beautiful.

When Mrs. H was confronted, she became hysterical. Eventually, she had to be hospitalized in the regional psychiatric hospital. She remained in the hospital six months. The boys went to stay with their maternal grandmother who lived in a Detroit suburb, far from the mother. Al wrote his mother several times a week. Neither boy liked the grandmother. She was strict and disapproved of their mother, saying she used to think she was just flighty, but now she knew she was crazy.

After their mother got out of the hospital, she went to therapy and visited the boys about once a month. The boys were seen by a male counselor and each was matched with a Big Brother. Al did not like the counselor or the Big Brother. Mrs. H also went back to work part time at her old job. Curiously, although people in the police department knew what she had done, they seem to have been understanding. She was befriended by a retiring police officer who was a widower. About a year after he retired, he married Mrs. H. After the marriage, the boys were allowed to stay with them during the summer. Al did not like his new stepfather very much, saying he was bossy and wanted everything done his own way.

Al graduated from high school when he was 18 and then was no longer under court jurisdiction. He moved back to the community where his mother resided so that he could be close to her.

In Al's case, he is very much the partner of his mother. He was old enough to appreciate the inappropriateness of the sexual abuse but clearly cared so much for his mother that he discounted the abuse. Treatment does not seem to have been very successful with Al as he evidences a lot of jealousy of his new stepfather. In addition, when Al himself became a stepparent, he sexually abused his stepdaughter.

D. Old Man Perpetrator

Another type of case is one where the perpetrator is an older man. The youngest man in our sample is 55 and the oldest 75. He may have a variety of role relationships to the child. He may be a grandfather, an uncle or great uncle, a close friend of the child's family, or a neighbor. Even though these are different roles, there are similarities in the characteristics of the sexual abuse.

Sometimes these men have a history of sexual abuse or sexual acting out, but in the majority of our cases we could obtain no such history. In contrast is a study by Goodwin et al. (1983) of 10 grandfather-granddaughter incest cases; in six of the cases the men had also sexually abused their daughters. What we found as a contributing cause was absence of an appropriate sexual partner in their current situation. Either the spouse was deceased, was no longer interested in sex, or was absent. For example, the 57-year-old wife of a 61-year-old perpetrator in our sample said she no longer wished sexual intercourse. She weighed about 190 pounds, and had diabetes and a heart condition. She stated that since her husband was older than she, she had just assumed he was not interested in sex anymore either.

The victims in our sample were between the ages of two and eight, and were both male and female. In a number of cases more than one child was involved. None of the cases involved genital intercourse. Most involved the perpetrator doing something intended to pleasure the child, hugging and kissing the child's body, fondling the genitals, or oral contact with the child's genitals. In many instances, the perpetrator was incapable of achieving a complete erection or of ejaculation. Often bribes such as candy or money were used to induce the children to cooperate, and in no case was force used. Usually there was some ongoing relationship between the perpetrator and victim. Victims, when asked to tell how they felt when the perpetrator was doing things to them, responded variously, "weird," "strange," "good," and "relaxed." Many of the children were not aware of the inappropriateness of the behavior when it occurred.

Parental response, if they discovered the abuse, appears to have been governed by the closeness of the relationship between perpetrator and family. If the person was a relative, usually the family attempted to handle it without involving outside authorities. Parents would tell the child to stay away from the abuser or would not allow the perpetrator to babysit anymore. We are also aware of several instances, but not from this case sample, where families put the abusers in nursing homes in order to protect their children. If the person was not a relative, the police were more likely to be called.

Intervention should focus on protecting the victim and future victims from the perpetrator, on helping the child to understand the meaning of the sexual abuse, and on dealing with any other issues the child raises. We have not found these offenders very good candidates for therapy. If they have a prior history of sexual abuse, it is naive to expect that such a long-standing pattern will respond to treatment when the man is in his sixties. We have also noted that it is difficult to get a man who is preparing for the end of his life to focus on his sexuality and on change. On the other hand, protection of victims by incarceration of the perpetrator seems inhumane. Often the men are infirm as well as aged. Their health may fail in prison and they may be brutalized by other prisoners.

The following example is fairly characteristic of this casetype.

EXAMPLE 7: Mr. G, age 55, moved precipitously into his daughter's home. He had been married for 35 years, but three years earlier his wife had had a hysterectomy. After that, according to Mr. G, she had no further desire for sex. Mr. G began going to dances where he would dance with "ladies." He would invite them to dinner and then to bed.

His wife discovered his infidelity and had him served with divorce papers. He had to immediately vacate the marital home. The first night he slept in his truck, but by the second night his daughter, Mrs. S, took him in. The S's have two children, Linda, eight, and Jane, four.

Mr. G had been laid off several months earlier and was living on unemployment. The S family began to use Mr. G as a babysitter. Both S's worked and had different shifts, but there were two to three hours when both parents were gone and the children were home from school. Both children loved when their grandfather babysat. He played games with them and he would make them pancakes for supper.

However, Linda began to complain of stomach pain and she had as sore throat. When her mother took her to the doctor, she was found to have pharyngeal gonorrhea. When the family was told this, they immediately challenged the doctor. He double-checked the results. The parents submitted to the necessary laboratory tests but initially would not allow any contact with Mr. G. The parents' and Jane's tests were negative, but it was a month before the grandfather went for tests. Initially Mr. G told the doctor to do a test for syphilis instead of gonorrhea. When he finally was tested for gonorrhea, the results were negative. Later it was learned that Mr. G had worked in a VD ward while in the armed forces and, contrary to his presentation, knew all about venereal disease, its symptoms, and how to get rid of it.

Linda was very reluctant to implicate her grandfather and actually did so only indirectly. From what could be discerned, the parents never confronted Mr. G, but they made him move out of the S household into an apartment. No treatment was ordered for the grandfather, but the S family sought and received treatment. The S's were told never to let Mr. G alone with the children, and other relatives of Mr. G with children were also warned.

In the case of Mr. G, we find that he was cut off from what were his ordinary sexual outlets rather abruptly and put into a situation where he had unsupervised access to his two granddaughters. Jane did not have gonorrhea but we do not know whether she was sexually abused because the parents would not allow her to be interviewed. What differentiates this case from others of this type is that the grandfather was more sexually active with appropriate partners (i.e., his "ladies") and he used the child to pleasure himself rather than vice versa. No treatment was ordered for Mr. G because he was a man of weak superego, little insight, and not very great intelligence. Criminal prosecution would have been unsuccessful because Linda would not have testified against her grandfather, and the parents would not have cooperated. In addition, prosecution would have induced more trauma for Linda than the sexual abuse. Finally, Mr. G did not seem to present a great risk to other children in the community. He did not appear to have a history of sexual molestation of children, and appeared to have been quite frightened by the consequences of his involvement with Linda. It was felt that fear of similar outcomes, should he ever be tempted, would act as an "external superego" (see chapter 4) for Mr. G and inhibit further sexual abuse.

E. Adolescent Abuser

Adolescents who become sexually involved with young children represent another case type. As with the older man, the adolescent can have different role relationships to the child. The abuser may be an older sibling, but is more likely to be a half-sibling or stepsibling, a cousin, an uncle, a babysitter, a neighbor, or a friend of the family. Most of the abusers in our sample are male but a small percentage are female. All of the sexual relationships were heterosexual, but this finding is not necessarily a characteristic of adolescent offenders in general (Knopp 1982; O'Brien 1986). The age of the perpetrators ranged from 13 to 20. Others (Knopp 1982) find perpetrators as young as 11. The victims were from three to eight years.

Adolescent sexual abuse can be distinguished from developmentally appropriate sexual experimentation which most children engage in. First, in adolescent sexual abuse, generally there is an age differential between the perpetrator and victim, usually of five years or more, whereas, with sexual experimentation, children are about the same age. Second, there is power differential—the perpetrator is, of course, more powerful. The abusive situation is not one of mutual exploration, where both parties play an equal role in deciding on the sexual play, but rather one where the perpetrator imposes his will upon the child or is in control of the sexual behavior. Finally, there is a differential in the level of knowledge about the meaning of the sexual behavior, the perpetrator being well aware of the exploitative nature of the relationship with the younger child.

Adolescent sexual offenders represent a substantial proportion of the sexual offender population. For example, the 1979 U.S. National Crime Survey report 21 percent of the forcible rapes were committed by adolescents (Becker et al., no date). One treatment program for child victims found that almost half the perpetrators were adolescents and as a result developed a treatment program for them (Knopp 1982:48). The research of Masters and Johnson (1970) indicates adolescence is a period of heightened sexual drive for males. At the same time most adolescents are not accomplished sexual performers. These circumstances may increase the risk of teenage males choosing sexual outlets where their performance will not be questioned, for example, children.

The severity of the adolescent's problem varies. At the less serious end of the spectrum is the teenager who sexually experiments with a younger child. As a rule the encounter is opportunistic—that is, the adolescent finds himself in a situation where he can take sexual advantage of a younger child and does so. However he does not plan the encounter nor maneuver himself into a situation where he can have unsupervised access to children. Usually these adolescent abusers are fairly young, 13, 14, or 15. There is generally one victim and usually one instance of sexual abuse. Force is not used. Sometimes the encounter is precipitated by reading sexually arousing material.

More serious is the young perpetrator who seeks out situations where children are available to him. He may be a babysitter or an adolescent who willingly plays with younger children. He often has difficulty with peer relationships because of his physical appearance or lack of social skills. He is particularly likely to have problems with peers of the opposite sex. With this type of perpetrator there are repeated instances of sexual abuse both with the same and different victims. Bribes and other inducements may be employed but force or threats are not ordinarily used. Sometimes the adolescent induces the child to cooperate by showing her sexually arousing material. The adolescent may cultivate the relationship with his first victim initially for his emotional gratification, someone who will look up to him. Then the relationship becomes sexual. With later victims, the adolescent consciously pursues liaisons that he intends to be both emotionally and sexually gratifying.

Next in terms of severity is the aggressive adolescent who also sexually abuses children. Sexual abuse is one of several areas in which the teenager acts out. He is likely to engage in physical assault of peers and sometimes parents, to be involved in destruction of and crimes against property, and may be sexually aggressive to peers as well as younger children. Often his lack of success with peers leads him to sexually accost younger children. Diagnostically he would be classified as character disordered. In general, anger and the desire to exert control over his victim play a prominent role in the sexual abuse. Thus force is likely to be used and physical injury may result. There may be multiple victims. This type of perpetrator makes little or no emotional investment in his victim.

Finally, there is the adolescent who is a pedophile (see section D, below for a fuller discussion of pedophilia). Pedophilia appears to have its onset during adolescence (Groth 1977; Abel, Mittelman, and Becker, in press). It is a compulsive behavior and therefore is characterized by multiple, repetitive sexual encounters with children.

With regard to intervention, the first step is safeguarding the victim by restricting the perpetrator from unsupervised access. For example, if the perpetrator has been the victim's babysitter, he should be so no more. If the two children live in the same household, in cases other than the first type described, separation should be effected. This usually means that the adolescent must move.

Minimal treatment may be all that is necessary for the victim. She will need to understand the meaning of the sexual behavior and why it is inappropriate. She will also need to be assisted in developing strategies for self-protection. More extended treatment is necessary when the sexual abuse has been traumatic or extensive or the perpetrator was a family member.

On the other hand, treatment of some duration with the perpetrator is essential. While some authors (Gagnon 1965; Roberts et al. 1973; Finkelhor 1979) have suggested that sexual offenses by adolescents usually represent sexual experimentation, others strongly disagree (Groth 1979; Becker et al. in press; Becker et al. no date). In any case it is not worth the risk to society of giving adolescent perpetrators the benefit of the doubt. Research (Groth and Birnbaum 1979; Becker et al. in press) indicates that the majority of sex offenders begin their abuse during adolescence, and that the abuse is likely to involve progressively more serious behaviors. Thus an adolescent who is caught committing his first offense may be beginning his sexually abusive career rather than merely experimenting.

Treatment of adolescent perpetrators generally involves a combination of individual, family, and group therapy (Knopp 1982; Becker et al. 1985). Emphasis is placed upon the teenager confessing the full extent of his abusive behavior and taking responsibility for it, sex education, changing values related to sexual behavior, teaching self control techniques, enhancing attraction to appropriate sex objects, social skills training, and understanding the contribution of the family to the sexual abuse (Knopp 1982; O'Brien 1986).

Some adolescent perpetrators, usually the aggressive adolescents and the pedophiles, require treatment in a closed setting, because they continue to be a threat while being treated, and their problems are so severe they require more intensive intervention than can be provided on an outpatient basis. Treatment programs for adolescent perpetrators are still experimental, but results so far are quite promising (Knopp 1982; Becker et al. 1985; Boulder County Protective Service 1983).

Two case examples will be cited below, one which does not appear to have been very serious and which has a good prognosis, and a second, much more severe and with a poor prognosis.

> EXAMPLE 8: Garred, 14, was a babysitter for Sophie, 6. Their parents are very good friends and frequently, when they would go out together, Garred would babysit for Sophie. One night when Garred and Sophie were watching television and lying on the couch, Garred told Sophie to close her eyes, that he was going to put his thumb in her mouth. Instead he put his penis in her mouth. Sophie knew it was a penis because she heard him unzip his fly, what he put in her mouth was not shaped and did not taste like a thumb, and when she opened her eyes she caught a glimpse of his penis as he zipped his fly back up.
>
> Sophie did not tell her mother, but told Jean, 7, who is Garred's sister. Jean told her mother who told Sophie's mother. Because Garred's mother did not believe her son would do such a thing, Sophie's mother brought Sophie to be evaluated so they could find out the truth. After the evaluation, the families were told Sophie was telling the truth.
>
> Garred admitted it to his parents when confronted and he was very ashamed. When he was seen by an evaluator he seemed to be a shy young man. He was a computer whiz, but did not have many friends. His father was a famous athletic coach, and Garred was a disappointment to his father because he had asthma and could not achieve at sports as his father had hoped. Garred had never gone out on a date, although most of his contemporaries had. When asked what put the idea in his mind to do this to Sophie, he said he and his friends had read about it in *Playboy* magazine.
>
> One session of therapy was conducted with Sophie in her mother's presence. It dealt with the meaning of Garred's behavior, its inappropriateness, and how to protect herself in the future. Garred was referred to a male therapist. He was seen separately and in the context of his family over a period of several months. No groups were available in the community where Garred lived.

Garred seems to be the first kind of adolescent offender, but he could have progressed to the second type if there had been no intervention. In many respects Garred was a model child, but his feelings of inadequacy inhibited his ability to form appropriate peer relationships. Both families responded quickly and sought help for their children. For Garred, treatment not only interrupted a potentially deviant sexual pattern, but also served to improve his relationships with peers and with family members, particularly his father.

The next example is very different.

EXAMPLE 9:   Karen, age three, was the youngest child in her family. Her mother, Mrs. C, actually had had two families, by two different husbands. The first husband deserted her and she abandoned his five children to foster care. She remarried and had twins, Sallie and Suzie, and then a year later a son, Art. It was 16 years later that she had Karen. She was not even aware she was pregnant until four months. She was 46 at the time. When Karen was born, Mr. C, Karen's father, had just had surgery for throat cancer and the prognosis was poor. Mr. C died when Karen was a year old. Art had had a very tempestuous relationship with his father, and, by his own admission, was not sad when his father died.

When Karen was three and Art 19, she told Suzie that Art had hurt her "pussy" while he was babysitting for her. Suzie examined her and found her vagina red and swollen. Suzie insisted, against her mother's protests, that they take Karen to the doctor.

The following facts emerged from the evaluation. Karen indicated with anatomically explicit dolls that Art had put his "dick" in her "pussy" and mouth, and that he put his fingers in her "pussy." She said this happened "lotsa times" and that she had told her mother.

Mrs. C responded that she had Karen sleep in her bed and there was a lock on the inside of the door so that Art could not get in. However, she also admitted that Art physically abused her, that she hid her money in her room so he would not get it, and that she slept with a butcher knife in case Art broke her lock. In general, she appeared to be a very low functioning mother.

Art already had two delinquency charges against him. When evaluated, he was dirty, his hair uncombed, and his teeth not brushed. He appeared to be a loner. He spent most of his time in the arcades playing video games. He had quit school without graduating and he did not work.

Initial intervention was that Art moved out of the home. Because Karen was really too young and immature to respond to treatment, her mother was instructed to put Karen in day care. Day care was to deal with the inadequacies of the mother's parenting and to provide some protection. Art was told by his probation officer, whom he had because of his delinquency offenses, to attend treatment or he might be prosecuted for criminal sexual conduct. He did not do this. Within two months he was arrested for breaking and entering. He was convicted and sentenced to a facility with a sex offender treatment program.

Art is best described as an aggressive adolescent who also commits sex offenses against children. He abuses his mother and she is so frightened of him she sleeps with a knife by her bed. He engaged in some delinquent acts prior to being caught for sexual abuse and a more serious offense afterward. The likelihood of his profiting from treatment is not great.

IV. TYPES OF SEXUAL ABUSE WHERE PERPETRATOR PSYCHOPATHOLOGY IS THE ORGANIZING CHARACTERISTIC

Four types of sexual abuse will be described for which the individual psychology of the perpetrator is the defining characteristic. While each represents a fairly small percentage of cases that come to the attention of social agencies, they are all problematic for professionals, and each requires a special set of interventions. The four types are cases where the perpetrator is psychotic, cases where one or both participants is (are) mentally retarded, polymorphous or polyincestuous families, and cases where the perpetrator is a pedophile.

A. Psychotic Perpetrators

Since cases where perpetrators are psychotic constitute only two percent of our sample, observations about them must be made with less certainty. However, our findings are consistent with those of other writers (e.g., Summit and Kryso 1978). In most instances, the abusers are schizophrenics, but in one case the perpetrator was manic-depressive. Perpetrators in our sample are both male and female. If one examines the sexual abuse literature for cases of female abusers, frequently the mother is reported as psychotic (Justice and Justice 1979). The perpetrator was in a parental relationship with the victims in all of our cases. The ages of the children were between two and eight.

The psychotic process plays an essential role in the sexual abuse. There are some commonalities in delusional systems of perpetrators. They are a mixture of persecution and grandiosity. Perpetrators often appear to deal with their own libidinous feelings, which are out of control, by projecting them onto others or the environment, while at the same time justifying their own sexual behavior. For instance, one mother in our sample reported fears that the FBI and the U.S. Government were inciting devil worshippers to sexually molest her four-year-old daughter. To counteract this, the mother would give the daughter enemas and douches, inserting her fingers in the girl's vagina.

Nonperpetrating parents who choose to remain with psychotic perpetrators are often fairly disturbed. Further, they are often strikingly unprotective despite their knowledge of the perpetrator's psychosis. For instance, in one of our cases, the mother was an attendant at a mental hospital. She would befriend male mental patients, bringing them home as lovers, and then she would use them as babysitters for her four-year-old daughter. She brought home a man who signed himself out against medical advice and thought he was God. He was convinced that the daughter also had special powers and had intercourse with her to protect her from others sapping her powers.

The best course of intervention in such cases is to hospitalize the perpetrator. With proper medication the delusions are likely to be dampened or they may disappear. However, it is our experience that frequently perpetrators are paranoid about and will refuse medication. Alternatively, once they are out of the hospital they will stop taking their medication. This means that unless their medication and mental illness are closely monitored, it is unwise to allow the perpetrator access to the child after hospitalization. Treatment of the child should focus primarily on understanding what is or was wrong with the perpetrator and why this led to the sexual abuse. Usually, treatment is also necessary for the nonabusive parent. It should focus on the lack of protection provided the victim. Often there are unconscious motives leading to failure to protect that need to be explored.

The following case example is of a black family and illustrates the characteristics common to cases where the perpetrator is psychotic.

EXAMPLE 10: Mrs. B presented herself at the local domestic violence shelter with her daughter, Bunny, 5, and son Silas, 8. She had left her husband of six years, not because he was physically abusive, but because he was driving her crazy. Some days he would think he was "the almighty pan-African leader" and he would spend his time drawing maps and making plans to free his people. Other days he was a sorcerer and would go around casting spells and putting potions in various parts of the house to ward off the evil spirits. On still other days, he would be preoccupied with his body, describing it as having a good side and an evil side, a live side and a dead side. On these days he would take four baths. He also slept very little. Mr. B never left the house and refused to work. He was the father of Bunny. Mrs. B had Silas before this marriage and was not married to his father.

Mrs. B, in order to prepare herself to get out of the relationship with Mr. B, had enrolled in a legal secretarial course. She was gone eight hours a day. She left the children in the charge of Mr. B. Silas went to school until 2:30, and Bunny was supposed to be in kindergarten. However, Mr. B would not send her there because he thought they were trying to poison her soul at school.

While the family was in the shelter, both children showed sexual precocity and spoke of their involvement in sexual activity. When the children were evaluated, Bunny, although initially reluctant to speak, was eventually fairly forthcoming. Silas was acutely embarrassed and did not acknowledge any sexual abuse.

Bunny said that her father would put his fingers in her ''vaginita'' and tell her he was getting ''bugs and maggots'' out of her. He also poured hot water over her genitals once to get the ''fleas out.'' When he did this, he also would be rubbing his ''ding dong'' to get the maggots out of his. When asked when this happened, she said when her mom and Silas were at school. Bunny also reported seeing her father getting the ''maggots'' out of Silas's ''ding dong.'' At that point during the evaluation, Silas hid under a chair and denied that anything had happened to him. Bunny said, ''You lie, Silas.''

Mrs. B, when questioned, said that she found her husband disgusting and would not have sex with him. She would sleep on the couch, and usually she went to bed before Mr. B. When she would waken in the morning, she would frequently find Bunny in the bed with Mr. B. When asked if she had ever tried to do anything about this, she said sometimes she would put Bunny back in her bed, but her husband would just get up and go get her again. His disturbed behavior had been extreme for a year, but three years prior to her leaving he had begun to exhibit symptoms.

With the support of the shelter staff, Mrs. B filed charges against her husband. He was arrested and she then returned home. At the arraignment, Bunny testified. Mr. B appeared totally disoriented. He kept bobbing up and down and bowing to the judge. When he took the stand, he said he was the almighty pan-African leader and did not know the infidel who had testified against him. Before going into court, he had put pepper in his shoes in order to fend off evil spirits.

The judge concluded he was incompetent to stand trial and remanded him to the forensic psychiatry unit for treatment. Mrs. B received treatment in her own right, for she, herself, was psychologically quite fragile from having lived with a man who was psychotic for three years. The children received treatment, and there were family sessions for Mrs. B and the two children. However, Bunny continues to present difficulties.

In the case described above, Mr. B's delusions about bugs and maggots are a projection onto the environment of his own out-of-control

libidinous feelings. They also served to justify his need to touch the children's genitals. The mother's failure to protect is strikingly illustrated by her giving total responsibility for child care to her psychotic husband. However, in her defense, she was very overwhelmed by her husband and his behavior. She appears to have been withdrawn and timid prior to her marriage and felt she was duped by her husband into marrying him.

B. Mentally Retarded Participant

In a small number of cases of reported sexual abuse, the perpetrator, the victim, or both, are mentally retarded. In some instances, where the victim is retarded, the abuser may actually be chronologically close in age to the victim, but developmentally more advanced. Such cases fit the definition of sexual abuse because perpetrator and victim are at different developmental stages. This type of sexual abuse is usually quite straightforward diagnostically but often problematic and even heart-wrenching in terms of intervention. While such cases represent only two percent of our cases, persons who work with the developmentally disabled find their population at high risk for sexual abuse (Goff and Demetral 1983).

Victims who are retarded are vulnerable to sexual abuse because they are more prone than other children to victimization. First, they may be less aware than other children of the meaning and exploitative nature of the sexual behavior. Second, often such children have many unrewarding interactions with their environment, for example, in the family, with peers, at school, and in the community. Therefore, when someone (an older person) engages them in a sexual relationship, they are less likely to view it critically and in fact, may be hungry for the positive attention that accompanies the sexual abuse. Moreover, the sexual experiences feel good and the partner is very appreciative. The child suddenly discovers that she gets positive responses and in fact may be sought out because of her willingness to do sexual things.

When the perpetrator is retarded, one often finds that his sexual behavior pattern actually originated in being victimized when younger (Goff and Demetral 1983), and as an adolescent or adult, the retarded individual takes on the role of the aggressor. Like the situation of the retarded victim, the perpetrator has few opportunities for gratifying and appropriate relationships and experiences. This lack of alternative outlets makes the retarded perpetrator at risk for sexual acting out and targeting naive sexual partners.

Serious dilemmas are faced by professionals trying to intervene in these cases. Traditional forms of therapy are of no avail with retarded perpetrators and victims. Attempts by other means to get them to give up behavior patterns which seem to them rewarding are likely to meet with minimal success. One cannot expect sustained change with this population.

The options then are strict monitoring of the individual's behavior and attempts to build alternative, appropriate, and gratifying experiences for the perpetrator or victim. An institutional placement may be a solution. Another possibility may be a sheltered living situation such as a specialized foster home or a group home. A sheltered workshop may also provide at least partial protection. A final option might be to have a guardian appointed to oversee the retarded person's activities. All of the environmental situations just mentioned could provide alternative appropriate experiences and relationships, but these are by no means guaranteed. Retarded persons are physically and sexually abused in institutions, and can also experience maltreatment in any of the other settings discussed.

An ethical dilemma that this type of case presents for professionals is whether or not to restrict the sexual behavior of retarded persons. Frequently, this means saying to the person who has a total absence of success and pleasure in her/his life, "No sex either." In certain relationships the professional's obligations and right to intervene are fairly clearcut—when the retarded victim is still a child and when the retarded perpetrator is clearly exploiting a younger person who is not free to resist. But do professionals also have a right to restrict consensual relationships involving older retarded individuals?

The additional complicating issue in the latter instances is the possibility of pregnancy. If the pregnancy were to go to term, would the baby also be retarded? Whether the baby is retarded or not, who would care for the baby? The prospect of pregnancy raises the option of contraceptives. However, one of the problems with retarded people is that they may not use contraceptives appropriately. Either they do not have the cognitive ability to do so or they actually want a pregnancy. The other method for preventing conception is sterilization. This option raises its own set of legal and ethical problems. We mention these issues not because we have the answers, but rather so the reader is aware of the complexity of intervention in cases of sexual abuse with retarded participants.

The case of Anna, described below, illustrates the characteristics of this type of case when the child is still young. How Anna will fare as she grows older remains to be seen.

EXAMPLE 11:   Anna was removed from her parents' care when she was nine years old. At the time, she appeared large for her age—plump, outgoing, and overly friendly. She had sporadically attended special education classes since she had been enrolled in school. The reasons for removal were gross neglect and the inability of the parents to control any of their four children, of whom Anna was the youngest. She and her brother Walter, 14, were removed at the same time. The other two children had already been placed, one in residential treatment and the other in a therapeutic group home.

Walter and Anna were placed in the same foster home. Within a week they had been caught in bed together having sexual intercourse. Walter was acutely embarrassed and told the foster parents it was Anna's idea. He said that this was the only time they had done it. Anna was not at all embarrassed, although she admitted with a smile that she knew she and Walter were not supposed to do it because they were not married. She said Walter had taught her how to do it when she was seven, and that at home they did it downstairs in the basement on the couch in front of the TV set. They did it every time they watched TV. When asked how she felt about doing this with her brother, she said she liked it with Walter but she did not like it with her dad.

She went on to explain that one time, when her dad—now extremely obese and with a heart condition—could still come down the stairs into the basement, he caught her and Walter. At first he was mad and said, ''Don't let me catch you doing that to your sister again.'' then he made Anna come to his room. He told her to take down her pants and she thought she was going to get a ''whupping.'' However, instead he took his ''wiener'' and put it in her ''pussy.'' She did not like doing this with her dad because he weighed too much on top of her. So she would have to lie on his bed with her ''butt on the edge'' and he would stand up to do it. Anna's mother slept in a separate bedroom and continually stated she wanted a divorce. She was of limited intelligence.

Anna and Walter were placed in separate foster homes after the discovery of their sexual relationship. Anna was very unhappy in her new foster home and longed to go home. She continued to act out sexually.

Clearly, Anna's case is a poignant one. Sexual encounters for her are an opportunity to get close to people, to be valued, and to experience physical pleasure. Her prospects for the future are not good.

C. Polymorphous or Polyincestuous Families

The polymorphous type of family is rare and represents a relatively small proportion of sexual abuse cases in most communities. About 18 percent of our sample consists of this type of case, but this is probably because communities, not knowing what to do with them, refer these cases to outside experts.

This kind of case is differentiated from the case where there are multiple victims, in that there are at least two perpetrators. They may be father and mother, father and older son, grandfather and father, father and an uncle, or father and some other adult, male or female, who plays an important role in the family.

In this type of family, many of the relationships will be sexual—that is, there may be father-daughter, mother-son, and father-son incest, and siblings may be sexually involved with one another. Sometimes persons outside the immediate family, usually relatives, are also included. These may be both perpetrators and victims. In some of the cases we have seen, family pets and occasionally other animals have been sexually misused by one or more family members. Sometimes everyone involved in the sexual abuse lives within one household, sometimes not.

Several different patterns of polymorphism can be found described in the literature (Summit and Kyros 1978; Justice and Justice 1979) and in our sample as well. In some instances, there are fixed dyadic sexual relationships and some family members are excluded. In others, sexual interactions are shifting but generally dyadic. Finally, some families engage in group sex.

Often it is difficult to differentiate perpetrators from victims because an individual who is sexually abused by one family member may in turn victimize someone else. Moreover, victims may be so successfully socialized into this family system that they accept the family values around sex or at least expect to be sexual with other people. For example, in one case a 13-year-old had a baby by her uncle with whom she declared she was in love. She wanted to keep the baby and raise it as she had been raised. The uncle was so pleased with the birth that he was going to declare paternity until he realized that would lead to his criminal prosecution. In that family, the uncle also had an ongoing sexual relationship with the 13-year-old's mother, and the father was sexually involved with two of his nieces, ages four and five. Because older children in such families may have "bought into" the sexual abuse, they may resist removal from the home, do poorly in foster care, and run home when they are placed. They are also often uncooperative if attempts are made to get them to testify in court against their families.

Some polymorphous families develop an ideology to justify the sexual abuse. This ideology may have a religious or cult component. Summit and Kryso (1978) describe this category of sexual abuse as "Ideological Sexual Contact" and mention the Rene Guyon Society as illustrative. They note that the Society claims as members more than

2000 parents and psychiatrists. Its motto is "sex before eight or it's too late." Its belief is that sex should be learned by children within the protective and loving atmosphere of the family through sexual interactions with adults. Sexual repression is believed by the Society to be responsible for many social ills: for example, delinquency, suicide, and warfare.

The cases in our sample with an ideological component are not so well developed. In one case the father—who was sexually involved with two sons, one adopted and one natural, and an adolescent daughter—asserted that sex was his way of showing his children how much he loved them. He could not show them by giving them gifts or money, because he did not have much money, so he showed his love by fellating his sons and engaging in cunnilingus with his daughter. His wife, who was 20 years younger than he was, often brought men into the home, which her husband allowed, and she had an incestuous relationship with their adopted son.

Intervention with the polymorphous family usually involves legal intervention. Our experience thus far with this type of family is that treatment is not successful. Furthermore the family may relocate to avoid treatment. Even when treatment is court-ordered, families will miss sessions or, when they do come, they will not deal with the issues. Further, as mentioned above, there may be relatively little discomfort with the sexual abuse. Because of this, and because the therapist must also be concerned with two or more perpetrators and a longstanding pattern of sexual interaction in the family, the prognosis is poor. Further, a crucial intervention with sexually abusive families is working with the nonabusive parent to enable that person to protect the children. In a polyincestuous family there may be no nonabusive parent.

Therefore, intervention should consist of protection by removal of those children who are uncomfortable in the polyincestuous family or who are young enough so that they can benefit from an alternative living situation. Removal is generally accomplished through the juvenile court where Protective Service cases are handled.

Placement of these victims requires taking into consideration the extent of psychological damage to the child and the amount of sexual acting out the victim is likely to display. Some children will need residential care. Others will need a group care facility because of difficulties they have with object relations. Such a child might have problems in forming a close relationship with a foster parent, because, for her, adults cannot be trusted. However, if a foster parent who can tolerate being kept at arm's length can be found, such an environment can be an appropriate placement. Some communities have therapeutic foster homes that handle children who have difficulties in object relations, and these homes can accommodate children who have been grossly sexually abused. A problem with such a placement is that it is temporary. These children need permanent homes. Thus, a foster home or relative placement that can be supported and that can become permanent may be preferable to a residential, group, or therapeutic foster placement. Whatever the placement, in cases of children who are older than toddlers, individual treatment for the child and supportive work with the child's caretakers should be anticipated for a year at minimum. If additional children are born into these families, they also should be removed. The case below is illustrative of polymorphous families.

> EXAMPLE 12:   Jane F, 8, and Melissa F, 7, were removed from their parents', care because of physical abuse. Melissa told her foster care worker that she was glad they were not at home because she was getting tired of what Uncle Ricky did to them when he babysat for them. He would take each child separately into the bathroom, undress the child, and make her masturbate and fellate him. He also let the man who lived next door do the same thing to them.
>
> The police then interviewed both girls, and their stories with regard to Uncle Ricky and the neighbor were consistent. Criminal prosecution of both men was begun. Jane testified at Uncle Ricky's trial, but Melissa did not because she appeared to be quite disturbed.
>
> In foster care the children began talking about their Aunt Penny, who is their mother's sister, and Uncle Cecil. They said they frequently spent the night with their aunt and uncle and would watch pornographic movies on their cable TV. Afterward, the girls would observe their aunt and uncle engaging in the various acts seen in the movies. Because two sets of relatives had been involved sexually with the children, because Mrs. F had been sexually abused as a child, and because the children exhibited an unusual amount of sexual behavior in foster care, there were concerns that perhaps the parents had also sexually abused the children.
>
> A mental health evaluation was initiated for the two girls. As they were being seen together and questioned, they made anatomically explicit dolls engage in intercourse, fellatio, cunnilingus, and breast sucking. But they denied that anything happened between them and their parents. When seen separately, Melissa with great hesitation showed how her mother would lie in the bathtub naked and have one of the girls lie on top of her and suck her breasts while mother and daughter manually stimulated each other's vaginas. As to where her father was, Melissa said he was there and "he helped out." She was then asked to show how he helped out. Melissa then demonstrated genital intercourse which she said he performed with both girls and their mother sequentially.
>
> When Jane was seen separately she continued to deny any sexual activity with her parents. She and Melissa were then seen together, and Melissa again stated what she had said alone. Jane began crying des-

perately, holding the evaluator's face to get her full attention, and saying, "she's lying, she's lying." Melissa retorted, "I am not and you know it." Jane ran out of the inteview room, losing her shoe on the way, and exited the building. When she was brought back, she curled up in a fetal position on the evaluator's lap and sobbed, occasionally saying, "My mommy would never do those things to us."

The children had been placed initially in an emergency foster placement and were not doing well there. They were moved to a potentially adoptive foster home and are doing much better. There are no other children in this placement and the parents share equally in the child care.

Treatment was initiated with both girls. Initially they were seen separately. After two months of treatment, Jane said she was starting to remember things and wanted to talk to the evaluator again. She revealed ongoing sexual abuse by both parents beginning when she was about three. She said what her mommy did felt good but what her daddy did hurt. Her mother encouraged their "education" at their aunt and uncle's. When Jane complained about Uncle Ricky, her mother told her to "shut up." Eventually, the foster parents were also involved in the treatment with both girls.

The parents did not attend the evaluation set up for them and, within a week of the allegations against them, disappeared.

In this case example, both children in the family were being sexually victimized, not only by both parents but also by an aunt and her husband, another uncle, and a neighbor, and there was group sex involving the parents and both children.

Since both children were young, they were removed from their parents' care, and termination of parental rights was initiated. While the children are doing fairly well at the present time, their functioning over time may not be so good.

D. Pedophilia

The fourth type of sexual abuse in which the classification is based upon perpetrator psychopathology is pedophilia. Such cases represent approximately five percent of our sample. The term pedophilia is defined differently by different writers. For example, Groth uses the term fixated pedophile or fixated molester for a person who is essentially this type of sexual abuser (Groth et al., in Conte and Shore 1982). However, Mayer (1985) employs the term to refer to extrafamilial sexual abuse. We use pedophilia to describe cases where the perpetrator's primary sexual orientation is toward children. The perpetrator may have liaisons with or even marry adults of the opposite sex, but those sexual relationships will be exceptions to the perpetrator's general sexual pattern and sexual preference.

All of the perpetrators in our sample are male, and there is no evidence in the literature of any female perpetrators who fit this classification. Most of the victims in our sample are male, a finding also reflected in the literature (Groth et al., in Conte and Shore 1982; Groth and Birnbaum 1979). This type of sexual abuse differs from those described thus far in which the preponderance of victims are female.

The perpetrators in our sample had all had sexual encounters as children, and there was evidence of a relationship between this childhood experience and sexual abuse of children as an adult. The sexual abuse had a narcissistic quality to it in that the perpetrator identified with the victim. The victim was usually the same sex as the perpetrator, and frequently the victim was approximately the same age as the offender when he was victimized, and in a number of cases the sexual acts were the same. In addition, the family backgrounds of perpetrators reflect deprivation and harsh treatment.

Pedophilia is also characterized by victimization of multiple children, and the perpetrator's relationships with his victims are fairly shallow. Seduction or subterfuge to induce the victims to cooperate is found rather than the use of force. There is a compulsive pattern in the sexual abuse indicated not only by the multiple victimization but also by a repetitive, ritualistic pattern in the sexual behavior. Furthermore, offenders often describe themselves as unable to control their sexual behavior.

Pedophiles often obtain positions where they have ready access to their victims. Thus, they may be scout masters, camp counselors, day care center providers, teachers, or big brothers (O'Carroll 1980). Some of these men appear to be quite well functioning in areas other than sexual, while others will have a number of areas of dysfunction. This group of perpetrators does not appear to abuse chemicals, a finding also made by Groth (in Conte and Shore 1982).

The case example below is an example of a pedophile with a fair amount of superego strength.

EXAMPLE 13:   Mr. H came to the attention of our project when he was about to be sentenced for sexually molesting 11 boys. Mr. H was 38 and had been married three years. The victims were his wife's 15-year-old brother and ten of the boy's friends, ages 13 to 16.

Mr. H said he had been emotionally and physically abused by both of his parents as a child. His father was a police officer and his mother worked as a secretary for the local mayor. He was beaten regularly, often having to cover up bruises when he went to school, blamed for ruining his mother's life (she became depressed and had to be hospitalized after his birth), and scapegoated by his older sister. When his mother was interviewed, she appeared to be a depressed, angry woman whose major concern was all the humiliation he son's behavior had brought upon her and her husband.

Mr. H said when he was 13 years old and had just been severely beaten for missing three houses on his paper route, he had a homosexual experience with a friend who was a year older than he. Although the older boy seduced him, he described the experience as tremendously satisfying. It began a pattern of sexual encounters with boys about 13 or 14 in which he was the initiator that persisted into his adulthood. He described himself as loving many of these boys but also indicated some encounters were with boys he hardly knew. He estimated he must have had sexual encounters with at least 100 boys.

He said because of his problem he decided not to marry. Initially he went out with his wife-to-be only when he needed a partner for a social gathering. Eventually, he stated he became emotionally and sexually involved with her. He indicated that she wished to marry. He did not want to because he was afraid eventually she would become aware of his sexual involvement with boys and would be hurt, or alternatively they would have children and he would molest them. He agreed to marry her but with the proviso that they would have no children. She could not understand his wish, because he was so active in raising money for children's programs and seemed to like other people's children. However, eventually she agreed to have no children and they got married.

Mr. H was a successful businessman and at one point was an administrator in county government. Mrs. H was a school teacher. About a year into their marriage, Mrs. H's mother died suddenly, and her father, who was a victim of emphysema, was so devastated by losing her that he was not able to care for their 15-year-old son, George. Mrs. H then asked her husband if George could come and live with them. Mr. H was reluctant because he feared he might sexually molest the boy. However, he agreed, assuming the boy would return to his father at the end of the summer, and feeling he would be able to control himself for a summer.

George stayed beyond the summer and began school. About that time Mr. H became sexually involved with him and in quick succession with ten of George's male friends. His pattern was the same in almost every case. He would begin by showing the boy *Playboy* magazine in the guise of sex education. He would then offer to teach the boy about masturbation by masturbating the boy. He did not ask that the boys touch him but only touched them. He said he was very fond of some of the boys and he would fellate those boys. With most of the victims there was only one encounter and never more than three.

Finally, one of the boys told his parents and soon all of the victims spoke with the police. Mr. H was arrested but released on bond. Mr. H confessed to all of the counts involving the 11 boys so that they would not have to testify in court.

In this case we find a harsh and punitive upbringing, a history of sexual misuse as a child, compulsive sexual activity with many boys who are about the same age as the perpetrator was when he had his childhood sexual encounter, and a repetitive pattern of sexual behavior. Mr. H's case typifies pedophilia in a man who has many other areas of his life in which he is well functioning.

V. CONCLUSION

In this chapter, we have discussed two related conceptual frameworks, the degree of intimacy between victim and offender and the role relationship between them, and four case types which are defined by perpetrator psychopathology. The purpose of this typology is to guide professionals in differential diagnosis and case management. We see this as a beginning. As we and others working in the field gain more experience, there will be refinements and developments in case classification that can lead to more sophisticated understanding of sexual abuse and to better case management.

CHAPTER FOUR

The Causes of Sexual Abuse

I. INTRODUCTION

Why do adults sexually abuse children? The answer proposed here will necessarily be incomplete because a great deal still needs to be learned about the causes of sexual abuse. In most cases the dynamics are complex and multiple factors lead to sexual abuse. However, perpetrators appear to share important characteristics that are prerequisites for sexual abuse. These are sexual attraction to children and the willingness to act upon that attraction. The probability of sexual abuse is increased by cultural, environmental, individual, and family factors. See figure 4.1 for a diagram of the conceptual model.

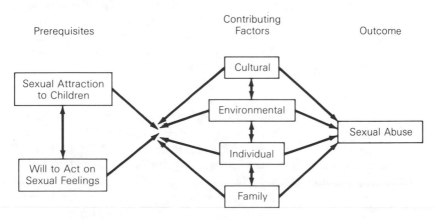

FIGURE 4.1. Model of the dynamics of sexual abuse.

This chapter will consider the prerequisites for sexual abuse, and will elaborate upon the above contributing factors. Emphasis will be placed upon critically examining the role of contributing factors based upon our own case experience. We feel it is important to do so because previous authors have often seen them as the primary causes of sexual abuse.

II. PREREQUISITES FOR SEXUAL ABUSE

As already noted the first prerequisite is sexual attraction to children. In our opinion, the majority of adults do not become sexually aroused by children. (However, there is no research to support this assertion.) Elements in the perpetrator's life experience lead to sexual feelings toward children. Exactly what these are is not yet fully understood. However, it is felt that sexual arousal patterns are learned responses.

Some perpetrators' primary sexual attraction is toward children, for example in the case of pedophiles (see chapter 3). For other offenders the sexual feelings toward children appear to be situational. For example, offenders may become aroused by child pornography; physical contact, such as a child sitting in their lap, evokes a sexual response; or they have sexual feelings toward children when they are feeling psychologically vulnerable and regressed. Still others are sexually responsive to a range of objects; adults and children, both male and female, and sometimes animals as well.

An example of the latter type of case was a man who was married three times. In his first marriage he sexually abused his three daughters and was observed by his son to engage in anal intercourse with a cow and to induce a heifer to suck his penis. He also brought women into the household when his wife was away and had sex with them. After his first wife divorced him he married a woman who had a 16-year-old daughter by whom he conceived a male child. He sexually abused this son. He allegedly killed his second wife and married her daughter. They had a second child whom he also sexually abused. He continued to have liaisons with other women even though he had three sexual partners at home.

The frequency and intensity of sexual feelings toward children will vary depending upon the offender. For some abusers they are persistent and very compelling. For others they are intense but intermittent. For still others they are frequent but not intense, and finally, for some feelings are intermittent and not strongly felt.

The second prerequisite for sexual abuse is the perpetrator's willingness to act upon sexual feelings toward children. This implies a lack of superego development. Some perpetrators have pervasive superego deficits, that is, they have few inhibitions against engaging in a range of socially questionable or unacceptable behaviors. Others have lacunae in their superegos regarding sexual activities or sexual abuse. The former will not only engage in sexual abuse but may also be involved in criminal activity, exploitation of others, and manipulations of institutions in their own interest. In contrast, the latter may be quite law-abiding and socially appropriate in areas other than the sexual abuse. In addition in some cases, poor impulse control leads to the willingness to act on sexual feelings.

Usually the essential dynamics of sexual abuse are related to the interplay between the intensity of sexual attraction to children and the willingness to act. A perpetrator who has rather mild sexual feelings toward children and poor superego functioning will become involved in sexual abuse. In contrast, a man with similar feelings but a more intact superego will not. There are also men with very intense sexual feelings and similarly intact superegos who nevertheless give in to their sexual urges because they are so pressing.

The following examples illustrate the interplay between sexual attraction and superego functioning.

> EXAMPLE 1: Mr. A is a 19-year-old stepfather who sexually molested his stepdaughters, ages 7 and 11. Although he had not had much sexual experience prior to his marriage, his sexual interest had been in women. He was caring for his stepdaughters while their mother was in the hospital. He would get down on the floor and wrestle with the girls. On one occasion, he became sexually aroused. He then fondled the girls' vulvas while he masturbated himself. When asked to describe his feelings when he touched the girls, he said for a second he thought that he shouldn't do it, but then he just did it anyway. This was the beginning of an ongoing pattern with the girls. Mr. A reports that he had no more bad feelings about what he was doing after his initial twinge of conscience and only felt bad again after he got caught.

> EXAMPLE 2: Mr. H was discussed in chapter 3. In his case, he had compelling sexual feelings toward 13- and 14-year-old boys which began in his adolescence. He felt that these feelings were wrong and tried not to give in to them. However, many times he would become quite overwhelmed and act upon his urges. When he did so he tried to choose boys who really enjoyed it.
>
> In discussing these events, Mr. H described an intense need for the sexual contact. This need would overcome his feeling that the behavior was wrong until he achieved orgasm. Then he would be overcome by feelings of revulsion and would apologize to his victim.
>
> When he was eventually caught, he said he was relieved and confessed everything so the boys would not be further humiliated by testifying in court. When he was evaluated, Mr. H showed great concern for the harm he had done to these boys.

In the first case, Mr. A initially had rather mild sexual feelings toward his stepdaughters but weak superego functioning. In contrast, Mr. H reports intense and frequent sexual feelings and a superego, though strong, not sufficient to prevent his sexually abusive behavior.

Without the two ingredients, sexual attraction and the willingness to act, sexual abuse will not take place.

Other factors to be discussed in the remainder of this chapter may play a role in the sexual abuse, but none of them is either a necessary or sufficient cause of sexual abuse.

III. CONTRIBUTING FACTORS

Four factors—cultural, environmental, individual, and family—are identified in the clinical literature as being causes of sexual abuse or have been noted in research as being correlates of sexual abuse. We will critically examine them.

A. Cultural Factors

It has been argued cogently by Rush (1981) and Herman (1981) that a culture that assumes dominance of men over women and children also gives permission for men to sexually abuse children (and women for that matter). Ample evidence exists historically for the socially superior position of men and the inferior position of women and children. Rush particularly points out certain historical and cultural contexts in which sexual relationships between adult males and children were condoned.

Both authors rightly note that at least until recently much professional writing tended to normalize men's sexual behavior with children, to minimize the impact of sexual abuse on children, and to place blame and responsibility with the victim and the mother. That is, there is literature that suggests men are expected to have sexual feelings toward children, that these are natural, and men will try to express them. Then it becomes the responsibility of the victim not to entice the perpetrator or the mother to protect the child, rather than the obligation of the potential abuser to control his own behavior (Rush 1980:134-141; Herman 1981:7-50). While this belief system is now changing, change is coming slowly. It is still easy to find a judge who thinks incarceration is too high a price for a man to pay for a little sexual acting-out with a child, to find a therapist who wonders whether an eight-year-old seduced her father, and to find a physician who will not report a case of sexual abuse because he does not think it has been all that harmful to the child. Furthermore, statistics on reported cases support the contention that sexual abuse is primarily a male problem and victims are largely female—about 90 percent of perpetrators are male and about 85 percent of victims female (Herman 1981, American Humane Association 1984; see also chapter 2).

Male sexual socialization is very different from the female counterpart. Men are socialized to believe that they should be the aggressor or at least the initiator in a potential sexual encounter. Further, they are taught to expect to have lustful feelings toward women; and if they do not, something is wrong with them. In contrast, women are usually socialized into a passive or even resistant role and, at least until recently, to believe that they should not have lustful feelings. By extension, the socialization experience of men could also lead to their rationalizing sexual behavior with children and acting upon sexual feelings toward them.

However, if the male dominance argument is carried to its logical conclusion, all men would be wife-beaters, rapists, and child abusers. Clearly they are not. It is also incorrect and simplistic to make the argument that the normative and social structure of our society is the only reason there is child sexual abuse. Further, as already noted, these norms are changing. There is increasing societal concern about women's rights and children's rights and a concurrent diminishing belief in male dominance. However, these changes come at a time when reports of sexual abuse are increasing.

Probably some men who become sexual abusers incorporate the belief system of male dominance to a greater extent than the general population does. Indeed, they may see that belief system being threatened by normative changes and defensively adhere to it. It is possible that being in such an embattled position leads them to be more abusive than they might otherwise be.

Clinical assessments of perpetrators in our sample indicate a large proportion believe that to be masculine means to be in charge and to be feminine means to be submissive. They think they should control what goes on in their families and have the right to take corrective steps when family members are not in compliance. In the case example below, this belief system is represented in an extreme form.

EXAMPLE 3: When Mr. and Mrs. C got married, Mrs. C already had two children, both boys, one by a previous marriage and one out of wedlock. The C's had two more children, also boys. At the time Mrs. C successfully left her husband—on her tenth attempt—the children were Bruce, 14, Steven, 12, Alex, 7, and Tony, 3 months.

Mrs. C said before they were married, her husband was "real nice." He would buy groceries and do things with her and the boys. They knew one another two months before they got married. After the marriage, things were different. He would make the boys stay in their rooms because he said they were in the way. He gave Mrs. C a limited allowance for food and raged when he did not like what she was able to buy for his meals. He allowed her only enough gas in the car to take him to work, take him his lunch at noon, and pick him up. He checked the gas gauge every day. He was pathologically jealous of her, and convinced she was cheating on him. He would not allow her to work or to see her family.

He physically abused everyone in the family. He beat up his wife regularly and knocked out her four upper front teeth. She stated that after one beating, it was six months before she could stand up straight. He would become particularly enraged when she tried to protect the children from him. When asked if he was assaultive to her sexually, Mrs. C said they never had much of a sexual relationship, because Mr. C openly stated he preferred men and boys as sexual objects. The two older boys were particular targets of abuse. He beat them with chains until there were marks all over their bodies. On one occasion, he was angry with Steven and attempted to drown him in the bathtub. When he was unsuccessful at this, he slammed Steven's head against the spigot, doing serious injury, and the mother reports brain damage.

He also sexually abused the two oldest boys. For two years prior to Mrs. C's and the children's successful departure, he would make Bruce fellate him. He often did this while holding a shotgun to Bruce's head. He also would hit Bruce with the gun butt. One time he attempted anal intercourse with Bruce but Bruce got away. He made Steven fellate him in much the same way, but this had gone on with Steven only about a year.

Alex was a lesser target. He was beaten regularly, sometimes with chains. When Tony was two weeks old Mr. C became enraged with him because his crying was taking Mrs. C's attention away from Mr. C. He attempted to smother Tony with a pillow. Mrs. C intervened and her husband attacked her, hitting her in the face with his fist, knocking her down, and kicking her. He told her Tony was his kid and he could kill him if he wanted. Mrs. C then ran away with the children.

However, Mr. C, enraged that his wife thought she had the right to leave him, pursued her to another state and threatened to kill the children if she did not return. She agreed to come back but instead escaped with the children to a domestic violence shelter in another county.

The C case provides a dramatic example of a man who believed in his right to control, subjugate, abuse, and even kill the woman and children in his family. He feels he has the right to physically assault his wife when she does not please him; he can limit her activities with the outside world as he sees fit; and he was outraged when she had the audacity to try and extricate herself from this situation. Similarly, his rights over the children, both natural and stepchildren, extended to the right to kill them if they displeased him, to abuse them horribly for minor infractions, and to sexually abuse them. The boys' sexual preference was not of any concern to him; his own preference for boys was the factor of importance when he made the boys perform fellatio.

One question to consider is, as women become more assertive about their sexuality, whether there will be an increase in females sexually abusing children. This might be a logical consequence of such a change in values.

B. Environmental Factors

There are a number of environmental factors that may play a role in the dynamics of sexual abuse. For our purposes, we will classify them as economic factors and social isolation.

1. *Economic factors.* The literature about the role of economic factors in sexual abuse is inconsistent. Early studies of incest frequently asserted that it was a problem associated with low socioeconomic status. For example, Sonden (1936), who looked at 241 incest families in Sweden, noted that all of the offenders were of the lowest social stratum. Similarly, Flugel (1926) in England and Guttmacher (1951) in the United States reported that incest behavior was inversely related to socioeconomic status. More recent authors (e.g., Weiner 1964) are critical of these conclusions, pointing out sampling biases since cases were limited to ones already successfully criminally prosecuted or to victims hospitalized in mental institutions.

Similar criticisms can be raised about any conclusions based upon current cases of sexual abuse coming to the attention of child protection agencies and the police (Walters 1975). These tend to be instances involving the poor, whose behavior is more likely to come under scrutiny of professionals who report sexual abuse (a welfare worker, a public health nurse, or a charity hospital physician). In contrast middle class persons are likely to seek assistance from helpers in voluntary agencies or private practice who are not so disposed to report them to authorities. Since most of our sample is referred by protective services, its poverty status cannot be used to argue that sexual abuse is associated with being poor.

Further, professionals may be biased against believing that a middle class person, particularly one who is presentable and persuasive, could sexually abuse a child. A case in point is that of a 16-year-old girl who asserted that her father had put his hand up under her blouse and fondled her breasts and had held her against him and rubbed his erect penis against her through their clothing. Later she recanted because she was very unhappy being placed with her paternal grandparents. The psychiatrist who evaluated the parents noted that the father was a banker and the mother a Sunday school teacher, that they had been married for 20 years, and that the family appeared economically stable and well functioning. Therefore, he did not believe sexual abuse could have occurred. He did not interview the child.

Moreover, even recent studies do not resolve the questions of socioeconomic status. Finkelhor (1984), in two samples, one of college students and another of a representative sample of parents from the Boston area, found increased risk for sexual abuse if the victim was in a household whose income was under $10,000. In contrast are Russell's (1986) most recent research findings. She found incest victims came from families with higher incomes than did nonvictimized females and victims of other types of sexual assault. Thus, more research is needed to understand whether there is a relationship between sexual abuse and economic factors.

However, if poverty is to be cited as a cause for sexual abuse, what is there about it that leads to sexual abuse? If there is a relationship, perhaps it is indirect rather than direct—that is, poverty is associated with other factors that contribute to the risk of sexual abuse.

One such factor might be physical overcrowding, which is also cited in the literature as leading to incest (Weiner 1964). However, such findings are reported in many of the studies cited above which have sampling biases. In our sample, we had cases where physical overcrowding caused a lack of privacy, which exposed the offender to sexually arousing situations, and necessitated sleeping arrangements, adults and children together, that were sexually stimulating to the adult. More numerous, however, were cases where the perpetrator violated the child's privacy, and situations where he insisted the child sleep with him or got into the child's bed even though there were sufficient beds. Moreover, in certain instances, overcrowding seems to have made available to others, including the nonperpetrating parent, opportunities to observe the sexual abuse. Thus possibly sexual abuse in overcrowded households is more likely to be identified and reported.

An economic factor that seems to play a more important role is loss of employment or unemployment. One reason is that employment loss can have a dramatic impact upon a person's, particularly a male's, self-esteem. In part, the sexual abuse may be a result of the perpetrator's reaching out to achieve some solace from this narcissistic insult or lashing out at a vulnerable child because of his own pain. Often in these situations wives are not very supportive of partners who have lost jobs. For example, one mother was totally exasperated with her husband for riding his motorcycle when he was drunk and having an accident. She stated he deserved to be in a full body cast and to lose his job. When he was physically able, he began to fondle his ten-year-old stepdaughter.

Another reason unemployment may be a causal factor is that it may result in unsupervised access to the child. For instance, a man who loses his job and may have to babysit while his wife works.

About a third of the perpetrators in our data set were unemployed at the time of the sexual abuse, and in most cases we were able to identify the specific impact of loss of employment upon self worth. In a number of cases there were other crises, such as a physical injury or illness, that had a comparable impact upon the perpetrator and/or led to unemployment. The case of Mr. B, which will be described below, is typical with respect to the role of unemployment and injury.

> EXAMPLE 4: The B's had been married 28 years. Mrs. B had never worked. Mr. B had always worked two jobs to support the family because they had eight children, four of them girls. Mr. B was a heavy-equipment operator.
>
> About three years before the reported sexual abuse, Mr. B fell at work and hurt his back. Because he was also obese, the injury was and is disabling. He became very bad tempered following the injury and began unpredictably beating the children with a razor strap. He also started sexually abusing three of his daughters, Gina, 18, Margie, 16, and Sally, 15. The youngest girl, Joyce, was seven, and was not abused. Mr. B's sexual abuse had a hostile, angry element to it. He would grab his daughters' breasts and pinch hard and would grab their vulvas.
>
> When he was evaluated, he spoke with great bitterness about his injury, loss of employment, and their effects on him. He said he never was lazy and always wanted to work, but now he could not even do work around the house. He said he still woke up at 6:00 A.M., the time he got up when working, and sometimes when he first awoke he did not remember he had nothing to do. He bemoaned the fact that all he could do was play cards, read the newspaper, cut out coupons from the paper, and help his wife prepare vegetables for canning. He couldn't even tend the garden. She had to do this.

Mr. B's description of his past and present life and his current feelings about himself document the impact of his injury and loss of employment. The quality of the sexual abuse suggests Mr. B was not seeking affection, but only expressing his anger.

2. *Social Isolation.* A second environmental factor that may play a role in sexual abuse is social isolation. Some of the early researchers (Sonden 1936; Sherrer 1959) found incest rates higher in rural than in urban environments, but other studies do not support this finding (Riemer 1940; Weiner 1964).

Our data indicate that while families may not be totally socially isolated, a substantial proportion were fairly isolated. In addition, consultations with child protection workers in rural areas indicate that child sexual abuse represents a higher percentage of their caseloads than it does of state and national statistics. Nationally, 13 percent of child maltreatment cases are sexual abuse (American Humane Association 1986), while rural child protection staffs report 25 to 30 percent of caseloads are sexual abuse. Isolation in rural areas results from low population density, lack of transportation, and inclement weather.

Social isolation may play a causal role in, may prolong, or may be an effect of sexual abuse. Furthermore, social isolation may be environmentally induced, imposed by the perpetrator, or imposed by the family upon itself. Environmental social isolation may result from geographical isolation or community avoidance of the family. As a causal factor, social isolation may mean the lack of access to appropriate sexual partners, or it may mean the family does not experience the normative pressure from society supporting the incest taboo. Social isolation may also lead to a prolongation of sexual abuse in that there is no interference in the family from the outside world. Outside interference might put a stop to the incest. Social isolation is an effect of sexual abuse when the community shuns the family because they know of the sexual abuse. Alternatively, the community may be the cause of the isolation in that its members may avoid the family because of, say, alcoholism, illegal behavior, or unusual behavior. This type of isolation may precede the sexual abuse and possibly be a causal factor, or it may succeed the sexual abuse and play a role in its prolongation.

Further, some incestuous fathers, even prior to the incest, are very controlling and limit their family's access to the outside world. After the incest behavior occurs, the isolation serves to protect the family from its detection, as was the case with the C family described in the preceding section. In other instances, the whole family senses its difference from other families and keeps to itself.

The example of the R family illustrates several types of social isolation.

EXAMPLE 5: Mr. and Mrs. R have been married for ten years. Mrs. R is of limited intelligence and Mr. R is frequently unemployed. They live in a rural area in northern Michigan. They are snowed in frequently during the winter, and their nearest neighbor lives on a farm half a mile away. Mrs. R does not drive and therefore is dependent upon her husband or her father who lives in the next county for transportation. Mr. R does not like Mrs. R's father to come around and take her places because he drinks too much. Mr. R also has objected to his wife's socializing with the neighbors because then she "didn't get her work done and she would drag the children with her." He has allowed his wife to attend church on Sunday and she enjoyed this very much for a time.

The R's had their first child, Sallie, two years after they were married. She was eight when the sexual abuse was discovered. Their second child, Alice, was born two years later. When Alice was three, her mother took her to the doctor because she was not yet walking or talking. She was also filthy and had terrible diaper rash. A diagnosis was made of mental retardation, and Alice was placed in foster care because it was felt the parents were not able to care for such a limited child. Within six months it became apparent that Alice was not retarded, but had been so poorly cared for that she was not developing normally. Parental rights were terminated.

Mrs. R was very upset during this time and appealed to church members for support. She shared much information with them about Alice and her efforts to care for the child. They became very aware of her limitations as a parent and began to avoid her. After termination of parental rights, she felt less comfortable at church as well as quite depressed and began to attend less frequently and eventually stopped going altogether. The only person to take notice of her absence was the pastor, who stopped by briefly. He then made a Protective Services referral because the house was filthy.

After the loss of Alice, Mrs. R was indeed despondent. She began to refuse her husband sex because she said that if she had another baby the State would just take it away. She spent substantial amounts of time in bed and cried a lot.

Mr. R had to care for Sallie because his wife would not. Frequently he would return from work and find Sallie sitting in a dark room with her mother. Mrs. R would refuse to eat. Mr. R and Sallie would have TV dinners by themselves sitting on the couch. Eventually, Mr. R initiated sexual contact with Sallie. First he had her fondle his penis until he ejaculated. He also had her suck the tip of his penis while he rubbed the shaft until he ejaculated. As the sexual relationship progressed, he would rub bacon fat around her anus and penetrate her anally.

When the sexual abuse finally came to light, Sallie said her father had started it when she finished kindergarten and that she had told her mother about it many times. She said her mother would either not pay any attention or say there was nothing she could do. It did not occur to Sallie to tell anyone at school, which she attended irregularly, because she said they did not like her. The other kids would not play with her and the teacher would not make them. She finally told her paternal grandmother when she was allowed to go and visit for a week.

The father and mother released their rights to Sallie to avoid criminal prosecution. She was placed in a specialized potentially adoptive foster home. She is also in therapy.

Several types of social isolation appear to be factors in the occurrence and continuance of Sallie's sexual abuse. Environmental isolation resulted from geographical isolation and community avoidance. Mr. R also limited his wife's access to social contacts by disapproving of them and controlling her transportation. In addition Mrs. R diminished her involvement with the church after she lost custody of Alice. Further, it is possible that the family's isolation decreased the availability of other sexual partners for Mr. R, and it appears to have increased the risk of sexual abuse because it led to a lot of unsupervised access for Mr. R to Sallie. Finally, clearly the isolation prolonged the sexual abuse because both mother and daughter felt cut off from outside help.

C. Individual Factors

Many clinicians and researchers have sought to understand sexual abuse from an examination of characteristics of fathers and mothers in families when it occurs. This extensive exploration has yielded somewhat contradictory results (Mayer 1983:28; Weiner 1964:6). This is particularly true of descriptions of incestuous fathers but somewhat less true of mothers. For example, perpetrators are described as being of below average intelligence, (Bender & Blau 1952), average intelligence (Meiselman 1979), and above average intelligence (Mayer 1984; Weiner 1964). They are diagnosed as being both psychopathic and pedophiliac (Justice and Justice 1979), but have also been described as not easily differentiated from the general population. They are defined as aggressive (Groth and Birnbaum 1979), passive/aggressive, and passive (Gottlieb 1980). Mothers are characterized as inadequate and dependent (DeFrancis 1971; Sarles 1975) but also sometimes as dominant (Stern and Meyer 1980). These inconsistencies reinforce a point made earlier—that a range of factors can contribute to sexual abuse, and the factors that are important vary from case to case. Paternal and maternal characteristics will be discussed in relation to the findings from our case sample.

1. *Characteristics of paternal caretakers (perpetrators).* A substantial proportion of fathers in our sample report a *harsh or deprived childhood experience.* This may include parental marital discord, parental separations, divorce, multiple caretakers—including foster care— alcoholism, and physical abuse, but it is most likely to include circumstances in which the child feels unjustly punished or scapegoated. In our sample, the problematic parent for the perpetrator is more likely to be the mother. This finding is consistent with that of Groth and Birn-

baum (1979) and the Justices (1979), but not with that of Knopp (1982). The mother may be punishing or rejecting or she may fail to protect the child from the father, stepfather, or her boyfriends. There appear to be at least two consequences of this deprivation. First, the men have deficits in the ability to develop intimate relationships and show affection. In adolescence they learn about interacting sexually as a way to demonstrate feelings. Consequently, their repertoire is limited to showing affection in a sexual way. Second, the perpetrator may have difficulties in his adult relationships with women. These relationships tend to be characterized by a need to express the anger they feel toward the mother and/or a need in their relationships with women to get the nurturance and protection they did not get as children. When they marry, one or both of these emotional needs may underlie the attraction to the partner. A common pattern is to find that the perpetrator initially sees his wife as the compensatory nurturer, but is disappointed either because his wife does not want to be his mother or because with the mothering comes control over his behavior. He may then express anger directly toward his wife. Or there may be minimal direct expression of his disappointment, and he turns to the child, where the sexual relation is both an attempt to obtain nurturance from the child and an expression of the anger he feels toward women, the anger which originated in his relationship with his mother.

A second factor which is common in the histories of men who become sexual abusers is having had a *traumatic sexual experience* as a child. Sometimes the abuse is not perceived as traumatic, but as neutral or positive. Our data suggest that pedophiles, fathers in classical incest cases, and noncustodial fathers are more likely than other perpetrators to have had such experiences. The sexual abuse may have been directly experienced by the father, or he may have repeatedly witnessed or been aware of sexual abuse of others, for example his sisters. Sometimes the perpetrator's abusive pattern is very much a reflection of his childhood experience. Other times the emotional tone of that experience is reflected in his sexually abusive behavior. For instance, if the childhood experience was perceived as humiliating, the perpetrator's victims may well be treated in a humiliating manner. In addition, sexual abuse may reflect an identification on the part of the perpetrator with his abuser.

The following case example illustrates both a harsh childhood experience and childhood sexual trauma.

> EXAMPLE 6: Mr. M decribed his childhood as "dramatic." His father was a lawyer of some renown who was described by Mr. M as always in a bad temper and always putting everybody in the household down, but particularly Mr. M's mother, whom he would call a whore and a slut, and

his sister, 14 months older than Mr. M. He hated his father and wanted to kill him.

Mr. M described his mother as an alcoholic, a drug addict, and a hypochondriac. A traumatic experience he recalls at about age three was when his father was in the army and his mother had to be hospitalized for detoxification. He and his sister were put in an institution. He does not know how long he was there, but he was terrified.

Mr. M related that when he and his sister were children, they were cared for primarily by a black couple. When the couple did not come, Mr. M would stay home from school and take care of his mother. She would be drunk and "slobber all over him" and repeatedly asked him if he loved her. He hated this and reported it went on "hour after hour, day after day." He said he kept thinking he could make a difference but he never could. In the end he hated his mother.

In addition, he said his mother had men around the house who stayed with them. His father did not stop this. He also described his mother as placing a barrier between the children and their father, trying to keep them on her side. Frequently, she would tell the children things that she said their father was not to know. She would then tell their father, but the children would not be aware of this. Their father would then question them about these matters at the dinner table, and they would lie to their father, not knowing their father already knew the truth. Because they had lied, they would be beaten by their father.

Mr. M confided that his mother dressed and undressed and took baths in front of him from the time he was little until he was about 20. She also had a bad back and hemorrhoids and would sit on the toilet with her legs up and spread apart. He would sit on the floor in front of the toilet and they would talk while he looked up at her vulva. From that experience he developed a distaste and fear of female genitalia. He remarked that when he looks at a woman and sees how small the vulva is, he is always surprised because his childhood memory of it is as being so large. When Mr. M was 19, his mother tried to come to bed with him in order to have sex, but his father intervened and prevented her from doing so.

Mr. M has been married twice. He said he did not love his first wife and she was physically unattractive. He married her in order to have children, even though her major concern was getting her PhD. They never had children. He found that the only way he could get sexually excited with her was by having anal intercourse because of his fear of female genitalia. She found this very painful and resisted.

Mr. M said he loved his second wife enormously but they fought bitterly all of the marriage. Mr. M said he had hoped his second wife would erase the bad feelings he had about women because of his mother and first wife. He would threaten suicide when his second wife tried to leave him. Toward the end of the marriage, he began to hate her. With her too he preferred anal intercourse. She did not wish it because she had hemorrhoids. When she was separated from him and they were fighting, he insisted on anal intercourse.

After they were separated, Mrs. M got pregnant. Although they did not really reconcile with the birth of their daughter, Annie, Mr. M took a leave from work for six months to care for her. Mrs. M returned to work to support the family. Later Mr. M quit work entirely to care for Annie. Mr. M was extremely possessive of Annie and did not like her to interact with his wife when he was responsible for her.

When Annie was about 20 months old, she began to say her dada was "eating my too too" and that she had "eaten his too too." She also said he did some painful things to her.

The perpetrator in this case was more disturbed than many are, having come from a very pathological family. At least with his second wife, Mr. M was seeking the nurturing his mother (and father) never gave him. However, his sadistic and disturbed behavior precluded the possibility of his getting nurturance from any adult. He then became involved in an extremely enmeshed relationship with his daughter in order to satisfy his unmet dependency needs. That relationship became sexual because sex was one of the few ways Mr. M could express positive feelings, but it also became sadistic as it was a vehicle for his expression of anger toward women.

Substance abuse may be a contributing factor in sexual abuse, although experts do not agree entirely about its role. Some assert that chemical dependency among sexual abusers is no higher than in the general population (Giarretto 1982 a and b). At the other end of the spectrum are those who insist that not only is there a substantial correlation between sexual abuse and subtance abuse (Carlson and Reibel 1977), but indeed that the sexual abuse itself is like an addiction (Carnes 1984). As a general rule, however, professionals believe that use of drugs and alcohol does play some role in a considerable number of sexual abuse cases.

Treatment programs that have collected data on substance abuse report that more than half of their families have such a history (University of Minnesota 1978; Janzen 1979), and include substance abuse treatment as an important component of their intervention. In more than half of our cases a substance problem was identified. The rate of alcoholism for adults in the general population is about four percent (Faller and Bauman 1980).

Substances serve two functions. Most commonly they are a disinhibitor that facilitates the sexual abuse, but they can also be used to blunt feelings of pain and guilt related to the sexual abuse. Sometimes chemicals serve both functions. When the first function operates, the offender either gets drunk and acts out sexual feelings or he gets drunk in order to have an excuse to be sexual with a child. This dynamic can operate on both conscious and unconscious levels. The alcohol does not engender any sexual feelings; rather it facilitates the expression of existing feelings.

Further, in some cases, alcohol or drugs play a central role in the early stages of the sexual abuse, that is, initially chemicals enable the perpetrator to do what he would not do when sober. However, later he no longer needs alcohol to facilitate the abuse. In other cases, men appear to be serious and chronic alcoholics and are always intoxicated when abusive.

The men who drink because of their guilt feelings about the sexual abuse appear on the whole to be better functioning than those for whom alcohol is a disinhibitor. The former tend to have more intact superegos.

The following case example illustrates the role alcohol can play.

EXAMPLE 7: Mr. A first had problems controlling his sexual feelings toward children when his two daughters from his first marriage ran away from their mother and came to live with him and his second family. At the time the girls were 13 and 14. He had not seen them since they were infants, as his wife had disappeared with them after the divorce. Mr. A had an alcohol problem that preceded the sexual abuse. When he came home from work about 4:00 he would begin drinking whiskey. He admitted that some evenings he would have the impression that he had only had a drink or two and he would discover the whole bottle gone.

One evening when he was babysitting for all of the children—Patsy, Todd, James, and Lucy , and his two older daughters, Gina, 14 and Lola, 12—he became aroused by Gina, who was walking around in babydoll pajamas. Initially he did not act on his feelings but later when he had a few more drinks, he went into the bedroom and lay down on the bed with Gina. She awoke and he got under the blankets with her and began to fondle her breasts and genitals. Gina did not say a word but told Mrs. A the next day. Mrs. A went to talk to a counselor who advised her to make arrangements for the two older girls to return to their mother. She did this.

Mr. A persuaded himself that the reason for his behavior was his drinking. He also thought since he had not raised Gina, he did not think of her as his daughter.

The next abuse occurred when Patsy turned 12. Mr. A got drunk and attempted to molest her. Patsy resisted her father's attempts and threatend to tell her mother if he bothered her anymore. He stopped accosting Patsy but they became sworn enemies. Patsy never told.

When Lucy was nine, Mr. A was responsible for her care while her mother was still at work in the early evenings. He would begin drinking right after work and would be drunk by 5 P.M. His sexual behavior with

Lucy consisted of fondling, oral-genital contact, and mutual masturbation. Usually for two or three days after the encounter, he would drink even more heavily, but would not bother Lucy.

When he was caught he was very upset that Lucy had to leave the home. He said it was all his fault and she was being punished by being taken away. Initially he blamed the entire problem on the alcohol, saying that whiskey made him lose his mind. However, he came to understand that he had a sexual problem as well, and part of the reason he drank was so he would not have to deal with it.

In the case of Mr. A, alcohol seems to be a disinhibitor as well as an analgesic to help Mr. A deal with his guilt about the sexual abuse.

2. *Characteristics of mothers (non-perpetrating parents).* Like fathers, mothers in situations of intrafamilial sexual abuse are frequently found to have been *sexually abused as children,* or they come from an incestuous family but are not actually victims. Much more needs to be learned about the role played by these sexually abusive childhood experiences, but we have formed three related hypotheses.

First, there is ample evidence in the psychological literature that individuals internalize images of male and female roles from their childhood experience. Thus, sometimes, on the basis of childhood experiences, mothers have an expectation that men are sexual with children. Furthermore, as adults, these women may be attracted to men like their fathers in some respects. This may mean unconsciously choosing a partner who will sexually abuse children. Similarly, because the mother's maternal role model was not protective, she may not be sensitive to situations where her children may be at risk. Sometimes she seems to have blind spots, for, even when dangerous situations and/or her role in the sexual abuse are pointed out to her, she does not perceive them. Finally, a related dynamic is that the mother's experience of sexual abuse as a child may make her fearful of sexual relationships with men. She may avoid mature relationships by choosing a man who will not make adult sexual demands upon her. In doing so she picks someone who is sexually attracted to children. The case of Mrs. L illustrates how the mother's being sexually abused as a child can play a role in her own children's abuse.

EXAMPLE 8: When Mrs. L reached the age of ten, her stepfather began sexually abusing her. Her mother was very religious and would attend church all day on Sunday. Mrs. L's stepfather was left at home to look after Mrs. L and her two stepbrothers, ages three and four. He would drink when her mother was away. During those times, he would take Mrs. L into her bedroom, make her undress, and lie on top of her, placing his penis either between her legs or on her stomach and rubbing until he ejaculated. This pattern persisted for about two years and stopped without any explanation.

Mrs. L met Mr. L when in high school. Although she was fearful of sexual intercourse, she nevertheless complied when Mr. L asked her to do it. Soon she became pregnant and they had to get married. They were both 17 at the time, but Mr. L was much younger looking than that. He had a cherubic baby-face and was only 5'4''. Mrs. L was 5'2''. However, he turned out to be an alcoholic and wife beater like her stepfather.

After Laura was born, Mrs. L quickly got pregnant again and had another girl, Sally. When the children were three and two, respectively, she caught her husband teaching them to French kiss. She told the girls not to do it anymore but never confronted her husband.

When the girls were three and four, they told their mother that dad made them kiss his "wiener" and "went pee" in their mouths. Mrs. L did not talk to her husband or do anything about the allegations. A year later when Mr. and Mrs. L separated, she allowed him custody of the older daughter and she took the younger one. When the older daughter was found to have gonorrhea, an investigation was conducted. Extensive sexual abuse had been taking place with both girls, with Laura on a daily basis and with Sally on her visits to her father every other weekend. Mrs. L was horrified and overwhelmed by the discovery.

In this case there are indications that Mrs. L married someone who on the surface appeared boyish and not threatening in the manner her stepfather had been. She thought this was so even though he initially made adult sexual demands upon her. Her compliance with his wishes regarding the premarital sexual behavior is very similar to her response to her stepfather's pressures. Mrs. L had clues that Mr. L's relationship with their daughters was not normal: his French kissing and their statements. While she could recall these at the time the sexual abuse was reported, she had difficulty understanding the importance of the clues.

In our sample, there were three types of cases where mothers are very likely to have been sexually abused: stepfather/LTP cases, single parent cases, and polyincestuous families. In the latter two types the mother is likely to be a perpetrator, and usually she had experienced extensive sexual trauma.

A second characteristic one finds with a fair amount of frequency among mothers of victims is some form of *incapacity*. Some mothers, like fathers, have drinking problems. Some are mentally ill or mentally retarded. Some have physical incapacities such as multiple sclerosis, heart conditions, or obesity. These kinds of problems mean that the mother is not available as a protector and in addition that she may not be a very gratifying partner to her husband. (For further discussion, see Section D, "Family Factors"). Mrs. E in the case below illustrates this type of mother.

EXAMPLE 9: When Mrs. E was 18, she had been in a serious automobile accident. She suffered a head injury as well as a broken pelvis and internal injuries. She was in the hospital for seven months, two months of which she was in a coma. It took her another year after the hospital discharge before she could care for herself. She was certified eligible for SSI because of her brain damage. She was easily confused and had blunted and inappropriate affective responses.

When she was 21, she met Mr. E. He was 31 and had recently obtained a divorce from his first wife. He was attracted to Mrs. E because she was "pretty and kind of helpless." He also seems to have been attracted to her SSI. They were married three months after meeting.

According to Mrs. E, because of her accident she was not supposed to be able to have children. But she decided to "try just to see if I could." She was successful in getting pregnant and Patty was born a year after the E's married. Mrs. E provided minimally adequate care for Patty but had to be reminded to do everything for her. A homemaker or a public health nurse stopped by every day. When Patty was about a year old, Mrs. E again became pregnant. The public health nurse and homemaker were quite concerned about Mrs. E's ability to care for two children. They discussed abortion and adoption with her. Mrs. E said she did not want an abortion because she wanted to "see what the baby was" (boy or girl), but she said she would put it up for adoption. However, when the baby was born, Mr. E did not want the baby adopted, and Mrs. E wanted to keep the baby, Robert, because he was a boy. It was recommended that the E's get someone to move in with them to assist Mrs. E. The E's chose an unemployed male friend of Mrs. E's, George.

When Patty and Robert were nine and seven, respectively, Patty told her teacher about some funny things that went on at home. They were made to watch their mother and father in sexual intercourse and their mother and George in sexual intercourse. Further, Patty and Robert were made to engage in sexual intercourse while the three adults watched. In addition, on special nights Patty went to bed with her dad. He was "stretching me with his fingers" so she would be able to have a "grown up peter go inside me." Patty also reported her daddy and George beat them with belts and George would tie Patty and Robert to a chair and leave them there for hours.

When Mrs. E was interviewed, she acknowledged that sexual abuse was taking place. Mr. E denied it, saying that you could not believe Mrs. E because she "did not have all her marbles."

In this case, there are two men with significant sexual aberrations. If Mrs. E had not suffered the head injury she might well have been protective of her children rather than being involved in the sexual abuse.

Other characteristics of mothers and perpetrators that are described in the sexual abuse literature will be discussed in the next section.

D. Family Factors

Many writers (e.g., Weiner 1964; Sarles 1975; Matchotka, et al.
1967; Lukianowicz 1978, Lustig et al. 1965; Mayer 1983) see intrafamilial
sexual abuse, especially incest, as caused primarily by family dysfunction. The argument is basically as follows. Mothers in incestuous families
are seen as inadequate, as having abdicated, or as being unable to fulfill
certain of their maternal and wifely role responsibilities. There is sexual
dysfunction in the marriage. Either there is infrequent sexual intercourse
between husband and wife or the sexual relationship is not emotionally
gratifyng (to the husband). Sometimes the mother does not like sex;
sometimes she is overwhelmed by having many children and has no time
or energy for sex; sometimes she is not sexually attractive to the husband.
Moreover, the wife is not performing other maternal duties, such
as childrearing and homemaking tasks. Into this breach comes the oldest
female child in the family, who not only takes over the sexual role with
the father but also has an abnormal amount of responsibility for other
traditionally maternal tasks. These tasks include caring for her younger
siblings, cooking meals, and deciding what chores other family members
should perform. She is a parental child, and there is role reversal between
mother and daughter.

role confusion

Finally, for incest to occur, there must be a father, who, when the
marital and sexual relationship with his wife is unsatisfactory, does not
endure this, go outside the family and form a more gratifying adult relationship, or divorce his wife, but rather seeks an alternate sexual partner
within the family, the oldest female child. When the oldest female child
reaches majority and extricates herself from the relationship with the
father, younger female children are induced to become sexually involved
with the father. Incest is regarded as a way individuals prevent family
disintegration. Mothers are seen as colluding in the sexual abuse of their
daughters. Daughters are described as seductive. Fathers are domineering, sometimes tyrannical, and overinvolved in the family. It becomes
their refuge from the external environment.

Our clinical experience does not entirely support this theoretical
formulation. We agree with Conte (1982) that this family structural
theory may be more in the minds of the analysts than in the functioning
of the families. The major components of this conceptual framework for
explaining incest will be discussed in light of our clinical findings.

1. *Inadequate mothers.* Both inadequate and very adequate mothers are to be found in our sample. Maternal incapacity, as described earlier, can lead to maternal inadequacy, as can characterological problems. Such mothers do not care for, nurture, or protect their children. Adequate mothers may play a part in quite a different dynamic. They not only fulfill expected roles as child caretakers and household managers but often compensate for their husband's inadequacies as well. In such cases, sexual abuse may arise in part out of anger the husband may feel toward his wife, yet dares not express directly. The A family, mentioned above, is a good example of an adequate, controlling wife who excites her husband's resentment.

> EXAMPLE 10:   Mrs. A came with her husband for evaluation after their ten-year-old daughter, Lucy, confided to her mother that Mr. A had been sexually abusing her for three years.
>
> Mr. and Mrs. A had been married 22 years and had four children widely spaced, Lucy being the youngest. Although Mr. A worked steadily and supported the family, he was an alcoholic. He drank every day after work, on Friday afternoons at work, and on weekends. He would come home late in the evening and drink, and sometimes would not come home at all.
>
> Mrs. A appeared to be a warm and caring parent. She cried when she talked about what had happened to Lucy. Mrs. A said that she had stayed with her husband for her kids' sake. They all loved him and he loved them. She had always figured there would be no risk of him sexually abusing them, but there might be a risk if there were a stepfather.
>
> She said early in the marriage, she had developed a pattern of coping with her husband's alcoholism. She never argued with him when he had been drinking. When he got paid, she went right down to the shop and got his check and they cashed it. She gave him ten dollars to go to the bar and put the rest in the bank. She paid all the bills and saw to it everyone in the family got the money they needed. She had the final say over how money was spent. Mr. A was particularly upset that she would not let him have the car he wanted. She kept liquor in the house for her husband. It was less expensive than his drinking in bars, and she did not have to worry about going to get him when he was too drunk to drive. She worked too and had for about 18 years so the kids would not suffer from the money Mr. A spent on alcohol. She tried always to work the shift when the kids were at school so she could be there when they were home.
>
> She reported that the sexual relationship with her husband had been good until she found out about the sexual abuse. Now she never wants to have sex again. Sometimes when her husband had been drinking, he would want to do "unusual" sexual things, but he was never inconsiderate.

In the A case, one of the dynamics of the sexual abuse appears to have been Mr. A's resentment at being controlled by his wife. When he was first seen, he described Mrs. A as a perfect wife and mother, and said that she was the best thing that had ever happened to him and that he was a terrible husband and father because of his drinking. This was three weeks after the discovery of the sexual abuse and he had not had a drink since. Mr. A was seen again three months later. By that time, he had gained a little more insight and was in touch with the resentment he felt about "always being the bad guy" in the family, although he acknowledged that his wife had been doing what was best for the family.

2. *Parental Children.* Victims of intrafamilial sexual abuse are described in the literature as parental children and involved in role reversal with their mothers (Brooks 1982; Justice & Justice 1979; Meiselman 1979; Kaufman et al. 1954; Machotka et al. 1967; Lustig et al. 1965). While a number of the cases in our sample fit this pattern, a much larger number of cases do not. One reason is, close to two thirds of intrafamilial cases have multiple rather than single victims. In such situations, the incestuous triad, with the victim being the oldest female and the parental child, cannot apply. Second, more than half of our victims were five or under at onset of the sexual abuse. Their young ages make it difficult for them to assume parental roles. Third, while a number of families had mothers who were quite dependent and did not fulfill traditional maternal role responsibilities, it was not usually the case that the victim then carried out the mother's tasks. The tasks were left undone. The case example below is as characteristic of our sample as the parental child configuration.

> EXAMPLE 11: The T family consisted of Mr. and Mrs. T, their two daughters, Sharon, 14, and Rene, 12, and Boyd, 8, a son. Mr. T had a history of about eight years of intermittently sexually victimizing Rene and Sharon. Rene was an extremely aggressive and hostile adolescent who was often truant from school, promiscuous, delinquent, and frequently ran away. Rene was in an emotionally and mentally handicapped classroom and was scapegoated by the family. She was a very needy girl, who seemed much younger than her 12 years.
>
> Mr. T worked steadily at an auto plant, but Mrs. T never felt they had enough money. Thus she was always applying for and accepting part-time jobs. She would hold several of these simultaneously and was not at home much. Mr. T appeared rather ineffectual. He played with his wife's hair with his face averted from the evaluator when the family was assessed.
>
> When the sexual abuse was discovered and the two girls went into care, both had very poor dental hygiene. Rene had a hearing loss because

she had experienced chronic ear infections. The family lived in a nice enough house, but it was very dirty and cluttered. The family tended to eat evening meals at fast food restaurants, and it was "every man for himself" during the day.

The first problem that presented itself when protective services tried to work with the family was Mrs. T's inability to attend therapy, make visits to the girls, accept homemaker services, and come to meetings with the caseworker because of her work schedule.

In this family, mother clearly has chronically avoided child and family care responsibilities, a pattern that continued after placement. Yet no one appears to have filled the breach. Sharon certainly is not a parental child and has engaged in a lot of acting out behavior outside of the home. Rene is a very dependent, sometimes pathetic child. Mr. T is so passive and unaware it does not appear to have occurred to him that he might do something about the condition of the house and the care of the children.

3. *Maternal collusion.* A frequent assertion is that mothers are aware of and collude in the sexual abuse of their daughters (Walters 1975; Henderson 1972; Sarles 1975; Machotka et al. 1967). Our data do not support this contention. The definition of collusion is a "fraudulent, secret understanding" (Concise Oxford Dictionary 1964:236), which implies conscious activity. Some unconscious factors, described earlier, and related to the mother's victimization as a child, may play a role in the incestuous family situation, but unconscious factors do not constitute collusion. In the very small number of cases where mothers did collude, they were also perpetrators, usually in polyincestuous families (see chapter 3).

However, mothers sometimes did not respond in a protective way when they were apprised of the sexual abuse, but that response also is different from collusion. Some professionals might argue that the absence of a protective response means the mother wants the abuse to continue, but we found that mothers either were persuaded by the perpetrator that it had not occurred, or believed they could protect the child without professional intervention. There were also some cases where mothers knew that the sexual abuse was gong on and chose to tolerate it. They did so because they were terrified of their spouses, cared more about keeping their spouses than protecting their children, or saw other options as more horrendous than the incest. In less than a third of our cases did mothers have knowledge of the sexual abuse prior to its discovery by professionals, either by observation or by being told.

Mrs. B, in the example below, is one of the most unprotective mothers in our sample but she does not appear to have been collusive. Events which played a role in Mr. B's sexual abuse of his daughters are described earlier in this chapter.

EXAMPLE 12:   Mr. and Mrs. B have been married 28 years and have eight children, four of them girls. Mr. B has sexually molested all but one of the girls. According to Gina, 19, and Sally, 15, their mother had observed their father when he would grab their breasts and vulvas. Sally said she would yell for her mom when her father started. Her mother would come into the room and tell him to stop, but he would continue for several minutes afterward. Gina moved out of the house at 15 into a room she rented in someone's house in order to avoid the sexual abuse. She worked after school and on weekends in a bakery in order to pay room and board. Margie, 16, did not acknowledge she was also being abused although the other two victims had observed their father molesting her. Sally said Margie was planning on getting married as soon as she finished high school and had told Sally she could stand it until then.

Mrs. B, when interviewed, denied ever having observed her husband touching the children inappropriately. She said Gina moved out because she did not want to do her chores and abide by family rules. She said that Sally was making these statements because her best friend was not getting along with her stepfather.

Mrs. B was facing the reality of a husband who was disabled and who would probably not live much longer. She and her children were also financially dependent upon his Social Security benefits. She had worked very infrequently during the marriage, and had no skills. In addition, although Mr. B could not chase anybody and hurt them, he was heavy, strong, evil tempered, and willful. She admitted that every time she had gone against him in the past, she ended up being sorry.

In the B case, not only was Mrs. B financially dependent upon her husband, but she was emotionally tied to a relationship she had been in for 28 years. In addition, she probably weighed the impact of the sexual abuse on her children against the impact on her husband if he should have to leave the home, and decided to lie and protect him.

4. *Sexual dysfunction.* Lack of sexual satisfaction in the marriage is cited frequently as the reason why the husband turns to the child for sexual gratification (Henderson 1972; Lustig et al. 1965). In fact, sexual dysfunction was found in a little less than half the families in our sample. Sometimes this consisted of the mother withholding or not wanting sex. However, at least as often it was the husband who had difficulty performing or did not wish sex with his wife. In one of our cases, the couple was married 12 years and had sexual intercourse only 20 times. After the birth of the second child, who was a girl, there was a four-year period when no sexual intercourse took place. This wife, a very attractive

woman, stated she tried everything she could think of to interest her husband in her, all kinds of sexy nightwear, pornographic movies, and techniques she had read about that were supposed to result in sexual arousal.

Moreover in many of the cases where there was marital sexual dysfunction, fathers had sexual outlets other than their children. Many of these men engaged in a lot of sexual activity including activity with children. Furthermore, the victimization of children was not necessarily confined to the family. The case example of the P family is characteristic of a fairly large number of men in our sample.

> EXAMPLE 13:   Mr. and Mrs. P had been married 21 years. They had three children: Vicki, 20, Tommy, 16, and Patti, 10. Patti reported to her school counselor that her father had been having sex with her since she was about six or seven. This included fondling, oral-genital contact, and genital intercourse. She also reported that he had done the same thing to Vicki, but her mother put a stop to it. In addition, two female cousins, one 16 and the other 18, who lived from time to time with the P's had also been victims. Patti knew this because she had observed it.
>
> Mr. P admitted to the sexual abuse of Patti. Mrs. P said that as far as she could tell, she was the only woman her husband did not want to go to bed with. She stated that for the last few years he had not been interested in her sexually, even though she tried to interest him.
>
> During the course of treatment, Mr. P admitted that when he turned 40, he went through a period of "midlife madness," during which he "went to bed with every woman I could, fat or skinny, blond, brunette, you name it." Now he said he had calmed down quite a bit and only had one or two women he saw on the side.
>
> When other women in the extended family were interviewed, in speaking of Mr. P, they said that women had to avoid being in the room alone with him because he could not keep his hands to himself. They asserted he had always been like that, not just since he turned 40.

Although Mr. P appears to reject what his wife has to offer, he is not at a loss for sexual outlets. Indeed, he is very promiscuous. Thus, our experience does not support the contention that the mother's withholding sex from the perpetrator is a prerequisite for sexual abuse. For further dicussion of sexual patterns exhibited by perpetrators, see chapter 7.

5. *Acceptance of the sexual role by the victim.* Victims are often described as seductive with the perpetrator, as enjoying the sexual abuse, or at least having tolerated it (Walters 1975; Sarles 1975; Lustig et al. 1965; Dietz and Craft 1980). Our experience suggests these contentions are gross distortions. As was reported in chapter 2, in more than half the cases some degree of force—including acts resulting in injury—was used to coerce children into involvement.

While some children who have been sexually abused may appear somewhat seductive, this is a result of the sexual abuse, not a cause. Victims are socialized by the perpetrator to interact with men in a sexual way. This is the behavior that is taught and encouraged by the perpetrator. Most victims have little awareness that their behavior is seductive and are distraught and bewildered when men accost them sexually.

Only a small percentage of victims in our sample reported, or indicated in some other way, that the sexual abuse was positive. Many of these children came from very deprived, neglectful environments, and all had severe superego damage. They enjoyed the closeness and the sensual pleasure of the sexual abuse even though they would describe it as bad or naughty. In addition, a few very young children—usually two or three years old—who did not understand the meaning of the behavior, did not have a detectable negative response to the abuse. However, for the overwhelming majority of our victims the negative aspects far outweighed any positive ones.

Finally, children who passively accept the perpetrator's attentions reflect the substantial power differential and role relationship between perpetrator and child. The perpetrator has the ability and frequently the willingness to coerce the child to comply should the child attempt to resist. Further, the perpetrator is usually the child's caretaker—that is, a nurturer, protector, and teacher. A child is not expected to resist requests of a person in this role.

The example that follows is characteristic of situations where children find pleasure in the sexual interaction.

EXAMPLE 14:   Katy was 3 1/2. Concern about possible sexual abuse was raised by her aunt who was caring for Katy while her parents were getting married, Katy said to her aunt "Tantie you fuck me." A referral was made to protective services.

The agency had been involved with the family at the time of Katy's birth when her mother, Mrs. G, had a postpartum psychotic break. Mrs. G thought Katy was possessed by the devil and feared leaving Katy with Mr. G because she thought he would rape Katy. At this time Mrs. G was observed tongue kissing with Katy, who was two months old. Protective services would not allow Mr. G to assume care of his daughter because of a history of indecent exposure and sexual assault. Mrs. G recovered after about a year and regained custody of Katy.

When Katy was evaluated regarding the current concerns, she exhibited a lot of sexual excitement and pleasure at the sight of the penis on the male anatomically explicit doll, caressing it and putting it in her mouth. When asked what the penis was, she called it a dick and volunteered her daddy had one. The evaluator then asked her if she had ever done the behavior she was demonstrating, fondling and fellatio, and she replied she did this with her daddy. She then engaged the dolls in sexual intercourse and said "it feel good." She picked up an adult female doll and began to suck its breasts. She was asked "who does that?" and she said "me, do, me do to my mom." She was asked what does her mommy say, and Katy stated, "her like it, her want me do it." She then hugged and kissed the mommy, daddy and Katy dolls and made them engage in a number of sexual acts.

Katy appears to have been socialized by both of her parents to expect sexual interaction with adults, and thus requests sex from her aunt. Because she is young and lacks information indicating sex between adults and children is inappropriate, she has a positive view of sexual abuse. In fact she becomes sexually stimulated by the anatomically explicit dolls. However, she cannot be characterized as seductive. As she becomes older and aware of the meaning of the sexual abuse, her perception of these events will change.

V. CONCLUSION

The causes of sexual abuse are multiple and complex. The professional should be aware that the abuse has its origins in some level of sexual feelings and superego deficits on the part of the perpetrator. In addition it is important to systematically examine the context of the victimization for cultural, environmental, individual, and family factors that contribute to sexual abuse. The role played by these factors will vary from case to case.

Our data suggest the need for some reformulation of the family dynamics theory of sexual abuse. There is far too much blaming of the victims—that is, mother and daughter—and not enough emphasis on the perpetrator's role. The perpetrator is the person who does the abusing, not the mother or the child. While his behavior is motivated by multiple factors, the underlying cause is whatever in his personality or functioning compels him to engage in sex with children. The propensity to abuse may be enhanced by cultural supports, environmental factors, maternal dysfunction, marital discord, and sexual dysfunction in the marriage. The sexual behavior may be prolonged by the mother's failure to protect and the daughter's unwillingness to disclose or fear of the consequences of telling. But the sexual abuse would not happen without there being an adult who has sexual desires toward children and the willingness to act upon them.

PART III: EVALUATION OF SEXUAL ABUSE

CHAPTER FIVE

An Overview
of the Assessment Process

I. INTRODUCTION

The purpose of this chapter is to provide the reader with a general orientation toward investigating an allegation of sexual abuse and to describe strategies for data gathering that maximize the probability of an accurate assessment.

In the first part of the chapter the issue of lying—the probability of a child, a perpetrator, and significant others lying—will be taken up. Then the structuring and sequencing of interviews will be discussed. In the final section the importance of data gathering external to the interview process will be described. Later chapters will deal with specific interviews of the child, the alleged perpetrator, and the mother of the victim.

II. A GENERAL ORIENTATION TO THE ALLEGATION

We approach an allegation of sexual abuse with a number of clinical assumptions. First, we believe children rarely make up stories that they have been sexually abused. Young children usually have neither the sexual knowledge to invent such stories nor a reason to do so. Rather, victims have many reasons for not telling when sexual abuse has occurred, particularly in cases where there is a close relationship between the victim and the perpetrator. The victim may suffer multiple negative consequences as a result of revealing the sexual abuse. First, for children who are aware of what sexual abuse is, there is the stigma of being identified as a participant in the sexual interactions. Further, the victim may be rejected by the perpetrator, and that person may be valued by the child. The child may also be ostracized if the family chooses to side with the perpetrator, or be "punished" by placement in foster care or an institution. The family may be torn apart, and the child may see herself as responsible for its demise. (For a discussion of treatment of these feelings, see chapter 11). She will have to tell the intimate details of the story to many people. If the case goes to court, the victim may have to describe the abuse to strangers with the perpetrator facing her, and she may be subjected to harsh cross-examination by the defense attorney.

In contrast, perpetrators are not likely to admit they have engaged in sexual abuse; in most cases they will deny it. The offender has a great deal to lose if a true allegation is believed. He will very likely face rejection by his immediate and extended family, and divorce may ensue. In some instances, his employment may be in jeopardy. He has reason to fear the juvenile court, which may deprive him of his child, impose treatment, and intrude in other ways into the family. The perpetrator has even more cause to fear the criminal courts, where he may be tried for criminal sexual conduct and sent to prison, or at least be placed on probation. In addition to the practical consequences of admission, there are psychological ones. Many perpetrators are so ashamed of their behavior they cannot admit it. For some the shame is so great they will continue to deny in the face of overwhelming evidence. However, others have character disorders. These men lie, and they may lie convincingly and persistently over a period of months and even years. Frequently they go to extraordinary lengths to persuade others of their innocence. The case cited below is illustrative.

EXAMPLE 1:   Mr. P had been involved in cunnilingus and fellatio with his four-year-old daughter. His wife attempted to divorce him when she caught him in the act. He sought custody of the child in the divorce settlement, stating that his wife was an unfit mother because she had induced the child to state the father had been sexually abusive. He went to a mental health evaluation and strongly asserted his innocence. He persuaded his family's minister and the minister's wife of his wife's craziness and his innocence. They made a Protective Services referral on the child's mother based on their belief that she was very disturbed. They thought she had made up stories about her husband and had coerced the child to say the sexual abuse had happened.

This type of response is fairly typical of men who are guilty of sexual abuse. Unfortunately many professionals incorrectly assume that men who go to these lengths must be innocent.[1]

Mothers may also have reasons for denying the sexual abuse and disbelieving their children, particularly in intrafamilial sexual abuse cases. First, to acknowledge that the incest occurred may be perceived by the mother as an indictment of herself as a mother and a spouse. In her eyes, she did not protect the child, and her husband preferred her child to herself as a sexual partner. This may be so painful that "putting on blinders" is a more tolerable solution. The mother may also be facing more concrete and practical problems. For instance, she may be financially dependent on the perpetrator. If she has to expel him or he goes to prison, she may have to seek other means of support. These include going on AFDC or seeking employment when she has never worked or has not worked for years.

Finally, should her spouse leave or be incarcerated, she will lose the emotional support he may have provided. To an outsider this may not seem much, but frequently he will be all the mother has, and she will not be able to imagine life without him. Further, she may feel sorry for him, as he experiences the consequences of his sexually abusive behavior.

Because of these dynamics, mothers of sex abuse victims may disbelieve their daughters' allegations, or ignore them when they are made, or try to deal with the problem without bringing in outside help. Alternatively, they may initially side with the child, but then switch their loyalties and side with the perpetrator as they experience the practical consequences of the spouse's anger and/or absence. Our assertions in this regard are based upon clinical experience and reports of other experts (see Jiles 1980; Summit and Kryso 1978; Leaman 1980).

The example below illustrates maternal ambivalence in sexual abuse.

EXAMPLE 2:   Laura S is the mother of four children—two by her husband, who is in a prison for the criminally insane, and two by her boyfriend who moved in shortly after her husband's incarceration. One rainy night she was returning to the trailer where they live and through the window saw her boyfriend attempting sexual intercourse with her oldest child, Sarah, age 6. She rushed in, grabbed a kitchen knife and threatened him. He desisted and she took all four children, went to the nearest neighbor and called the police. They came and arrested him, and Laura was seen throwing all of his belongings out of the trailer into the rain.

Her boyfriend was to be criminally prosecuted and she was the main witness. However, on the stand she stated that she was not sure he was sexually abusing Sarah because his back was to her. He was acquitted. Later she admitted that she felt sorry for him because he had only one arm, and she had been fearful that he would go to prison where her husband was and that her husband would have killed him. Six months later she sent her daughter to live with the maternal grandparents. It was learned subsequently she did this because her boyfriend was moving back in and she wanted to be sure her daughter was safe.

Laura's behavior reflects her attempt to reconcile protecting both her children and her boyfriend, as well as her preference for having her boyfriend rather than her daughter in the house.

Therefore, we begin our investigation with the assumption that a victim who claims to have been sexually abused is very likely to be telling the truth. On the other hand, a perpetrator who denies the allegation is likely to be lying. Finally, mothers who disbelieve or discount the allegation have a number of conscious and unconscious motives for doing so, despite the veracity of the child's allegation.

III. WHEN MIGHT AN ALLEGATION BE FALSE?

Although, in general, children do not make up stories about being sexually abused, there are circumstances where the allegation may be false. False accusations can come from either adults or child victims, but are more likely to come from adults (Goodwin et al. 1980; Jones 1985). False accusations from adults will be described first, followed by a discussion of untrue statements coming from a child.

A. False Allegations from Adults

There are circumstances where the mother, father, grandmother, or someone else close to the child may make a false accusation. These may result from misinterpretation, lying, or psychosis.

1. *Misinterpretation of behavior or statements.* A significant other or a professional may observe fear of the alleged perpetrator or reluctance to go with that person, may note sexual behavior on the child's part, or may be aware of certain statements the child has made and wrongly assume they indicate sexual abuse. This type of misinterpretation of data is somewhat more common with increased awareness of sexual abuse. The example that follows illustrates an incorrect allegation made by professionals based upon a child's sexual behavior and statements.

> EXAMPLE 3: Lucy, 3, spent several hours a week in a day care home while her mother worked. Her father was a physician's assistant. The day care mother noted that Lucy masturbated when she took a nap, which disturbed her, so she began to chart Lucy's masturbation and praise her when she did not masturbate. The chart was sent home to Lucy's parents

weekly. Because the charting system did not eliminate Lucy's masturbation and the parents did not seem sufficiently concerned, the day care
mother made a referral to protective services for possible sexual abuse.

The protective services worker went to the day care home and interviewed Lucy. Lucy described playing doctor with her father. They did
this in her father's bed. Her mother was downstairs. Lucy told the worker
her father had a buzzer with which he used to touch various parts of her
body. These included her arm, her cheek, her stomach, and possibly
lower down, that is, her vulva. Lucy also said her father had two buzzers,
and he only took them out when it was time to play doctor. The worker
thought that the buzzer was a vibrator which the father had used to
stimulate his daughter's genital area.

Because of her concerns, the protective services worker asked an
expert to evaluate the child. The mother, very distraught about the allegation and the fact that her husband had to move out of the home, asked if
she could bring her husband's and her daughter's doctor kits for the
evaluation. This request was granted. The mother also said she had noted
occasional masturbation by Lucy but never had considered it extreme.

During the course of the evaluation the child did not evidence any
sexual behavior even though sexual matters were discussed. In the
father's doctor kit was a tuning fork, which the child identified as the
buzzer. She showed the expert how it works by striking it and then
touching various parts of her and the evaluator's body with it, mostly the
arms. Direct questions were asked about a range of sexual touching, including touching with the buzzer. These questions elicited negative
responses and the child showed no distress or concern at these questions.
The conclusion was that the child most likely had not been sexually
abused.

In this case, it seems that the day care provider may have exacerbated a fairly normal response, masturbation at bedtime, by paying
special attention to it. The protective services worker's suspicions were
aroused by the finding that the child played doctor in her father's bed
away from the scrutiny of the mother, and the threshold of suspicion was
heightened by the description of the buzzer game. The concerns of both
professionals were legitimate, but the interview data from the expert
demonstrates how important a careful examination of evidence is.
Techniques for the examination will be described in the next chapter.

2. *Fabrication.* On rare occasions an adult will completely fab-
ricate an accusation of sexual abuse. The cases of this type in our sample
involved disputed custody and visitation after a divorce. Slightly more
common is embellishment. An adult, usually a parent or grandparent,
genuinely believes another adult is sexually abusing a child and augments
the supporting data. The example below illustrates both types of fabrication.

EXAMPLE 4:   Mr. J originally made allegations of neglect of Angela, 3, against his former wife. He said the child was being left unsupervised and that she was not receiving proper well child care. There was an investigation by the Friend of the Court, who determined that Mrs. J was using a responsible 16-year-old babysitter when she was seen with her new boyfriend by Mr. J. Angela's shots and medical checkups were up to date. Mr. J then said he thought Angela was being sexually abused by the boyfriend, Carl. He said Angela masturbated when she visited him and told him she didn't like Carl. Further he said he had heard that Carl beat and raped his former girlfriend and beat her kids. He did not want Carl around his daughter. The Friend of the Court asked for an evaluation of Angela by an expert in sexual abuse.

In the meantime Mrs. J said Angela was having bad dreams and waking up crying, "Don't hit me Rhonda." Rhonda was Angela's father's new wife. Mrs. J also said Angela complained that her pee pee hurt and said Rhonda hurt her pee pee. A medical examination revealed no evidence of trauma or infection.

Before the evaluation, Mr. J withdrew his complaint that Angela had been sexually abused by Carl and requested Mrs. J cancel the appointment. She went forward with the evaluation in order to "get to the bottom of this."

The evaluator got no information that would support that Angela had been sexually abused. She did say her pee pee hurt sometimes but no one had touched her. She said she didn't like Rhonda or Carl too much and responded "yes" when the evaluator asked if she wished her mom and dad were back together. When Mrs. J was interviewed she changed her story somewhat, stating that Angela had only said her pee pee hurt. She said she thought Angela told her aunt that Rhonda hurt her pee pee. Mrs. J was very relieved to find her daughter had not been sexually abused.

In this case, it seems likely that Mr. J fabricated his accusation against Carl. The allegation does not have much substance to it and he dropped the complaint. The findings of the evaluation support the probability Mr. J did not want his wife to go forward with the evaluation because he would have to bear the expense rather than because he had something to conceal. Mrs. J seems initially to have embellished the facts by adding that Angela told her Rhonda hurt her pee pee. The fact the mother evidenced relief at the findings of the evaluation suggests she genuinely did believe something had happened to Angela. How to evaluate statements made by significant others will be discussed later in this chapter.

3. *Delusions of sexual abuse.* Finally, as noted earlier, sometimes a psychotic adult will have delusions that a child is being sexually abused. This type of false accusation has also been noted by others (Lustig et al.

1965; McDonald 1971; Goodwin et al. 1980; Goodwin et al. 1982). Both our research and the literature indicate that the accuser is usually a female, most often the alleged victim's mother. The parent has a lot of sexual content in her thought process, including the specific delusion related to the child. There may be a symbiotic relationship with the alleged victim. The parent is herself likely to have been sexually abused as a child, and in the delusional structure the child becomes the parent. The alleged perpetrator may be someone who has sexually misused the parent. In the example below, the mother had delusional thoughts about her employer sexually abusing her daughter.

EXAMPLE 5: Mrs. P was one of four children in a middle class family. When she was 16 her parents took her to a psychiatrist because she was alleging her uncle had had intercourse with her. No finding of sexual abuse was made by the psychiatrist who saw her at that time, but he prescribed anti-psychotic drugs.

Mrs. P reports having been promiscuous during her adolescence and at 20 giving birth to a son, who was adopted by her oldest brother. She was hospitalized about every year during her twenties for psychotic episodes. She married a very disturbed man and had two children. He obtained custody of the children when they divorced because Mrs. P was in a psychiatric hospital.

Mrs. P developed a relationship with a man she met while hospitalized and became pregnant. She had a daughter, Flower. When Flower was almost a year old, Mrs. P took a job as a housekeeper for a retired man, Morris. She and Flower lived with him. Mrs. P remained his housekeeper for three years, but there were many ups and downs.

At some point Morris decided he wanted more than a business relationship with Mrs. P. He began to treat her like his girlfriend. Flower called him DaDa. Morris bought clothing and other presents for Flower and her mother, he took them out to dinner, and he established a savings account for Flower's education. He asked Mrs. P to marry him. She refused. Sometimes Mrs. P said there was no sex between them. Other times she would say that Morris made sexual advances but she rebuffed him. Yet there were times she told her after care worker that they had a good sexual relationship. Further, at one point Mrs. P accused Morris of raping her. She was then quite psychotic and left him and went to a battered women's shelter. When she got to the shelter, Mrs. P began saying that Morris had sexually abused Flower, that he stuck his finger in "her little pee pee." Mrs. P was observed several times inspecting Flower's vagina and putting vaseline on it.

An evaluation of Flower was conducted. She appeared to be a precocious child who was accustomed to taking care of her mother. When asked if anyone had ever touched her pee pee, she looked at the evaluator and responded, "No, my mommy asked me that, too," in a very matter of fact voice. She replied negatively to questions about other sexual activities in the same calm manner. She stated that she slept in the same bed with her mother, but denied any sexual contact with her mother. Her mother had Flower sleep with her to protect her from Morris. Flower did say one time she got into bed with her DaDa. She touched his back and it was cold. She denied any sexual touching while in bed with him.

At a later time, when the mother was less psychotic, she said she did not think Flower had been sexually abused by Morris. When asked why she had alleged that in the past, she described that time as one when she feared everyone, including Morris. However, she continued to talk compulsively about sexual matters and her concern about Flower's sex education. The evaluator concluded that Morris had not sexually abused Flower.

In this case we have a mother and a daughter who are very much fused. For the mother, her daughter is her identity. At the time Mrs. P went to the shelter, she perceived Morris as being sexually assaultive toward herself. Therefore, in her delusional system Morris was also assaultive toward Flower. When the mother is less psychotic, she no longer has these delusions. But there still is a lot of sexual content in her thought process.

B. Untrue Statements Made by Children

Researchers examining allegations of sexual abuse find approximately 2 percent of children's assertions they have been victimized are untrue (Goodwin, et al. 1980; Jones 1985); about 3 percent of children's allegations in our sample appeared to be false.

Several types of situations where the child's statements might be untrue will be discussed. First will be two types of situations where children may be falsely stating they have been sexually abused: social desirability responses and untrue allegations made by older children. Second, two situations where children lie to conceal the sexual abuse will be described, situations where children lie because they fear telling the truth, and situations where children do not reveal all aspects of the sexual abuse. Finally, the issue of children fantasizing will be considered.

1. *Social desirability responses.* Sometimes children indicate there has been sexual abuse to gain approval from the interviewer. These situations often arise because of an inappropriate line of questioning. For example, the interviewer asks the child leading questions, such as "were you in his bed when this happened?" The child may answer yes to

the question when that may not be so. This type of false positive is more likely to be found with very young children who do not understand the questions. (More discussion of questioning techniques can be found in the next chapter.) Other times children will not remember or know certain facts and will make facts up in response to repeated questioning. The children whom we have found engaging in this type of lying were fairly disturbed. We have seen no cases of this type where children made up an entire scenario of sexual abuse, but only cases where they make up some details.

The highly publicized case in Jordan, Minnesota *(Minneapolis Star & Tribune*, May 26, 1985) may be one where the questioning techniques and multiple interviews led to some social desirability responses. The example below is one where a fairly disturbed child, among other things, gives social desirability responses.

> EXAMPLE 6: Sally, 9, her sister Lisa, 4, and brother George, 10, had been removed from their mother's care for intractable neglect. The mother was mentally retarded and had a drug problem. She alternated between living with her husband and a boyfriend. Both of her men were physically assaultive to her and the children.
>
> The children were placed with their maternal grandfather and his wife. Sally and George were also enrolled in day treatment programs. The grandparents, on numerous occasions, found George attempting intercourse with the girls, but more frequently with Sally. The children could not be left unsupervised and had to be locked in separate bedrooms at night.
>
> The grandparents initially asked that Sally be seen for an exploration of possible sexual abuse. During that interview Sally said George had sex with her all the time and she could not stop him. She did not evidence any particular psychological discomfort regarding the intercourse with George and said it felt good. Sally also described all three children being in the bed with their mother and either their father or their mother's boyfriend and observing the adults having sexual intercourse. The grandparents were convinced that sex with the children had also occurred.
>
> The second interview involved both Sally and Lisa. Sally was eager to talk but Lisa was reticent. Sally said that her father put his "wiener" in her "pussy" and her mouth. When asked if anyhthing came out of his wiener, she looked to the evaluator for direction and asked, "Did anything come out of it?" The evaluator said, "I don't know; I wasn't there." Sally then said yes. When asked what color the stuff was, she said, "Red? Green?" When asked if the stuff was wet or dry, she said it was dry.
>
> When questioned about her mom's boyfriend, Sally said he also put his wiener in her pussy and in her mouth. Sally asserted that both men had done the same things to Lisa. Lisa denied any sex with the boyfriend but admitted to sexual abuse by the father.

A case like this one is confusing for the evaluator. On the one hand we have extensive sexual behavior by all three children while in placement which strongly suggests the children were sexually abused. It is highly unlikely that this type of sexual behavior could result from casual observation of sex. It is possible that it could be the consequence of having made intimate observations, such as would occur if the children were in the mother's bed while she was having sex. But it is more likely to be the result of actual sexual contact. There are also statements by both girls that sex occurred with their father. The activities with the boyfriend are more questionable, both because Lisa does not accuse him and because Sally states he engaged in exactly the same sexual acts her father did—sometimes an indicator of a false allegation. Further, we have some responses by Sally that appear to be social desirability responses. She wants to know from the evaluator whether the desired response is yes or no to the question of whether something came out of the penis. She does not know the color of semen and she incorrectly guesses that semen is dry. These responses suggest there was no observed ejaculation. Therefore, in this case we can say the children experienced sexual abuse at the hands of their father, most likely in the presence of their mother and probably observed their mother engaging in sexual activities with both father and boyfriend. But we cannot confidently go beyond that.

2. *Suspect allegations with older children.* On rare occasions children will assert that they have been sexually abused when this is not the case (Goodwin et al. 1980; Sgroi 1982).

These situations have identifiable characteristics.[2] First, the children are older, usually adolescents, and have some sexual knowledge (thus they possess enough prior information to make up a story). Secondly, they are usually children who are fairly damaged psychologically, particularly with regard to their ability to form attachments. This means they are less likely than more intact children to be troubled by the enormity of the accusations they are making. Often they display a range of delinquent behavior. Third, there is generally a short term instrumental gain which will result from the allegation. This may be revenge against a physically abusive stepfather, avoiding punishment for truancy or another offense, or being allowed to go live elsewhere. Frequently the child has been sexually or physically abused in the past and has experienced some relief from that abuse when it was revealed. Finally, the child is likely to have difficulty describing the specifics surrounding the incident and the abuse and may be quite inconsistent from one interview to another.

However, even in such cases, the evaluator should explore carefully. Children who come from chronically sexually abusive situations usually have difficulty forming trusting and close relationships. They engage in such acting out behavior as promiscuity, truancy, and stealing, and they finally tell about the sexual abuse in an effort to extricate themselves from the sexual relationship or the family. The example below was a difficult one to sort out but turned out to be false.

EXAMPLE 7: Christie, 14, had been removed from her mother's care and placed with her grandmother at the age of 7 because of fondling by her father and physical neglect by both parents. Her father had also been physically assaultive to the mother and had an alcohol problem.

Christie remained with her grandmother until she was 13. In the meantime her parents had divorced and her mother married a widower who had two sons, both somewhat younger than Christie. Christie's grandmother was obese and had a heart condition. She also drank a fair amount. She did not provide much supervision and bought Christie whatever she wanted within her means. Christie had a 10-speed bicycle, her own waterbed, and a pair of Jordache jeans. Contact with her mother had been intermittent over the years.

When Christie was 13, her grandmother had a heart attack and could no longer care for her. Christie was returned to her mother's care. Her stepfather was rather strict and disapproved of the way the grandmother had raised Christie. He told Christie and her mother that all the children would receive equal treatment. The first example of this was to sell Christie's waterbed and spend the proceeds equally on all three children. Christie got a bed that would fit into her new bedroom and the boys got school clothes. Christie was furious.

There were numerous other conflicts between Christie and her stepfather. He disapproved of her dating and forbade her seeing an 18-year-old high school dropout. There were also some instances when he hit Christie with his belt. He left a belt buckle mark on her neck in one abusive encounter.

Six months after returning to her mother's care, Christie told her school counselor that her stepfather had raped her. She reported that one night when her mother had taken the boys to Cub Scouts, her stepfather threw her down on the couch, pulled off her jeans and raped her. As evidence she showed a linear bruise on her lower back. She said that the bruise occurred when she landed on the couch. When the physician stated he thought it was inflicted by a whip or belt, Christie said her stepfather hit her with a belt because she resisted the sexual abuse. The stepfather admitted to hitting with the belt, but denied sexual abuse.

Christie was removed from the home and placed in foster care. She had difficulties responding to the limits in the foster home, and she asked to be allowed to live independently or with her grandmother; neither plan was regarded as appropriate. Within a month Christie was thoroughly disillusioned with foster care and ran away to her mother and stepfather's.

At that point she said her stepfather had not sexually abused her, that she had made it up to get placed back with her grandmother. She said she couldn't stand it that all of a sudden there were all those rules and her stepfather could boss her around even though he was no relation of hers. Her real dad was never like that even though he had sexually abused her. However, she said it was even worse in foster care because they were always going to church and there were lots of rules.

Christie's mother wanted her to stay with them and her stepfather was willing to give it a try. The whole family was sent to family therapy, and a children's services worker met with Christie regularly to monitor how things were going, specifically being alert to other concerns regarding sexual abuse.

Things went reasonably well for the next two years, although there were periodic flareups because Christie did not like the rules. There were no further allegations of sexual abuse. At 16, Christie became pregnant by her boyfriend who was 18. The parents granted permission for them to marry.

In this case, we find an adolescent who is quite distressed about the living situation she is suddenly thrust into. She had experienced sexual abuse at age seven, which led to her removal to what she regarded as quite a pleasant circumstance. It appears she made another allegation in order to return to her grandmother's. Nevertheless, the children's services worker kept a close watch on the family situation to make sure this was an accurate assessment.

3. *Lying because the child fears the consequences of being truthful.* Children frequently deny sexual abuse has taken place when in fact it has. They do this because they like the perpetrator or fear the perpetrator or fear the consequences of admission. The example below is illustrative.

EXAMPLE 8:   Jackie, 6, returned from visits with her father, who was divorced from her mother, with evidence of vaginal trauma on three separate occasions over a year and a half. Yet she anxiously and steadfastly asserted no one touched or hurt her. She both loved and feared her father who was alternately loving and violent with her. Ultimately it was learned he slept with her at night and sometimes put a ruler in her vagina.

In the above case, there is physical evidence which tells us something sexual is happening to the child. Yet the child denied any abuse, even when questioned for a lengthy period of time.

Another very common occurrence is for a child to state that sexual abuse happened but subsequently to retract the statement. This happens so frequently that professionals now consider it an aspect of the "sexually abused child syndrome" (Lloyd 1982; Summit 1983). Sahd (1980) asserts that in a third of cases where there is sexual abuse, there is a later false retraction. There are many reasons why children withdraw their assertions. Young children often do not initially understand the meaning of the behavior or that it is taboo. If the reaction they receive to their statements suggests the behavior was wrong, they may change their story because they don't want to be regarded as "bad." Alternatively, they may like the perpetrator and may want to protect him. In other instances they recant because of threats from the perpetrator or coercion from the family. Also, sometimes children withdraw the accusation because of shame and embarrassment. Finally, retraction may arise if the child does not want to be removed from the home, does not want to have to go to therapy, does not want to have to testify in court, or does not want the perpetrator to go to jail. Two examples below illustrate the dynamics of recantation, one with a young child and the other with an adolescent.

> EXAMPLE 9: Emma, age 4 1/2, stated that she and her father would take baths together and she would suck his penis. She asserted that he did not make her do this, that she wanted to do it, saying, "I did it so much I loved it." She missed him and would ask repeatedly why she could not see him. She was told because he "did those bad things." She changed her story, stating, "He didn't do anything bad. I made it all up. It's a story."

Because Emma loved her father and wanted to see him, she reversed her story. He did, in fact, abuse her.

> EXAMPLE 10: Debbie, age 16, told her school counselor that her father had been having sexual intercourse with her for several years. He was an accountant with a part-time income tax business and had his office for the tax business at home in the basement next to her bedroom. He would enter her room at night and have sex with her. He vehemently denied the sexual abuse, but based upon Debbie's statements the juvenile court took jurisdiction and placed Debbie in foster care. She felt she was being punished by the placement.
>
> There was also a criminal investigation during which the police seized Debbie's night clothing and bedsheets. The day before the criminal trial, her father left a note for Debbie's mother to deliver to her. In it, he said he would commit suicide if she testified against him. Debbie at first refused to testify and then got on the stand and said that she had lied, that her father would only come in and talk to her at night. She said she didn't know how his semen got on the bedsheets. Later in treatment she spoke of her inability to tell the truth in court beause she did not want to be responsible for her father's suicide. He was a psychologically very fragile man who well might have committed suicide.

Potentially devastating negative consequences for telling the truth caused Debbie to lie on the stand.

In general, denial and reticence in revealing the sexual abuse, a delay in telling about it, and recantation are to be expected when there has been sexual abuse. They are not indications that an allegation is false. Children may become more forthcoming after they have spent a period of time in a safe, nurturing environment.

4. *Partial revelation of sexual abuse.* Sometimes victims will admit to elements of the sexual abuse, but not to the full extent of it. There are a number of reasons why this lapse may occur. Children may have been told not to tell about some aspects of the abuse, but not others. Alternatively, they may find certain types of sexual behavior especially repugnant, for example oral-genital contact, and not tell about these. Sometimes they conceal acts for which they feel responsible, for example having sex with a younger child. Or, they may not know what sexual behavior is and what it is not, and therefore give incomplete information out of ignorance. Finally, they may simply forget about some instances when being questioned. In the example below the victim initially withheld certain information.

> EXAMPLE 11:   Teresa, age 6, lived with her father and her grandfather, both of whom drank heavily. Teresa said both her father and grandfather put their fingers in her vagina. When her grandfather did this it hurt, but when her father did it it felt good. Sometimes they put medicine in her when they did this. She denied ever seeing either man's penis and insisted that nothing else had happened.
>
> Later during treatment, her father admitted that he regularly engaged in interfemoral intercourse with Teresa. Teresa eventually told her foster mother about the intercourse. This was terrifying to Teresa because her father lay on top of her and she could hardly breathe.

Teresa seems to have given incomplete information because the interfemoral intercourse was too frightening to describe.

Related situations are ones in which children have stated correctly that they have been sexually abused but have implicated someone other than the perpetrator. They may do this because they fear or love the actual perpetrator more than the person they have implicated. A young child may give a completely implausible statement. For example, a five year old girl told us a one and a half year old girl taught her about intercourse. Another child, age three, said it was a lion and a monster who gave her a red vulva. Stories told by older children are more plausible, as in the case that follows.

> EXAMPLE 12:   Helen, age 15, initially reported she had been raped by someone whom she could not identify because, she said, he jumped out of the bushes at night. When taken to the scene of the alleged crime, she

could not decide which bushes he had been behind and described the perpetrator as a black man, something she had not mentioned before.

Later she revealed that her stepfather was making passes at her, such as asking her to go to bed with him, telling her how her mother no longer would have sex with him, and making sexual remarks about her body. On one occasion he put his bare feet between her legs and underneath her nightgown until they were under her buttocks. Before these sexual advances Helen had been very close to her stepfather. Frequently he took her side in arguments with her mother. When asked why she had lied in the first instance, she said she was trying to get her mother's attention so she'd know something was wrong and thought maybe if her stepfather thought she'd been raped, he'd leave her alone.

In the above case the victim implicated someone who did not even exist in hopes that doing this would bring some help. When this did not work, she related the true nature of the victimization.

Similarly, when there is more than one perpetrator, the child may speak of the abuse by one but not by the other. Often there is greater reluctance to talk about victimization by maternal than paternal figures.

5. *Oedipal and other fantasies.* Until relatively recently many allegations of sexual abuse were dismissed as children's fantasies. In part, this response is a legacy of Freud, who assumed that allegations of sexual abuse were primarily a product of a wish to have sex with a parent, usually the parent of the opposite sex (Summit and Kryso 1978; Herman 1981, chapter 7; Masson 1984). In fact, oedipal fantasies are usually easily distinguished from allegations of sexual abuse. They are likely to be expressions of a general desire for closeness to one parent and exclusion of the other, and do not have explicit sexual content. In addition, the child perceives them as desired events and experiences. The following are examples of oedipal wishes:

EXAMPLE 13: Jennifer, 4, said she was going on vacation just with her daddy and would leave her mommy at grandmother's house. She also said that her mother would want to stay at grandma's after the vacation "because she likes it better there, and daddy likes it better with me."

EXAMPLE 14: Nellie, 3, played out her oedipal wish. She would proclaim upon waking in the morning, "I'm awake." Then she would get out of her own bed and crawl in between her parents in bed and kick her mother, saying, "You get up, ma. Me and daddy want to snuggle. You go 'way!"

The examples above differ greatly in content from the following allegation of sexual abuse.

> EXAMPLE 15: Leann, age 3, said her daddy peed in her mouth. His "dinky" would be big and he would make her suck it and after a while he would go pee and say, "Ahh, ahh." The pee was white. He told her not to tell anybody or he would get in trouble. She did not like it; so she told her mommy.

Leann demonstrrates explicit sexual knowledge and was repulsed by the experience, not desirous of it as is usually the case with an oedipal wish or fantasy.

Comparable differentiations between fantasy material and accounts of sexual abuse can be made with allegations made by children beyond the oedipal stage or against people outside the oedipal triangle, as illustrated in the following case, also mentioned in chapter 3.

> EXAMPLE 16: Sophie, 6, made a report about her 14-year-old male babysitter. She said they were lying on the couch and he told her to close her eyes and suck his thumb when he put it in her mouth. She closed her eyes and heard him unzip his fly. What he put in her mouth didn't feel or taste like a thumb. It was bigger and rounder. She opened her eyes and saw his penis. He quickly withdrew it and zipped his pants back up. She thought this was "gross" and told her best friend, who was her babysitter's seven-year-old sister.

The explicitness of the child's account and her emotional reaction to the event indicate it is not a fantasy.

IV. THE STRUCTURE OF THE INTERVIEWING PROCESS

In this section guidelines regarding the order for interviewing those involved in the allegation as well as the physical arrangements for interviews will be described.

A. Sequencing Interviews To Answer the Assessment Questions

A range of questions needs to be answered in the course of the assessment of an allegation of sexual abuse. First and foremost is, "Has the child been sexually abused?" This question must be addressed in all cases, both intrafamilial and extrafamilial, and most often can be determined by an interview with the child. Questions that follow from the first one are "What is the victim's general functioning level?" and "Does the child need treatment in her own right?" These questions too need to be addressed in all cases. Chapter 6 will cover interview techniques to be employed with the child.

The next series of questions is more likely to be asked about intrafamilial sexual abuse. They are "Why did the sexual abuse happen?" "What kind of treatment is indicated for the family?" and "What is the treatment prognosis for the offender?" The reason questions of causality are raised more often about intrafamilial than extrafamilial cases is that in the former treatment is usually considered, while in the latter criminal prosecution is more frequently the primary intervention. Answers to the question of causality and treatment prognosis in intrafamilial sexual abuse are obtained primarily from information related to the functioning of individual family members, particularly the perpetrator and nonperpetrating parent, and from an understanding of family functioning. With extrafamilial sexual abuse, the best strategy for understanding etiology and prognosis is interviewing the perpetrator, with consideration of significant others in the environment. Interviewing perpetrators and mothers of victims is covered in chapters 7 and 8.

If the first question to be answered is whether or not the child has been sexually abused, then it follows that the alleged victim should be interviewed first.[3] There is no point, for example, in interviewing the alleged perpetrator first if he turns out not to be a perpetrator. On the other hand, if he does turn out to be a perpetrator, the evaluator will once again have to confront him, if this status is not known at the time of the initial interview. Interviewing the child first is particularly important in intrafamilial sexual abuse, when the family is just becoming aware of the allegations. A delay in interviewing the child may mean that pressure will be placed upon the child not to reveal the sexual abuse.

It is less important which of the adults is interviewed after the child. However, if the mother is supportive of the victim her information may be useful in confronting the perpetrator. In intrafamilial sexual abuse cases where the family intends to remain intact it is helpful to have an opportunity to see the parents together. Similarly, it is useful to observe the mother-victim relationship and the perpetrator-victim relationship (assuming the male parent is the perpetrator). However, these sessions should not be opportunities for either parent to confront the child, and they should be forgone at the assessment stage if they may be potentially traumatic for the child. Individual assessment of nonvictim children and a family interview can also be informative. As a rule, interviews with the victim and individual parents are essential for case planning while the other interviews will be useful. Assessment interviews with non-victims can be integrated into the treatment process.

B. Should the Child have an Ally During the Interview?

An issue which arises frequently is whether the child should have a support person during the interview. The answer is "that depends." The relationship of the perpetrator to the support person must first be taken into account. If the perpetrator is not known, or known only slightly to this person, then having the ally present can reduce trauma to the victim. However, if the perpetrator is the father and the support person is the mother, that is another matter. Even in situations where the mother is supportive of the child, including the mother throughout the interview may inhibit the child. The child may not want to create more problems between the parents or may not want to upset the nonabusing parent. If the support person is another professional, such as a school counselor, his presence is likely to facilitate the child's ability to talk. However, our general practice, regardless of who the support person is, is that the child should be interviewed both with and without that person. Usually the interviewer begins with the support person present, but as the child becomes comfortable the evaluator asks the child if it is all right if the person leaves for a while.

A related issue is whether or not to interview children together when there are two or more suspected victims in a family. As a rule, when interviewed together, one child will talk more readily than another, and the more verbal child can help the other to talk more easily. In the example below, a rather timid little girl was able to affirm her victimization in the presence of her big brother.

> EXAMPLE 17:   George, age 10, was the alleged victim of fondling by a 15-year-old neighbor boy. He was interviewed with his sister, Tanya, age 6, who was also an alleged victim. After George showed with anatomically explicit dolls how he had been handled by the boy, Tanya was able to point on the girl doll to where the boy had touched her.

In addition sometimes one child will tell how another was victimized. In some cases the child who talks is a nonvictim; in others the child is able to describe another child's victimization, but not her own. The example below is illustrative.

> EXAMPLE 18:   Rachel, 4½, and Lisa, 3½, were both made to engage in fellatio and submit to cunnilingus with their father. They were also made to watch their father and his girlfriend in various sexual acts. At the trial, each girl testified only as to what their father had done to the other.

In addition, the interaction between two children as they respond to questions can often help assess the credibility of the children's statements.

However, as in instances where significant others accompany children to interviews, it is usually important also to interview the children separately when there is more than one alleged victim. For a variety of reasons, the presence of another child may inhibit a victim from giving a complete account. The example below is illustrative.

EXAMPLE 19:   Carol, 8, and Sally, 4, were sexually molested by their stepfather. He babysat for them while their mother worked in the evening. Carol was angry and forthcoming during the joint evaluation. She said that her stepfather had rocked her on his lap until he "got hard" and then he "treated me like a wife." When asked what "treated me like a wife" meant, she said "he put his peter in me." She had suffered physical trauma as a consequence. Sally said during the interview, "he touched me, too." She would say nothing more at that time and her mother concluded she was saying that something had happened to her in order to get attention. The father initially admitted to the abuse of Carol but denied abusing Sally.

Subsequent separate interviews with both girls revealed the following additional information. When Carol had initially told her mother, her mother had slapped her face and told her "don't say nasty things about your father." Sally revealed that her stepfather would get in bed with her and they both would be naked. On several occasions, perhaps as many as five, he placed her on top of him and put his penis between her thighs, engaging in interfemoral intercourse. He denied this and agreed to take a lie detector test. After he failed the lie detector test, he admitted to sexually abusing both girls.

Without the separate interviews, the sexual abuse of Sally would probably not have been known nor would the extent of the family problems have been understood.

C. Who Should Interview?

No profession is automatically best suited to interview children in cases of sexual abuse. Physicians, nurses, mental health experts, law enforcement personnel, protective services workers, and attorneys are all likely to be in situations where they must talk to the children, although the purposes of their interviews will vary. It is important to anticipate what the subsequent intervention is likely to be so that appropriate professionals are involved.

There are, however, two personal characteristics which interviewers must possess if they are to be successful. They must be comfortable with their own sexuality, with sex generally, and must have achieved some resolution of feelings about sexual abuse. In addition, they must have an interest in and capacity to relate to children. We recommend that protective services units and police departments use one or two people to interview in sexual abuse cases rather than requiring that all staff do it. Those interviewing should want to do this kind of work and choose it.

Another concern raised quite often is deciding who should interview is the sex of that person. Specifically, if the child has been sexually abused by a man, is the child likely to "clam up" in the face of a male interviewer? Probably on the whole it is preferable for interviewers to be women, but there are many exceptions. First, in some cases the perpetrator is a woman. Second, in some families the father is nurturing even though he is sexual with the victim and the mother is cold and rejecting. Both instances might argue for a male interviewer. Finally, nurturing men make very good interviewers in cases of sexual abuse. For the victim, encountering such a man may be very important in therapeutic resolution of the sexual abuse. The example below, noted earlier in this chapter, is illustrative.

> EXAMPLE 20: Teresa, 6, refused to give any information to a female evaluator about her father and grandfather who had sexually molested her. However, she finally agreed to talk in the presence of the evaluator if she could sit on the male protective services worker's lap and he could ask her the questions. She saw him as her protector because he had removed her from the abusive environment and placed her in a nice foster home. In addition, her mother, who was not in the home any more, had been brutally physically assaultive to Teresa.

This is a somewhat surprising case because the perpetrators of the sexual abuse were two men.

D. How Many People Should Interview the Child?

One of the dilemmas frequently faced in a sexual abuse evaluation is that many people may need to know the facts first hand. These may include the physician, the child protection worker, a mental health expert, the child's therapist, the police officer, and the prosecutor. A central aspect of the trauma experienced by many children is having to repeat the story many times. Therefore, it is important to minimize the number of times the child must tell it. At the same time having two, three, four, or more professionals involved in the evaluation can be quite overwhelming. It may itself induce trauma and make the child unwilling to speak. How many interviewers the child can tolerate will depend upon her age and state of mind. The younger and the more upset the child, the riskier it is to have several interviewers. If several people must be present during the interview, often it is best to have only one of them questioning the child, and the others on the sidelines.

One of the uses of a one-way mirror and a video or audio tape of the interview is to allow key persons direct access to the child's statement without having them present during the interview. In those cases where such persons need additional or direct information from the child, the observation or video information usually will decrease the supplemental questioning.

Another reason for recording the interview is exact recall of what has taken place; the verbatim statements of the child will be crucial in the interpretation process. For more extensive discussion of videotapes, simulcast, and one-way mirrors, see chapter 15.

E. Allow Enough Time

The customary 20 minute or half hour interview by a police officer or a protective services worker is rarely adequate to elicit a statement about sexual abuse. Two or three hours, and sometimes several sessions, will be necessary for many children to feel comfortable enough to talk and for all the data to be gathered.

After the interviewer has achieved some experience conducting sexual abuse interviews, she will be able to gauge when to stop the interview and resume later. However it is time to cut the interview short when the child becomes too upset to proceed, becomes silly and starts giving nonsensical responses, or when she cannot be focused upon the sexual abuse. If the interview is terminated under any of these circumstances, the evaluator should say, "I want you to come back another time so we can talk some more about what happened." If the child is upset, the evaluator needs to comfort the victim and help her calm down before she leaves.

F. Where to Interview

The best setting for interviewing the child will vary depending upon the type of sexual abuse case. For a situation of extrafamilial sexual abuse, where parents are supportive, the child's home is likely to be ideal. A good example of such a case would be one where the child has been sexually abused in a day care center. In contrast, if the situation is one of father-daughter incest, the child's home is often the worst possible setting, particularly if the perpetrator is in the house at the time. The child's day care center or a room in the child's school may be a good neutral environment. However, access to the child in such settings will often depend upon the setting's policy about parental consent for an interview. Sometimes a meeting can take place at a relative's or supportive neighbor's house when the evaluator has chosen to talk to the child without prior parental permission. Persons interviewing under such circumstances are usually protective services or law enforcement personnel, and they should check local statutes to be sure such a strategy is in compliance with the law.

Special interview rooms, with audiovisual equipment and one-way mirrors, are also very useful for assessing these cases. These may be located in hospitals or other health care facilities, mental health facilities, departments of social services, or police stations.

G. Equipment

Some of the equipment found in a traditional play therapy room is quite useful in evaluating sexual abuse cases. A dollhouse with furniture and family members is an excellent tool. The dolls should include male and female adults and children whose clothes can be removed. Having both black and white family members is also helpful. Hand puppets and paper dolls are valuable additions. Dolls with whom the victim might identify should be part of the evaluator's collection. Baby dolls, both male and female, black and white, blond and brunette, are suitable for children three and under. The evaluator should have baby bottles and blankets, and the dolls should have removable clothing. Little girl dolls and little boy dolls are useful for older children. Anatomically explicit dolls are very important tools for evaluation.[4] In ideal circumstances, the evaluator should have eight—an adult male and female, a boy and girl, both in black and white. If possible, dolls which have anal, mouth, and vaginal openings, penises, and fingers should be available. Dolls which come with clothing and can be undressed are superior to naked dolls.

Paper, pencils and crayons are also essential parts of the evaluator's equipment. So too are pictures that can be used projectively to elicit stories. While standardized instruments such as the Children's Apperception Test (CAT) and the Rorschach can be helpful, we have collected our own set of pictures for sexual abuse evaluations. (Examples appear in chapter 6).

Other items which may be found in a play therapy room can augment the items just described. These include a toy telephone, blocks, Legos, toy soldiers, guns, and trucks and cars. These additional items just mentioned are particularly important if the evaluator is assessing not just whether the child has been sexually abused but also her overall functioning.

With older children toys are less important, but paper and pencil tasks, games, puzzles, and such items as comic books can be useful devices for diversion and release of tension. Persons such as police officers and protective services workers need to have a "traveling kit," which should perhaps consist of anatomically explicit dolls, one or two other items, and paper, pencils, and crayons.

V. DATA-GATHERING EXTERNAL TO THE INTERVIEW

Although interviews with the victim, the alleged perpetrator, and the mother are the major data sources for the evaluation, certain information relating to all of these parties, which might be available from other sources, should be sought. Ideally these data should be available to the evaluator before the interviews. However, sometimes efforts to acquire this information ahead of time unduly delay the interview, and it is optimal to do the evaluation as soon as possible after there are concerns about sexual abuse.

The reason it is essential to gather information about the child is because the child may be quite reticent in an interview with a stranger, but more spontaneous and forthcoming in other contexts. Similarly, the perpetrator and sometimes the mother may fail to report events, may distort information, or may lie outright during the evaluation. Reports from other sources can help the evaluator interpret the data supplied in the interview by the offender and mother.

In a sense, validating an allegation of sexual abuse is like fitting together the pieces of a puzzle. Evidence comes from diverse sources and may span a considerable time period. Further, some information is quite ephemeral. The child may inadvertently mention a happening which causes concern about sexual abuse and then recant. Others, including witnesses, parents, and sometimes even professionals, may change their stories when pressured. The evaluator must systematically collect and weigh data from a range of sources, and then attempt to integrate this information to formulate a conclusion.

A. Information Relevant to the Child

The evaluator will want to collect evidence about the victim related specifically to concerns about sexual abuse as well as information about the child's overall functioning. Data related to the sexual abuse can be divided into five categories: (1) any physical evidence, (2) statements made by the victim to significant others, (3) information about unusual sexual behavior on the victim's part, (4) sexual knowledge beyond that expected for the child's developmental stage, and (5) nonsexual symptomatic behavior. Sexual behavior, sexual knowledge and symptomatic behavior may also be observed in the interview, but it is still good practice to explore these areas with other sources.

1. *Physical evidence.* There are two types of physical evidence: medical findings and evidence collected by law enforcement personnel. A discussion of medical findings can be found in chapter 9. The forensic pelvic exam, which is indicated in some situations, weds medical and law enforcement efforts, for the evidence is usually gathered by a physician but analyzed in the State Police crime lab. Circumstances which affect the likelihood of medical evidence as well as the types of evidence police can collect will be discussed in this section.

a. *The probability of physical findings.* It should be noted that physical findings are not common. Of the cases in our sample, in only 16 percent was there any physical evidence. Jiles (1980) notes, in 20 to 40 percent of his cases where the abuse was later substantiated, there was a total absence of physical findings. Thus the absence of physical evidence is not indicative of the absence of sexual abuse.

The likelihood of physical findings will depend upon the type of sexual abuse and the context in which the case is being seen. Cases of attack by someone external to the family more frequently generate physical evidence. This is because force is likely to be employed and therefore physical injury may occur. Further, the child frequently tells immediately, and the family generally seeks medical intervention right away (therefore evidence of the injury, semen, etc., will still be there). In contrast, incest cases less often yield physical findings. Force is not usually employed, intervention may well occur when the most recent incident is quite remote, and the sexual behavior may well be something short of penetration, precluding the presence of semen in or significant damage to the anal, vaginal, or oral orifice.

The child's age also has an impact upon the probability of physical evidence. The younger the child, the more likely there is to be physical injury because of the small size of the child (including that of her apertures), and her diminished ability to avoid what is painful. Furthermore, individuals who abuse very young children may be more disturbed and therefore less sensitive to the physical harm they are inflicting.

Finally, cases which are seen in medical settings and by law enforcement personnel are more likely to have physical findings than those which are seen in mental health settings or even by protective services.

b. *Evidence from a police investigation.* Evidence gathered by the police is somewhat more stable than that sought by the physician because it is less likely to shortly disappear.

Police can confiscate, with a warrant, bed sheets, the victim's clothing and the perpetrator's clothing. These items may have semen stains, blood stains, body hairs, or other physical evidence which support the allegation. In some situations, an investigation of the scene of the crime will yield physical evidence. The following case is one where the evidence gathered by the police was crucial.

> EXAMPLE 21: Becky, age 8, and in a special classroom, alleged that her 19-year-old uncle would take her into his basement, where there was an old mattress. He would make her lie face down and would stick his penis between her buttocks and rub back and forth until he ejaculated. No physical evidence was found on Becky's person. But a laboratory examination of the mattress revealed semen stains, hairs from Becky's head and the uncle's head, and pubic hairs. These findings led to successful criminal prosecution of the uncle.

In some cases of sexual abuse erotic pictures or pornographic literature may be employed either to stimulate the child or the abuser. This type of evidence may be found at the scene of the crime. In cases of child exploitation for pornography, photographic equipment, the pornographic pictures, or other paraphernalia may be confiscated by the police.

Some abusers use instruments in the process of their abuse and these may be identified and taken into evidence by law enforcement personnel. In the case below, on the basis of the child's statements, the police obtained a search warrant.

> EXAMPLE 22: Sandra was 6 years old and often left in the care of her mother's boyfriend, who thought he had special powers. She was placed in foster care when her mother had to have gall bladder surgery. She told her foster mother that Johnny, her mother's boyfriend, was teaching her how to become a man. She told the foster care worker, "he would put a carrot in me and told me some day it would take root." The police investigation uncovered several carrots in the refrigerator, one with evidence of vaginal secretion on it.

Other professionals who are investigating allegations of sexual abuse, for example, protective services workers, should not attempt to confiscate material evidence. Their seizure of evidence may be illegal and they do not have the capabilities for preserving the chain of evidence law enforcement has. The police have a locked facility for evidence and procedures for documenting that evidence is not tampered with.

2. *Statements made to significant others.* A very important aspect of the investigation of an allegation of sexual abuse is inquiring into statements the child makes to family members, friends, or professionals. Most often the case comes to the attention of authorities because the child has revealed the sexual abuse to someone close. Furthermore, all too often the child offers some information and later recants the statement.

The perpetrator may assert the significant other has some vested interest in accusing him or in some way inducing the child to say she has been sexually abused. This claim is most likely to be made when the significant other is an estranged spouse, relative, or family friend.

The evaluator should speak with these significant others for two reasons. First, it is very important to know precisely what the child has said. The range of possible sexual behavior and potential perpetrators is very wide. Narrowing the focus of concern can facilitate the evaluation process. The second goal of the evaluator is to assess the credibility of the significant other as a reporter. This may be an issue when the significant other is a nonprofessional and there is hostility between the perpetrator and that person.

Two dimensions are important for the evaluator to explore in assessing credibility: the nature of the story and the reporter's emotional reaction. First, the evaluator should be looking for a story which is idiosyncratic and seems consistent with a child's viewpoint. The following example is a credible story from an estranged spouse.

EXAMPLE 23: Mr. and Mrs. Jones were in the process of getting a divorce and there was much animosity between them. Their two sons, Jim, 5 and George, 3, were spending alternate weeks with each parent. Mr. Jones reported an incident that occurred on the 4th of July weekend just after he had resumed custody of his sons. It was very hot and he was reading his two sons a story, wearing only cut-off jeans. George was sitting on his lap and reached over and began to fondle his father's nipples, stating, "I play with your nipples, Daddy." The father reports he asked, "Who else's nipples do you play with?" To that George responded, "We play with Mommy's nipples in the bath." Mr. Jones reported Jim quickly interceded, stating, "Ssh, we're not supposed to tell."

The explicitness of the father's story led the evaluator to believe that what the father related had occurred. It is unlikely that a parent would make up such a unique scenario. Further, this incident between the boys and their father was witnessed by two other members of the father's family, to whom the evaluator also talked.

The second factor in evaluating a significant other's credibility is that individual's reported emotional response to the child's statements. The two examples below illustrate different emotional responses.

> EXAMPLE 24:   Mrs. S was divorced and remarried. Two and a half year old Ruth was the legal child of her first husband, Barry, although she claimed Ruth was the biological child of her second husband, Terry. Ruth was allegedly forcibly taken by Barry to live with him and his cousins.
>
> About a month later, Ruth was returned to her mother and there was physical evidence of vaginal trauma. Mrs. S reported the following: she said Ruth told her, "Barry hurt my pee pee," and began to cry. Mrs. S said, "I didn't ask any more because I was crying too. I just put my arms around her."

> EXAMPLE 25:   Mrs. A described her three-year-old, Sue, asking her boyfriend to put peanut butter on his thumb so she could lick it off. When he complied, Sue said, "I do this with grandpa, except with his dicky." Mrs. A stated that at first she couldn't believe it and got upset with Sue for making the story up, but later on it made sense to her.

In the first example, the significant other describes being so upset she cried, and the second indicates disbelief, both common responses to the discovery of sexual abuse. Another common emotional response is anger. It is unlikely that a parent would make up both a scenario and his/her emotional reaction to it.

3. *Sexual behavior on the victim's part.* A third characteristic the evaluator needs to probe for is sexual behavior displayed by the child. Sexual acting out takes different forms at different developmental stages and, as a rule, is more likely to be observed in children too young to completely understand its meaning. Parents may identify these patterns, as may foster parents, teachers, or others who have considerable contact with the victim. Sexual behavior may also be noticed when children are hospitalized, in day care, or in school. Alternatively the evaluator may note these patterns when interviewing the child.

There are four categories of sexual behavior of concern: (1) excessive masturbation; (2) sexual interaction with younger children, peers, or adults; (3) seductive behavior; and (4) sexual promiscuity.

a. *Excessive masturbation.* It is normal for children (and, in fact, for adults) to masturbate, but children who have been sexually abused sometimes are preoccupied with masturbation to the point where they cannot control it, or masturbate in contexts which are sexually stimulating. The case below, also described in chapter 4, is an example of what would be defined as excessive masturbation.

EXAMPLE 26:   Patty, age 9, and her brother Robert, age 7, had been made to watch their parents have sexual intercourse and had been induced to engage in intercourse themselves. There was also a suspicion that Patty's father had had coitus with her, and that a male friend had also been involved.

The evaluator took both children to the store for treats prior to the evaluation. Patty began to rub her vulva on the corner of a box in the store. The evaluator quietly told her to stop. Five minutes later Patty was rubbing herself on the corner of the box again, but this time from behind.

Patty's foster mother also commented that Patty masturbated frequently. Sometimes Patty would go to bed early and would then be found masturbating in bed.

Professionals have some hypotheses about why sexually abused children masturbate excessively. They do so because they have been sexually overstimulated at an early age and become preoccupied with their genitalia. The masturbation may also be a way of either reliving or working through sexual abuse.

b. *Sexual interaction.* Children who have been sexually abused will often engage in sexual encounters in other contexts. Sometimes they will take on the role of the aggressor and victimize smaller or younger children. Other times the sexual interaction with their peers. In still other situations, victims will attempt to recreate the pattern of power distribution in the sexual abuse; thus they may attempt to be sexual with an older person. It is common to find the latter happening with an adult whom the victim likes. The three examples below illustrate the three different types of sexual interaction.

EXAMPLE 27:   Bill, age 5, was hospitalized for minor surgery and tests. On three separate occasions he got in bed with a younger child, one boy and two girls, and attempted to feel their genitals.

The protective services worker discovered Bill was the only child of a single parent. Bill and his mother slept together. Protective Services thought Bill's mother was fondling him at night. However, it was not until two years later that the abuse was substantiated.

EXAMPLE 28:   Kirsten, 6, was observed by the babysitter to be putting a toothbrush in her seven year old sister Jean's vagina. Kirsten also masturbated and urinated on her sister and herself. When she urinated upon herself, she lay on her back with her legs up over her head. These behaviors were traced to sexual experiences with a 10-year-old-boy and girl. Their sexual precociousness was later traced to interactions with a mentally retarded man.

EXAMPLE 29:   Emma, 4, was very fond of her uncle and on one occasion demanded he take off his clothes so she could see his penis. It was discovered that Emma had had an incestuous relationship with her father.

In all three of these cases the initial concern was related to the sexual interaction. This led to investigations that revealed sexual abuse.

c. *Seductive behavior.* Seductive behavior is less overt than the sexual interactions already described and tends to be characteristic of somewhat older children, latency aged or adolescent. Older victims are likely to be aware that the sexual abuse is abnormal and therefore are less likely to engage in overt sexual interactions. However, they have been socialized by the perpetrator to relate to adults on a sexual level and are often deficient in other ways of relating. It is important not to blame the victim for this behavior but to recognize that its origins lie in the socialization process. Frequently the child is totally unaware that she is perceived as seductive and often thinks of herself as ugly or fat or stupid. The example to follow illustrates seductive behavior.

EXAMPLE 30:   Terry, 16, had been placed in foster care. She had been sexually abused first by her father, then by her stepfather, and most recently by her mother's boyfriend. Terry was an extremely well proportioned 16-year-old and wore tight Levis and tight sweaters.
 She called her therapist saying she was getting nervous around the foster father, particularly when they were alone together in the house. She said, "I know he's a nice man, but I'm scared." The therapist went to the foster home to discuss the problem. The foster parents, Terry, and the therapist were present. It was a cool October day. Suddenly in the middle of the interview Terry said, "It's hot in here," and left in the room. She returned in a couple of minutes having removed her jeans and put on a pair of brief shorts. During the rest of the interview she sat with one long leg draped over the arm of her chair and the other on the coffee table. Terry, because of her background, did not perceive her behavior as being provocative. Yet she could sense the foster father's response. She also was bewildered beause of the trouble she had at work with men making advances.

Terry is a fairly overt example of seductive behavior. Other children may be described as very feminine and coquettish.

d. *Sexual promiscuity.* Finally, the evaluator should be alert with adolescent victims to reports of a lot of sexual activity. This may be an outgrowth of the seductiveness just described. An irony is that frequently the promiscuity is used to discount the allegation of sexual abuse. Another irony is that frequently the victims are frigid. Sometimes the sexual relationships are with older men. Other times they are with age-mates. In the example below the victim had sexual encounters with both adults and peers.

EXAMPLE 31: Selma, age 14, was a very disturbed teenager. She reported having "affairs" with a number of different men and boys. She described having sexual intercourse several times with a 15-year-old cousin during which he would also suck her breasts. She described two sexual encounters with a male friend of her father's. On one occasion, when she and her sister were spending the night with the male friend's family, he asked her to take off her night clothes, which she did. He then rubbed his penis against her body until ejaculation. On another occasion he took her for a ride in his truck and had her masturbate him to orgasm. Her school was quite concerned about her "sexy talk" in which she would invite boys to have sexual intercourse with her. Both Selma and her 12-year-old sister had longstanding incestuous relationships with their father.

Selma's promiscuity is not atypical of children with an ongoing sexual relationship with an adult. It and her emotional disturbance were used to discount her allegations regarding her father. However, both were a result of the sexual abuse by the father.

4. *Sexual knowledge beyond that expected for the child's developmental stage.* With young children often a clue that they have been sexually abused is intimate and explicit knowledge of sexual behavior. Examples include knowledge about fellatio and cunnilingus, analingus, and intercourse, that the penis gets big and hard when rubbed, that the penis goes in the vagina during intercourse, and that something white comes out of the penis. Such knowledge conceivably could be gained in ways other than in sexual encounters, such as by observing sexual acts or pornographic movies. However, for such information to come from observation, the child would need to be quite close, and pornography on cable television does not show such explicit material. In any case, caretakers who afford children opportunities to see these things are being sexually abusive. Further, mere observation is not sufficient to relay information regarding certain details, for example how the sexual behavior feels and what semen tastes like. If a child possesses sexual knowledge, the evaluator needs to pursue the source of the child's information. Two examples follow.

EXAMPLE 32: LeAnn, 3, during an interview was examining an anatomically explicit male doll. When asked what the penis was, she said, "That's the daddy's dinky." The evaluator then asked, "What do daddies do with their dinkies?" LeAnn replied, "They go pee with it," simulating urination with the doll. She was then asked if daddies do anything else with their dinkies. She said, "Girls kiss it."

Both she and her 4 1/2 year old sister had been made to commit fellatio on their father and to watch him and his girlfriend in sexual acts, including fellatio.

EXAMPLE 33: Sandy 3 1/2, had been complaining to her mother over a six month period that her bottom hurt. She was taken to the doctor and the doctor suspected sexual abuse. Sandy was then seen for evaluation. When asked how her bottom got hurt, she picked up a male doll with a penis and placed his penis in her crotch, moving him back and forth, and said, "It hurts real bad."

Eventually it was dicovered that her father had been attempting intercourse with her when he had responsibility for her care and the mother was out of town.

In both cases we find sexual knowledge beyond that found with most three-year-olds. In the first case knowledge of fellatio, and in the second information about intercourse. In the first case the information could have possibly come from observation, and in fact part of the sexual abuse was making LeAnn watch. In the second case, the fact the victim describes intercourse as painful tells us her experience went beyond mere observation.

5. Nonsexual behavioral indicators of stress. The fifth area the evaluator should explore is symptomatic behavior. Children who have been sexually abused may present with a range of problem behaviors of a nonsexual nature.

Among these are *sleep disturbances*, including inability to sleep, night-waking, sleep-walking, night-wandering, fear of the dark, nightmares, unwillingness to sleep in their own beds, and nocturnal enuresis. The victim's fear of sleeping in her own bed may be because the child is being molested in bed at night. The example below is typical of sleep disturbances.

EXAMPLE 34: Julia, 6, was being sexually abused by her estranged father on visits to him. She began having terrible nightmares in which she would wake up screaming. Frequently she would wet the bed. She would not remember the content of the nightmares but they preceded visits to her father. Often she would have three in one night.

In addition to being *enuretic* at night, as in Julia's case, some children wet their pants during the daytime, and some are *encopretic* (incontinent of feces). Some of these victims have never managed to control elimination, but others were toilet trained and become enuretic or encopretic with the onset of sexual abuse. The former situations are often ones of chronic family dysfunction and chronic sexual abuse. In the latter, the incontinence is a regression to an earlier developmental stage. Encopresis tends to be associated with anal penetration. Other symptoms of *regression* are also seen. A child who has given up a transitional object (a teddy bear or blanket) will insist on having it again or will demand a pacifier again. Some children will resume baby-talk. Sally in the example that follows regressed as a consequence of sexual abuse.

> EXAMPLE 35: Sally, 7, had been sexually abused by her grandfather during a two-month stay with him during the summer. When she returned home, she insisted on having her "blankie" again and begged to be allowed to take it to school. The older children at school made fun of her, so she would hide it in her desk.

In addition, children may also develop *eating disturbances,* sometimes overeating, other times loss of appetite, anorexia, or refusal to eat certain foods.

School and learning problems may be associated with sexual abuse. These include developental lags, inability to concentrate, school failure, and truancy. Sometimes developmental lags are so marked that children are placed in special programs or classrooms. However, in such cases the sexual abuse is longstanding and there are other problems in functioning present in the family. In fact in contrast for some children, school is a refuge from the pathological home situation, and they may excel in school. The example that follows is of a child with marked symptomatic behavior including school difficulties.

> EXAMPLE 36: Ruth, 9, was placed by her father in voluntary foster care when she was eight because he said he was unable to handle her. Ruth was functioning academically at a five-year level. She had been in an emotionally impaired classroom for two years. She had a very brief attention span, and she did not obey. She often became agitated and did not seem to hear what was being said to her.
>
> Prior to placement she had lived with her father, who sexually abused her, her mother, who was chronically mentally ill and spent about half her time in the mental hospital, and her three older brothers. Her oldest brother, Tim, 19, also sexually abused her, and Bobby, Ruth's 15-year-old brother, was very assaultive. He beat up both his mother and Ruth.
>
> In foster care Ruth began to describe cunnilingus, fellatio, genital intercourse, and digital penetration by both her father and Tim. Ruth did not know there was anything wrong with this and described it as feeling "oh so nice."

Ruth's school difficulties are serious enough that she is in an emotionally impaired classroom, and she had other behavior problems. The severity of her dysfunction is related not only to the extensive sexual abuse, but also to other family problems, for example her mother's psychosis and her brother's assaultive behavior.

Children who are being sexually abused may present with *personality and interpersonal difficulties*. Some will undergo personality changes with the onset of the sexual abuse. An outgoing, happy child may become withdrawn and depressed. Some children have difficulty relating to peers. This problem may arise out of a need to be guarded in order to keep the incest a secret. Sometimes the victim states she feels that her life experience is totally different from that of her peers or she feels much older than they. In other instances, this difficulty has its origins in an inability to form attachments because of poor bonding in the nuclear family. The example below is illustrative.

> EXAMPLE 37:   Stella, 8, was sexually abused on three separate occasions by her best friend's father. She and her friend would play at the friend's house on Saturday, when the only person home was her friend's father. He worked nights as a security guard and slept during the day. He usually would drink whiskey while in bed. He persuaded Stella to allow him to engage in cunnilingus with her. Stella's mother said she knew something was wrong because Stella, whom she described as "motor mouth," suddenly became noncommunicative. Subsequently, Stella told her mother about the abuse and her mother filed a criminal complaint.

Stella experienced a personality change as a result of the sexual abuse.

Older victims may engage in a range of *acting out behaviors*. They may truant from school and violate curfews. They may be belligerent and defiant in the school context, and often they are aggressive with peers, beating them up and carrying weapons. They may lie, steal, and frequently they run away from home. The example below, a case discussed earlier in this chapter, illustrates the kind of acting out characteristic of some older victims.

> EXAMPLE 38:   Terry, 16, was being sexually accosted by her mother's boyfriend. Her mother was bewildered by Terry's angry demands that her mother make him leave. (Terry had not told her mother about his attempts to become sexually involved with her). On one occasion Terry became enraged with her mother for putting up with the boyfriend's drinking buddies and initiated a fist fight with her mother. The boyfriend then smacked Terry and she jumped out of a second story window, and reported her mother and her mother's boyfriend to protective services. Terry had also run away from home six times and refused to go to school. Terry's anger and indignation are focused not only on the boyfriend, but also on her mother.

In this case we see assault of the mother, rage sufficient to lead to a report to protective services, running away, and school truancy.

Other victims *"turn against the self"* rather than acting out their anger against others. They are depressed and frequently suicidal. They engage in self-destructive behavior, such as acts of self-mutilation, drug addiction, and alcohol abuse. Some victims will become psychotic during adolescence or in later years, as in the example below.

> EXAMPLE 39:   Linda was 24 years old when her sexual victimization first became known to protective services. Her father, then 75, had been sexually abusing her since she was 6, had had sexual encounters with her two sisters and Linda's three-year-old son, and would masturbate the family dog. Linda's mother, 52, had never been told of these activities.
>
> At 24 Linda had her first psychotic break and was hospitalized. Her two children, Darryl, 3, and David, 1, were placed with her parents. Linda became very upset with this arrangement and signed out against medical advice to place her children with her sister.
>
> Her psychotic break was precipitated, according to her, by drug abuse. She said she had used drugs so she could deal with life, especially her father. She also confessed to two suicide attempts.
>
> She still had a sexual relationship with her father, who claimed to be "in love with me." She steadfastly refused to allow the worker to tell her mother about the sexual abuse, claiming it would kill her mother.

Linda is a prime example of a victim who "turned against the self" by abusing drugs, attempting suicide, and becoming psychotic. It is also not unusual to find both acting out and self-destructive behaviors exhibited by the same victim.

The evaluator should be cautioned that nonsexual behavioral indicators of stress can result from other types of traumatic experiences and therefore cannot by themselves be taken as indicators of sexual abuse. Thus, unlike the other four types of victim characteristics, which by themselves are highly indicative of sexual abuse, nonsexual indicators need to be buttressed by more sexually explicit supportive evidence if they are being used to validate an allegation.

B. Information about the Alleged Perpetrator and the Victim's Mother

By the time the perpetrator and the victim's mother (in intrafamilial sexual abuse cases) come for evaluation, they usually are aware of the accusations of sexual abuse. For that reason they may be quite guarded in the evaluation, failing to disclose certain types of information, distorting the facts, or lying about some events. Furthermore, the offender may have spent many hours anticipating how to respond to disclosure of the sexual abuse and may have a carefully thought out sequence of lies to deal with the situation. Most mothers in intrafamilial sexual abuse cases do not know about the abuse prior to disclosure, but when they hear of the allegation they may defensively develop an interpretation of the situation to persuade the evaluator (and sometimes themselves) their children were not sexually abused. Because of the predilection of one or both adults to be less than candid, it behooves the evaluator to collect information about them from other sources. Often an important source of information about the alleged perpetrator is the victim's mother or vice versa. Other sources of information, both professional and nonprofessional, can also be enlightening.

While observations that relate specifically to the sexual abuse allegations are very valuable, data related to other aspects of the perpetrator's and mother's functioning will also be very useful. These include substance use, mental illness, criminal activity, sexual functioning—including prior history of sexual abuse—marital relationship, and the relationship between the victim and the adult. The relevance of these data to diagnosis will be discussed in chapters 7 and 8.

This information may come from hospital records, court files, police records, mental health agencies, schools, and departments of social services. Sometimes striking inconsistencies are found between information from other sources and that gathered in parental interviews. The example below, also cited in chapter 5, is typical of the kind of distortion a parent may offer and illustrates the value of information from other sources.

> EXAMPLE 40: Mrs. P said she had never been mentally ill but sometimes checked herself into the hospital when she needed a rest. Mrs. P also denied a substance abuse problem. With Mrs. P's permission, the evaluator obtained her hospital records. She had been hospitalized six times for psychotic episodes and had been given a diagnosis of paranoid schizophrenia.
>
> At discharge from one hospitalization she was referred to a substance abuse program. That hospitalization had been the result of an automobile accident. When the police arrived, Mrs. P was quite incoherent and was transported to the mental hospital. After observation, hospital staff felt Mrs. P's condition was in part the result of intoxication, although she also had some delusional thoughts.

Thus external data clearly indicate Mrs. P was hospitalized for more than a rest.

Given how much impact the results of the evaluation can have on the future of the parents, it is to be expected that they will present themselves in a favorable light. It would be naive of the evaluator to take all of the parents' statements at face value.

VI. SUMMARY

Much preparation needs to precede the interviews to assess an allegation of sexual abuse. First, the evaluator must understand that a child has almost nothing to gain and often much to lose by truthfully alleging sexual abuse. In contrast, the perpetrator and sometimes the victim's mother may have a great deal to gain by persuading professionals that the sexual abuse did not take place, that the child is mistaken, fantasizing, emotionally disturbed, or lying. However, the evaluator also needs to be cognizant of those rare situations where adults and children make false accusations.

This background information leads to an understanding that, as a rule, the truth or untruth of an allegation of sexual abuse is established by interviewing the child. What is understood by interviewing the alleged perpetrator, the victim's mother, and others are the dynamics of the sexual abuse and the prognosis for treatment. Further, the sequencing of interviews should place the child interview first so that the evaluator has made an assessment of whether or not the sexual abuse took place before investigating its dynamics and treatment prognosis. The context of the child interview is also important; it should take place in a setting that is conducive to the victim's talking and appropriate media should be available to facilitate candid discussion by the child.

Finally, there are crucial data about the victim, perpetrator, and mother the evaluator should attempt to gather external to the interview. For the child, they consist of any physical evidence, statements the child has made to others, sexual behavior, precocious sexual knowledge, and nonsexual symptoms. The types of data the evaluator should collect about the perpetrator and the mother include evidence related to mental illness, substance use, criminal activity, sexual functioning, marital relationship, and the relationship to the victim.

NOTES

1. We disagree with Goodwin (1984) who views the fact that alleged perpetrators make themselves available for interviewing and cooperate with the professionals involved as indicative of their innocence.

2. Our observations with regard to characteristics of suspect allegations differ somewhat from those of Sgroi et al. (1982) who find the absence of a gradual progression of intrusiveness (see chapter 3) and the inability of the child to be precise about the sexual behavior indicative of a false allegation. A progression of intrusiveness is likely to be found in classical incest (see chapter 3), but is not particularly characteristic of other types of sexual abuse. The majority of the children we have seen are quite young, meaning the abuse has been identified before such a progression can develop. Children may also have difficulty being explicit about the sexual behavior because they block the details of the traumatic event, cannot bring themselves to speak of them, or merely because they close their eyes during the abuse.

3. Therefore, we are in agreement with Sgroi et al. (1982), and disagree with Sheurer et al. (1980) who think the assessment of a case of in-household sexual abuse should begin with a family meeting, after which individual family members should be interviewed.

4. We use the term anatomically explicit rather than "anatomically correct," as some of these dolls' parts only remotely resemble human parts.

CHAPTER SIX

Interviewing the Child

I. INTRODUCTION

Because a diagnosis of sexual abuse is usually made from the interview with the victim, this interview is the most crucial part of the assessment. However, it is sometimes very difficult. Many children will not want to to talk about the sexual abuse, and the interview can be traumatic for the child, particularly if the interviewer has to press the child in order to gather the information. The goal of the evaluator is to get the child to disclose as much as possible about the sexual abuse while causing the minimum of trauma to the child.

In this chapter a range of interview techniques will be discussed: strategies for assessing children who are willing to talk as well as those who do not want to, techniques of utility with younger children and those better suited to older children. However with a child younger than two, the evaluator usually must rely on other information: physical evidence, corroborative statements, confessions or partial confessions, or observation of the sexual abuse by a third party.

All of the techniques to be described are appropriate for mental health professionals, and some to be discussed, particularly the use of anatomically explicit dolls, might be suitable for anyone who has to question the child: a law enforcement official, a physician, a protective services worker, an attorney, or a judge.

II. ESTABLISHING A RELATIONSHIP

There are three reasons for taking the time and making the effort to establish a relationship with the victim before initiating a discussion of the sexual abuse. To begin with, the evaluator is usually a stranger to the child.

It is unlikely the child will "betray" to a stranger someone close. The evaluator must attempt to build trust before approaching the issue of sexual abuse. In addition, if the child feels she knows the questioner somewhat, she is likely to describe more fully what took place. She may provide more details and be more spontaneous once a relationship has been developed. Finally, the interview will induce less trauma to the child if there is a relationship. Thus it is less frightening to reveal stressful information to someone whom the child knows as an accepting and warm human being.

At the beginning of the interview a tension exists for the evaluator between the need to identify the purpose of the interview and the need to develop a relationship with the child. How this should be handled will vary depending upon the case and the age of the child. In most cases the person who brings the child to the interview will have said something to prepare the child. Often a good approach is initially to introduce oneself and assume the child has some idea why she is there. With a younger child, the evaluator then helps choose a toy or game and involves her in play. After a time the evaluator begins to ask general questions about the child's family, school, and friends. When she feels the child is comfortable enough, the evaluator can then ask the child why she thinks she is there. Thus, there is a time to develop a relationship before clarifying the purpose of the interview.

Another strategy is to make a brief initial statement about the purpose of the interview and then move on to more general topics or play. For example, the interviewer might describe herself as "a doctor, but not a shot doctor, who helps kids when they have problems or worries." Or the interviewer might say, "I help kids when grown-ups do things they shouldn't" or more specifically that "Your mom thought I could help with the problem you've had with Uncle Billy." After a brief statement about the reason for the interview, the evaluator can say, "But first maybe you'd like to play with some of the toys" or "but we don't have to talk about it right away. We can get to know each other a little first."

With older children, particularly adolescents, it is necessary to be explicit about the purpose of the interview at an earlier stage. They are not likely to be enticed with toys, and they will be aware that being interviewed by someone previously unknown is an unusual situation and one that must have a purpose. Therefore, in order to reduce the child's anxiety, at the beginning information must be provided regarding the purpose of the interview. However, having done that, the evaluator can then switch to other topics, such as how the child is doing in school, how she gets along with siblings, what her hobbies are, or what she does after school, and return to the sexual abuse later.

III. SEXUAL CONTENT IN CHILDREN'S ACTIVITIES

One of the dilemmas of evaluating young children is their lack of ability to communicate in words. They express themselves more readily in activities. In addition, communicating material in an indirect way, such as in play, is less traumatic, so that the child is more likely to be forthcoming. A variety of activities can be used, but we will specifically discuss techniques for using doll play, picture drawing, and storytelling.

As a rule, doll play will be employed with very young children, those from two to about six or seven; picture drawing requires some fine motor development and is useful with children beginning about five; and storytelling requires language skills and vocabulary, and therefore is most useful with children of school age. The evaluator will track the number of times sexual content appears in the child's doll play, pictures, or stories relative to other content. If expert testimony about the meaning of sexual themes is going to be necessary, a person who can be so qualified should do the evaluation.

A. Doll Play

Normal children engaging in doll house play will have the dolls fix breakfast, watch TV, clean up, go to the movies, and so forth. Likewise, in doll play with baby dolls, nonabused children might feed the baby, put the baby to sleep, scold the baby, give the baby a bath, and cuddle the baby. Sexually abused children, on the other hand, may repeatedly undress the dolls, peer between their legs, make sexual comments about them, or make them go to bed in configurations suggestive of the sexual abuse; they may also make the dolls touch one another's intimate parts, touch the dolls in a sexual way, or make them engage in sexual intercourse or other sexual activity. The examples below illustrate sexual content in play with a play therapy doll house.

> EXAMPLE 1:   Lee, 3, began playing with dolls in the doll house. She took off the daddy doll's clothes stating he likes to walk around naked. The evaluator then asked what he did when he walked around naked. She

said, "Goes potty," making him sit on the toilet. She then got a little girl doll and made her sit straddling the daddy on the toilet. She did this four times, once substituting a black daddy and little girl for the white daddy and girl. She then took the white daddy and began rubbing him against her vagina.

EXAMPLE 2:   Selma, 5, had much guilt about the sexual relationship she had with her uncle and ambivalent feelings about him. She wanted to see him yet was afraid of being sexually abused. She refused to admit that any sexual abuse occurred when she visited him, although he stated he slept in the bed with her and on one occasion mistook her for his girlfriend and fondled her.

In doll house play, she put the daddy doll and the little girl doll in bed repeatedly, sometimes clothed and sometimes naked. After each encounter, she would spank the daddy doll and say, "bad, bad man." She then put them on the couch, head to foot, and spanked the little girl, saying, "Bad, Selma." Somewhat later in the interview she took a boat with a tall mast and pressed the mast between her legs.

In both examples children play out content which is preoccupying them at the time of the evaluation. These behaviors are suggestive of sexual abuse. They give the evaluator cause for concern and indicate the need to further pursue these matters in the interview. In both of these cases sexual abuse was substantiated with further information.

B. Picture Drawing

There are many different ways picture drawing can be employed in assessment. We generally ask children to draw one or more of three types of pictures: (1) a picture of anything; (2) a picture of their family; (3) a picture of themselves.

Some sexually abused children will draw pictures that indicate heightened awareness of sexuality, for example they will draw breasts on themselves, or will put penises on animals or humans. Occasionally they will draw persons involved in sexual acts. Other times the sexual content will be more subtle; there may a focus on the genital or abdominal area, for example a zipper drawn in detail; or when they are asked to tell about the picture, sexual meaning emerges. Children who have been sexually abused may also make drawings that depict their emotional reaction to being sexually abused, such as anger or helplessness (Stember 1980). Finally, pictures sometimes indicate an avoidance of sexuality. An example of this might be an older child, perhaps 10 or 11, who when asked to draw her mother draws her as a stick figure (see also Yates et al. 1985).

Figure 6.1 is an example of a drawing with sexual content. It is discussed below. The family is also described in chapter 3.

> EXAMPLE 3: Figure 6.1 represents the picture Bunny, age 5, drew when asked to draw a picture of anything. She covered the paper with her arm and admonished the evaluator, "Don't look," while she was drawing. When finished, she said the picture was of her father. When asked what various parts of the picture were, she identified his "peanuts" (penis), and his "balls." Most five-year-olds do not draw their fathers' penises unless they are for some reason preoccupied with them. In Bunny's case, her father was psychotic and part of his delusional system was that Bunny had maggots and bugs in her vagina. He would put his finger inside in order to find them while fondling himself.

In this example, the child's drawing is very explicit. In the next example, when the picture was discussed with the child, sexual content emerged.

> EXAMPLE 4: Sandra, age 5, repeatedly drew pictures of herself with her legs apart (figure 6.2). Sandra had been very traumatized when a friend of

FIGURE 6.1. When asked to draw a picture, Bunny, age 5, drew this picture, which she said was of her father (see example 3).

FIGURE 6.2. Sandra, age 5, repeatedly drew pictures of herself with her legs apart (see example 4).

her father's took off her panties and spread her legs and took a picture of her perineal area. He later apparently sold the picture as child pornography.

When Sandra's therapist asked why the legs were so far apart in the picture of herself, she first said, "I don't know," but then added, "This is the way I was when Sam took the picture. I am screaming."

In this case the picture that does not have any obvious sexual content does in fact represent not ony sexual abuse but the child's feelings about it.

C. Storytelling

Another well-respected method for eliciting traumatic material from children is storytelling. Standardized projective tests such as the Children's Apperception Test (CAT), and the Thematic Apperception Test (TAT) and the Rorschach, consisting of pictures the respondent is asked to tell a story about, may be employed. We have used pictures that might be more readily construed as depicting material related to sexual abuse. Figure 6.3 shows an example of these pictures. Again the evaluator is looking for material such as sexual comments about the figures in the picture (she is sexy; she has big tits); statements about sexual thoughts the figures may be having; indications that the figures are engaged in, will engage in, or have engaged in sexual acts; and admissions that the pictures evoke sexual thoughts and feelings in the child. Figure 6.3 elicited the following story from a seven-year-old girl.

> EXAMPLE 5: A seven-year-old, Susie, gave this explanation. "That's a girl. Her name's Sally. She got raped." (What's "raped"?) "That's when they take your pants down and put it in your butt." (What's "it"?) "Oh, I don't know. Whatever they feel like sticking in you. They're taking your temperature." (What happened to Sally after she was raped?) "She told her mom, but her mom didn't believe her. So she told God, but he didn't do anything either."

The story told by Susie not only revealed precocious sexual knowledge regarding rape but turned out to parallel her own experience when her mother's boyfriend abused her.

While one or two observations that could be construed as sexual are not sufficient to make the diagnosis, they should be noted. We recommend the use of several different media in the data gathering. Thus the evaluator might employ doll house play, picture drawing, and anatomically explicit dolls in order to fully assess sexual themes.

Another important point is that the themes elicited will be those things which are salient to the child at the time, that is, those things which are preoccupying the child and which may be "worked through" in play, pictures, or storytelling. The evaluator, by stating why the child is being interviewed, may sometimes trigger the sexual content and concerns the child has about the abuse, but not always. The frequency of sexual contact, the length of time since the last incident, and the trauma involved will all influence the likelihood of sexual content. The example below is illustrative.

> EXAMPLE 6:   Sarah, 6, was sexually abused by her mother's boyfriend (described in chapter 4). She and her three brothers were subsequently placed in three separate foster homes. After six weeks of placement, she was evaluated. One assessment tool used was TAT. Themes in her responses suggested loneliness, isolation, and a desire to be returned to her family. There were no sexual themes in her responses.

In Sarah's case the experience of loss of family is more preoccupying than the sexual abuse that had ocurred six weeks previously. A naive evaluator might mistakenly assume no sexual abuse had taken place based upon the TAT results.

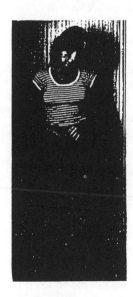 

FIGURE 6.3. A seven-year-old girl, when shown this illustration, told the story described in example 5.

IV. TECHNIQUES FOR MOVING FROM SEXUAL CONTENT
TO VALIDATION OF THE ALLEGATION

Observations of sexual themes in the child's play, pictures, or stories tell the evaluator that the child has had some sexual experiences, but ordinarily the data are not specific enough to validate an allegation of sexual abuse. Sometimes progressing from such content to specifics regarding the abuse can be done simply by asking the child how she came to know about rape or that "yucky stuff comes out of the dick." Other times the information in pictures and stories can be pursued. The evaluator can ask the child what the bear's name is that hurt her pee pee or whether what she said happened to the little girl in the picture ever happened to her.

However, in many instances the evaluator will not feel comfortable in asking such questions, or the sexual content will not be present in unstructured play. Then a technique that can be tried is structuring the play context so that it simulates what is known about the context of the sexual abuse. The evaluator might make this move after playing with and observing the child for 15 to 20 minutes. To illustrate, if the case were one of father-daughter incest, the evaluator might remove all dolls in the doll house except a little girl and a father of the same race as the victim and perpetrator. The evaluator might ask the victim, "Is this a daddy?" "Is this a little girl?" "What's this daddy's name?" "Is this Barry?" (the father's name). The evaluator notes carefully the child's response in terms of affect, behavior, and statements. The evaluator might also ask what this daddy and the little girl do together. If the room where the abuse occurred is known, the evaluator might put the dolls in that room in the doll house and ask what the daddy and the little girl do in the room. Perhaps the evaluator thinks the abuse happened when the father was babysitting for the victim. The child might be asked what the daddy and the little girl do when he babysits. Similar strategies can be employed with other types of dolls, including anatomically explicit ones. In the example below, no sexual themes emerged in unstructured play. However, restructuring led to important revelations.

> EXAMPLE 7: Lucy, 4, and her brother, David, 6, allegedly had been fondled by their mother's boyfriend when he was babysitting for them, and there was a possibility he had induced them to attempt intercourse. As the interview started, David began to play with a toy truck and Lucy started looking in the drawers of the evaluator's desk. She said she was looking for candy. The evaluator joined David in play and answered Lucy's questions about the various items in her desk. After a time the evaluator

said to them, "Look, here's my doll house. You can play with it too if you want." Both children went to the doll house and busied themselves putting the furniture in place, deciding who slept where, and asking questions about various items in the house. David went back to his truck but then brought the truck to the doll house. The evaluator then removed all the dolls except a boy, a girl, and a man, and put the TV set in the bedroom. The sexual abuse was alleged to have occurred while all three were watching TV in bed. David asked, "Who's the man?" The evaluator responded, "Well, who do you think?" David said, "I think he's the ma's friend. He's not the kids' friend." Lucy said, "He's a bad man like Leroy." The evaluator said, "Leroy's your mom's friend, isn't he? What does he do that's bad?" David said, "Real bad stuff, but we're not supposed to tell." The evaluator said, "Well, maybe you can show me with the dolls." David shook his head, but Lucy began showing how Leroy had taken off David's pants and rubbed his penis and made her take off her nightgown, and "put two fingers inside, and it hurt like H!" She demonstrated also how he had made them do "like you do to get a baby" putting the boy doll on the girl doll.

In this case the scenario set up by the evaluator elicited responses from both children, but the younger and less inhibited child actually demonstrated what had happened.

Another tactic is to take a doll which looks somewhat like the victim and say, "This little girl (boy) is very worried, upset, angry, or confused (depending upon the child's emotional response to the abuse). Why do you suppose that is?" Probes can be added if the child does not respond or says, "I don't know." For example the evaluator could say, "Maybe she's having trouble with her uncle." In the example below (this case is also mentioned earlier in this chapter) the evaluator employed a doll the victim could identify with.

EXAMPLE 8: Lee was a three-year-old girl with blond curly hair. The evaluator took a doll that looked like Lee and gave the doll to her, saying, "Do you want to play with this little girl? She looks like you but not as pretty." Lee took her and began feeding her with a baby bottle and making her go "nignt, night." Then she took off the doll's pants and looked and felt the doll between her legs. The evaluator asked, "Is that little girl hurt and worried?" Lee looked up and nodded gravely, saying, her "pee pee hurt." The evaluator then asked, "How did it get hurt?" Lee said, "A man doed it." The evaluator asked, "What man was it?" Lee answered, "Don't know." Then the evaluator asked if it was a daddy or someone else, and Lee responded, "Not her daddy, friend's daddy, Jenny's daddy." The evaluator asked what the little girl doll's name was and Lee responded "Lee," then she said "Jenny." It turned out that both Lee and Jenny had been molested by Jenny's father.

This example well illustrates the importance of media other than language with young children. Lee both showed and stated where the doll was hurt.

Dolls can be used in other ways. The child can recount the victimization by having a doll or puppet tell about the sexual abuse. The evaluator may also try using a doll or puppet to ask the questions. Thus the evaluator may have a puppet say, "Did you hear what happened to Julie (the victim)?" The child may then respond with another puppet who tells what happened. After this sequence, the evaluator should step out of the role and confirm with the victim that what she has said is what happened to her.

Picture drawing can also be used to move progressively closer to the sexually abusive situation. The evaluator can move from asking the victim to draw a picture of anything, to a picture of herself and a picture of the alleged perpetrator. Pictures of the perpetrator may be quite revealing. The evaluator can then ask about the picture and about the perpetrator and child.

> EXAMPLE 9:   Mary, age 8, was asked first to draw a picture of her family. She protested, "I can't draw. I'm not good at drawing." She was told it didn't matter, whatever she drew would be interesting. She then drew a picture of her family in stick figures, including her parents and all nine children. This was interesting because all family members except Mary and one brother, age 18, are quite obese. When asked about this inconsistency, she simply said, "I can't draw." She then was asked to draw a picture of herself. She drew a tiny figure with breasts surrounded by large trees. When asked about why she had breasts in the picture, she said, "someday soon I will have them." She was then asked to draw a picture of her father, who was alleged to have fondled her and two other daughters. She drew a picture of him from the back. When asked why she drew him from behind, she said, "So I don't have to see his angry face and his front part." Although she refused to discuss her father any more at that point, later she stated he had fondled her saying he was seeing how her breasts were developing.

In this case no sexual content was present in Mary's initial drawing but when asked to draw herself the blatant content of breasts emerged. Similarly, there is sexual content in her discussion of the picture of her father, the use of the term front part for penis.

Another strategy is to ask the child to draw a picture of what happened or of part of the scene. Alternatively, a child who is older may be willing to write down what happened but will not say the words. Figure

6.4 is a picture drawn by a six-year-old girl of "the thing" her daddy was putting inside her. Later the object was identified as a ruler.

The technique of storytelling can also be focused more specifically on the sexual abuse. For example, if the child is telling how the girl in the picture was frightened, the evaluator might ask if anything had happened recently to frighten the victim. Sometimes the child will tell a story with many parallels to her own sexually abusive situation, and the evaluator can ask the child if anything like that ever happened to her, as was done in the case that follows.

> EXAMPLE 10:   Shari, 10, told a story about a picture of a man sitting in a chair and a child (sex unclear) who looks worried (figure 6.5). She said, "The girl is scared. The old man is thinking bad thoughts." The evaluator asked what bad thoughts and Shari answered, "About murder, rape, and pillage." She was asked what rape and pillage meant. She said, "Rape was something old men do to girls and pillage is the same thing." Shari was then asked if the girl in the picture was like her, and she said, "No. The girl in the picture didn't get it done to her. I did. My grandpa raped and pillaged me."

In this case, the word "rape" is sexual in content. It leads the evaluator to question whether the child in the story represents the victim, and indeed "she" does.

In summary, important techniques for assessing allegations of sexual abuse are those that might elicit sexual content. However, just because no sexual material emerges, the evaluator should not conclude no sexual abuse has taken place. Rather, the absence of findings indicates the need to try additional strategies.

FIGURE 6.4. A six-year-old girl drew this picture; she said it was "the thing" her daddy was putting inside her.

V. USE OF ANATOMICALLY EXPLICIT DOLLS

Anatomically explicit dolls can enormously facilitate interviewing. They allow the evaluator to validate the allegation both by what the child does with the dolls and by what the child says. They can be employed with children of all ages but have their greatest utility with younger children. The evaluator should have the dolls in evidence during the interview. Some children will spontaneously turn to them and undress them. Others need to be introduced to the dolls. Usually the evaluator says "I want to show you my dolls, they're a little different." As the child examines the dolls, the evaluator gets the child to identify the differences between male and female, adults and children, and attempts to elicit the child's names

FIGURE 6.5. Shari, 10, told a story about this picture
(see example 10).

for the intimate parts. These terms are then used during questioning about sexual experiences.

A. Responses of Sexually Abused and Nonabused Children to Anatomically Explicit Dolls

Because these dolls are anatomically explicit, they are likely to elicit both unusual responses and more sexual content than ordinary toys. With children who have not been sexually abused these dolls excite curiosity and sometimes ridicule. Children will pinch and poke the dolls' private parts, make them urininate and defecate, and ask questions about why the evaluator has such dolls. However, usually their interest will dissipate and they will move on to other toys.[1]

In contrast, some children who have been sexually abused will react to these dolls differently. They may become frightened or upset at the sight of anatomically explicit dolls. They may refuse to go near or touch the dolls. In addition, sometimes the dolls elicit anger, statements that dolls are bad, or such responses as attacking them, throwing them, or placing them outside the interview room. Alternatively, sexually abused children may deny ever having seen any of the intimate parts on a person or that they have names for the parts, when the evaluator knows these assertions are not true. Such children, when asked what is different about the anatomically explicit dolls, may not acknowledge any differences. Children are particularly likely to have these emotional responses to the adult male doll. The example below is illustrative.

> EXAMPLE 11: Libby was 2½ when she was sexually abused by her father on visitation (the parents were separated). He had a history of drug abuse and believed in witchcraft. Libby would sleep in the bed with him, and after one visit was bleeding from the vagina. When police investigated, they found a bloody sock under her father's bed. When Libby observed the naked anatomically explicit dolls, she became very upset and hid under a table. Her mother, who was assisting the evaluator, then tried to approach her with the dolls, and she ran to the door of the interview room crying, "No, no,no" and tried to get out.

Libby's response of terror at the sight of the dolls is consistent with her own experience of sexual abuse, which was painful and led to physical injury.

Alternatively, the presence of anatomically explicit dolls may immediately elicit sexual use of the dolls by children who have been victims. This response is likely to be noted in very young, or emotionally disturbed children. The case below is illustrative.

> EXAMPLE 12: Donna, 9, came from a very chaotic and disorganized
> family where she had been involved in sexual activity, including inter-
> course with a brother. She was in foster care and her brother in residential
> treatment, but there were concerns that her father might be sexually abus-
> ing her on weekend visits.
>   When Donna was being evaluated, she chose to play with a toy
> sewing machine. She took the trousers off an anatomically explicit boy
> doll to sew them and discovered his penis. She immediately disrobed both
> the boy and girl doll and with gusto made them kiss and engage in sexual
> intercourse. This she did repeatedly for the next 45 minutes. When the
> evaluator asked what the dolls were doing, Donna replied, "Smooching."

Thus, there are two divergent response patterns to anatomically
explicit dolls that may be elicited from children who have sexually
abused. Victims may exhibit emotional reactions to the dolls or they may
act out their sexual experiences with them. However, the absence of these
characteristic responses does not mean the child has not been sexually
abused.

B. Techniques for Using Anatomically Explicit Dolls

In addition to observing children's responses to anatomically explicit dolls, there are a number of ways they can be employed in asking
questions about the sexual abuse.

After the child has named the private parts, the evaluator might
take a doll who could represent the perpetrator and ask the child, "Did
you ever see one of these?" — pointing to the penis. If the child responds
affirmatively, the evaluator can then probe, asking "Whose? When?
What happened when you saw it?"

Similarly, the evaluator can take a doll which could represent the
victim and say, "Let's pretend this doll is you. Has anybody ever touched you on any of the parts of your body you just named?" If the child
says yes, the evaluator then queries, "Which parts? When? With a hand
or another part of the body? Who did this? Were your clothes off or
on?" The example below demonstrates the use of the dolls with a child
who was moderately reluctant to talk.

> EXAMPLE 13: Ruth, 5, was shown a male doll with a penis and asked if
> she'd ever seen one. She nodded gravely and said, "But the hair was
> brown." (This doll had black hair on both head and pubis). When asked
> whose penis she had seen, she said, "It was yukk. I don't want to talk
> about it." With further urging, (her mother insisted she had to talk about
> it), Ruth said it was her retarded 16-year-old half-brother's. As to when

she had seen it, she first said when he went to the bathroom. When the evaluator asked what what was so ''yukk'' about that, she said, ''Nothing, but he showed me it another time when it was all big and red. He made me hold it for him and he rubbed it back and forth in my hands. He liked it, but I didn't.''

In this case a doll with a penis was very important. Its color and the pubic hair color stimulated the child to give a description of a tumescent penis, which is indicative of sexual knowledge beyond that expected for her developmental stage.

Another way of using the dolls is to have the evaluator ask, ''What do daddies do with this part of their body (penis)?'' or ''What do girls (boys) do with this part (genitals)?'' or ''What do people do to this part of girls' bodies (vagina)?'' In the example below (also mentioned in chapter 5) this approach was employed.

EXAMPLE 14:   Lisa, 3 ½, was being evaluated with her 4 ½-year-old sister. Both had been shown the anatomically explicit dolls, but then Lisa moved off to play with the doll house. The evaluator then asked, ''What do daddies do?'' Lisa said, ''I'll show you.'' She returned to the anatomically explicit dolls and took a man and woman doll, first making the woman suck the man's penis, then having the man suck the woman's breasts, and finally having them engage in sexual intercourse. She and her sister then stated they had been made to watch their father and his girlfriend engage in these acts.

Again we see the dolls eliciting evidence of sexual knowledge beyond that expected for the child's age.

The evaluator can also ask the victim to show what happened with the dolls. This is useful both with victims who are willing and those who are unwilling to talk. The example below illustrates the use of this technique.

EXAMPLE 15:   Betty, 6, and Wendy, 4, who were in foster care because of chronic child neglect, told the foster mother that Betty slept with dad and Wendy slept with mom. They also engaged in a lot of sexual play in the foster home, including French kissing and simulated intercourse.

During the evaluation for possible sexual abuse, they admitted to the sleeping arrangements, but Betty would say, ''Wendy will tell you what happened,'' and Wendy would say, ''Betty will tell you what happened.'' The evaluator then asked if they would show with the dolls, and both steadfstly refused saying, ''Daddy said he would go to jail if we tell.'' However, a little later, when the evaluator was playing with Wendy, Betty took three male dolls and laid them on their backs and took three little girl dolls and laid them on the male dolls' stomachs, taking care to put all three penises in the female dolls' vaginas. When the evaluator asked if anything like that had ever happened to her, she shook her head. When asked what was happening and if she had ever seen people do these things she did not answer. Yet she continued to play in this manner, switching the partners and at one point making an adult male and female doll engage in cunnilingus and fellatio. She then took two girl dolls and one adult male and made them engage in a range of sexual acts, saying in the process, "Hold on sister."

In this case the victim did not respond to the evaluator's questions about what she was making the dolls do and whether she was ever involved in such activities because she had been expressly prohibited by her father. Yet she took her cue from the evaluator, who asked her to show what she could not tell, and demonstrated a series of sexual encounters.

Two final techniques that can be employed are to ask the child to show on the dolls where she was touched and to have the evaluator touch the dolls in various places, asking the child if she was touched in any of these places. The latter is a close-ended technique and possibly can lead to social desirability responses. In an effort to avoid such responses, the evaluator should ask questions about many parts of the body and intersperse these with questions about the intimate parts. In addition, if the child gives an affirmative response to touching any of the intimate parts, the evaluator can then ask more open-ended questions.

VI. DIRECT QUESTIONING ABOUT THE SEXUAL ABUSE

Even when the evaluator is relying heavily upon media such as doll play, picture drawing, or anatomically explicit dolls, some direct questioning about the sexual abuse will be necessary. Moreover, in cases with older children, primary or total reliance will be upon their direct verbal communication about the sexual abuse. It is important to employ questioning techniques that maximize the likelihood of obtaining complete and accurate information while minimizing the trauma to the child. In this section general guidelines for questioning will be discussed.

A. General Questions

In exploring the sexual abuse, the evaluator may begin by asking general questions about the person, context, or symptoms that might be related to the sexual abuse. Usually the evaluator has some clue about the context of the sexual abuse which can guide the framing of the questions. Examples might be: "How do you get along with your dad?" or "Your teacher says you've been talking about secrets at school. You dont't suppose you could tell me your secrets?" or "You know you have a soreness in your vagina. Do you know how that could have happened.?"

At this point most children will be hesitant. However, we will deal first with cases of children who are willing to talk. Even in the latter cases, the evaluator should proceed so as not to induce trauma in the interview. The example of George below is illustrative.

> EXAMPLE 16: George, 8, had been sexually accosted by his Cub Scout leader. He did not understand the meaning of the behavior when it occurred and persuaded himself it was a dream, since the Scout leader had wakened him in the night to molest him. His parents became aware of the abuse only when the police questioned their son. Both of his parents came with him to the evaluation, but George had told only his mother what had happened.
>
> When the evaluator asked George if he knew why he was there, he said,"To talk about the weird things Mr. K did to me." The evaluator nodded and asked him if he wanted his parents to stay. He thought for a while and then said, "Yes." The evaluator then asked him about his family before querying how long he had been a Cub Scout, and how many kids were in his den, and how long Mr. K had been a den leader. The evaluator next said she had talked to the police and understood that some of the "weird things" had happened when George spent the night with Mr. K's son. Could George tell about that night, beginning when Mr. K picked him up after school?

This approach allowed George to start with less emotionally laden material and gradually work up to the material that was harder to talk about.

B. Asking About the Last Time it Happened

When the child is willing to talk and there have been multiple instances of sexual abuse, a good strategy is to ask the child to describe the last time it happened. The reason for starting with the last incident is that recall is likely to be more complete with the most recent sexual encounter and the evaluator will be able to elicit material important in validation of the sexual abuse.

There are three hallmarks of a true allegation which need to be explored. While a fabricated allegation is rare, a conscientious evaluator nonetheless looks carefully at the child's story to be sure it contains characteristics of a true allegation. The first characteristic is the child's *ability to describe the context* in which the sexual abuse took place or its surrounding events. These might include where the sexual abuse took place; approximately when it happened (whether it was warm or cold outside, in the daytime or at night, on a weekday or weekend, before or after supper); what the victim and perpetrator were wearing; where other family members were; and whether or not the perpetrator did anything to induce the child to cooperate or to keep the abuse a secret. Sometimes, in describing the context, the child will include a unique or idiosyncratic event that adds credibility to the child's statement.

The second hallmark of a true allegation has to do with the victim's *description of the sexual behavior* itself. The evaluator will be looking for an explicit description of sexual behavior, not, for example, "He molested me," but "He put two fingers in my pee pee hole." If the child says "He molested me," the evaluator needs to ask, "what does 'molest' mean?" In addition, the evaluator will be looking for sexual knowledge beyond that expected for the child's developmental stage. Examples of such knowledge are described in chapter 5. Finally, in exploring the sexual behavior, the evaluator will be alert for a description of the sexual behavior consistent with the child's developmental stage. This will vary with the child's age. For example, a 4½-year-old boy, in describing being fellated, said, "He tried to suck pee out of my wiener." The victim knows nothing of such activities for sexual pleasure, but he does know that there is pee in his wiener. He also probably knows that if you suck on the nipple of a bottle that has liquid in it, the liquid will come out.

The final hallmark of a true allegation relates to the child's *emotional response to the sexual abuse*. The evaluator is looking for both the child's description of her emotional state when the victimization took place, and her affective reaction to having to speak about the sexual abuse. Regarding the former, it would be very unlikely for a child to manufacture both an incident of sexual abuse and a description of how it made her feel. As to the latter, emotional responses children are likely to manifest as they describe sexual abuse include fear, revulsion, anxiety, anger, and embarrassment. Fear is characteristic of young children and children who have been physically traumatized or threatened. Latency aged children are more likely to display revulsion. Adolescent girls may show a lot of anxiety and distress, often crying as they speak. Anger may be demonstrated behaviorally, for example by attacking or throwing the anatomically explicit male doll, or by attempting to mutilate his penis. Occasionally, anger will be focused on the evaluator. Often children who do not have a full appreciation for what has happened to them will exhibit embarrassment.

These are usually younger or disturbed children. Occasionally, naive or emotionally disturbed victims will evidence sexual excitement. The example below contains the hallmarks of a true allegation.

> EXAMPLE 17:   Sixteen-year-old Sally finally "blew the whistle" on her father who had been having intercourse with her for close to ten years because she feared she would get pregnant. When asked about the most recent incident, she readily located it in time as the morning she came back from Junior Achievement Camp, August 30. The abuse began at about 9:30 A.M. Her mother had taken her 11-year-old sister to get a hair cut, and Sally was left to babysit for her two- and four-year-old siblings.
>
> She then hesitated, embarrassed and distressed, and the evaluator said, "What did your dad do?" She said, "He came out of the bedroom and asked me to go in there with him. I said I couldn't leave the other kids, but he said to put them both in the little one's crib. I put them in the crib together and they screamed the whole time he was doing it to me. I finally said I had to go and take care of the kids and he stopped."
>
> Sally was then asked what exactly her father did to her. She said he had sexual intercourse with her. The evaluator then asked whether her clothes were on or off. Sally said he took off her jeans and her panties and pulled up her shirt and her bra above her breasts. Sally was asked where in the bedroom this happened. He made her lie on the bed and got on top of her. The evaluator then asked Sally if she knew what ejaculation meant and she said she did. She was not aware of whether her father ejaculated or not. As to how she felt at the time, Sally said, "dirty."

Sally's replies have the indicators of a true allegation. Sally was able to describe the context of the sexual abuse (August 30, 9:30 A.M., while her mother was taking her sister for a haircut, in her father's bedroom, on the bed, while her siblings were screaming), was able to be explicit about the sexual behavior with questioning (intercourse with her jeans and panties off and her shirt and bra pulled up, with her father on top), and described feeling dirty at the time, and appeared upset, embarrassed and reluctant to talk during the interview.

While the evaluator looks for information in the three areas just described as indicators the allegation is true, she need not necessarily find confirming evidence in all three areas in order to be convinced the child's statement is valid. Moreover, there are certain situations in which the child will not provide the expected data even though the allegation is true.

First, with regard to the child's ability to describe the context of the sexual abuse, very young children will not have sufficient language to verbally communicate this information. Also, as already noted, if the sexual abuse occurred in the distant past, the victim may not have recall of all of the surrounding events.

Second, when assessing the child's ability to describe the sexual abuse, the evaluator must bear in mind that the child may have closed her eyes, it may have been dark, or the child and perpetrator may have been under the bedclothes. Also, sometimes the victim will repress the sexual abuse. This is more likely to happen when the sexual abuse occurred sometime in the fairly distant past. The entire scenario may be repressed or just parts of it. For example, the mother of one of our victims knew she had been sexually abused as a child, but all she could recall was lying on her back on the dining room floor and looking up at the trim around the ceiling. In addition, the utility of sexual knowledge beyond the victim's developmental stage will be limited to young children.

Finally, there are certain situations where the child will not exhibit a notable emotional reaction while describing the sexual abuse. First, very young children, who do not understand the meaning of the abuse and its transgression of normal adult–child interaction, may not have any emotional response to telling. Second, boys often do not exhibit as much overt distress, not because they are untraumatized, but because they are socialized to conceal indications of such vulnerability. Third, some latency aged children who are psychologically damaged will show little emotional response, or they will evidence sexual pleasure and/or mild embarrassment. Fourth, children who have already told their story several times may describe the particulars of the sexual abuse without any emotional reaction.

C. Directive Questions

Most children will not readily describe the abuse, and require support and directive questioning. Although the optimal report is a spontaneous blow by blow account, in most cases questions must be employed to cue the child throughout the information gathering. However, the evaluator should try to use open-ended questions. The best type of question is one like "What happened next?" or "Who did it to you?" However, sometimes the child does not respond to such a question or it is hard to ask for the information in such an open-ended fashion. Then the evaluator must try a question which gives the child a range of alternatives, such as "Were you wearing your day clothes or your night clothes?" In the example below, questions were necessary to prompt the child.

EXAMPLE 18:   Amanda, 8, had told her mother of some scary things that happened when she visited her dad. Her parents were divorced.

However, when her mother took her to tell the Friend of the Court what happened, she refused to say anything.

Her mother then brought her for an evaluation by an expert in sexual abuse. After the evaluator asked Amanda about her school, her dog, and her friends, her relationship with her mother was discussed. Then the subject of her father was raised. Amanda said she did not like visits with him except when he took her to stay at her grandmother's. Amanda was then asked if she went to her grandmother's on the last visit, and she said, no. The evaluator said, "Could you tell me what happened on your last visit?" and Amanda said, "Scary things." "What kind of scary things?" was the evaluator's next question. Amanda responded, "I don't like to talk about it." The evaluator asked Amanda what would make it easier to talk about it, and she said if the evaluator would ask more questions like, "Did this happen?" "Did that happen?"

The evaluator then asked if the scary things had happened to someone else or to Amanda. She said they had happened to her. The next question was whether they had happened in the daytime or the night, and Amanda said night. The evaluator asked whether it was before she went to bed or after, and Amanda said, before she got up in the morning. She was asked what room she was in, and she replied, in her bed. The evaluator asked who did the things to her, and she said, "My dad." The evaluator then asked Amanda what parts of her body these things happened to, and she spread her legs and pointed to her vagina. Amanda was asked how her dad did this, and she said, with his wiener. Next the evaluator wanted to know what it felt like, and Amanda replied, "Real bad, I begged him to stop. He said, 'in a minute', but he kept on doing it for a long time." The evaluator said, "That must have been pretty scary, huh?" and Amanda nodded vigorously. The evaluator asked Amanda if she noticed if anything came out of his wiener and Amanda responded, "Blood, there was blood on his wiener when he took it out of me." The evaluator then asked if any blood came out of her, and she said, "Yes, it was all from me but it got on his wiener. He wiped it up with his undershirt."

In this case Amanda gives an account of the last abuse which describes the context, the specifics of the sexual abuse, and labels the event as scary. Yet she would not have been able to give the details without being asked directive questions. The evaluator took care to avoid leading questions.

D. Allowing Digression

Children's discomfort during the evaluation may cause them to digress or to state directly that they don't want to talk about the abuse.

The evaluator should allow them digression and diversion but then gently bring them back to the topic. Further, sometimes children will want to play or occupy themselves while talking about the sexual abuse, and this behavior should also be tolerated. The example below is typical of a child reducing anxiety by doing something while talking about the mistreatment.

> EXAMPLE 19:   Tessie, 10, had been living alone with her father for four years and he had been sexually abusing her for at least that long. A very disturbed child with a high activity level, she was functioning cognitively at the six-year level. She said she was afraid to tell about the sexual abuse because her father would spank her. However, she was able to talk once she sat in the evaluator's chair and began straightening up things in the evaluator's desk drawers. Thus, her story about naked games with her father, in which she straddled him and he penetrated her, was interspersed with inquiries such as, "What's this?" or "Where does this go?"

Tessie's need to have some control and to relieve tension are played out as she takes over the evaluator's desk, interrupting the interview periodically. Thus she takes a role which is not only adult but also that of a person asking questions.

E. Gathering Data About the Extent of the Sexual Abuse

Once the child has described the most recent instance the evaluator will want to gather data about the full range of sexual abuse—that is, the duration, frequency, and type of sexual behaviors. Questions that may be helpful in eliciting information about duration are: "How old were you when it first started? Do you remember where you lived when it started? Was it before or after your little sister was born? What school were you going to when it started?" The evaluator will also try to get an account of the first incident and some sense of intervening encounters.

If the child is young or the abuse has happened multiple times, the child will not be able to give an estimate of frequency without helpful questions. With victimization of long duration, the evaluator can ask how many times a year or how many times a month the encounters took place. Sometimes a question like: "Did it happen once a month, once a week, or more than once a week?" will be useful. With young children the evaluator may be limited to a question such as: "Did it happen one time, two times, or lots of times?"

It is important to explore for other types of sexual abuse because they are an index of the extent of damage to the victim and the pathology of the perpetrator. In addition, sometimes the perpetrator engages in progressively more intrusive sexual behavior, a factor Sgroi et al. (1982) employ in validating an allegation. In our opinion, this certainly lends authenticity to the child's account in many cases of intrafamilial sexual abuse of long duration. Another reason for inquiring directly about other sexual behavior is that children may not know the difference between what is sexual and what is not, and may find some behaviors so repulsive that they avoid recounting them, as noted in chapter 5.

To inquire about additional sexual abuse the evaluator should begin with general questions such as whether the perpetrator "did any other sexual things" (in the case of older children) or "did anything else to your privates or with his privates" (in the case of younger children). If these questions do not elicit any data, the evaluator should then query about specific sexual behaviors. With older children the evaluator might ask, for example, whether the perpetrator "ever licked, kissed, or sucked your vagina," and then proceed through a range of sexual behaviors. With younger children anatomically explicit dolls can be used to demonstrate a range of sexual behaviors and ask the child if she has ever seen them or if anyone has ever done with them with her. The evaluator should explore genital intercourse, fellatio, cunnilingus, anal intercourse, digital penetration, fondling (including mutual maturbation). In addition the evaluator should ask about picture taking and making the victim engage in sexual behavior with others if there is any indication of such activities. Our experience has been that asking about other sexual abuse, which follows whatever spontaneous statement the child makes, elicits additional information about victimization in 40 percent of cases.

Furthermore, frequently the affective reaction, important in validating an allegation, is present when the child must discuss types of sexual abuse not previously revealed. The reader will recall that if children have to describe sexual abuse several times, their emotional reaction to the subject may be muted. The example below is illustrative not only of a child's response when revealing hitherto undisclosed sexual abuse but also of progressive intrusiveness which is an indicator of a valid allegation in cases of longstanding intrafamilial sexual abuse.

EXAMPLE 20:   Janice, aged 15, was not believed when she alleged sexual abuse by her mother's boyfriend because of the matter of fact way she described the events. She was alleging that he had fondled her intimate parts and had told her he loved her.

During evaluation Janice readily disclosed the fondling behavior, which involved his putting his hand inside her pants and indicated it had happened as often as once a week over a three year period beginning when she was 12. She showed little emotional reaction as she described the incidents.

The evaluator then asked whether she could remember the first time her mother's boyfriend did anything sexual to her. She hesitated and said, ''Well, it wasn't really sexual, but when I was five or six and we lived in Alabama, he made a hole in the bathroom wall so he could watch me in there and I was supposed to watch him.'' Janice said she developed a habit of sitting with a towel covering her lap when she went to the toilet so that the boyfriend could not see her genitals. Janice showed visible distress while describing these incidents, adding that this made her feel filthy and in fact she rarely bathed and would try and use the toilet at school or at a friend's house. Janice said this stopped when they moved to Michigan when she was eight and there were no holes in the bathroom wall.

The evaluator asked if the boyfriend did any sexual things to her during the time she was eight to twelve. Janice replied that at that time he didn't bother her much. Occasionally he would touch her private parts when wrestling with her or when they went swimming, but mostly he left her alone. However, he was having full intercourse with her older sister. She had observed this on two occasions. When Janice was 11, her older sister ran away from home.

After her sister's departure, Janice said the boyfriend began touching her more frequently but outside her clothes, which she described as not too bad. However, he then began demanding she take her jeans off or coming into her bed at night and putting his hands under her nightgown.

The evaluator asked if he ever tried to do anything else to her and Janice quickly shook her head. The evaluator then asked about specific sexual behaviors, beginning by asking if the boyfriend ever wanted her to touch his penis. She said he had wanted her to touch him, and she had done it two or three times but recently had refused to touch him. The evaluator then asked if he had ever wanted to or had put his penis in her mouth. Janice looked down and opened her mouth as if to speak but no words came out. She then began to cry and shake. Finally, she was able to talk and said that he had done this one time and she had practically choked. He ejaculated in her mouth and she had vomited. She said it was horrible and had precipitated her telling, although she had been too upset about the fellatio to reveal it.

In Janice's case, although the initial allegation was just of fondling, the behavior that Janice spontaneously described, probing by the evaluator elicited additional findings, voyeurism and exposure, digital penetration, and fellatio. Further, there emerges a pattern of progressive intrusiveness of sexual behavior beginning with noncontact behaviors, progressing to fondling outside the clothing, then inside the clothing, next digital penetration, and finally fellatio. There is a hiatus in the sexual abuse while the mother's boyfriend has genital intercourse with Janice's older sister.

Some professionals may be concerned that by asking about specific sexual behaviors the evaluator puts ideas into the child's head. This is a possibility and often the evaluator will conclude that the child's affirmative answers to these questions are less reliable than the child's more spontaneous statements earlier in the interview. However, if the child also gives detailed information about the behaviors the evaluator asks about directly, as in Janice's case, then the evaluator can conclude the child is not merely giving social desirability responses.

F. Asking About Other Victims

Once the evaluator understands the extent of the sexual abuse with the victim, she will want to know whether the perpetrator has sexually abused other children. The victim may have observed the sexual abuse of other children, may have participated in group sex, may have been told by another victim, or may have been told by the perpetrator. Sometimes perpetrators tell of other victims in their attempt to persuade the current victim to cooperate, or they brag about other sexual abuse. Recall from chapter 2 that multiple victims are the rule rather than the exception.

There are good reasons for asking about other victims. The first is to be able to protect them. The second is that in attempting to persuade various people that the sexual abuse took place, having more than one child stating that she has been victimized may be very important. Finally, the more promiscuous the perpetrator, the poorer the treatment prognosis. The case below, also discussed in chapter 4, is a case in point.

EXAMPLE 21:   Patti, 10, reported having had intercourse with her father since she was six, but was not believed by social workers who had been involved with her family for several years. In addition, the police doubted Patti's story. However, Patti said her father had also sexually abused Vicki, her older sister, who was then 20, but her mother made him stop. She also cited two cousins, Susan, 18, and Sandy, 16. He had put his hand inside Sandy's bra and felt her breasts. Vicki denied any abuse by her father, but both Susan and Sandy asserted their uncle had sexually molested them when they stayed with his family.

The corroborative statements of other victims were very important in Patti's case. Furthermore, the finding that the father had been involved with multiple victims suggests he may not be treatable.

G. Finding out Whom the Victim has Told

The evaluator will also want to know whether the victim told her mother or another caretaker and what that person's response was. Determining how protective the child's primary caretaker was to the child's revelation of sexual abuse will be important in treatment planning, as will be discussed in chapters 8 and 10. The maternal response in Patti's case is illustrative. When Patti told her mother, her response was, "Don't tell anyone else." Patti decided her mother was not going to protect her and told her teacher.

H. Gathering Information About Other Perpetrators

Another important question is whether anyone other than the already identified perpetrator has sexually abused the child. This question should be asked, first, because in rare instances one finds that there is general permission given by the family for the child to be sexually exploited. If this is so, the situation is obviously an extremely deviant one and the prognosis for maintaining the family intact is, of course, very poor. Secondly, children who have been sexually abused once are vulnerable for subsequent sexual abuse (see chapter 2). Third, it makes a great deal of difference with regard to treatment recommendations depending on whether the child has been sexually misused by only one perpetrator or more than one person. Fourth, often an argument used by the perpetrator is to acknowledge that the child has been sexually abused but to assert someone else is the perpetrator. The evaluator needs to rule this out. The example below is one where the knowledge that there were multiple perpetrators was quite important.

> EXAMPLE 22: Denise, 8, was removed from her parents' care because of alleged sexual abuse by her father. She reported that she told her mother and that her mother ignored her statements, acting as if she hadn't heard what Denise had said.
>
> While being evaluated, Denise talked about two other men who had sexually abused her. The abuse included fellatio, intercourse, and digital penetration. These were men whom her parents used as babysitters. One of them had sexually abused his own daughter and his parental

rights had been terminated. Denise said she had complained to her parents about this sexual abuse and they had not responded. Later it was learned both men paid Denise's father to "babysit" for her. Denise also described having sex with a 12-year-old boy who took her for walks in the woods.

In this case, condoning of sexual abuse with "babysitters" by the father (as well as the mother's unprotectiveness) indicates extremely poor prognosis for parental treatment. The repeated abuse also suggests that long-term treatment for Denise will be necessary. Denise's acquiescence to a sexual encounter with a 12-year-old boy is reflective of her vulnerability because of past victimization.

I. Strategies Used to Maintain Silence

In most cases the perpetrator will attempt to persuade the child not to tell. Such a finding is considered by many experts as an indication of a valid allegation (Jones and McQuiston 1985; DeYoung 1985). The victim should be asked if the perpetrator said anything to her concerning telling or not telling about the sexual abuse. Some admonitions are threats of physical harm to the victim; others relate to consequences of revelation for the perpetrator (he will go to jail; mommy will divorce him; he'll have to leave the family); and still others are threats to other people, as in the example below.

EXAMPLE 23: Jean, 10, was forced to have intercourse with her mother's boyfriend over a six month period. He warned her not to tell her mother, saying if she did, her mother would take Jean and her brother and go to her grandmother's trailer. He would then come and burn down the trailer, killing them all.

J. Finding out the Victim's Wishes Regarding Outcome

It is also important to ascertain what the child thinks should happen about the sexual abuse. Recall the discussion in chapter 1 of a victim-centered approach. Knowing the child's wishes will assist in following a victim-centered approach, although it may not be possible to do exactly what the child wants. Nevertheless, if the child says she wants the perpetrator to get help, that suggests one avenue of intervention, whereas if the child wants the perpetrator to go to jail, that suggests another. Sometimes it is appropriate at this point to discuss issues such as the need to testify in court if the child wants the offender to go to jail, so the victim can begin to consider this prospect.

VII. STRATEGIES TO BE EMPLOYED WHEN THE CHILD WILL NOT TALK ABOUT THE SEXUAL ABUSE

The child who willingly and readily talks about the sexual abuse is the exception rather than the rule. Thus the interviewer should approach an evaluation of a victim with an expectation the child will be resistant to talking. We will describe techniques we have found useful in eliciting information from children who do not want to speak about their experiences.

A. Use of Reasoning

Sometimes reasoning with the child will persuade the child to tell. Assuring the child she will be protected or letting her know that protecion cannot be assured without full knowledge of the abuse may work. Telling children there is risk of sexual abuse with younger siblings if something is not done will sometimes be persuasive. Giving the child hope that telling will assure the perpetrator will receive help or will be made to desist may be important to other children. Assurance that professionals will shield the child from the wrath of the perpetrator or the family may induce some children to talk. Others may want the perpetrator to be punished or made to leave the home, and that potential will lead them to talk. The example below illustrates the use of reasoning.

> EXAMPLE 24:   Katie, a seven-year-old black child, had been taken to the walk-in clinic at the local hospital by her mother because she had a cold. During the course of the medical examination, Katie was found to have gonorrhea. Katie denied any sexual contact. Her mother denied any knowledge of how Katie could have contracted gonorrhea. In the household lived Katie, her mother, her mother's boyfriend, Katie's three younger siblings (two of whom had been subjects of past protective services referrals), and Katie's aunt, uncle, and three cousins, who had recently been evicted from their own apartment. In addition, there were many people who visited the home. Katie's mother was on AFDC, her boyfriend was unemployed, and Katie's aunt and uncle had recently applied for public assistance.
>
> Because it was felt Katie was unsafe at home, she was hospitalized. She remained in the hospital for three days during which time she was seen by a social worker, psychiatrist, and psychologist as well as numerous medical staff, all of whom tried to discover the origin of the gonorrhea. Her mother and mother's boyfriend were also interviewed. No

further information was forthcoming, and Katie was discharged to her mother's care but with the understanding that she would attend an after school program and would not be left alone with any men.

Within a week the protective services worker visited Katie at her after school program and tried to get her to say how she contracted the gonorrhea. After an hour and a half, the worker gave up. Katie would only say, "I don't know," and specifically denied contact with all likely male suspects.

Katie was referred for evaluation to a mental health expert. She came to the interview with her mother. Initially they were both brought into the playroom. Katie's mother was a short, overweight young woman who appeared very excitable. She spoke repeatedly of the fact that people were saying that Katie had a disease and what she had wasn't a disease; it was an infection. She said Katie was very upset that people were saying she had a disease. Katie, a slim child with large, dark eyes, sat silently while her mother spoke in this agitated way. The evaluator told the mother that the most recent medical examination had revealed no sign of infection, so that whatever gonorrhea was, a disease or an infection, it had been cured by the penicillin. The evaluator then asked Katie if it was OK if her mom went back in the waiting room while they talked. Katie said that would be fine. Her mother was then ushered somewhat reluctantly back to the waiting room.

In the interview with Katie, the evaluator first asked her about her new after school program, then about school: what grade she was in, what she liked best in school (recess), and what she liked least (math). The evaluator then said, "I hear you're the big sister in your family," and asked Katie about her brothers and sisters. She learned Katie's youngest brother had a heart problem and her sister had fits, usually when her mom forgot to give her sister medicine. The evaluator asked about Katie's mother's boyfriend and her aunt and uncle and their children. None of this information yielded any clues about who might be the sexual abuser.

Then the evaluator said, "You know, Katie, I'm worried about your infection. Are you?" Katie nodded. The evaluator continued, "It's all gone now but I'm afraid it'll come back unless I know who gave it to you and we can tell him to stop." Katie did not respond. The evaluator added, "I need to know his name." Katie replied, "Or maybe he'll move away." The evaluator then asked, "Where does he live?" and Katie gave the address next to her own. The evaluator then asked what the person's first name was and Katie responded "Bobby." The evaluator then asked Katie if she knew Bobby's last name and Katie gave it. As to how old Bobby was, Katie said, 15.

The evaluator then produced anatomically explicit dolls and asked Katie if she had ever seen dolls like them before. Katie said, yes. The evaluator asked Katie if she could show what Bobby did with the dolls. Katie demonstrated intercourse. In response to questions, she said Bobby did this to her one time in her bedroom when he was babysitting for her. Her mom was at Bingo. Her brothers and sisters were asleep. Bobby did not tell her not to tell, but she was afraid to tell because her mom would be mad at her. The evaluator told Katie she didn't think her mom would be mad and asked Katie if she thought she could tell her mom. Katie said, "You tell her."

Katie's mother was then asked to come back in and the evaluator recounted what Katie had said. Katie's mother was quite distressed because Bobby was a boy she had befriended when he had gotten in trouble with the juvenile authorities. She was also upset that Katie had been afraid to tell her, saying repeatedly to Katie she should come to momma when people hurt her.

The evaluator asked Katie what ought to happen to Bobby and she said, "Get some help." Her mother agreed that she wanted Bobby to get treatment. Katie and her mother were told that Bobby should not come over to their house any more and that protective services would be talking to Bobby and his mother that day or the next. Katie was praised lavishly for telling.

In this case, the victim had not revealed the sexual abuse despite multiple efforts to get her to talk. Her reluctance to talk probably was related to her race and fear of the white establishment, her fondness for Bobby, and her concern her mother would be mad. Because Katie had not been responsive to anatomically explicit dolls during previous interviews, initially the evaluator did not use them, but tried to think of ways to motivate Katie to speak about the sexual abuse. Thus, taking her cue from the mother's discussion of disease and infection, the evaluator said she didn't want Katie to get another infection. Another move by the evaluator that probably facilitated Katie's telling was excluding her mother from the interview. This was done for two reasons, the mother's highly agitated state and a concern that the perpetrator might be someone the mother wanted to protect.

Bobby and his 17-year-old girlfriend were both found to have gonorrhea.

B. Asking About the Context of the Sexual Abuse First

Another strategy that may be effective in gathering information from children who are reluctant to talk is to inquire about the context of the sexual abuse and then to ask about the act itself. This technique can be useful when the child responds, "I don't know," "I can't remember," "I don't want to talk about it," or "I can't tell" when the evaluator asks what happened. The evaluator might proceed by saying,

"Well, maybe you could just tell me where you were when it happened," and then perhaps, "Do you remember whether it was day or night?" and so forth. In the example below this technique was employed.

EXAMPLE 25:   Jennifer, 4, was one of 15 possible victims of sexual abuse by a volunteer in a day care center. She became very subdued when asked about Tommy, the alleged perpetrator, and replied "I don't remember" to questions about things Tommy did to her.

The evaluator then asked if Jennifer could remember whether things happened in the morning or the afternoon, and she replied in the afternoon. She was then asked whether it was at naptime or another time; and she responded naptime. The next question to Jennifer was where were the teachers. She said the teachers were at the desk, but they couldn't see her cot from the desk. She was then asked who napped near her and she stated Todd and Mike but they were usually asleep. The evaluator then queried how many times Tommy did these things and she replied "lotsa times."

The evaluator then said, "Boy, Jennifer, you remembered a whole lot! Do you think you could remember exactly what Tommy did, too?" Jennifer hesitated and the evaluator suggested she might be able to show with the anatomically explicit dolls. Jennifer nodded and placed the adult male doll's penis in the little girl doll's mouth. She was asked if that was what Tommy did to her and she nodded. She added "Something come out of him, too," pointing to the penis. She was asked what it tasted like and she said, "yucky."

In this case, the evaluator was able to overcome Jennifer's reluctance to talk by asking her about less distasteful aspects of the situation and then returning to the sexual abuse.

C. Giving the Child a Choice of Responses

The following approach can be employed if the interviewer has some idea of the sequence of events of the sexual abuse. After first attempting to get the child to respond to open-ended questions, the evaluator might then go through the suspected scenario, giving the child a choice of responses. The example that follows is illustrative of this approach.

EXAMPLE 26:   Cleo, 10, had been digitally penetrated by her uncle, who gave her candy and allowed her to steer his car for her cooperation. This occurred when she visited her uncle and she went for drives in the country with him. She had told her 12-year-old cousin who then told her teacher at school. Cleo was reluctant to talk. In the first interview all she would say was that her uncle did something naughty. For the second interview the evaluator made the following list of possible responses:

Uncle	*Grandfather*
Fingers	Toes
Mouth	Pussy
Bed	Car
Clothes on	Clothes off
Drive car	Stay up late
Popcorn	Candy

The evaluator then asked questions and had Cleo point to the right answer. "Was it your uncle or your grandfather who did the naughty things?" "Did he use his finger or his toes?" "Did he put them in your mouth or your pussy?" etc. Cleo answered all the questions and corroborated what her cousin had said, adding, "He did it to my sister when she was 10, too, but now she says she's too big to play games."

In this example the evaluator avoided eliciting social desirability responses by giving the child a choice of answers.

D. Asking Questions with "Yes" or "No" Answers

Sometimes, however, children will not respond to questions when they are given a choice of answers. Then, as a last resort, the evaluator goes through the sequence of events asking the child to respond yes or no to questions. In the following case this technique was used.

EXAMPLE 27:   Ellen, 6, loved her father and had been told repeatedly by him that if she told about their special games, he would be sent to the hospital. Her mother said she sensed something funny would be going on when her husband took Ellen in the spare bedroom with him to watch TV. He often did this when the mother was having a Tupperware Party. She became suspicious on one occasion when he received a telephone call and emerged from the bedroom flushed and seemed to be tryng to hide an erection. Ellen had told her mother when questioned that she and her dad played special games but when asked what they were, said, "I don't know, ask him." Instead of asking him, the mother brought Ellen to be evaluated.

After being unsuccessful in trying a number of other strategies, the evaluator used a "yes and no" format. She asked:

Do you like your mom?	Yes
Do you like your dad?	Yes
Does your dad ever do anything scary to you?	No
Does he ever do anything that makes you feel funny?	Yes

Does it happen when you watch TV with him?	Yes
Sometimes in the spare bedroom?	Yes
Are you on the bed?	Yes
Do you have your clothes on?	No
Do you have them off?	No
I don't understand.	Some are on and some are off
What ones are off?	My panties
What happens?	No answer
Does he touch you where your panties would be?	Yes
In the front?	No

Ellen then took her hands and placed them between her legs saying, "In between. I lie on his tummy and he puts his thing in between my legs. He likes it. He said I'll like it when I get bigger but I don't. I want him to stop. I can't watch TV when he does it."

In this case the child was responsive to the yes-no format and then the evaluator tried more open-ended questions. Toward the end Ellen became quite spontaneous, both showing and telling what had happened. Further, she volunteered information about how her father rationalized his behavior, his emotional state in the process, and her own emotional reaction to the sexual abuse.

There also will be cases where children refuse to talk or deny the abuse. However, it should not be assumed the abuse did not take place because the child did not talk. In such situations, evaluators may be able to validate the allegation on the basis of other sources of information as described in chapter 5. In cases where no conclusion can be reached after multiple strategies have been employed, sometimes treatment which involves further diagnostic work can lead to an understanding of whether or not the child has been sexually abused. In some cases, however, children remain in or return to environments where they may be victims of sexual abuse.

VIII. CONCLUDING THE INTERVIEW

At the end of the interview, the evaluator should reassure the child and let her know what will happen next. The child should be praised for disclosing the sexual abuse and told she did the right thing. For example, the evaluator may tell the child she was brave, did a very good job, or talked about something that was really scary, and that was good. Other types of reassurance which may be needed will be described in chapter 11.

At this point the child needs only to know about the immediate future, and, in fact, it will be hard to know the long-term future at this early stage. Thus, the evaluator may say, "You'll stay at grandma's tonight. She'll take care of you until we can get things straightened out", or "We're going to find a foster home for you, so you won't have to worry about your dad spanking you," or "You are going to stay here for a little bit while Mrs. Jones goes out and talks to your parents."

IX. CONCLUSION

This chapter has described a range of strategies an evaluator can use in interviewing an alleged victim of sexual abuse. Some, those which elicit sexual content in doll play, drawing, or stories, are better suited to younger children. Anatomically explicit dolls have a unique role to play in this field because they may stimulate the child to express latent material and they allow the expression of a range of information the child may not be able or willing to speak about. With older children, the evaluator will need to rely primarily on statements about what happened.

Various techniques are described separately for the purpose of clarity. In interviews they are usually employed concurrently. The keys to good interviewing are patience, staying in tune with the respondent's feelings and level of functioning, and flexibility and creativity in interview techniques.

NOTES

1. Because there is almost no literature about using these dolls, nor the responses non-sexually-abused children have to them, I have systematically included them in assessments of normal children, and children whose maltreatment is not sexual, in order to gather information about the responses of other populations.

2. I disagree with Sgroi and colleagues, who ask the child to begin with the first time it happened (Sgroi 1982).

CHAPTER SEVEN

Interviewing the Perpetrator

I. INTRODUCTION

The content and process of interviews with alleged perpetrators will vary depending upon the context in which they are done. Sometimes they are undertaken by mental health professionals, sometimes by the police, or they may be done by the police and a child protection worker. We will describe a strategy which is best suited for a child protection or other type of children's services worker, a mental health expert, or a multidisciplinary team.

In some respects, evaluations of perpetrators are similar to other types of mental health evaluations. However, the reasons for covering certain content areas in the interview may be different, and some aspects of functioning that might be dealt with superficially or not at all in other mental health evaluations are very important in sexual abuse cases. In this chapter topics that should be discussed with the alleged perpetrator will be described and the rationale for examining them will be explained.

In most cases, the evaluator will already have decided on the basis of interview data from the child whether or not the child has been sexually abused (see also Sgroi 1982 and McCarty 1981). Thus the purposes of the interview with the perpetrator are to gain an understanding of the dynamics of the sexual abuse, to obtain a direct or indirect admission from the perpetrator, to make some predictions with regard to prognosis, and to gather data which will be helpful in posing an intervention plan. Of special interest will be information regarding such important factors for prognosis and treatment planning as the perpetrator's overall functioning, superego functioning, and the extent of his sexually abusive behavior (see chapter 10). In a few cases, the evaluator may not be sure from the child's interview that the child has been sexually abused or who the perpetrator is. In such instances, this interview will be used to address these questions as well.

II. PROCESS AND CONTENT OF THE INTERVIEW

The likelihood of obtaining desired information from the interview with the perpetrator is enhanced by making efforts to form an alliance with him and by gathering data about a range of aspects of his functioning. This can be done by employing the following approach. First, the evaluator briefly states the concerns about the sexual abuse and the way in which the information gathered in the interview will be used. Having made this initial statement, a good strategy is to deflect any protests of innocence and tell the perpetrator that the most helpful thing right now is to "get to know you a little," or "for you to tell me a little about yourself." The evaluator then asks questions of the offender which progress from material which should be fairly neutral to that which should be emotionally laden. It is likely the perpetrator will deny the sexual abuse. If the evaluator initially confronts him on this issue, he will probably become angry and alienated and will withhold information about other aspects of his life. The other information is essential to diagnosis, prognosis, and treatment planning.

The following information will be useful: (a) demographic data (age, race, ethnicity, religion); (b) education and employment history; (c) family composition and parental functioning; (4) family of origin and social supports; (e) relationship with the spouse or significant other; (f) description of a typical day; (g) substance-use history; (h) history of mental illness or retardation; (i)   history of criminal activity;   (j) sexual history; and (k) discussion of the sexual abuse. These topics are ordered roughly from the least to the most stressful.

A. Demographic Data

To some, demographic information may not seem important, and little attention has been paid to it in the literature on sexual abuse. We do not believe that sexual abuse is more prevalent among certain races or religions. However, clinical evidence suggests that there may be some variation in type of sexual abuse by subculture. For example, our experience and the research of Pierce and Pierce (1984) indicate that, compared with other racial groups, in black families the abuser is more likely to be someone other than the biological father and the family is more likely to take decisive action to protect the child. Furthermore, it is a commonly held belief that incest is more prevalent among whites in certain parts of the South, where families tend to be isolated. Indeed, in our sample, 45 percent of family, where previous location was known, were originally from Southern Appalachian states. Probably more significant, however, is the fact that there tended to be multiple incestuous relationships in families of Southern origin. Thus, information regarding ethnicity can assist the evaluator in understanding the dynamics of the sexual abuse and alert her to patterns that may be present.

In addition, it is useful to explore with the perpetrator his religion and the meaning of religion for him because it may have a role in the dynamics of sexual abuse. Two patterns have been noted in our sample. First, some perpetrators are members of marginal religious cults, sometimes of their own invention, which may provide some ideological underpinning for sexual abuse of children. A few cases involved the sanctioning of sex with children. One perpetrator had a throne and required all the family members to worship him.

The second pattern we have noted is that some perpetrators turn to religion as a reaction formation, or in order to cope with the guilt and shame they feel about the sexual abuse. Some men for whom religious involvement is a reaction formation have alternating periods of religiosity and acting out behavior including sexual abuse. However, sexually abusive, behavior does not appear more prevalent among religious people. The example below illustrrates the first pattern described. Mr. Jones has developed religious beliefs that support sexual abuse.

EXAMPLE 1:   Mr. Jones had over the years refused to send his seven children to school. Finally, he was ordered to do so by the court. When they appeared, the children were very neatly dressed and clean, but very far behind in all school subjects. Seven year old Keyana was sent to the school nurse because she kept rubbing her vulva. Lateral bruises on her back, legs, and upper arms were found when she was undressed. Protective services was called and Keyana was taken for a full medical exam. She was found to have no hymen and an enlarged vaginal opening. Keyana was very frightened and would say nothing.

When Mr. Jones was interviewed, he immediately informed the worker his title was Father, not Mr.. The worker discovered he had two wives and was not sure which children were from which wife. He stated that the children were beaten regularly because otherwise the devil would possess them, and then they would do the devil's will instead of his own. The female members of the family, wives and children, slept in one bedroom, in two double beds pushed together. Father Jones would come and join them and "bless them" from time to time (he said he "blessed" merely by being present). He adamantly denied having had intercourse with anyone but his wives and said this went on in another room. He said no one had sexually abused Keyana.

All of the children were given physical exams and were found to have injuries resulting from excessive discipline. Joni, four, had a vaginal tear. All seven children were placed in foster care. Later in foster care, Jacob, 12, described how he was being taught how to ''bless'' female members of the household, (by having sexual intercourse with them) including one of his father's wives. However, he said that the wife he had ''blessed'' was not his mother.

In this case, Mr. Jones developed an elaborate belief system that justified sexual abuse as well as having two wives, physical abuse, and not sending the children to school. This case fits the definition of a polyincestuous family as described in chapter 3.

B. Education and Employment History

Information about the offender's education and employment is important because it tells the evaluator a good deal about his overall functioning. While these are fairly good indices of overall functioning for men, they are not so useful in assessing women. Sometimes it is useful to think of homemaking and parenting abilities as the female counterparts of employment for men. Understanding overall functioning is useful primarily in assessing prognosis. A man who was unsuccessful in school and has a poor work history is not, to our knowledge, more likely to sexually abuse children, but if he has chronically malfunctioned in these areas, his treatment prognosis is less good. In contrast, achievement in school and a good employment history may be indicative of more strengths and the ability to be successful in therapy. The two cases cited in the example below are illustrative.

> EXAMPLE 2:   Mr. A had worked steadily during 20 years of marriage and had just completed college by attending school part time. He also had been having sexual intercourse with his 14-year-old daughter for five years.
>
> Mr. B occasionally worked as a truck driver or he chopped wood. He frequently lost jobs for lateness, absences, drinking on the job and physical fights with other workers. He also had been fondling his 12-year-old daughter for two years.
>
> Mr. A responded well to treatment and the family was reunited within a year. Mr. B only sporadically attended treatment, and often was intoxicated. After six months of attempted treatment, termination of his parental rights was sought.

In the cases above Mr. A's sexual abuse was more serious and more damaging to his daughter. Yet he responded better to treatment. Mr. B's fondling behavior was less severe and probably less damaging to his daughter. However, he made no investment in treatment.

In addition, it is important to investigate employment because, in a considerable number of sexual abuse cases (27% in our sample), one can mark the onset of the sexual abuse with unemployment or some other stress which has an impact upon the perpetrator's self-esteem (see chapter 4). Thus, identifying such stresses can help the evaluator understand the dynamics of the sexual abuse. Further, cases that have a precipitating stress are fairly amenable to treatment. The Z case described below is illustrative.

> EXAMPLE 3:   Mr. Z and his wife met while working at a small-parts factory. Her divorce from her first husband was in process and she had two children ages six and three. The Z's were married as soon as Mrs. Z's divorce became final, and they continued to work together for about six months. Then Mr. Z took a better paying job as a truck driver. Since he worked days and Mrs. Z worked evenings, he hardly ever saw his wife except on weekends. He would babysit for the children while his wife worked. After two months as a truck driver, he was laid off, and was reduced to intermittently pumping as as his only means of livelihood. During that period he describes his life as being very lonely, being alone all day and at home with the children at night. His wife was also very impatient with him. During the time he was babysitting, he sexually abused both children.

Mr. Z's unemployment, which affected his feelings of self-worth, his lack of access to his wife, and his unsupervised access to his stepdaughters, contributed to the sexual abuse.

C. Family Composition and Parental Functioning

Information about family composition can be extremely useful: it will enable the evaluator to explore for other possible victims, who will need to be interviewed later; such information will help the evaluator understand the context of victimization and future risk; finally, these data will help in assessing the perpetrator's object relations.

In pursuit of his last goal, the interviewer should ask the alleged perpetrator to describe the children in the family. In cases where the victim and alleged perpetrator do not live in the same household, he should be asked to describe not only children in his own household but also the victim. The interviewer might ask what the child is like and then use probes such as the following: What about the child pleases you, displeases you? What are the child's interests? What do the two of you do together? What do you do when the child misbehaves? What does the child do when upset? How do you know when the child is happy? What are the child's strengths? Weaknesses?

The offender's responses should be assessed according to: (1) his ability to individualize children in the family so that they are described as separate people with personalities; (2) the affective tone of the relationship with children; (3) the accuracy of the respondent's perception and description of the children, based upon the evaluator's contact with them and the opinions of others, and (4) the presence or absence of inappropriately sexual descriptions of the children. Information in these four areas is of greatest utility in understanding the dynamics of the sexual abuse and predicting prognosis, but also can augment information supporting a diagnosis of sexual abuse.

The first two qualities, the ability to individualize and the quality of affect are important in determining whether the offender considers people, particularly children, as objects to be used or manipulated for his interests or needs, or whether he sees them as individuals with their own needs who are valued and loved for themselves. The two cases that follow show men of quite divergent capacities in this area.

EXAMPLE 4:   Mr. S was being interviewed as a possible sexual abuser of his eight-year-old daughter. The maternal grandfather was also a suspect. When the father was asked to describe his daughter, he said, "She's real smart. She has perfect attendance and she hates to miss school. She's a real talker, she'll talk your ear off, and she likes to play games; bingo and checkers. She can beat me at checkers. She doesn't like dolls; she likes to ride her three wheeler and she likes to ride on the tractor with me when I mow the lawn. She's an affectionate kid with me and the wife, but she doesn't get along too good with her sister. Of course her sister's 4 years younger and kind of babied. We're a very close family. I'm very proud of her."

EXAMPLE 5:   Mr. T, who had required his three and five-year-old daughters to fellate him and who had a history of criminal activity and drug use, described his three-year-old as "an OK kid," and his five-year-old as "OK, too." He could not tell what they were like or what they did during the day, even though he babysat for them while his wife worked. All he was finally able to state specifically about them was, "Sometimes they want a sip of my beer."

Mr. S's capacity to individualize his daughter and the appropriate affective tone of his remarks about her indicate the capability of good object relations and were useful factors in arriving at the conclusion that the father was not the perpetrator. In contrast, Mr. T shows no appreciation of his daughters as individuals. This quality and his dysfunctional behavior in other areas made him a poor candidate for therapy. Nevertheless, some fathers who can describe their children appropriatrely, and love them, also sexually abuse them; but they are less likely to do so, and when they do, their treatment prognosis is much better.

Turning now to descriptions by offenders that are inconsistent with others' perceptions, these may be more fitting to an older child, or reflect a perception of the child as being on the same level as the offender. The child also may be described in negative terms or in a manner that suggests the victim is to blame for problems associated with the allegation of sexual abuse. These reactions are indicative of poor treatment prognosis, which, however, may moderate over time or as a result of treatment. The case of Linda is illustrative of this kind of discrepant description of the victim.

> EXAMPLE 6:   Linda, 14, had been sexually abused by her father for 10 years. She was described by her mother as an intelligent, responsible child, who worried about others more than herself. She told about the sexual abuse when she learned her father was sexually abusing her 12-year-old sister as well. She had not told earlier because she was worried about the complications for the family if the sexual abuse were known.
>
> Her father described her as lazy, saying she could do better in school if she wanted. He said she manipulated other people, especially her younger sister and she was "always sitting on her pitty pot" (feeling sorry for herself). He denied the sexual abuse and said the whole thing was Linda's fabrication to get attention. The evaluator's perception of Linda was consistent with Linda's mother's.

Linda's father response is indicative of poor prognosis because he describes her very negatively and projects blame onto her.

Finally, the evaluator should be alert to sexual connotations in perpetrator's descriptions of victims. These may be speculations about the child's future sexual functioning or projections about how other men or boys regard the victim. In other situations, the victim's alleged sexuality provides an excuse to the perpetrator for the abuse, as in the following example.

> EXAMPLE 7:   Mr. L sexually abused a nine-year-old neighbor, Lisa, whom he described as "outrageously seductive." As an illustration, he described pre-adolescent boys clustering around her when she came home from school and his sons always wanting to go over to her house and play. He refused to allow this because he said her mother was a tramp, but he allowed Lisa to play at his house and on several occasions fondled her. He also said he was sure he was not the first one because Lisa didn't even scream.

Mr. L's description of Lisa did not fit with her presentation, which was that of a normal, outgoing nine-year-old.

D. Family of Origin and Social Supports

There are two major reasons for speaking with the alleged abuser about his family of origin and social network. The evaluator will want to get some sense of what it was like for the alleged perpetrator growing up and will want to assess the extended family and others as sources of social support.

Many factors related to the perpetrator's upbringing may shed light on the dynamics of sexual abuse and predict prognosis (see chapter 4). The evaluator will want to find out what kind of people his parents were and how he experienced them. A common pattern in childhoods of sexual abusers is one where there was little nurturing, significant trauma, and much deprivation. Their histories may indicate a lack of experience of closeness so that the only kind of intimacy they know is sexual. Further, persons who become sexually abusive were often physically abused as children. In addition, many sexual abusers were themselves sexually abused or had unusual sexual experiences in their childhood. In other cases, they have fathers or other relatives who are role models for exploitative behavior, including sexual victimization. Paradoxically, there may be little discussion of sex in the sexual abuser's family of origin. It is a taboo subject and a potential source of fascination. At the same time, because of lack of sexual knowledge, the perpetrator may lack guidelines for acceptable sexual expression. The case of Mr. M, described below, illustrates the kind of background found in some sexual abuse cases.

> EXAMPLE 8: Mr. M's mother had worked as a barmaid when he was growing up. He was the only child she was allowed to keep; three of his siblings were placed with relatives. His mother was both an alcoholic and very promiscuous. He recalls over his childhood there being six men who lived with his mother and whom he was supposed to call father. A number of these fathers severely physically abused him. He also remembers his mother getting into numerous drunken brawls over men and ending up in the workhouse. He would wake up in the morning to an empty house. He would then go find his older sister and they would go get his mother out. Finally, the most frightening experiences he recounted were when his mother had no man available, for then she would take him to bed and make sexual demands upon him. This began when he was about 6 and continued until he left home at 16. Mr. M had sexually abused his ten-year-old daughter. He was extremely remorseful and made a full confession.

Mr. M experienced emotional deprivation, physical abuse, and sexual abuse as a child. Given his disastrous childhood, it is not surprising that he had little knowledge of how to show his love for his daughter.

Social isolation and the absence of social supports play a role in the dynamics in some situations of sexual abuse. As noted in chapter 4, social isolation can have several functions. It may facilitate, prolong, or be the result of sexual abuse. In addition, the social network can be a resource in working on the sexual abuse problem.

Aside from questions about extended family members, relationships with them, and frequency of contact, the evaluator might ask the alleged perpetrator who he relies on when he or the family needs help. For example, who can you turn to when you have a financial problem? Who can you rely on when you have a problem with one of your children? And who would help out if there was sickness in your family?

In the case below social isolation played a role in the sexual abuse.

EXAMPLE 9:   Mr. J lived in a cabin in the woods with his three daughters, ages 13, 10, and 6, and a son, age 8. He supported his family marginally by working in a sawmill. The family moved from a house in a small town to the woods after Mrs. J deserted the family. She left town with a man five years younger than she, headed for Detroit.

Mr. J was regarded by the community as a righteous man and a caring father, but with unusual ways. His children always came to school clean, on time, and having done their homework. They were a close knit group and did not make friends at school. They were not allowed to participate in after school activities and did not go to church. When Mr. J was questioned about this, he said his children needed after school time to do their homework and chores, and that the family prayed at home every night.

On one occasion, a new neighbor went to call on Mr. J and was greeted by Mr. J with a shotgun. Mr. J apologized saying that no one had "just dropped by" his house before and living in such an isolated area he had to protect himself.

Mrs. J returned to town two years after her departure, but Mr. J refused to have anything to do with her. She took a room in a hotel. The J's 12-year-old daughter, Sarah went into town to see her mother one day after school. She told her mother that she now slept with her father every night and that he treated her like his wife. When confronted, Mr. J confessed and asked that he be incarcerated. He also said the children should go to an orphanage or a foster home, and not be allowed to ever see their mother or him again.

In this case, social isolation probably had several functions: the lack of access to other outlets played a role in the father's gravitation toward his daughter; the isolation facilitated the continuance of the incest; the father avoided outside contacts because of fear or discovery; and the community shunned him because of his unusual ways.

Relationship with the Spouse or a Significant Other

Information about relations with significant others can be of
benefit in understanding the dynamics and prognosis of sexual abuse.
Specifically, these relations are another aspect of the perpetrator's object
relations; they may shed light on the mother's functioning, an important
factor in treatment planning for intrafamilial sexual abuse; and marital
problems or difficulties may play a role in sexual abuse. Some of the
commonly seen marital problems are as follows: (1) husband tyrannizes
his wife; (2) wife is coercive and cold with the husband; (3) there is no
communication between the partners; (4) the spousal relationship is a
hostile one; (5) there is no sexual relationship between the partners or it is
not emotionally gratifying. Such problems in adult relationships may
contribute to a gravitation toward children for emotional and sexual
gratifications. Finally, information about the state of the marital relationship and parental wishes about continuing it is necessary for treatment planning.

A good way to approach this part of the assessment is to employ
questions similar to those asked about children: (1) What is your partner
like or what kind of a person is she? (2) What about her pleases you? (3)
What displeases you? (4) What kinds of things do you do together? Do
you enjoy these? (5) Do you ever do things together without the children?
(6) Are there things about your partner you would like changed? (7) Do
you tell her things you don't tell anyone else? (8) How do you show her
when she pleases you or you are happy with her? (9) How does she show
you when you please her or she is happy with you? (10) How does she
know when you are displeased? (11) How do you know when she is displeased? (12) What do you have arguments about? (13) Have you ever
used physical force with each other? Describe. The evaluator may choose
to ask about the couple's sexual relationship fairly early in the assessment or wait until later during the taking of the sexual history.

The interviewer will be interested in dimensions similar to those
of interest in the respondent's relationship with children: the quality of
the relationship, the ability of the perpetrator to see his spouse as a
separate individual with her own needs, and the extent to which the
description of his spouse is consistent with input from other sources. In
the case below Mr. A was asked what his wife was like.

EXAMPLE 10:   Mr. A, 22, in describing his relationship with his wife said
they had married when both were 16 and she was pregnant. He wasn't
sure how long he had known Renee, his wife, beforehand, but maybe
about three years. (In fact, it was one year). He said that she wasn't too innocent because her stepfather had sex with her. He felt that pretty soon
after their oldest daughter's birth, Renee started running around on him,

and that was the part of her he wanted changed. (In fact, he had been cheating on her since their honeymoon). He couldn't describe what Renee was like except to say he always gave her his paycheck, and she was supposed to pay the bills. (Renee stated that she had to beg him for money for food). When asked how he showed her he was pleased with her, he said, "I give her a good lay, like most men," but stated she didn't appreciate this. (Renee described sex as "rough and painful" and tried to avoid sex with him). As to whether he ever hit her, he said, "Only when she deserves it." The therapist found Renee to be a warm and supportive mother who was very frightened of her husband.

Mr. A's responses to these questions show a lack of empathy for his wife, a superficial relationship, and a perception of her as an object. Moreover, some of his assertions were contradictory to statements by his wife and other persons. His statements also reveal lack of sexual access to his wife which probably was a contributory cause in the sexual abuse.

F. Description of a Typical Day

Having the alleged perpetrator describe a typical day may be useful in assessment and treatment planning. It may yield information regarding the perpetrator's access to the victim, his overall functioning, and possible intervention strategies.

The interviewer asks the alleged perpetrator to describe a typical day beginning with when he gets up in the morning. In cases of intrafamilial sexual abuse, the evaluator will be asking where the spouse and children are at various points in the day and whether the respondent has the company of other persons during the day. Important information includes time with the victim(s) without another adult being present, who in the house goes to bed when and with whom, and who gets up in the night. The evaluator should also ask if weekends are any different and, if so, obtain as much detail about weekend activities as weekday ones. The evaluator should be sure to ask about a typical day as it was before the report of sexual abuse, as family patterns are likely to be disrupted by its discovery. It may be useful to compare this to the child's and mother's descriptions of their typical days.

EXAMPLE 11:   Mr. G described his typical day as follows:

Time	Activity	Who Else Present
5:30	get up, fix own breakfast	no one; wife and 2 daughters asleep

6:30	work: drives a truck, hauls parts back and forth between 2 plants	alone with radio in truck
9:00	15 min. break; has coffee	sometimes goes to a cafe
11:30	lunch: 45 min. eats in truck	no one
12:15	back to work	no one
1:30	15 min. break	no one
3:30	goes home	no one
4:00	at home: plays games with kids; helps them with home-work	2 daughters; wife is at work from 3:30 to 11:30
5:30	finishes fixing supper; father and daughters eat	2 daughters; 8 yr. old sets table
6:00	does dishes	2 daughters; they help
7:00	watch TV with kids	2 daughters
8:00	gives them their baths	2 daughters
9:00	all three go to bed; daughters sleep in queen-sized bed with father.	

This case illustrates not only the father's extensive unsupervised access to the children but also lack of access to the wife. Both parents often worked on weekends and never did anything together without their children. Further, as Mr. G's report indicates, when the couple would be together, at night in bed, both children were also in the bed. Frequently Mrs. G slept in the youngest daughter's bed because there was not enough room in the parental bed.

Nevertheless, just because the alleged perpetrator's account indicates no instance of unsupervised access to the victim does not mean he did not abuse the child. Some men are remarkable in their ability to find opportunities and skillful in not getting caught. Further, the respondent may be aware that the evaluator is looking for access to the victim and lie about this. The example below is of a case of a father who had minimal access but nevertheless sexually abused his daughter over a long time period.

EXAMPLE 12: Sixteen-year-old Lucy described her father as having intercourse with her over a period of years, when her mother was cooking, doing chores, or shopping. Her mother totally disbelieved her daughter. Later the father confessed.

In addition, in many cases of sexual abuse, the sexual encounters are intermittent, once a month or less often, and in such cases, information about a typical day will not be so useful.

G. Substance Use

Understanding a respondent's history of substance use can be helpful in assessing the dynamics of sexual abuse, making treatment recommendations, and assessing prognosis (see chapter 4). The exact role substance use plays in a particular case varies. Sometimes it is a disinhibitor that is, it facilitates acts the perpetrator would like to perform but does not do when sober. In other cases, the sexual abuser feels ashamed and guilty about his behavior and drinks in order to dampen these feelings. Alcohol is the most common substance reported. Clinical histories from our sample suggest that when other drugs are involved, the sexual abuse is more severe.

Taking a history is often difficult because many substance abusers will deny they have a problem or lie about how much substance they use. There are two strategies which can be useful in overcoming this difficulty. The first is to ask a lot of questions to get as much detail as possible. The second is to look for inconsistencies, either in his statements or between his statements and information from other sources.

Taking a Substance Use History. Since alcohol is a legal drug and its use appears more highly correlated than other substances with sexual abuse, it is usually best to begin questioning about alcohol. What follows are sample questions.

1. What kinds of alcohol do you use?
2. How much of each?
3. Do you mix drinks?
4. How many times a week do you drink?
5. Approximately at what time during the day do you take your first drink?
   Before lunch?
   At lunch?
   Before dinner?
   During dinner?
   After dinner?
6. What is your pattern of drinking after the first drink of the day?
   How many drinks at lunch, between lunch and dinner, etc.?
7. Are weekends different? If so, how?
8. Do you ever get drunk?
   How much does it take to get you drunk?
   What do you do when you get drunk?
9. Do you ever get hangovers?
   How much does it take to give you a hangover?
   What kinds of drinks give you a hangover?

What do you do to cure a hangover?

How long does the hangover last?

10. What is the most you ever drank?

11. Was there a time in your life when you drank more or less than you do now?

12. Does alcohol ever make you or or allow you to do things you wouldn't do otherwise?

Do you drink when you are upset?

13. Do you ever have times when you can't remember exactly what happened when you were drinking? (blackouts)

14. Does it take more to get you feeling good than it has at times in the past? (increased tolerance)

15. Do you ever need to take a drink in the morning?

16. Has your alcohol use ever interfered with your work, care of the children, etc.? How?

17. Have you ever been stopped for drunk driving?

18. Does your spouse (or anyone else in your family) ever worry about your drinking?

19. Have you ever tried to stop drinking? What's the longest you were able to stop?

20. Have you ever been in an alcohol treatment program?

When?

How many times?

How long did you stay away from alcohol afterward?

21. Have you ever had the DT's?

When?

How many times?

22. Does anyone else in your family have a drinking problem?

Who?

Of what sort?

Note that the list of questions represents a general progression from less serious to more serious alcohol use. The evaluator in deciding on a line of questioning will build upon the client's previous responses. For example, if a client responds that he does not drink at the present time, the interviewer should move on to ask about past drinking and holiday drinking.

In order to elicit information about drug use, the evaluator might begin by asking if the respondent ever uses any drugs while drinking. If not, does he ever use drugs at other times. Specific questions may be asked about the following drugs:

1. Marijuana

2. Hashish

3. Amphetamines

4.   LSD, other hallucinogens
5.   Cocaine
6.   Heroin, morphine, codeine
7.   Prescription drugs
8.   Barbiturates
9.   Airplane glue, lighter fluid, paint thinner, nail polish
       remover
10.   Over the counter drugs.

Questions similar to those related to alcohol should be asked about those drugs the respondent says he uses.

Examples of inconsistencies that might be found between the abuser's statements and other sources of information are as follows: A client may deny any but social drinking, yet have a history of arrests for alcohol-related offenses such as drunk driving or giving alcohol to a minor. Substance use is denied, but the welfare caseworker reports complaints to the agency of drunken parties. The respondent may deny alcohol or drug use while appearing high or smelling of alcohol. Sometimes heavy drinkers douse themselves with aftershave or cologne, but the evaluator will usually be able to detect the odor of alcohol underneath. Drug and alcohol use may be denied but the perpetrator has intimate knowledge of the effects of various illegal drugs. The evaluator may note the client has a ruddy complexion resulting from multiple broken veins or the interview elicits a history of liver disease. Information which counters the alleged perpetrator's statements may also come from significant others. In the case below the evaluator noted inconsistencies between the respondent's statements and information from several other sources.

EXAMPLE 13:   Mr. G was alleged to have fondled the genitals of his six-year-old daughter of whom he had custody. He came for an evaluation at 8:30 A.M., reeking of alcohol. When questioned about alcohol use he said he drank ''a couple of beers after work.'' The evaluator said she was sure he had more than a couple in the recent past because of his smell. He acted incredulous and then said lamely that the day before had been pay-day, and he had had four beers to celebrate. The evaluator said she was sure he had a little more to drink than four beers, and also pointed out that one of the allegations in the juvenile court petition was that he took his daughter to bars and kept her out late at night. He responded that these were restaurants. The evaluator noted that the petition specifically mentioned a bar which sold only peanuts, potato chips, and alcohol, and that on at least two occasions he had not taken his daughter home until closing time. Subsequently, information from a friend of the family confirmed the father's alcoholism.

In Mr. G's case his appearance during the interview, his public behavior, and other's statements about him indicated he was not being truthful.

H. History of Mental Illness/Mental Retardation

There are three reasons for exploring the offender's history for mental illness. First, mental problems must be taken into account in assessing overall functioning, a key factor in treatment planning and the prognosis. In addition, certain kinds of mental illness are indicative of poor object relations, and can affect the offender's ability to relate to children and partners. Finally, in a few cases mental illness plays a key role in sexual abuse. A psychotic perpetrator may have specific delusions which justify his sexual abuse (see chapter 3). Also, in a small percentage of cases the perpetrator becomes significantly depressed and his depression plays a role in the sexual abuse. (See also Goodwin, undated, who finds the characteristics of persecutory fantasies and grandiosity in sexual abusers.)

To obtain information about mental illness the evaluator may choose to conduct a mental status exam and should be generally alert for indications of psychotic process. However, in addition the perpetrator should be asked whether he ever has difficulty sleeping, and if so, what the patterns of the sleep problems are; whether he has ever been on medication for sleep problems or his nerves, and if so, the particulars; whether he regards himself as anxious, easily upset, or sad, and if so how he has coped with these feelings; whether he has ever seen someone for personal problems and the specifics of these sessions; and finally, whether he has ever been hospitalized in a mental hospital and, if so, the details. The frequency, duration, and severity of the mental problems will determine their effect on the prognosis. If psychotic delusions have played a role in the sexual abuse, the perpetrator may be psychotic at the time of the evaluation. Questions regarding the victim may well elicit recognizable delusional content. Similarly, significant depression will be easily noticed in the evaluation, for the respondent will evidence a sad affect, will report feelings of hopelessness, and will describe symptoms such as sleep difficulties including early morning waking, loss of appetite, and problems having bowel movements. The evaluator should query how long the depression has existed to determine whether it in part precipitated the sexual abuse or whether it is a result of the sexual abuse or its discovery. It is also very helpful to obtain records of psychiatric hospitalizations and reports from others who may have knowledge of the perpetrator's mental health, because he may either be intact at the time of the evaluation, may be able to "pull himself together" for the interview, or may not be candid about his mental history. In addition a referral to a psychiatrist for further exploration of the perpetrator's mental status may be useful.

The example that follows is one where the evaluator discovered a history of significant mental illness during the assessment.

EXAMPLE 14: Mr. V was accused of sexually molesting the daughters of his girlfriend—Melissa, 3 and Candy, 4. When the girls' mother was interviewed she spoke of how much she relied upon Mr. V for advice about how to manage the children. She felt that the allegations of sexual abuse were all a big mistake and talked about her impending marriage to Mr. V. She said that Mr. V liked the kids and they planned to have a few of their own. She also stated she and Mr. V got along very well, "like two peas in a pod." She did say that sometimes Mr. V had a problem with his nerves.

When Mr. V was interviewed, the first thing that was notable was a thought disorder. His speech was tangential and often what he said did not make sense. When asked what his means of support was he said Social Security. He told the therapist that he qualified for benefits because his father had worked. Though Mr. V was 30, he had never worked. He could not give a reason why, but said he liked tinkering on cars. He said he didn't know why he was considered disabled. The evaluator later asked him about his nerves, indicating that his girlfriend had said sometimes he had bad nerves. He admitted that he did have bad nerves. The evaluator then asked if he'd ever gotten any help for them, and he said "No, unless you count the time I was in the hospital." Further probing revealed that Mr. V had spent the last six years in a mental hospital. He had first been hospitalized at 14 and was in and out several times during his adolescence and early twenties.

The evaluator asked Mr. V if he would sign a release so that she could get his medical records. He agreed although he said he didn't understand why the evaluator needed to see them. Medical records revealed a diagnosis of chronic schizophrenia in remission. In the past he had been episodically quite violent and had attacked hospital personnel. He also had a history of drug use.

In this case, based upon the interview with the children's mother, one would not conclude that Mr. V had serious and chronic mental illness. She described Mr. V and their relationship as if he were a fairly normal person. His presentation during the interview was the first indication of his serious dysfunction, and ultimately a history indicative of very poor prognosis was uncovered.

There are two reasons for exploring mental retardation. Any indication that the offender is mentally retarded means that his overall functioning is significantly impaired, so that the prognosis is not good. Furthermore, the perpetrator's retardation usually means he has few other positive experiences in life and also has impaired judgment, which may lead to repeated incidences of sexual abuse (see chapter 3).

The best way to ascertain mental retardation is by means of an IQ test administered by the evaluator or someone else. However, other indicators may be readily available. The perpetrator may report having attended special education classes or in his responses during the interview indicate his limited intellectual capacity.

I. History of Arrests and Criminal Activity

Knowledge of illegal activity can be useful in understanding the sexual abuse, developing a treatment plan, and in predicting prognosis. The existence of other sex crimes may help the evaluator understand the sexual abuse and prognosis. Criminal behavior may need to be one focus of treatment, and the perpetrator's attitude toward his crimes is indicative of his superego functioning, an important factor in prognosis. On the whole, having a criminal history usually means the prognosis is less good.

Sometimes the alleged abuser will be forthcoming and admit to his past history of criminal activity, but often the evaluator will have to rely upon a police check or data from other sources for this information. A strategy for questioning that sometimes is helpful in eliciting this information from the perpetrator is as follows:

Ask about both adolescent and adult illegal activity.

Ask, first, about anything unlawful that he didn't get caught for. Use probes, as appropriate:

1. Did you ever take something from a store or someone's house?
2. Did you ever joy ride or steal a car?
3. Did you ever damage property?
4. Did you ever physically hurt someone?
5. Did you ever threaten or use a gun, knife, or other weapon on someone?
6. Were you ever involved in a sexual crime?

Second, ask about any times the police were called. Use probes above as appropriate.

Third, ask about arrests. Use probes above as appropriate.

Fourth, ask about being prosecuted. Use probes above as appropriate.

Fifth, ask about convictions and sentences.

The perpetrator in the example below, also discussed in chapter 3, was quite candid and even bragged about his criminal activity.

EXAMPLE 15:   Art, 19, had sexually abused his three-year-old sister. He admitted to "the part with my finger" but not "the part with my dick." When asked whether he had ever been in trouble with the law, he described having been caught stealing a pair of boots from the K-Mart, for which he was on probation. He also bragged about "beating up this mug who made a pass at my girl." For that incident he did 10 days in the county jail. When asked what jail was like, he said he didn't mind it because he "learned some new tricks," "except for this dude who tried to fuck me in the butt." He also bragged about "stealing booze from the liquor store" and not being caught and outracing a policeman who tried to stop him for running a red light.

While Art's crimes are not egregious, his young age, his attitude toward his criminal activity, as well as his other areas of malfunction (not described in this vignette) make his prognosis poor.

J. Sexual History

The perpetrator's sexual history can be very important in confirming a diagnosis of sexual abuse, understanding the dynamics of sexual abuse, making treatment recommendations, and predicting prognosis. Furthermore, attitudes toward sexual behavior can help assess superego functioning; and if the perpetrator is candid, the sexual history can help the interviewer assess the extent of the sexual abuse. In this section, the types of sexual problems found in cases of sexual abuse will be desccribed and illustrated. Following that, techniques for taking a sexual history will be outlined.

Sexual patterns characteristic of some sexual abusers can be generally categorized as presence of atypical sexual behavior and the absence of typical sexual activities. In the former the presence frequently represents a lack of inhibition against and sometimes a compulsion toward sexual behavior of all sorts, including sexual abuse. In the latter, there is an absence of normal sexual outlets, either because they are not available or the abuser cannot negotiate a normal sexual encounter.

The first type of atypical sexual pattern that may be found is a history of having been sexually abused as a child or coming from a sexually abusive family. The dynamics of such a history are described in detail in chapter 4. The case below is an interesting example because the perpetrator was able to make the connection between past abuse and current abuse.

EXAMPLE 16:   Mr. P engaged in interfemoral intercourse with his step-daughters, ages 5 and 7. He reported that when he was about 4 and his sister was 13, she ''used me to masturbate herself.'' He stated that she would take him into her bedroom, undress him and herself, then place him on her stomach and rub his penis against her clitoris in order to gratify herself sexually. This went on for about a year, after which time she told Mr. P it was ''nasty'' and they wouldn't do it again.

Mr. P saw his pattern with his stepdaughters as parallel. He said he used them to ''masturbate myself on.''

A second pattern which may be found in histories of sexual abusers is one where the perpetrator reports experiences of sexual involvement with persons noticeably younger or older than he. While relationships with younger people are usually indicative of sexual attraction to immature childlike objects, relationships with much older people often represent the wish for a parent figure, someone to take care of him. Although perpetrators with the latter type of relationships may perform sexually with partners, often there is not much sexuality in the relationship, and the perpetrator prefers sex at an immature level, with children.

To assess whether there are age differentials between the respondent and his sexual partners, the evaluator in taking his sex history asks, "How old was the youngest person with whom you have ever had sexual relations?" "How old was the oldest person with whom you ever had sexual relations?" The evaluator is looking for an age differential of five years or more. Sometimes a man in his thirties admits having had a relationship with a 17- or 18-year-old. Other times the respondent describes a pattern during late adolescence of having sexual encounters with 11-, 12-, or 13-year-olds. The respondent may reveal this type of sexual relationship fairly freely, but remain guarded and secretive about a more specifically sexually abusive relationship. When asking about older partners, the evaluator is looking for a series of such relationships and sometimes a stated preference for older women. The respondent in the case below denied the sexual abuse but admitted to statutory rape.

EXAMPLE 17:   Mr. L, age 35, who was accused of fondling a seven-year-old neighbor child, related that the youngest girl he had ever had sex with was 13. He said that he had met the girl at a roller skating rink he frequented, ''mostly just to watch the kids skate.'' About a year before the involvement with the seven-year-old, he met the girl at the rink and had sex with her in the back seat of his car in the process of taking her home.

He did this on several subsequent occasions until he was confronted by her father. Mr. L said it was only then that he found out the girl was 13. He said he thought she was at least 16. Her father was younger than he was.

Mr. L's admission of pleasure in watching children skate is strongly suggestive of pedophilia. Moreover, the age differential between himself and the 13- or even 16-year-old skater is very great.

A third pattern for which the evaluator needs to probe is unusually promiscuous behavior. For some men who sexually abuse children, many interpersonal interactions are sexualized. They may speak of having sex several times a day with their wives, often at awkward times, such as when the children are demanding attention or when the wife is attempting to engage in some other absorbing activity. They may engage in semi-public sex, such as fondling their partners' intimate parts in a bar or having sexual intercourse in a park. They may describe having concurrent affairs with several women and report sexual experimentation such as nudism, mate swapping, or group sex. Mr. H was fairly forthcoming when being questioned and evidences a pattern of unusually promiscuous sexual behavior, as described below.

> EXAMPLE 18:   Mr. H admitted to fellating his 10- and 12-year old sons and to teaching them to masturbate while reading *Playboy* magazine. In responding to questions about his sexual history, with no hesitation he described having to "suck my wife off" all of the time because she preferred that to sexual intercourse. He would do this 3 to 5 times a week but states it left him "horny" so he would "bang the maid, Elsie."
>
> When Mr. H divorced his first wife, he reported that he was "giving it to every kind of woman, black or white." He met his second wife in a bar and took her that night to a motel. He reported the motel had pornographic movies, and from that time on, he regularly took her to motels with pornographic movies. They also took part in group sex encounters which Mr. H readily described, relating that "watching two women making it really turned me on and then I could keep going all night."
>
> He described following his second wife into the basement and engaging in posterior entry intercourse while she was attempting to fold the laundry. The bedroom in his home had pornographic posters, and one of his sons reported watching his father masturbate the family dog to ejaculation. When asked about this, he said he liked the dog and felt sorry for him because he didn't have a girl dog.
>
> In trying to explain his sexual activities with his sons, he first said that it was his duty as a father to educate his sons sexually. Later he cried and said he was drunk and confused when he did these things and just wanted to show his sons how much he loved them.

Mr. H was unusually candid both about his sex life and his sexual abuse. His statements help us to understand that sex for him was the way he related to anyone (including the dog) for whom he had positive feelings.

A fourth and related pattern to look for in evaluation is unusual or bizarre sexual practices. Sometimes these are encounters in which the perpetrator is very regressed. Other times they are patterns of sexual deviation such as transvestism, sadistic or masochistic activities, coprophilia and coprophagia, zoophilia, fetishism, or certain kinds of homosexual encounters. Mr. H, described in the above case example was, among other things, a zoophiliac. Mr. D in the case below enjoys wearing women's clothes.

EXAMPLE 19: Mr. D had been married three times. He had two sons by his first wife. She reported that he got her to make him shifts which he wore around the house. He also liked to wear ladies' undergarments, especially panties and stockings. She divorced him because these practices began to bother her. After the divorce, their older son, age 6, said his father would fondle his penis. Mr. D's first wife successfully prevented further contact between father and sons.

Mr. D moved to another state and married a woman who had two daughters. They had a third daughter. Mr. D and his second wife worked the line at an auto factory, but they worked different shifts. One night she came home early because she was feeling sick and surprised Mr. D in a pair of queen-sized pantyhose and high heeled shoes. She then recalled that her panties had kept disappearing. With questioning Mr. D admitted to taking them and wearing them under his coveralls to work because "they gave me a good feeling." He gave them all back and promised to stop cross-dressing.

Soon thereafter the D's daughter complained that her pee pee hurt and eventually told her mother that her father played with her pee pee when they watched TV. This caused the second Mrs. D to divorce her husband. He took all her underclothing when he packed and left.

Mr. D married for the third time. He was by then 40. The second Mrs. D told the third Mrs. D what her new husband's habits were. The third Mrs. D did not believe it. However when they had been married a year, she found a black lace teddy, size extra large, stuffed into a pillow case inside a container hidden in the basement rafters. About four months later she borrowed her husband's truck because her car was in the shop. She reached down to adjust the seat and discovered four pairs of lace underpants (baby blue, black, and red), two lace camisoles, a petticoat, all size large, and a pair of high heels, size 12. She confronted her husband, accusing him of having a girlfriend, a large one. He denied any knowledge of the clothing but said he let his buddy borrow the truck at lunch time to take his girl out. Mrs. D did not pursue the matter.

Soon both of the third Mrs. D's children began to complain of fondling by Mr. D. At that point, the third Mrs. D decided that perhaps allegations by the second Mrs. D of Mr. D's transvestism and sexual abuse were not merely vicious lies.

The case of Mr. D is somewhat extreme because his pattern of cross-dressing and sexual abuse persisted over three marriages. It appears that both the feel of women's garments on his body and the touching of children's genitals are exciting to him, but one does not precipitate the other. A finding of unrelated sexual aberrations has been made on other cases in our sample.

A fifth type of sexual behavior the evaluator should be sensitive to is sex crimes (other than the sexual abuse). These include rape, exhibitionism, voyeurism, obscene phone calls, and sexual exploitation of adults or children. The two cases, briefly described below, are illustrative.

EXAMPLE 20:   Mr. J, also cited in chapter 3, sexually abused his 12-and 14-year-old stepdaughters. He engaged in anal intercourse on one occasion with the 12-year-old and had genital intercourse with the 14-year-old on four separate occasions. He had two previous convictions for rape. One involved a 16-year-old girl, when he was 23, for which he had served six years in prison. The other victim was about his age.

EXAMPLE 21:   Mr. K had an incestuous relationship with his daughter beginning when she was about 9 months old. When she was about 3, he began making pornographic movies in which they both performed along with three other men and their daughters.

The two cases just cited both suggest a general absence of superego controls related to sexual exploitation.

In the category of absence of sexual outlets, the first pattern to be observant for is one mentioned already, sexual dysfunction in the marriage. If the couple is questioned together, however, frequently they will not give a candid response. More accurate information is likely to be provided in the context of a sexual history, as in the case example below which is also discussed in chapter 4.

EXAMPLE 22:   Mr. and Mrs. B, ages 47 and 48, had been married 28 years, and have had eight children. Mr. B's 15-year-old daughter alleged he had engaged in fondling of her breasts and genitals and that he had done this to two of her sisters. Mr. B suffered from diabetes, a heart condition, and a bad back. He was also very obese. He could not put on his shoes and could not climb stairs. In a joint interview, when the B's were asked about their sexual relationship, Mrs. B described it as "very good" adding that they both enjoyed sex and had intercourse about three times a week and that this had been their pattern throughout the 28 years of their marriage. When asked if her husband's multiple disabilities affected his capacity, at first she said "somewhat" but then said, "not really very much." Her husband said nothing but when directly questioned he grunted agreement with his wife.

In contrast in responding to questions about sexual activity in an individual interview, Mr. B said that he could no longer maintain an erection. Therefore, he and his wife had not had sexual intercourse for the last 3 years. He said 3 years previously he had injured his back on the job and was now certified as disabled. Before that time he had suffered with diabetes and a heart condition which had reduced his sexual function but usually he could "manage it about once a week or so." After his accident, he was at home all the time. He said that his wife then became more sexually demanding, but he was "even more put off by her than before," adding, "She don't interest me 'tall."

Mr. B had a passive-aggressive component to his personality which was quite compatible with his inability to satisfy his wife sexually. Further, a pattern of impotence is consistent with the type of the sexual abuse which consisted of fondling.

Finally, the history of some abusers will reveal no sexual outlets and/or little sexual experience. The absence of sexual outlets is found in perpetrators of all ages, while lack of sexual experience is more frequently the case with young offenders. Often men of this type feel inadequate sexually or overwhelmed by the prospect of a sexual experience with an adult and as a consequence fall into or seek out sexual relationships with young children. Other times their circumstances or change in circumstances lead them to approach children. The following example also mentioned in chapter 4 is illustrative.

EXAMPLE 23:   Mr. A was 19 and had just married a woman of 32 who had four children, including daughters 7 and 11. He reported having sexual intercourse three times before being seduced by the woman who later became his wife. When he was 16, he had a girlfriend whom he dated for about 6 months. They had intercourse once and after that they never spoke again. His two other encounters were at parties with girls he did not know. He was quite overwhelmed by his wife and her sexual experience. They married within a year of their meeting, and before they had been married a month his wife was hospitalized with uterine cancer and had a hysterectomy. While taking care of the children when she was in the hospital he began to fondle the two girls.

Mr. A had little sexual experience before being thrust into a situation of constant sexual activity. This and his wife's illness, which no doubt he associated with their sexual activity, probably triggered regression and sexual attraction to the children.

Taking a Sexual History. The sexual history taking might be prefaced by a statement like: "Now I'm going to ask you a lot of questions about your sex life. Some of them might seem irrelevant, but they help me a lot in understanding you as a person." Since there is strong

likelihood that the respondent will be guarded, the evaluator tries to promote candor by dealing with the material in a matter of fact manner. In
addition, as with substance abuse, probing with a lot of specific questions and being alert for inconsistencies are techniques that can document a problematic sexual history. A chronological approach is helpful,
asking the respondent to describe his activities in a sequence of five year
time blocks, starting with the first five years of his life and ending with
the present (see table 7.1).[1] These questions should be employed in a
manner similar to the substance use history. They are sample questions
and it is not necessary to ask all of them. Further, it may be advisable not
to deal in depth with this sensitive area in the initial interview with the
perpetrator.

   In the case below, asking about incremental periods of five years
reveals quite a lot of important information.

> EXAMPLE 24:   Mr. F had been married four times and had sexually
> fondled two daughters, one stepdaughter, and a son. He also had been
> caught masturbating in his car at a school playground. He was asked what
> he learned about sex as a child, and he said his parents never brought it
> up. His first information came from an eighth grade health class. He had
> no awareness growing up that his parents had a sexual relationship.
> Although he was nine when his youngest sister was born, he had not
> known how babies were made.
>   When asked if he could remember any sexual experiences during
> the first five years of his life, he recalled a man fondling him in the park in
> exchange for candy. This happened several times and eventually his
> father followed Mr. F to the park and caught the man. Mr. F could recall
> being very frightened that his father would seriously injure the man. His
> parents never reported the matter to the police and never discussed it with
> him. He said when he thinks of it now he has "no emotion."
>   Between the ages of 6 and 10, he could recall having a crush on a
> female cousin a year older than he. They showed one another their
> genitals. This happened once at a family gather and she was wearing a
> pink lace dress. Everytime he sees pink lace, he is reminded of this en-
> counter. He admitted that he went to school playgrounds hoping to see lit-
> tle girls in lace.
>   When asked about experiences between 10 and 15, Mr. F recalled
> masturbating with a group of friends in a carpentry shed. He denied any
> sexual contact with the other boys and asserted he was not sexually
> aroused by them. He insisted that this group masturbation happened only
> once. He did not date during this time period.
>   Between the ages of 15 and 20 Mr. F reports his first intercourse.
> He said he liked it and was orgasmic. He does not know if his partner en-
> joyed it. He was smitten by the girl but she dropped him after the first sex-

Table 7.1 Sex History

Age Block	Questions and Probes	W/Whom	Sex/Age of Partners	Relation-ship	Activity	# of Times	Comments
0-5	1. Up through the time you were 5 yr do you remember or were you told about any sexual experience you had?						
	a) This is a time most children "play doctor." Did you ever engage in this type of game or activity?						
	b) Did any older children do sexual things to you or with you before age 6?						
	c) Did any adult do sexual things to you or with you before age 6?						
	d) A lot of kids start to masturbate during these years. Did you?						
6-10 yr	2. From 6 through 10 yr old do you remember or has anyone told you about any sexual experiences you had?						
	a) This is a time when children often sexually experiment with each other. Do you remember being involved in any sexual experimentation?						

b) Did you have any sexual experiences with older children before 11?

c) Did you have any sexual experiences with adults before age 11?

11-15

3. Up through the time you were 15 yrs old, what sexual experiences did you have?

a) Many people have their first sexual intercourse during this time. Was that true for you?

b) This is a period of time for many people of first really getting interested in sex. Many people experiment quite a bit sexually. This may involve both homosexual and heterosexual activities with relatives or non-relatives. Did you engage in any of these kinds of activities before the age of 16?

c) Did you have any sexual experiences with adults before you were 16?

d) Did you have any sexual experiences with younger children before you were 16?

(Table 7.1 Continued)

Age Block	Questions and Probes	W/Whom	Sex/Age of Partners	Relation-ship	Activity	# of Times	Comments
16-20	4. Up through the time you were 20 what sexual experiences did you have?						
	a) If you did not experience sexual inter-course earlier, did you during this time period in your life?						
	b) If you did not experiment sexually earlier, did you in this time period of your life?						
	c) During this time were you involved with any homosexual sex?						
	d) Did you have any sexual experiences with person five years older or younger than you?						
21-25	5. Up through the age of 25 what sexual experiences did you have?						
	a) If you did not experience sexual inter-course earlier, did you during this period in your life?						
	b) Did you experiment sexually during this period in your life?						

c) Did you have any steady partners during this period of your life?

d) Did you have sex with anyone five or more years older or younger than yourself?

26-30 6. Up through the age of 30 what sexual experiences did you have?

a) If you did not experience sexual intercourse earlier, did you during this period in your life?

b) Did you experiment sexually during this period of your life?

c) Did you have any steady partners during this period of your life?

d) Did you have sex with anyone five or more years older/younger than yourself?

Table 7.1 Continued

In case we have missed some activity, there are a few more questions I would like to ask:

1. How is your sexual relationship with your wife?
    Can you describe the kinds of sexual activity you engage(d) in and their approximate frequency?
    Has this relationship been more or less the same over the years or changing?
2. Have you had extramarital affairs? If so, please describe.
3. Have you had any homosexual experiences you haven't mentioned so far?
4. How old was the oldest person you ever had a sexual encounter with? How old were you at the time?
5. How young was the youngest person you ever had a sexual encounter with? How old were you at the time?
6. Have you ever paid for sex? Or have you ever been paid for sex?
7. Have you ever been involved in group sex?
8. Have you ever been involved in mate swapping?
9. Was there ever a time when you had a sexual encounter with an animal?
10. Do you ever do sexual things to your partner in public places?
11. Have you ever been arrested for a sex crime?
12. What were you taught about sex when you were growing up?

ual encounter for someone else. He was devastated and followed the girl and her new boyfriend around for almost a year. He described feeling extremely frustrated sexually during this time.

From the information he provided in the remainder of the sex history, it appeared that his behavior toward his first girlfriend was repeated in his four marriages. He would fall madly in love with a woman and marry her after a short courtship, (two weeks to six months). The marriages lasted only a short time. Then his wives would leave or have affairs. He would badger them or beg them to return. These would be very frustrating times for him. He said when he did not have a partner or his partner was being unfaithful, he would be desperate for sex. It would be during these periods that he would sexually abuse his children.

Mr. F's sexual history was instructive in understanding his attraction to children on the playground, in uncovering the prototype of the sexual abuse of his children, and in appreciatring the dynamics of his multiple marriages.

K. Discussing the Sexual Abuse

It is usually advisable to discuss the sexual abuse at the end of the interview. At this point in the evaluation process the interviewer should know whether or not the perpetrator committed the sexual acts. In substantiated cases the evaluator asserts her belief that the perpetrator sexually abused the child.

If the evaluator has obtained an audio or video tape of the victim in which the child makes the allegations in a straightforward way, this should be played. The tape may lead to a confession. Further, the alleged abuser's emotional response to the tape is useful in predicting prognosis. Those who became upset and agitated are more likely to respond to treatment than those who do not. When a compelling tape does not exist, the evaluator should summarize the child's statements.

Most perpetrators will respond to confrontation with denial. In such instances, there are some arguments the evaluator can employ, although they may not precipitate confession either. The evaluator can query what the child's motivation might be to lie, pointing out that there is rarely any benefit to the victim from making the allegation. The offender's response here can be predictive of prognosis. If the perpetrator derogates the victim by describing her in very negative terms, his prognosis is poor. If the abuser can give no reasons for a child making up such a story or describes the child in positive terms, the prognosis is better. An appeal to the offender to think about the child and how difficult this is for the child, not only to be sexually abused but then to have him deny it, is another approach that may be effective.

The interviewer might also point out that she has seen many victims of sexual abuse and they do not make up stories. In contrast, persons who engage in sexual abuse of children very frequently deny it. This argument may be persuasive, or it may lead the perpetrator to ask about other cases. He may ask what happens to offenders or what the consequences of sexual abuse are for children. This line of discussion affords the evaluator the opportunity to discuss treatment for the abuser and the victim. The evaluator may feel comfortable suggesting that ultimately the family could be reunited. Or the evaluator may be able to say that she will try to prevent criminal prosecution so the respondent can get treatment. But in some cases, the evaluator will not be willing to give such assurances.

The evaluator may want to assert her belief that sexual abusers are not monsters, that many people who love their children become confused or have problems which lead them to sexually abuse children. Further, an observation that many abusers are afraid to admit because of what others will think of them may lead to a confession.

A more coercive tack can also be taken. The interviewer may say that the case must be reported to the police, and describe the police investigation. The evaluator may also discuss lie detector tests and juvenile or criminal court action.

Any of these approaches may lead to a confession on the part of the perpetrator, but admission is not common. Sometimes these statements will cause delayed responses. For example, if the evaluator describes in some detail the court process, a day before the trial, the perpetrator may confess.

There are, however, a variety of kinds of admission that may be forthcoming at the time of the interview. For example, there may be an indirect admission. An indirect admission is one where the offender in some way communicates the truth of the child's statements while not confessing. The following are examples of indirect admissions.

EXAMPLE 25: Mr. A who was a drug abuser said he didn't remember what he did when he was high.

EXAMPLE 26: Mr. B said he had rolled over in bed at night and fondled his daughter's vulva, thinking she was his wife.

EXAMPLE 27: Mr. D said he would admit to some of the allegations in the petition so his daughter would not have to testify.

EXAMPLE 28: Mr. E who was accused of genital penetration of his three-year-old daughter on multiple occasions said that one time while giving her a bath, she slipped and his finger went up her vagina.

From the clinical standpoint statements of this nature are tantamount to an admission. The evaluator should so label them for the perpetrator. In communicating with other professionals, such as attorneys, police, judges, and child protection staff, such statements should be interpreted as the equivalent of admissions. The prognosis is fair when there is an indirect admission.

In other instances, the perpetrator will make a partial confession. He may admit to a less serious type of sexual abuse where the criminal penalties are not as severe.

EXAMPLE 29: Mr. F, who was accused of intercourse and fellatio with his 12-year-old daughter, admitted to fondling. His attorney assured him he would only get probation and be required to go to treatment for fondling.

Another type of response is a direct admission by offenders who do not deny the sexual abuse because they do not see anything wrong in it, as in the case below:

EXAMPLE 30: Mr. O engaged in a game with his four-year-old daughter and ten-year-old stepdaughter which was called "pussy." He would chase the children until he caught them and then make them lie on the couch and rub their vulvas. He told the evaluator he did not know what the fuss was about.

Yet another response to confrontation is to blame the victim, asserting that she seduced him or that she wanted to do it. Alternatively, offenders may blame their wives. In the example below, the wife was blamed.

EXAMPLE 31: Mr. P said that his wife would refuse him sex when he would try to wake her up at night. Because of this he would have to go to his 14-year-old daughter. She didn't mind being wakened.

When the offender discounts the behavior or denies his responsibility as in this case, the prognosis for intervention is not very good, and his response suggests poor superego functioning.

Another response by the abuser is to feel some guilt, but not to be extremely sorry or repentant. He may feel it is sufficient to acknowledge that he did something wrong, but then want people to forget about it and let him go about his life. These offenders usually believe they will never do it again. The likelihood of their abstaining without any treatment is not good.

Finally, in response to confrontation, some men will confess and feel terribly guilty. They accept responsibility and are very worried about the effect upon the victim and others. These responses are indicative of good superego functioning and good prognosis. Mr. H's response is illustrative. His case is also discussed in chapter 3.

EXAMPLE 32: Mr. H confessed to sexual abuse of eleven boys. He admitted to all the charges against him so that the boys would not have to testify. He made arrangements for his wife to go to Florida to be with her family and agreed to have no further contact with her if that was her wish. He attempted to commit suicide by driving his car over an embankment. He was sorry when he was not successful, but from prison made arrangements to see an expert in sexual abuse to come to understand how much he had damaged the boys and why he had molested them. He also made arrangements for treatment of the boys.

In Mr. H's case, not only did he feel guilt but he actively sought ways to reduce the impact of his sexual abuse on those affected.

CONCLUSION

Interviewing alleged sexual abusers is psychologically very difficult for
most clinicians. Feelings about people who sexually abuse children and
about sexual behavior can interfere with the evaluation. If the evaluator
responds to these feelings she may not systematically explore crucial
topics and fail to assess the workability of the perpetrator.

A methodical and thorough history taking of the alleged abuser
can protect the evaluator from inappropriate reactions. By beginning
with fairly neutral information such as that concerning family composition, work history, social supports, and the respondent's family of
origin, the evaluator can get to know the alleged perpetrator as a person
and find out about his overall functioning and his superego functioning
before addressing more sensitive issues, particularly the extent of his sexual deviancy and sexual abuse. Placing the respondent's deviant behavior
in such a context assists the evaluator in developing a more objective
view of the offender as a person, in predicting prognosis more accurately, and in making a better intervention plan.

NOTE

1. For a useful guide to sexual histories, see Pomeroy et al. (1982). We have used
their work in developing our own procedure.

CHAPTER EIGHT

Interviewing the Mother

I. INTRODUCTION

The mother of the victim will be a key figure in understanding the sexual abuse, and her role and functioning will have considerable influence on case handling. In most cases, the mother of the victim is not the perpetrator; therefore, the assumption being made in this chapter is that the mother is the nonabusive parent. If there are allegations against the mother, the interview process should combine topics found in this chapter with those just described in chapter 7.

The closer the mother's relationship is to the perpetrator, the more necessary an in-depth interview with the mother becomes. Thus very extensive exploration of her functioning is crucial in intrafamilial sexual abuse cases. If the sexual abuser is someone who is outside the family, does not have much contact with the victim, and the mother has responded appropriately, an in-depth interview with the mother is usually not necessary. The contents of this chapter are therefore most applicable in cases where the mother has a primary relationship with the offender.

There are several goals for the maternal interview. These are to assess the mother's overall functioning; to obtain the mother's view of the perpetrator; to assess the level of the mother's dependence upon him; to evaluate the quality of the relationship between the mother and the victim(s) and incidentally, between her and nonvictim children; and to determine how protective the mother has been of the victim(s) in response to knowledge about the sexual abuse. These last three areas—independence, nurturance, and protectiveness—are discussed at length in chapter 10. The interviewer will use data gathered in this interview to understand the dynamics of the sexual abuse, to plan intervention, and to make a prediction regarding prognosis.

II. PROCESS AND CONTENT OF THE INTERVIEW

As noted in the discussion of the perpetrator interview, a good rule is to begin with generally less threatening material and progress to more emotionally laden material. The content of the chapter progresses in this fashion. However, the mother's emotional reaction to topics will vary from case to case. For example, if the mother believes the child's statements regarding the sexual abuse, it may be quite natural and even tension reducing to talk about these early. In contrast, if the mother does not believe them, discussing the child's assertions and the interviewer's belief that they are true can be quite threatening and should be delayed until an alliance with the mother has been established.

The following topics should be covered in the maternal interview: (a) current living situation; (b) level of education and employment history; (c) family background; (d) social supports; (e) relationship(s) with partner(s), including the alleged perpetrator; (f) children and relationship with children; (g) substance use, mental illness, and illegal activity; (h) sexual history; and (i) the sexual abuse. The reader will observe there are many parallels with the data gathered from offenders. Techniques for gathering these data will be discussed as well as the rationale for needing the information.

A. Current Living Situation

The interviewer needs to ascertain who is living in the household and how family members are financially supported. While these data may come from other sources, the mother is likely to be the most reliable source of such facts and her information may be quite enlightening. Her statements will help the evaluator assess whether there was opportunity for sexual abuse, possible perpetrators, if there is still a question about this, other potential victims, the adequacy of the living situation, and how independent the mother is of the alleged perpetrator.

Sometimes discrepancies arise among the reports various people provide about the living situation. These may be between reports from children and parents, between statements of spouses, or between community observations and those offered by family members. Types of cases where discrepancies commonly arise are noncustodial parent cases and stepfather-LTP cases.

The following case in which the parents are separated and the father is the alleged perpetrator illustrates the type of discrepancy that might be found.

EXAMPLE 1: Mr. P's two daughters, aged four and six, alleged that their father made them play a game called "peanut," in which they fondled his penis until it became erect and then he would ask them to eat the "peanut" (suck his penis) until the juice came out.

Mr. P stated that he hardly ever saw his girls, that his wife prevented him from having his visits by making plans for the children on his weekends. He mentioned particularly that his wife sent the kids to her mother's on his weekends. He also said that when he did have his kids, he took them to his mother's because his wife would not allow his mother to see the children at other times.

When Mrs. P was interviewed, she stated that not only did her husband have the children every other weekend from Friday night until Sunday afternoon, but also that for about six months he had been their custodian and she saw them only on weekends. She said this came about after her husband made a complaint that Mrs. P was living with her boyfriend, who was an ex-convict. The Friend of the Court investigated and found this to be the case. He gave custody of the girls to Mr. P. At the time, Mr. P was unemployed and got AFDC while the girls were there. According to Mrs. P, when Mr. P returned to work, he gave the children back to her but did not pay child support.

A check with the Friend of the Court substantiated the change of custody reported by Mrs. P. It also revealed no complaints filed by Mr. P regarding his visitation but charges made by Mrs. P of nonpayment of support.

In this case example, not only did the information provided by Mrs. P allow the evaluator to determine that Mr. P had opportunity to play the peanut game but it also enabled the interviewer to make a determination that the mother's statements were more credible.

As noted above, data on current living situation also will assist the evaluator in determining the potential of the mother to be independent of the alleged perpetrator. In one case in our sample the mother and her living-together-partner, who was the father of the youngest of four children, resided in a house which was being purchased in the mother's father's name. The down payment had been made by her father, and the mother was making the house payments from her AFDC. Her boyfriend was unemployed and did odd jobs. When she came to believe two of her daughters had been fondled by him, she ejected him from the house.

This case is in contrast with another in our sample. A ten-year-old girl was fondled and subjected to cunnilingus by the mother's living together partner. The mother was attending beauty school and her tuition was being paid from a loan in her LTP's name. Although initially she believed her daughter and took her to the psychiatric emergency clinic when she found out about the abuse, she later persuaded her daughter to say the sexual abuse was a dream. She allowed her daughter to be seen briefly by a therapist, but she then married the LTP and refused to take her daughter back to therapy.

In both of these cases, the economic situation played a key role in the extent of the mother's independence. For additional discussion of the importance of independence/dependence of the mother, see chapter 10.

B. The Mother's Education and Employment History

While a mother's education and employment history are not as salient to overall functioning as they are for perpetrators, they are nevertheless good indicators of ability. A mother who reports an eighth or ninth grade education is telling the interviewer that she had encountered significant difficulties in a major arena of childhood functioning. It is then necessary to explore why she did not go further in school. Such a finding has different implications for different types of clients. If the mother is of minority status, particularly if she was raised in the South, low educational achievement is a less negative finding than if she is white. Similarly, if she was raised in poverty, such a finding is not so worrisome as it would be if her family had adequate income. Lack of education may also be a result of early pregnancy or psychological or behavioral dysfunction during adolescence. Conversely, if the mother finished high school or has some education beyond high school, that tells the evaluator that she has some strengths in an important area.

Her work history is additional information for assessing her overall functioning. A history of employment commensurate with her skill level suggests to the interviewer that the mother can hold her own in the world of work. However, if she has many children, it is unrealistic to expect her to have a substantial work history. In addition, as mentioned in chapter 4, extensive employment may indicate underinvolvement in the family and therefore may not be a strength. For this reason, it is important to assess why the mother works.

Education and employment, in addition to being indicators of general functioning, are indicators of the mother's capacity to act independently of the perpetrator. If she has a means of supporting herself, she will be able to be more independent in other ways, including resisting his sexually abusive behavior, extricating herself from the relationship with him, and supporting herself and the children.

C. Family Background

The mother's family background can be quite useful in providing indicators of overall functioning, in understanding the dynamics of the sexual abuse, and in making treatment plans. The interviewer explores material customarily covered in any mental health assessment, but with more emphasis placed upon the mother's relationship with each parent and sexual experiences during the mother's childhood. With regard to parental relationships, discipline techniques of each parent, the nature of the relationship with each parent, and the relative closeness to each parent are areas that should be investigated. Clinical literature (Lustig et al. 1965; Kaufman et al. 1954) suggests that many mothers whose children are sexually abused come from harsh, unprotective backgrounds. Further, some authors (Machotka et al. 1967; Kaufman et al. 1954) report mothers in sexually abuse families had distant and cold relationships with their own mothers, and this experience is then reflected in their relationships with their daughters. Moreover, the mother's father may have been a domineering man who was physically abusive to his wife, and sometimes his children, and the mother chooses a similar partner who also sexually abuses her children. Although there is some disagreement in the literature (Borgman 1984; Sarles 1975; Lustig et al. 1965; Herman 1981; Lukianowitz 1978) about the prevalence of these dynamics, they appear to play a role in some cases.

The case of Sally J below is an extreme example of the kind of deprivation and harsh childhood some mothers experience, and of the role of a traumatic sexual experience.

EXAMPLE 2:   Sally J, 19, is white and has a biracial daughter, Debbie, age 3. Some of the information about Sally's background comes directly from her. The rest was added by her adoptive mother.

When asked about her family, Sally said, "Which one? I lived with lotsa families." She said, "There's the one that adopted me when I got out of York Woods (a psychiatric hospital for adolescents). There's my real mom. She used to beat me with a broom. Then they took me away when I was ten. There was lotsa different people I lived with before I went to York Woods."

Sally's adoptive mother, Mrs. J, said that she understood that Sally's biological mother was an alcoholic and a prostitute. Sally had been made to stay outside when her mother had men in the apartment. This could happen any hour of the day or night. Sometimes Sally would have a place to go but other times she would have to sleep in the hall.

Sally missed a lot of school because she had no adequate clothing. When Sally was removed from her mother's home, she was placed in a shelter where she stayed for three months before going to foster care. She was in many different foster homes. In one home she was beaten by the foster father for stealing. In another home, she was sexually victimized by two black youths who were three years older than she.

When she was thirteen she was hospitalized at York Woods. Two years later she was discharged into an adoptive home. Initially she did reasonably well there. Then she then began drinking and using drugs. Soon thereafter she ran away to live with her boyfriend. However, she still maintained contact with her adoptive mother.

When sexual abuse of Sally's three-year-old daughter was reported, initially it was not clear whether the child's father or one of the other men Sally had relationships with, all of whom were black, had sexually abused her.

In Sally's case, not only was she rejected and neglected by her mother, but she formed no attachments in foster care because she was moved so many times and was victimized there. It was really too late for her to compensate for this deprivation when she was adopted. There is also a significant relationship between her victimization by two black youths in foster care, her choice of black partners, and later victimization of her daughter by a black man.

Clinicians and researchers (e.g., Greenberg 1978; Goodwin 1982) have found that the mother's traumatic childhood sexual experiences can be an important factor in the sexual abuse of her own children. The dynamics of the mother's sexual trauma are discussed extensively in chapter 4. However, they may result in her choosing a partner who is sexually abusive and can affect her ability to protect her children. This is a difficult area to explore, and the evaluator may wish to delay this discussion until later in the interview during the sexual history taking.

D. Social Supports

Understanding the mother's support system is another important area of assessment. This may help the evaluator to assess the dynamics of the sexual abuse, be of assistance in treatment planning, and aid in predicting prognosis.

As noted in chapter 4, social isolation may play a role in causing or prolonging sexual abuse. On the other hand, if the mother does have a support system, she usually will be better able emotionally to handle the sexually abusive situation. When the people available to the mother are professionals, they may be able to provide treatment. If she and her children need to leave the perpetrator for their protection, her support system may be able to offer her a refuge. Finally, if she had good social supports, she will be less dependent upon the perpetrator and more able to seek what is best for herself and her children.

If the evaluator has just completed an exploration of the mother's family background, questions about her current relationships with her family can follow. How the mother gets along with her husband's/partner's family is also relevant. In addition, the interviewer might explore relationships with friends, work mates, and neighbors. Inquiry into contacts with agencies and helping professionals should also be pursued. Such queries as "Who have you told about the sexual abuse and what were their responses?" and "Is there any other person you and your children can go to stay with during this crisis?" may provide pertinent information. More general questions like "Who can you go to if you have financial problems?" "Who do you turn to if you are having difficulties with your children?" and "Who would help if you got sick or had to go to the hospital?" can assist the evaluator in understanding the mother's ongoing social supports.

The case example of the F family illustrates how important social supports can be.

EXAMPLE 3: Psychologically Mrs. F was very dependent upon her husband. She had quit high school in the eleventh grade to marry him and for most of the 14 years of their marriage, he worked steadily. He was very physically and verbally abusive to her and her three children, but Mrs. F stayed with her husband because she wanted her children to have a father and she had an unconscious need to be told what she could and could not do. Mr. F was very good at fulfilling that need. Mrs. F said that her husband was much smarter than she and could "talk circles around me." He always won their disputes because he could convince Mrs. F that he was right and she was wrong. Mrs. F did not tell her parents or sister about her husband's behavior beause she was afraid they would tell her to leave him.

After eleven years of marriage, Mr. F lost his job because of absenteeism related to excessive drinking. The reduced income would have imposed considerable hardship except that Mrs. F was able to call upon her parents to take over their house payments. As her husband continued to be unemployed, he drank more and and Mrs. F did start complaining to her sister, but told her sister not to tell her parents.

Then Mrs. F's daughters, ages eleven and twelve, told her their father had been fondling them and making them fellate him for two and three years respectively. Mrs. F immediately fled, taking her children to her sister's house. After she had been there three nights, her husband showed up and threatened to shoot everybody. He said he had a gun in his car. The police were called but Mr. F left before they got there. Mrs. F and the girls then went to her parents' house, which was less isolated. With their assistance, she filed for a divorce and got an order for him to vacate the marital home.

In the F case, having reliable and supportive relatives seems to have been crucial. It is questionable whether Mrs. F could have responded protectively to the discovery of the sexual abuse without the availability of her relatives.

E. Relationships with Partners

The mother's relationship with partners, including that with the perpetrator if he is or was a partner, should be explored. However, even when the alleged perpetrator is, say, a grandparent, her pattern of intimate relationships with men should be examined.

Understanding these relationships can be helpful in several ways. First, they are an indicator of the mother's overall functioning. Second, her information regarding the offender can assist the evaluator in assessing her level of dependence upon him, his personality and functioning, and his treatment prognosis. Third, the evaluator may discover a pattern in the mother's relationships with men that is related to the dynamics of the sexual abuse and her prognosis for protecting the children. One pattern found in some cases is a mother who has relationships with a series of men who are sexually and otherwise exploitative of children. (For a discussion of these dynamics, see chapter 3). If this is the pattern the diagnosis uncovers, her relationships with men will need to be a focus for treatment. Another pattern one may find is one where previous partners have been quite dysfunctional and the present one, despite his sexually abusive pattern, is on the whole better functioning. In such cases, the mother may side with the perpetrator and discount the child's statements (again see chapter 3 for additional discussion). Uncovering these patterns helps the evaluator understand the mother's nonprotective response, and helping the mother develop insight into these dynamics becomes one focus of treatment.

At the time the mother is interviewed the information she provides about her current partner, if he is the alleged perpetrator, may be distorted by her reactions to the sexual abuse. If she has decided to support her partner, she may obscure his faults and lie about material related to the sexual abuse. Alternatively, if she has decided to align herself with her children, the picture she may present of him may overemphasize his negative qualities. The former response poses a greater obstacle to diagnosis than the latter. Because the data regarding the abuser may be colored, it is important also to explore the mother's relationships with other partners. This information should enable the evaluator to obtain a more accurate view of the mother's intimate relationships, to determine trends in these relationships, and to compare the functioning of the different partners.

Areas of the relationship that should be explored are how the couple met, the length of time between meeting and sexual intimacy, the division of labor in the relationship, the quality of the relationship, good aspects versus bad ones, their sexual relationship, the partner's relationship with the children, any violence with her or the children, his work history, his use of drugs or alcohol, his involvement in criminal activity, and the reason they parted, if they have. The reader will note that a number of these areas are ones also explored directly with the offender.

The following case example illustrates patterns in a mother's relationships with men.

EXAMPLE 4:   Jane got pregnant at 15 and married the father of the baby, Mr. G, under pressure from both his parents and hers. He was 17 and they moved in with his parents. He continued in school and Jane was responsible for all household chores in his parents' house, as both of them worked. She cleaned the five bedroom house, prepared all meals, cleaned up after them, and cared for two younger children, ages 5 and 7. Her mother-in-law bought the groceries and told her what to cook and how to cook it.

Mr. G would treat Jane civilly while in his family's presence, but when they were alone in their bedroom, he would castigate her for the dumb things she said, for not being as good a cook as his mother, and for not being sufficiently grateful for all that his family had done for her. He began slapping her face when she was about six months pregnant, saying he did not want to really beat her up because that might hurt the baby.

After their daughter, Sally, was born, he began physically assaulting her whole person. Her in-laws attempted to get the couple into counseling but their son refused. Mr. G began coming home later at night and Jane discovered he was going out with her best friend. He told Jane he was not interested in her anymore because she had gained weight when she was pregnant. He said he wanted her out of his parents' house and that the marriage was over. Her in-laws assisted Jane in applying for AFDC and finding a place to live. They told her they did not approve of their son's behavior but did not feel they could put him out of their house and let her stay.

She describes the next man she became involved with, Mr. H, as someone she rented a room to because she could not afford her entire rent; however, he did not pay for his room. She was then 18 and divorced from her first husband. This man soon persuaded her to marry him. They had known one another two months when they got married. She remained with him five years. He beat her and her daughter severely and sexually abused her daughter. Sally said she was afraid to tell her mother what Mr. H was doing because he would hurt them even more. Mr. H was eventually arrested for dealing in cocaine and his incarceration broke up the marriage.

Soon after that Jane met Mr. I through mutual friends. They began going out and soon moved in together. Mr. I worked as a private contractor laying brick. He had Jane serve as his secretary, taking telephone calls, typing estimates and contracts, and sending bills. He got on pretty well with Sally although he thought she was spoiled and attempted to remedy that by giving her specific chores. He also took her with him on some of his jobs after she came home from school. There were a fair number of rules for both Jane and Sally around the house. Jane had to make the beds, straighten the house, do the breakfast dishes by 9 A.M. when she had to be available to answer the phone. However, Mr. I was just strict. He was not abusive.

When Jane and Mr. I had been together about six months, Sally told Jane Mr. I had told her he wanted to make love to her and fuck her. On two occasions when he was babysitting for her, he had come into her bedroom and taken off her pajamas and licked her vagina.

Jane's initial response was to take Sally to a psychiatrist because she thought Sally must be crazy to say such things. When the psychiatrist told Jane she thought Sally was telling the truth, Jane did not take Sally back. When it became apparent Sally was not going to return, the psychiatrist made a protective services referral. Jane was furious. At this point, Sally denied the sexual abuse had taken place, stating she had made it up because she did not like to be left at home alone with Mr. I. Protective services told Jane not to leave Sally with Mr. I, and not to let her accompany Mr. I on his jobs. Two months later, Jane, Mr. I, and Sally moved to another part of the state.

This case indicates a pattern. Jane is a dependent woman who is accustomed to being victimized by men. She cannot imagine a different role for herself or her child. She regards herself as very fortunate to have found Mr. I because he is not nearly as exploitative as her past spouses. She aligned herself with Mr. I and probably pressured Sally to change her story.

F. The Children and the Mother's Relationship with Them

The evaluator will be interested in gaining some understanding of each child's history as well as assessing the quality of the mother's relationship with each one, particularly the victim(s). The mother is generally the consistent caretaker and can provide the most complete historical information about the child.

The interviewer will want to know the victim's background because it will help in understanding the child's overall functioning, perhaps why the victim may be dealing with the sexual abuse as she is, and her mother's reaction to the victim in this situation. The evaluator will be sensitive to whether the statements about each child convey positive or negative feelings. Of particular concern will be the parent's perception of and feelings about the victim and the possibility of scapegoating. In addition, it will be important to note whether the mother can see the child as an individual having needs separate from the mother's and to assess the accuracy of the mother's perception of the child by comparing it to the evaluator's and that of others, factors also important in assessing the perpetrator's relationship with the child.

The mother should be asked whether the child was planned or wanted, what the family situation was like at the time of the child's birth, and what the significant events have been in the child's history. Questions similar to those asked of the alleged perpetrator can be pursued to gather information about the relationship between the mother and victim. These can include, "Tell me about Jenny" or "What is Jenny like?" or "What do you like about Jenny?" or "Are there any things you don't like?" Further questions might include, "How does Jenny do in school?" "What are her likes and dislikes?" "How does she get along with the other kids in the family?" "How does she get along with you? Your husband?" "What kinds of things do you do with Jenny?" "How do you discipline her when she misbehaves?" A series of questions like this should be asked about each child.

The description by Mrs. A of her daughter, Lucy—a case also cited in chapter 4, is illustrative.

> EXAMPLE 5: Mrs. A said that even though Lucy, who was her fourth child, was not planned, she was cherished. She said, "I love all my kids and wouldn't change any of them really, except to take away some of their pain." She admitted that Lucy was "not an angel" and sometimes fought with her brothers. She described Lucy as "spirited," saying that she admired that quality in Lucy very much. It helped her not to be affected by her father's alcoholism.

> Lucy was alleging her father had engaged in cunnilingus with her
> over three years and had fondled her genitals. Lucy had not told her
> mother because she was afraid her mother would kill her father, whom
> Lucy loved.
>
> When Mrs. A did find out, she said she had "a lot of hate" for him
> because of what he had done to Lucy. She was willing to try to stay with
> him because the kids loved him and the professionals told her he was
> treatable. But if he ever touched a child again she would castrate him.

Mrs. A could accurately describe what kind of child Lucy was, spontaneously stated that she "cherished" Lucy, and was able to consider Lucy's feelings about her father.

When the mother of a victim has a warm and caring relationship with the victim, the psychological damage from the sexual abuse is less pervasive, and treatment prognosis for child and mother is good. The child has an anchor as well as someone who will look out for her needs in the fraught situation that surrounds the discovery of the sexual abuse. In contrast, if the mother is rejecting and chooses to place her own interests above the child's, the psychologiocal damage is severe and pervasive and the treatment prognosis is not good.

G. History of Substance Use, Mental Illness, Retardation, and Illegal Activity.

Obtaining information about the mother's substance use, mental illness, retardation, and illegal activity will assist the evaluator in understanding the dynamics of the sexual abuse, ascertaining what intervention is going to be appropriate, and determining prognosis. Moreover, information about these areas will assist the evaluator in understanding the mother's general functioning and her ability to protect the child.

Substance abuse may have a variety of functions in sexual abuse. Chemicals may be either alcohol or drugs or both, and their roles vary. Using either drugs or alcohol may cause the mother to lose her attractiveness to the perpetrator. Alternatively, she may not be sexually responsive because of her intoxication. Further, when the mother is high or passed out, she will not be available to protect her children. Frequently, the abusive spouse moves in to attend to the children's needs, and this unsupervised intimate involvement provides the opportunity for sexual abuse.

With drug use there is the additional problem of acquiring funds sufficient to buy drugs. In cases where the mother is actually addicted, she may engage in illegal activities to obtain money for drugs. Sometimes this is prostitution, which may expose children to men who may sexually exploit them. Other times illegal activities necessitate periods of time away from the home, when children are vulnerable to victimization.

In order to collect data about substance use, the interviewer can use questions from the outline suggested in chapter 7. However, since substance abuse by the mother is less common than by the offender, an extensive investigation may not be necessary.

The case example below illustrates some of the dynamics when alcohol is the chemical being abused.

EXAMPLE 6: Mrs. Q had three daughters, 4, 13, and 16. She had divorced the father of the two oldest girls when she found out that he was putting his fingers in their vaginas and then licking his fingers. He moved out of state and remarried. She allowed the girls to go and visit him in the summer despite the reason for the divorce.

After the divorce, Mrs. Q began to drink more. She would invite friends over and they would have drinking parties. Often various combinations of people would end up in bed together.

When the older girls were 8 and 11, a man moved in with Mrs. Q. He stayed for about a year and left because of Mrs. Q's drinking. Two months after he left, Mrs. Q had his daughter. Two or three other men in succession moved in and left after a few months.

Then Jake moved in. Within two months, Linda, then 13, told her school counselor that Jake was sexually abusing her. She complained he had gotten on top of her and "tried to hump" her. He admitted to this. He said that he and Mrs. Q had been drinking and "fooling around" on the living room couch. He became quite aroused and they went into the bedroom. However, Mrs. Q passed out "leaving him high and dry." He then went into Linda's room and got on top of her. He said, "Maybe I thought it was Maimie" (Mrs. Q).

It was discovered by protective services as they investigated that a previous boyfriend of Mrs. Q had had a sexual relationship with her 16-year-old daughter, Nadine. When Mrs. Q had found out about it, she threw him out. However, Nadine said she was in love with this man and continued to see him. Nadine described this man to the worker as "wonderful," "a college graduate" and said he got sick of her mother because her mother was a "drunken slob."

In this case, it seems that the mother's drunken state made her at least temporarily unavailable to her partners and also perhaps unaware of what they were doing to her daughters.

The mother's mental illness can have a range of functions. First, as noted in chapter 5, sometimes false accusations of sexual abuse come from a mentally ill parent (Goodwin et al. in Holder 1980; Goodwin et al. 1982). Occasionally a mentally ill parent who has some sexual dysfunction will develop delusions that her partner is sexually abusing the child. Second, there are situations where the mother's mental illness leads to her facilitating the sexual abuse. That is, her own sexual thoughts and behavior may become very disorganized, cause her to encourage the child or perpetrator, and sometimes lead her to participate. Third, the circumstances of the marriage, including the sexual abuse, may precipitate mental illness on the part of the mother. Fourth, mentally ill parents, like alcoholic parents, may be psychologically unavailable to others. Thus a psychotic or severely depressed woman is not likely to be able to meet the needs of her partner, including sexual needs, nor of her children. Fifth, mental illness is likely to cause the parent to be unavailable to protect the children because she is hospitalized.

It is important to carefully assess the role of the mother's mental illness. Too often mental health professionals accept the perpetrator's explanation that the mother is crazy, and that is why she believes he sexually abused the child, when the reality is the mother is very distraught or actually mentally ill because of the discovery of the sexual abuse. Too often also, the subtle or overt role played by the mentally ill mother in the abuse is overlooked. Acute and chronic mental illness appear to play different roles. Acute onset is more likely to be related to the trauma of discovering the sexual abuse or delusions that there is sexual abuse when there is not. Chronic mental illness is more often associated with the mother's psychological or physical inability to protect the victim. In addition, when the illness is chronic the probability that the mother will in the future be able to protect and parent children is much less hopeful than when it is acute.

The same techinques described for use in ascertaining the perpetrator's mental state can be used with the mother. Thus, the mental status exam and questions regarding sleep disturbance, nervousness, depression, racing thoughts, hearing voices, use of medication, counseling, and hospitalizations can be employed, as can the mother's presentation during the interview and records from agencies who have provided her mental health services.

The following case example illustrates one of the roles of emotional illness.

EXAMPLE 7: Mrs. G was described as ''flaky'' by people who knew her. That is, she was a very emotional person who tended to worry a lot about whether she was doing the right thing. She had a nervous breakdown when she separated from her physically abusive husband and filed for divorce. She said she fell apart because he threatened to kill her and her son, Tom, if she did not return to him. He would lurk outside her house and watch her at night and would send subtly threatening notes. The therapist she was seeing described her as paranoid. When she contacted the police, they did not take her concerns seriously.

Mrs. G alleged that when Tom was three, he told her his dad, during visitation, had put his pee pee in Tom's butt. Tom was evaluated by a psychologist who concluded Tom had been sexually abused by his father and recommended the visits be supervised. The divorce court had evaluations of the parents done, and the psychiatrist concluded that Tom had not been abused. He said the mother was emotionally unstable and had fabricated the allegation. He did not interview Tom. Tom continued to have unsupervised visits with his father for three more years. During these, he was sexually abused many times by his father, who also allowed an uncle to fellate Tom.

In this case the mother's "flakiness," nervous breakdown, and paranoia were in part a result of the relationship with Tom's father. The psychiatrist naively assumed that her instability had caused her to make up an allegation. If he had interviewed Tom, he probably would have arrived at a different conclusion.

The reasons for concern about mental retardation of the mother are as follows: She will probably have significant deficits in overall functioning including parenting ability, and specifically in being protective of her child. Retarded mothers tend to be focused upon getting their own needs met and the needs of the child become secondary. Furthermore such parents have marked deficiencies in judgment and may place their children in jeopardy, including situations where their children might be sexually abused. The most extreme example in our experience was a retarded mother who allowed a male friend to suck her two-year-old son's penis several times even though she said she knew it was grossly inappropriate. She also agreed to sell her son to this man for $2000. However, the man could not raise the money.

Ascertaining the mother's mental capacity is accomplished in the same way as for the perpetrator, by means of formal testing, by a history indicating retardation, and by the evaluator's observations.

Finally, the evaluator will want to explore the mother's criminal activity. While a criminal history generally bespeaks problems in functioning, it is necessary to understand the causes of illegal activity. Sometimes mothers break the law to support their children; in other cases, a history of assaultive crime indicates an antisocial personality. In addition, the evaluator must determine any implications for sexual abuse. If the mother has been on the run or incarcerated for periods of time, her absence may leave the child at risk for sexual abuse. Furthermore, if the mother is involved in crimes such as prostitution, pornography, or other types of sexual exploitation, her children may be vulnerable to victimization by the mother's companions (or the mother).

To ascertain any criminal activity, the evaluator can use the approach described in chapter 7 for the offender, asking first about incidents which have not come to the attention of authorities and then progressing to those which involved her more deeply in the legal system.

H. Sexual History

While the sexual history of the mother is not so salient as that of the perpetrator to understanding why the sexual abuse took place and what the treatment prognosis is, the mother's history can nevertheless be enlightening. Patterns that may be found include not only her own childhood victimization but also more proximate sexual assault that may promote risk to her children or suggest lack of maternal protective capability. Moreover, just as the perpetrator may reveal sexual patterns in the marriage that might support his looking for sexual gratification elsewhere, so might his wife. Finally, a discussion of sexual practices in the marriage may uncover sexual deviancy often associated with sexual abuse, as in the example below.

> EXAMPLE 8:   Mrs. C. was the mother of two boys, ages 8 and 5. She said her husband divorced her because he did not find her an adequate sexual partner. She said when they married they were both sexually inexperienced. However he soon began educating himself through pornography and urged her to do likewise. Practices he was particularly taken with were oral sex, especially analingus, group sex, and bondage. Mrs. G submitted to bondage and did comply with his requests for oral sex but refused group sex. However, she was not sufficiently sexually enthusiastic to please her husband. He also made her go to pornographic movies with him, which she found embarrassing.
>
> After the divorce her children had regular visits with their father, but did not like to go. After one visit, Mrs. C caught her five-year-old son engaging in analingus with his best friend as they were taking a bath together. He said this was a game his daddy taught him. Further questioning of both sons revealed extensive sexual abuse including group sex involving themselves, their father, his girlfriend, and the girlfriend's daughter.

In this case we find a direct relationship between the father's unusual sexual appetites in the marriage and his sexual abuse of his sons. The sexual history outline found in chapter 7 can be used as a guideline for interviewing mothers about their sexual experiences.

I. The Sexual Abuse

The discussion of the sexual abuse will vary depending upon the mother's position concerning the allegations at the time of the interview. However, the evaluator will want to determine whether or not the mother believes the child and how protective of the child she has been in response to knowledge about the allegations. An effort should be made to persuade the mother of the veracity of the child's complaints, if she does not believe them, for at this point the evaluator should have substantiated the allegation. There are many ways to approach this topic. The evaluator might ask the mother what she believes about the sexual abuse allegations at that point. In addition, she should be asked how she felt when she first learned about the allegations and what she did in response to them.

As with the perpetrator, if the evaluator has obtained a good audio or video tape of the child's statements, this can be played for the mother. The evaluator will want to explore the following: Is she moved or upset? Does she evidence some anger? If so, at whom: the child, the alleged perpetrator, or the professionals involved? Does she believe the child or does she try to explain away the child's statements?

The evaluator can use arguments similar to those with the offender to attempt to persuade the mother the victim is telling the truth. She might be told that only about two percent of allegations made by children are untrue (Jones 1985; Goodwin et al. 1980). It may be worthwhile to go through the litany of pressures which the child experiences that may prevent her from telling and militate against her making false allegations (see chapter 5). The evaluator also might describe various aspects of the story which are indicators that it is not made up (see chapter 6). Sometimes there is more than one victim and the fact that two or more children are asserting the perpetrator sexually misused them may persuade the mother. The interviewer also might point out what a devastating position her disbelief puts the victim in. It is common for the mother initially to have difficulty accepting the sexual abuse, but as she obtains and assimilates more information she may come to believe the child. Her realization of the problem is a process. Thus the evaluator should not despair if initially the mother resists believing.

At the end of the interview, the evaluator will note the level of the mother's commitment to the child's story. The higher the commitment the more hopeful the prognosis for mother and daughter staying together or being reunited, and the better the prospects for family treatment. Furthermore, if the mother believes the child, the psychological damage to the victim is less severe.

Similarly, if the mother was protective in her response to knowlege of the allegations, regardless of whether she completely believes them, the prognosis for keeping the child with the mother is quite good.

Mrs. K, whose case is discussed below, goes through several different stages with regard to her belief about her daughters' allegations of sexual abuse.

EXAMPLE 9:   Mrs. K's daughters, Kay, 10, and Lisa 8, told her of the sexual abuse by their stepfather. She was very distraught by these accusations and confronted her husband and asked him if it were true. Mr. K staunchly denied ever having done anything sexual to either child. He asserted that Kay, who was alleging cunnilingus, fellatio, intercourse, digital penetration, and penetration with a vibrator, had made all this up and had persuaded Lisa, who was alleging only fondling, to go along with her. He said that the motivation of the children was that they wanted him out of the house so there would only be the two children and Mrs. K at home, and Mrs. K could have any boyfriend she wanted.

Mrs. K seemed to believe her husband's rather illogical explanation but sought assistance from protective services to help her deal with children making such allegations. When protective services interviewed the girls, they thought the children were telling the truth, and removed them from the home. In addition to questions about Mrs. K's ability to protect the children were concerns that Mrs. K was allowing her husband to give the children alcohol and marijuana.

Mrs. K said she still did not believe that the children had been sexually abused. They had lied about so many other things. She said she wanted an expert to evaluate the children. This was done and the expert was of the decided opinion that the children were telling the truth. She then met with Mrs. K, who at first reiterated that she could not believe her children because Kay, in particular, lied so much. She said she wanted Kay placed in a separate foster home from Lisa because Kay was a bad influence on Lisa. However, when the expert told her that the children were telling the truth, she said well she had hoped she wouldn't find out the worst. Yet she knew that the hope was a slim one. She then asked what she should do in order to get her children back. When told she would have to separate from her husband, she appeared extremely upset but said she guessed she knew that too.

In this case the mother gives some indication initially she believed the children in that she was upset by the allegations and then asked the stepfather about them. However, he apparently was able to persuade her that the children were lying. Some part of her must have doubted her husband's innocence, as she went to protective services, albeit under the guise of obtaining assistance with the children who made up stories.

(Why did she choose to go to protective services rather than some other mental health agency?) Yet she continued overtly to say she didn't believe the children. However, when the expert revealed her opinion, Mrs. K immediately changed her stance, stating she realized the chances were slim her husband was telling the truth. She also appeared to accept the necessity of separation if the children were to return to her. Nevertheless, it would be a mistake to interpret the current situation as one where Mrs. K is firmly committed to believing her daughters.

III. CONCLUSION

The interview with the mother provides crucial information about what lies in the future for the child that is, whether one should be hopeful or pessimistic about the long-term prospects for the child. If the mother has a caring relationship with the victim, is protective of the child, and believes her child, the victim's prognosis may be fairly good. Alternatively, if the mother is rejecting the victim, has not been protective, and disbelieves her, the child will suffer psychological damage from these maternal reactions as well as from the sexual abuse.

The mother's perspective on and information about the various family members and the family as a whole will be valuable input for the evaluator. The mother will provide essential information about the children, the alleged perpetrator, and the family history.

Finally, understanding the mother's strengths and weaknesses and her overall functioning will assist the evaluator in planning for the child and helping the family.

CHAPTER NINE

Behavioral Characteristics and Physical Findings: A Medical Perspective

Mary Steinberg, MD and Mary Westhoff, MD

I. THE PRIMARY CARE PHYSICIAN'S PREPARATION FOR THE MEDICAL EXAMINATION

At some time during their careers, most primary care physicians will be called upon to examine a child or adolescent who has been sexually abused The patient may come to the physician specifically identified as a victim of sexual abuse, accompanied by parent, relative or law enforcement official. In less obvious cases, the victim may present with seemingly unrelated complaints or conditions, and the abuse will be discovered during the course of the evaluation.

Just as the victim may find the genital evaluation traumatic and frightening, so may the physician. For both parties the anxiety is founded on a fear of the unknown. Neither may know what to do or what to expect. It will greatly benefit the physician to approach this clinical problem just as she would any other—with an organized, careful, and thorough process of history-taking, examination, documentation, and appropriate followup. In addition, significant barriers between physician and patient can be avoided by attending to the location of the examination, the approach to the problem and the child, the timing of the examination, and communication with the child and family.

The hustle and bustle and lack of privacy in a busy emergency room or clinic will intimidate many children. Providing the child and family with a quiet, nonthreatening environment will make her feel safer and less restrained. The child will appreciate any available toys, dolls, or drawing

A Medical Glossary appears on pg. 405.

materials as play objects, whereas the physician can utilize these as adjuncts to the evaluation process.

It is very important to allocate adequate time for the evaluation. If the practitioner is aware that she is to do a sexual abuse evaluation, it is wise to set aside a large block of time—more than an hour may be necessary. If the alleged assault has occurred within the last 72 hours, the examination should be done as soon as possible, as there may be collectible evidence present. After 72 hours, since there is little likelihood of finding prostatic secretions of sperm, it is appropriate to delay the exam for as long as a day to a time that is convenient and of sufficient length.

Physicians, as well as other health care personnel, must not let their personal beliefs affect their professional judgement. Some doctors, astonished by the increase in reports of child sexual abuse, attribute this to "media hype." Others feel that many cases are invented by embittered parents during custody battles. For certain individuals, the whole issue of sexual abuse is so difficult to accept that they choose to believe that nothing like this can really happen. These misconceptions and biases must be put aside, to keep them from influencing objectivity. Similarly, an adult may view penile penetration as the most serious sexual act that could be committed against children. From the child's point of view, although the physical harm from fondling may be minimal, the psychological effects can be devastating. The physician should not minimize the child's situation. Each victim deserves respect and compassion, no matter what the circumstances or allegations.

It is essential that the child, family, and physician be able to communicate—especially with regard to sexual issues and anatomy. If the doctor uses the word "vagina," but a little girl regards this part of her body as "bootie," there will be confusion and misunderstanding. It is helpful to find out from the child or caretaker what terms are used to identify body parts.

Given comfortable surroundings, a relaxed and unrushed atmosphere, and a common language with the interviewer, many children will not find it difficult to tell of their experience. But there are many victims who, even under the best of circumstances, are unable or unwilling to discuss the abuse. It is not uncommon for a child to unexpectedly divulge her secret to a trusted person, never again to repeat it. The ramifications of disclosure can cause significant family upheaval. Upon detecting the tension and stress, the youngster may recant her story, hoping to restore order to her world.

Because young children's concept of time is self-centered and immature, it is helpful to explore instances or duration of sexual abuse in terms of significant events in the child's life such as birthdays, holidays, or vacations. Noting the approximate date of the most recent occurrence may make it easier to determine whether the physical findings are compatible with the history. If the child has already told the story three or four times, and the law enforcement officials or child protective services workers have the crucial information, it is unnecessary to press the child for details.

II. SIGNS AND SYMPTOMS OF SEXUAL ABUSE

Knowledge of behavioral and physical indicators of sexual abuse is essential to performing an adequate medical evaluation.

A. Behavioral Indicators

Behavioral indicators may be the only clues that sexual abuse has occurred or is occurring. The presence of any one or a combination of these signs is not diagnostic of sexual abuse. Many are transient changes common in childhood and reflect the developing individual. However, if the changes persist and significantly interfere with normal functioning, an underlying emotional conflict, and possibly sexual abuse, may be present (McHugh 1985).

In preschool children, any *change in bowel or bladder habits* may represent the emotional sequelae of sexual abuse, or actual physical changes resulting from the abuse. Young victims may exhibit *changed sleeping patterns, nightmares, fearful behavior, or excessive separation anxiety. Developmental regression* in areas such as toilet training or speech and language, if persistent, merits evaluation and may be the result of sexual abuse. *Self-manipulation, or masturbation* is an almost universal activity at some time during childhood. However, the child who *excessively masturbates* may have been sexually abused or raised in a severely emotionally barren environment.

Probably the most striking manifestation is *sexualized behavior or inappropriate sexual knowledge* for the child's age. A child normally has no point of reference regarding such behaviors as French kissing or simulated intercourse, unless that child has been inappropriately exposed to or participated in sexualized activities.

The example below is illustrative of the kinds of signs and symptoms that may be present.

EXAMPLE 1: Because of several allegations of physical abuse and neglect, A.M. had been closely followed by social service agencies. At age 6 years, she was severely growth retarded, microcephalic, mute, and appeared to be mentally retarded. Concerned persons notified the local child protective services agency after noting incidents where A.M. would approach male strangers, grab their genital areas and say "DA." She was subsequently evaluated by a multidisciplinary team. Although she could not speak, she was able to differentiate between the anatomically explicit "mommy," "daddy," and "A.M." dolls. She then clearly demonstrated multiple sexual activities between all three dolls. Physical findings consisted of perihymenal erythema, a generous vaginal introitus and multiple rounded hymenal remnants.

Following molestation, latency age children may become extremely *anxious, hyperactive,* or develop *problems in school,* both in academics and attendance. They may drift into *social isolation* or *depression. Conversion hysteria* is an unusual but alarming presentation and is found in the following case.

EXAMPLE 2: E.J., an eight-year-old girl arrived in the emergency room early one morning complaining of severe facial pain. She had awakened during the night with the pain, which appeared to be worse when she attempted to open her mouth. The physical examination was entirely normal. Upon further questioning, her mother admitted that there had been a great deal of stress in the family recently. Exactly two weeks earlier, the little girl's stepfather had attempted to force her to commit fellatio. E.J. had resisted and kept her mouth tightly closed. Her mother had arrived home unexpectedly that evening, and discovered the activity. Appropriate actions were taken against the stepfather. Upon reassurance that her mouth, as well as genital area, were quite normal, E.J.'s symptoms promptly resolved.

Nearly every primary care physician has been frustrated by the child who recurrently appears with *multiple somatic complaints* as well as frequent *school absences.* These complaints may include *abdominal pain, headaches, fatigue, malaise, weakness* and so on. Once serious illness has been ruled out by a careful history, examination, and appropriate lab tests, an in-depth psychosocial evaluation is called for. Since many physicians are not extensively trained in this area, referral to a social worker or psychologist should be considered. Failure to pursue the possibility of a nonorganic etiology for the complaints may condemn the youngster to lifelong debilitating emotional and psychological consequences and possibly continued sexual abuse.

Adolescents, more than any other age group, risk disbelief on the part of professionals, or even their own parents, upon disclosing that they have been abused (Kempe 1978). The allegations may be attributed to the teenagers' attempt to "get even" with someone, or an effort to cover up forbidden sexual activity. Under these circumstances the health care professional's obligation to the client makes a thorough evaluation imperative.

Symptoms teenagers may exhibit include *depression, loss of self esteem, or extreme preoccupation with their body image* (May 1978; Kaufman et al. 1954; Faller 1986; Cleveland 1986). Adolescent victims may become increasingly *socially isolated,* develop problems with *substance abuse* or even attempt *suicide.* Others react by becoming *sexually precocious* (Nakashima and Zakus 1977). In the following case example divergent responses to a sexually abusive environment are found.

> EXAMPLE 3:   T.M., age 15, was sexually abused by her natural brother and her stepfather. Her stepsister, S.L., was not molested by her father, but was aware of what was happening. Her mother told her that once she "came of age" her father was likely to include her also.
>
> T.M. presented as an outgoing provocative teenager who easily struck up conversations with strangers. She was noted to almost press her body against people as she spoke to them. T.M. boasted of many "boyfriends," most of whom were casual acquaintances who barely knew her. S.L., paradoxically, was submissive and dour. Her hair was severely pulled back. On a hot summer day she wore a long sleeve blouse, black skirt, and nylon stockings. She appeared to carry the weight of the world on her shoulders.

There can be a significant overlap of signs of sexual abuse among the various age groups. Inappropriate sexual play is not limited to small children, nor depression to adolescents.

B. Physical Indicators

Actual physical symptoms of sexual abuse include *recurrent urinary tract infections* or *urinary tract complaints,* including *enuresis.* In patients with these problems a thorough urologic evaluation is necessary. However, if the symptoms persist, without evidence of urologic dysfunction, the physician should consider emotional or psychological issues such as sexual abuse as the source of the disorder. A psychosocial evaluation or behavioral assessment may prove just as helpful as an intravenous pyelogram or voiding cystourethrogram.

Encopresis can also be a manifestation of emotional turmoil including sexual abuse, although not exclusively so (Levine 1981). Those children whose stooling difficulties are not greatly improved by appropriate medical management may require concurrent attention to psychosocial and stress-related issues.

Intermittent *vulvovaginitis* is not an uncommon occurrence in young girls. Its most frequent causes are poor hygiene, local irritants, retained foreign bodies or skin disorders (Altcheck 1981). Many organisms transmitted from extra-genital sites (rectum, skin, nasopharynx) can cause purulent vulvovaginitis (O'Connor and Oliver 1985). However, recurrent, persistent, or severe symptoms especially if associated with other physical or behavioral evidence of sexual abuse warrant thorough investigation. This same approach should be taken with *unexplained difficulties in walking or sitting and bruising and irritation of the perineum.*

The physician who diagnoses *pregnancy* in a child age 12 years or less, can be quite sure that sexual abuse has occurred. This is also true if *sperm or acid phosphatase* are found on a child's clothing or body. The presence of *sperm in the urine* of a little girl is also strong presumptive evidence of abuse.

In adults, the following diseases; *gonorrhea, syphilis, genital herpes, venereal warts, trichomonas vaginalis, and urogenital chlamydia* are considered to be sexually transmitted. Gonorrhea infection in prepubertal children (Committee on Early Childhood, Adoption and Dependent Care 1983) as well as syphilis are also accepted to have been acquired by sexual contact. However, the link between other venereal infections and sexual abuse is not as consistently entertained; yet there is no reason to believe that children should contract these diseases in a different way from adults. Only with persistent efforts to increase awareness among health professionals in many disciplines will these contagions be appropriately identified and investigated (American Academy of Dermatology Task Force in Pediatric Dermatology 1984).

Physicians must be concerned about children who present with *unexplained bleeding from the vagina or rectum.* If, after a thorough evaluation and examination, no apparent etiology for the bleeding is identified, sexual abuse must be strongly considered.

Finally, the youngster who gives a *consistent and detailed description of a sexually abusive situation* or event is very unlikely to be lying. Although there are a few cases of fictitious or exaggerated allegations, the physician's role remains constant: to comprehensively gather a history, perform an examination, and obtain the necessary laboratory studies. It is the responsibility of protective ser· ices or law enforcement officials to proceed with appropriate investigations or actions.

III. MEDICAL EVALUATION

History Taking

As with any pediatric evaluation, a comprehensive medical history is indicated. This should include developmental milestones and sleeping patterns as well as bowel and bladder habits. Investigation of prior illnesses, injuries, or hospitalizations may provide helpful information. For example, recurrent urinary tract infections may result from sexual abuse.

When there is a possibility of pregnancy, the date and character of the last menstrual period are critical information. Adolescents may prefer to give the history and be examined in the absence of their parents or caretakers. Certainly when touching on such topics as birth control and sexual activity, consideration to confidentiality is paramount.

All information gathered during the evaluation must be meticulously documented. This includes any of the youngster's drawings, a description of play with dolls or toys, as well as any pertinent statements made by the child or parents.

B. The Physical Examination

The physician should always have an assistant, such as a nurse or aide, present in the room during the examination. This assistant can help with the process of the examination, as well as protect the examiner from allegations of abuse or impropriety.

1. *General Physical.* Just as a thorough history may reveal critical information regarding the child and her environment, so may a complete physical examination. Growth retardation or abnormalities in head size can be detected by carefully measuring and plotting height, weight, and head circumference. The child's maturational stage can be closely estimated by using the Tanner Classification System. Other findings that might be detected by the astute examiner include pharyngitis due to Neisseria gonorrhea or patchy hair loss due to either trichotillomania or violent hair-pulling. A careful perusual of the skin may reveal bruises, lacerations, abrasions, scars, or bitemarks (Ellerstein 1981). All such findings should be carefully documented on a skin map. The color and clarity of the margins of bruises provide some idea as to their age. If possible, these findings should be photographed; these visual records

along with a physician's detailed notes might prove invaluable in future reviews, such as court proceedings.

2. *The Genital Exam: Techniques.* Each child reacts differently to the examination of the genitalia. Some sexual abuse victims are appropriately modest, others become hysterical, and still others are overly submissive, or unusually comfortable with the procedure. Although it is impossible to draw any firm conclusions as to whether or not sexual abuse has occurred simply on the basis of the child's response to the exam, this behavior should be noted, as it may correlate with other indicators of sexual abuse.

There are a number of techniques helpful in reducing children's anxiety regarding the genital exam. As previously mentioned, a non-threatening relaxed setting is beneficial. Many of the child's fears may be related to her lack of understanding of the examination process. It is well worth the examiner's effort to explain what is about to happen. Dolls may be used to demonstrate the examination. The child should be allowed to touch or inspect any instruments to be used. A support person remaining in the room can serve to comfort the child. Allow the child to keep on her underclothing during the general physical examination. By moving in a sequential, systematic manner from the general to the genital exam, the child is less likely to regard the genital exam as "different" and thus fearsome.

Throughout the examination the child should be constantly reassured about the integrity and normality of her body. It is not uncommon for children who have been sexually abused to view themselves as "damaged goods" (Sgroi 1982). Assuring the child that her body is just like any other child's may relieve her of a tremendous burden, as in the case example that follows.

EXAMPLE 4:   M.B. had been repeatedly sexually abused in a day care center. When the situation was discovered his parents brought him for physical examintion. They were told by the doctor that the exam would be "too traumatic" for the child. Over the next year, M.B. had serious behavioral problems, including encopresis. He made little progress in therapy. At the therapist's urging, a physical examination was arranged. M.B. initially resisted the exam, until he was told that the reason for the check up was to determine if his body had been hurt in any way. M.B. then readily submitted to the inspection; in fact, he repeatedly pointed to his penis and rectum, asking if they were all right. This reassurance apparently greatly benefitted M.B. He subsequently made great strides in therapy, and the encopresis improved.

Despite all best efforts, there are children who refuse examination. They should not be forced or held down. If the examination is critical, such as in acute assault cases, sedation or general anesthesia is indicated. In situations where the exam is not urgent, sequential visits can be arranged. These repeat visits, over time, may enable the child to grow comfortable with the doctor and the examination process.

There are several positions recommended to examine the female perineum. The knee-chest position, with the head and upper chest on the table and the knees tucked under the abdomen, probably offers the best visualization. Because the abdominal contents fall forward into the abdominal cavity, the vagina often balloons open spontaneously. The usefulness of the knee-chest positon is lessened by the fact that many children feel very vulnerable and unprotected when assuming it. As an alternative, the standard lithotomy position also provides excellent exposure. The abdominal contents can be shifted upward by placing a pillow under the child's buttocks. In some cases, the child will only allow examination while sitting on a trusted person's lap. The child's legs can be flexed, spread and held closely to the chest by the person holding her. Security assured, the patient can then be examined, although in a less than optimal position.

Just as a surgeon insists upon excellent exposure of the operating field, so must the doctor doing sexual abuse evaluations insist on adequate exposure of the vulvar area. It is not sufficient to briefly glance at the perineum while the child's legs are slightly parted. With the legs widely spread, the labia majora should be gently grasped and pulled outward, toward the examiner, and laterally (Cowell 1981). This technique will maximize visualization of the vulvar area and encourage the hymenal orifice to gape open. Relaxation techniques, such as panting or deep breathing may facilitate the spontaneous appearance of the opening. At times, moist redundant hymenal tissue will stick together, giving the appearance of an intact hymen. Gentle pressure on the area with a moistened Q-tip often demonstrates a hymenal orifice, when separated, assumes surprisingly large dimensions.

In documenting any abnormalities of the perineal area, it is helpful for the examiner to view the perinium as if a clock face were superimposed upon it. Thus findings can then be described as occurring at 6:00, 9:00, and so forth (Woodling et al. 1977).

There is a tremendous amount of variation in the appearance of the female perineum. The female infant has prominent labia majora and thick, engorged mucosal tissue. Newborn females may even have a milky white or lightly bloodstained vaginal discharge. This is a response to the maternal estrogen effect. Tags and bands on the newborn females external genitalia are not uncommon and tend to regress as the child grows older (More et al. 1983).

The shape of the hymenal opening may be cribriform, septate, punctate, eccentric, and so forth. Usually the hymenal ring is a thin, parchment-like web of tissue that forms a ring around the vaginal orifice. The examining physician should be able to differentiate normal anatomy and its variations from the abnormal (figure 9.1, Normal Anatomy). Pediatricians and family practitioners have ample opportunity to inspect the prepubertal child's genitalia during the course of routine physicals. The genital area deserves attention, just as do the heart and lungs. The inclusion of an examination of the external genitalia in the child's check-up must not be misconstrued as deviant or perverse, but rather appropriate and necessary.

A thorough general examination is imperative. Any signs of physical violence should be noted, such as scratch marks, bites, bruises, grip marks, or broken fingernails. There are patterns of injury in sexual abuse for the examining doctor to be aware of. Coital injuries commonly result in posterior tears, transections and avulsions of the hymenal tissue between 3:00 and 9:00 (see figure 9.2, Coital Injury). Deep tears between 5:00 and 7:00 are especially common after penile penetration, and often extend into the posterior fourchette (Woodling & Kossoris 1981).

When digital or noncoital manipulation occurs, the angle of entry is usually from the front of the child's body. This usually results in the presence of injuries anteriorly, between 9:00 and 3:00 (see figure 9.3, Digital Manipulation). Fondling may result in erythema only, or small abrasions. In some cases there are no physical findings at all. Autostimulation and insertion of tampons will not result in tearing of the hymen (Woodling, et al. 1977).

Damage due to sexual abuse may be attributed to a straddle injury, and vice versa. When a child falls onto a hard surface, the dissipation of force will occur where there is underlying firmness, such as cartilage or bone. In the female perineum, the underlying bones form a diamond-shaped support structure from which the perineal contents are suspended. The symphysis pubis is anterior, extending posteriorly only as far as the body of the clitoris. Laterally, the ischial tuberosities are surrounded by the gluteal muscles. The sacrum is located posteriorly, but at a much higher level than either the symphysis pubis or ischial tuberosities. Isolated injuries to the posterior vulvar area, with no accompanying lateral or anterior injuries are highly suspicious for sexual abuse. (See figure 9.4, Straddle/Coital Injuries).

When forced penetration of the rectum occurs with a rigid object, fissures and abrasions can result. An abrasion incurred in this way is likely to be widest outside the perianal ring, and narrowing internally. In contrast a lesion due to the passage of a large firm stool is more likely to

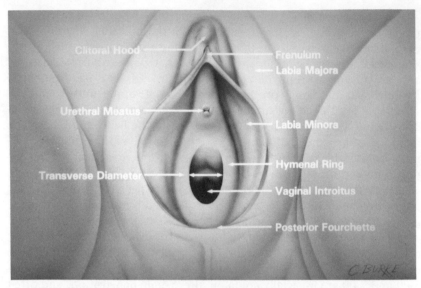

FIGURE 9.1. Normal anatomy of the prepubescent female external genitalia.

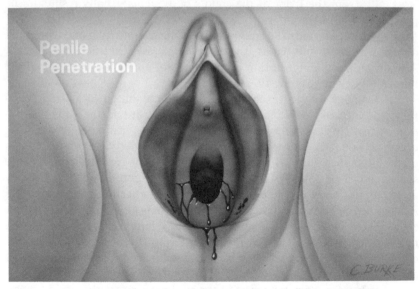

FIGURE 9.2. Coital injuries most often result in generalized erythema as well as hymenal injuries between 3:00 and 9:00. There may be extension of the tearing into the posterior fourchette.

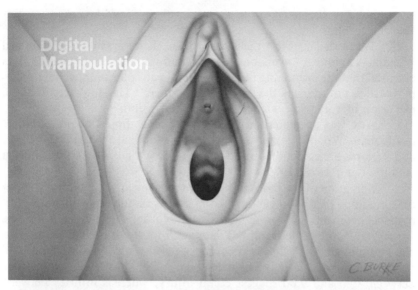

FIGURE 9.3. Digital or noncoital manipulation most often results in erythema, tears or abrasions between 9:00 and 3:00.

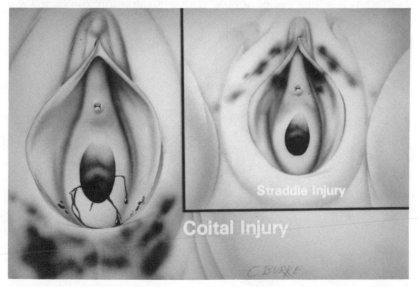

FIGURE 9.4. Straddle injuries can be differentiated from coital injuries by their proximity to underlying bone, such as the symphysis pubis.

have its widest diameter within the perianal ring, and be narrower outside the rectum.

When dealing with the victim of an acute assault, the standard "Sexual Assault Kit" available in most communities should be used. It is essential that the examining physician handle all collected specimens properly, so as not to break the "chain of evidence." This could result in the exclusion of valuable evidence from the courtroom.

Any foreign material in the genital area should be collected. If available, a Wood's Lamp can be used to illuminate the vulvar, rectal, and perioral areas. Seminal products fluoresce a greenish color under a Wood's Lamp (Paul 1975).

Palpation of the mons pubis may reveal exquisite tenderness. Specific findings in the vulvar area after acute assault may include perihymenal erythema as well as abrasions, avulsions and lacerations (see figure 9.5, Acute Molestation). Traumatic injuries to the vulvar mucosa can be highlighted by lightly painting the area with toluidine blue, and decolorizing the K-Y jelly (Lauber et al. 1982). Hymenal transections between 3:00 and 9:00 suggest coital injury, whereas injuries between 9:00 and 3:00 are more consistent with noncoital injury. Pooled secretions may be collected with a sterile dropper. Vaginal washings can be obtained by instilling 2 cc of nonbacteriostatic saline into the vagina with

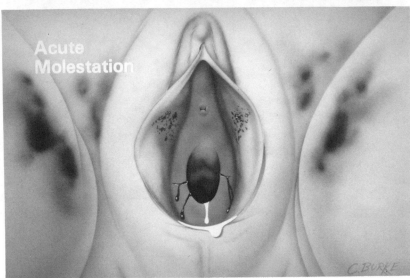

FIGURE 9.5. Acute molestation with penetration may result in bruising, abrasions, erythema as well as transections of the posterior hymenal tissue. Pooled secretions may also be present.

a transfer pipette and aspirating back. These washings can then be analyzed for the presence of sperm, acid phosphatase, or infectious agents. A wet mount may reveal trichomonas. Nonspecific vaginitis, caused by Gardenerella vaginalis, is relatively uncommon in normal children, but can be acquired after sexual abuse. In a study by Hammerschlag et al. (1985), nonspecific vaginitis was found to be the most frequent cause of vaginitis in a group of 31 girls who had been sexually abused. Nonspecific vaginitis is diagnosed by finding "clue cells" (epithelial cells laden with bacteria) in vaginal washings, and by the detection of a fishy odor upon mixing a drop of KOH with a drop of vaginal fluid. The vagina, rectum, and throat should all be cultured for Neisseria gonorrhea. New enzyme immunoassays are now also available for the rapid detection of urogenital chlamydia infection (McMillan 1985). A serum VDRL is indicated, and in post-menarchal females, a serum pregnancy test. This latter test is done to determine whether the victim was pregnant at the time of the assault.

If there is any physical evidence or a history given of penetration, an internal exam must also be done. An otoscope with a long veterinary speculum can be used, or a variety of more sophisticated instruments, such as the Huffman-Graves speculum, the Pederson bi-valved speculum, the Killian Nasal Speculum, or even fiberoptic vaginoscopes (Cowell 1981). Following an acute assault there may be vaginismus. This spasm of the pubococcygeal muscle can last up to a week and may make internal examination of any sort difficult unless heavy sedation or general anesthesia is administered. Findings during vaginoscopy may include hemorrhagic abraded areas of the vaginal walls or cervix, or even perforations of the vagina.

After acute sodomy there may be perianal erythema, contusions, lacerations, and fissures. (See figure 9.6, Acute Molestation Rectal). If serious injuries within the anus or rectum are suspected, an anoscope or lubricated 10 ml test tube can be used to visualize the inner mucosa. Because rectal spasm frequently occurs after sodomy, it is often necessary to treat the patient with a stool softener.

Oral-genital contact can result in abrasions and petechiae of the posterior palate. If ejaculation has occurred into the mouth, scrapings taken from behind the upper front incisors are most likely to harbor sperm (Woodling et al. 1977). In male victims the penis should be carefully inspected for erythema abrasions, bite marks or swelling. Any discharge from the urethra should be cultured for Neisseria gonorrhea and chlamydia.

Since medical problems can arise following the assault, it is not inappropriate to request a return visit in one to two weeks. A repeat VDRL

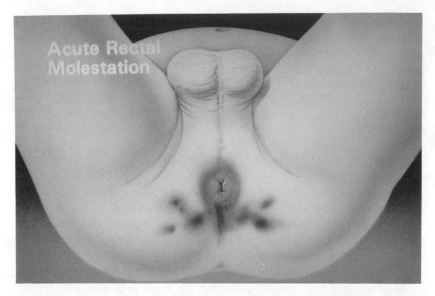

FIGURE 9.6. Acute sodomy results in erythema and bruising with tears and fissures of the rectal mucosa.

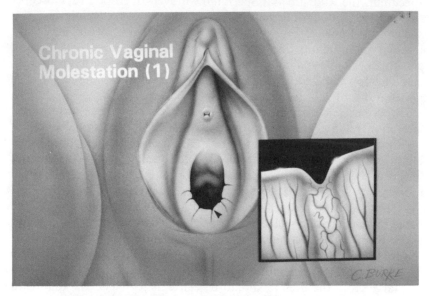

FIGURE 9.7. Chronic vaginal molestation may result in hyperpigmentation of the labia majora. There may be multiple healed transections of the hymen. Inset demonstrates colposcopic view of neovascularization.

and pregnancy test, if indicated, can be obtained. It is very important for a knowledgeable, compassionate health care professional to be available to attend to both the medical and emotional needs of the child and family.

Children who have been chronically sexually abused may have no physical findings at all, or very significant and striking findings. Chronic irritation of the perineum can result in hyper or hypopigmentation of the perivulvar skin (see figure 9.7, Chronic Molestation). This skin may also appear thickened and hyperkeratotic. The vulvar mucosal tissue, including the hymen, may also become thickened and edematous as a response to inflammation or constant irritation. Both digital manipulation or "dry or vulvar" intercourse may have this effect. Dry or vulvar intercourse, also known as interfemoral intercourse, is performed with the penis clasped between the child's upper thighs and against the vulvar area; penetration does not occur.

The female perineum has a tremendous capacity to heal. Ruptures of the hymen have been reported to heal completely in as few as nine days (Teixeira 1981). In addition, not all hymens are rounded and symmetric. Fimbriated or fringed hymens may conceal tears or lacerations within their fringes. Some hymens are more compliant than others and will have enough elasticity to permit penetration of small objects without tearing.

When tears of the hymenal tissue have occurred the examiner will note irregularities in the contour of the hymenal rim, as well as healed transections extending into the hymen itself (Woodling and Heger 1986).

The use of the colposcope is an important innovation in medical evaluations of sexual abuse. Colposcopic examination magnifies 5 to 30 times, is non-invasive, and can clearly define evidence of both old and recent trauma. Many colposcopes have photographic capability, which makes it an especially useful technique. Colposcopy can identify the hymenal transections as well as the neovascularization that occurs with healing. The inset within figure 9.7 shows the organized weblike capillary network in the undisturbed hymenal tissue. Neovascularization, the process of vessel regrowth within healing areas, is often chaotic and disorganized.

The colposcope is also very useful in identifying synechiae. Synechial bands are thin adherent webs of tissue that form in response to inflammation or irritation (see figure 9.8, Chronic Molestation 2). Labial adhesions are probably the most common form of synechiae in preadolescent females; however, their presence is not necessarily indicative of sexual abuse. A patulous urethra may result after prolonged digital manipulation of the periurethral area (see figure 9.8).

It is very important for the examiner to determine the horizontal

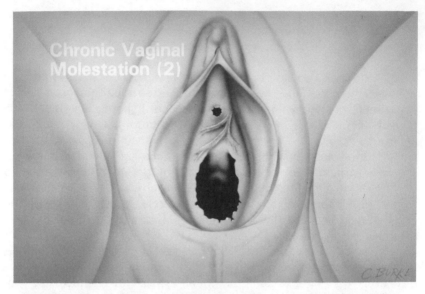

FIGURE 9.8. Chronic vaginal molestation with synechial bands, patulous urethra, and spacious introitus with multiple rounded hymenal remnants.

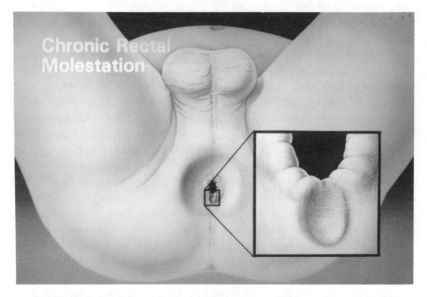

FIGURE 9.9. Loss of gluteal fat with reflex gaping of anus following chronic rectal molestation. Inset demonstrates colposcopic view of focal liponecrosis of anal ring.

width of the vaginal introitus. There is very little medical literature defining the normal diameter of the hymenal orifice at different ages. Cantwell (1983) suggests that any opening greater than 4 mm in a prepubertal child is suspicious of sexual abuse. However, in the author's opinion, the orifice may vary considerably in size. Equally significant is the appearance of the surrounding vulvar and hymenal tissue. A slightly enlarged orifice (up to 7 mm) with a perfectly smooth hymenal ring is less disconcerting than is a smaller opening accompanied by many irregularities of the hymenal tissue. A spacious introitus surrounded by multiple hymenal remnants is consistent with chronic abuse. Most sexually active females, regardless of age, are able to voluntarily relax the pubococcygeus muscle. This response can be enhanced by stroking the introital area. In contrast, the sexually inactive female's pubococcygeus muscle is quite tense and tends to contract with manipulation.

Children who are repeatedly sodomized may develop loss of the gluteal fat surrounding the anus (see figure 9.9, Chronic Molestation, Rectal). On visual inspection this will appear as a hollowing-out around the rectum. The impact of a firm object at the perianal ring may result in focal liponecrosis. This thumbprint-like impression (see insert, figure 9.9) is visible to the naked eye, but greatly enhanced with the colposcope.

Repeated anal penetration will result in thickening of the perianal skin. The buttocks should be retracted laterally for 30 seconds to one minute. There may be spontaneous gaping of the anus. This phenomenon can be stimulated by stroking the perianal ring with a moistened Q-tip. There will be an initial wink, and then reflex opening of the anus. Digital examination often reveals remarkably lax rectal tone.

IV. CONCLUSION

The spectrum of activities constituting sexual abuse ranges from exhibitionism through fondling to actual intercourse. It is not surprising, then, that the physical findings also vary greatly. Upon completion of an examination where no physical findings of abuse are detected, the examiner must not conclude that sexual abuse has not occurred. Instead, a statement such as the following clearly states the results of the exam, but allows for the possibility that abuse may have occurred, despite the negative findings.

"The physical examination at this time shows no evidence of sexual abuse. However, since many forms of sexual abuse do not leave physical findings, a normal examination does not exclude the possibility that sexual abuse has occurred."

PART IV: INTERVENTION IN CHILD SEXUAL ABUSE

CHAPTER TEN

Case Management

I. INTRODUCTION

Appropriate case management in child sexual abuse is difficult and challenging. Problems arise because many systems are involved: the police, the child protection agency, the hospital, the juvenile court, the criminal court, and evaluation and treatment agencies. An additional obstacle relates to the emotional reaction experienced by both professionals and nonprofessionals when confronted with cases of sexual abuse; how could an adult do such a thing to a child? As noted in chapter 1, this reaction can lead a person to expend energy explaining away the child's statements or the physical evidence, or alternatively, if a person believes the sexual abuse occurred, pursuit of retribution. These reactions are usually not in the victim's best interest.

In this chapter, case management in intrafamilial sexual abuse will be considered. Such decisions as when to try to maintain the family intact, when to try treatment and with whom, when to remove children, when to criminally prosecute, and when to terminate parental rights will be considered.

II. PARENTAL CHARACTERISTICS AND INTERVENTION

Certain parental characteristics should be considered when making decisions about interventions. These are not the only factors to be taken into account, but at minimum, these factors must be assessed. The characteristics are somewhat different for mothers and fathers. For mothers these are the level of her dependency (particularly upon the perpetrator), the degree to which she loves and is nurturing of the victim (and other children), and the extent to which she has been protective of the victim after discovering the sexual abuse. For fathers, characteristics to be examined are his overall functioning, the extent to which he feels guilty about the sexual abuse, and the extensiveness of the abuse. See also chapters 7 and 8. In each of these areas there can be considerable variability.

A. Maternal Factors

In assessing *maternal dependency* the clinician should first look at the mother's capability to be economically independent of the perpetrator. Does she now work? Does she have a work history or a skill? Alternatively, she may receive an AFDC check in her own name or be willing to apply for AFDC as a strategy for extricating herself from the sexually abusive relationship. Some mothers are made less dependent upon the perpetrator because they have friends or relatives who will take them in and support them when that is necessary. Other indicators of the mother's independence are her capacity to confront the father, to disagree with him, to act despite his objection, and to intercede on behalf of the children against his wishes. In general, maternal independence is a strength and improves the case prognosis whereas maternal dependence is a weakness and means the prospects of the mother's being able to protect the victim are lessened.

The second characteristic of mothers which is important to assess is the extent to which she has an appropriate and loving *relationship with the victim*. This is assessed in the interview with the mother (see chapter 8) and by making observations of the mother and child together.

Clinicians are likely to find that these relationships vary a great deal. Some mothers appear to be very close to the victims and are devastated when they learn what has happened. Others will have ambivalent feelings. Still others are distant and somewhat cold in relationships with their children, including the victim. And in other cases there is competition and jealousy between the mother and daughter. Sometimes a mother will express her dislike for the victim. One mother described her daughter, who was on the honor roll at school and a candy striper, as "lazy, selfish, and greedy." She said her daughter had "a fat ass and a funny face" and that it was absurd for social workers to believe "this liar" when the daughter said that her husband preferred "this stupid kid" to herself.

The warmth and appropriateness of the mother–victim relationship is important as a predictor of whether the mother and children can stay together. In addition, the better that relationship is, the less psychologically scarred the victim will be as a result of the sexual abuse.

Finally, the extent to which the mother has a *protective response* to discovery of the sexual abuse will be important. Again, the mothers' reactions will vary from case to case. What follows is a range of possible maternal responses, from least to most protective.

1. Mother observes the behavior and actively encourages it (very rare).
2. Mother observes the behavior and ignores it, perhaps walks out of the room.
3. Victim reports the abuse; mother accuses her of being a liar, having a dirty mind, etc.
4. Victim reports, mother tells her to avoid the perpetrator, but not to tell anyone.
5. Victim reports, mother confronts perpetrator, he denies, and mother believes perpetrator.
6. After confrontation, mother initially sides with victim, believing and supporting her, but subsequently sides with the father.
7. Upon discovery (observation or report) mother believes and supports victim and insists perpetrator get treatment.
8. Upon discovery mother supports victim, leaves the father and takes the children; calls protective services or police; throws father out; or seeks a divorce.

The more protective the maternal response, the more certain the mother and child will be able to stay together and the better the prognosis for family reunification, should the mother wish it. However, a mother can be protective without entirely believing the sexual abuse happened and can safeguard the child even though she ultimately reconciles with the perpetrator.

The three factors just described, taken together, are predictors for the workability of the mother. Dependent mothers who are hostile toward the victim or blame her, and who are unprotective of their children are not likely to make changes sufficient to become appropriate parents. In contrast the mother who is independent, nurturing, and protective will be able to make the necessary changes.

B. Paternal Factors

As already noted the first perpetrator characteristic to assess is his *overall functioning*. The clinician looks at his education, his work history, his mental health, his substance use, his functioning in the community, any criminal activity, his behavior as a spouse, and his relationships with his children. Some sexual abusers are model citizens in most respects. They work steadily and are regarded as exemplary in their jobs and are active in community affairs. They are attentive husbands who support their families, and they are concerned about their children even though they are sexual with them. Sometimes these fathers are described as overinvolved in their families. At the other end of the continuum is the incestuous father who works sporadically, and who, when working, may keep the money for himself and expect his wife to support the family. He may have a history of mental illness, but more often has a history of violence, criminal activity, and incarceration. He is often physically abusive of his wife and his children, and has an alcohol or drug problem. The perpetrator whose overall functioning is good is a much better prospect for treatment than the man who has significant problems in functioning.

The second aspect of paternal functioning, superego functioning, is related to the one just described. Particularly important here is his guilt about the sexual abuse. Some men who feel very guilty will state they are glad that they have been caught. Others will have suicidal feelings. It will be important to differentiate whether suicidal thoughts arise from the consequences of being caught or from a genuine sense that what they have done is wrong, concern about the damage to the child, and acceptance of responsibility for the sexual behavior. On the other hand, many men who are sexual abusers will feel little or no guilt. They may rationalize or discount their behavior. They may blame the victim, stating she was seductive or needed sex, or they may blame their wives, asserting the wife was withholding of sex or drove them to sexual abuse by nagging. Alternatively, they may describe the abuse as sex education or may state that it is normal behavior for fathers and daughters. One father in our sample claimed he was kicked by a mule and made sterile. It was therefore safe for him to have intercourse with his 14-year-old, and in doing this he sexually satisfied her so that she would not be tempted to have sex with boys her own age.

The prognosis for the father is better the more guilty he feels about the sexual abuse. However, sometimes it is difficult to assess guilt because the perpetrator has not admitted the sexual abuse. In such a situation, guilt and responsibility the perpetrator feels about other aspects of his behavior may provide an indication of the extent of his superego functioning.

The third characteristic to be explored is the *extent of the sexual abuse*. Several factors go into an index of extensiveness of sexual abuse. They are the intrusiveness of sexual abuse ("sexy talk" being the least intrusive and penile penetration the most intrusive), the number of different types of sexual abuse, its duration, its frequency, whether or not force was used, number of victims, and whether they were both intrafamilial and extrafamilial victims. The more extensive the sexual abuse, the poorer the prognosis.

When these three factors of paternal functioning covary they are even stronger predictors of workability. For the man who has few areas of appropriate functioning, evidences no guilt feelings about the sexual abuse, and had engaged in extensive sexual abuse, the prospects of him making sufficient change to play a parenting role are exceedingly remote. Such men are usually psychopaths, for whom successful modes of treatment do not really exist. On the other hand, if he has many areas of appropriate functioning, much guilt about the sexual abuse and has engaged in minimal victimization, the prospects of his being rehabilitated are very much better.

C. Decision-Making Matrix

These maternal and paternal characteristics just described can be put into a decision-making matrix that can be employed to choose appropriate interventions (see table 10.1). Four case types can be identified on the basis of maternal and paternal factors. These and their intervention guidelines are discussed below, with case examples also provided.

Table 10.1 Paternal Figure (Perpetrator)

	Many Areas of Appropriate Functioning; Feels Guilty About Abuse; Sexual Behavior not Extensive	Few Areas of Appropriate Functioning; No Guilt About Abuse; Sexual Behavior Extensive
Maternal Figure	*I*	*II*
INDEPENDENT; LOVES VICTIM; PROTECTIVE	Family should remain intact; or be reconciled when victim will be safe; family therapy but usually also individual, dyadic, and group treatment	Remove paternal figure, usually through arrest and criminal prosecution; treatment for mother and children; may also use individual, dyadic, and group treatment
	III	*IV*
DEPENDENT; POOR RELATIONSHIP WITH VICTIM; NOT PROTECTIVE	First, place children and attempt individual treatment of both parents and marital therapy; if unsuccessful, children should be placed long-term; parental contact may be maintained	Remove children; terminate parental rights; treatment for children; consider criminal prosecution

TYPE I CASES

Type I cases are those where both the mother and perpetrator have many strengths; the mother is independent, loving, and protective when she discovers the sexual abuse, while the perpetrator has good overall and superego functioning, and minimal sexual involvement with children. Type I cases are the most promising and in some instances these families voluntarily seek treatment when the father confesses or the children tell the mother about the sexual abuse. The mental health professional treating the family is legally obligated to make a referral to protective services. However, there is usually no necessity for court involvement. The role of protective services is to assure that the treatment personnel have skills appropriate for dealing with child sexual abuse, that the victim does not need further protection, and that the family continues in its resolve to address the sexual abuse.

Other families with fairly well functioning maternal and paternal caretakers may be overwhelmed by the shame involved in violating the incest taboo and thus may find treatment very painful. They may vacillate in their commitment to treatment or avoid it. They convince themselves "this will never happen again" and thereby persuade themselves that the humiliation of treatment is unnecessary. Such cases need juvenile court intervention to assure the child is protected—that is, the child or perpetrator may need to be out of the home temporarily— and to see that the family follows through on treatment.

In providing therapy to families that fall into Type I, a range of treatments is usually necessary, the final one being some type of family therapy. This may be preceded by individual, dyadic, or group therapy, which, in some cases, can be employed concurrent with family therapy. (For a discussion of treatment see chapters 11 through 13.) The example below is a Type I case.

EXAMPLE 1: Mrs. T remarried a man some eight years her junior after divorcing her first husband. Her second husband was 23, she was 31, and he was sexually inexperienced at the time of their meeting. She had two daughters, 11 and 8, by her first marriage, in whom she seemed very invested. Shortly after their marriage her mother became quite ill and Mrs. T went to take care of her.

Mr. T was left alone to babysit for the two children. After Mrs. T returned from her mother's, her two girls told of instances when their stepfather had rubbed their vulvas. Both children said they had been roughhousing with their stepfather while watching television, and in the process he put his hand inside their pants and rubbed their vaginas. He was fully clothed during these encounters.

Immediately after the children related these events, Mrs. T called her husband at work and demanded an explanation. He denied the allegations, but when he came home from work, he confessed, apologized to the children, and was very shaken. The next day Mrs. T made an appointment for the whole family at Catholic Social Services. The worker from Catholic Social Services called protective services, and the protective services worker joined the family meeting.

In describing how the sexual abuse came about, Mr. T said he was trying to be an appropriate and loving father by roughhousing with the kids when he became sexually aroused. Before he could think it through, he found himself fondling the children. He said at the time he knew it was wrong and was very upset with himself because he did it anyway. He stated that he was glad in a way that the kids had told because he did not think he would have had the nerve to tell Mrs. T. Now at least he would get some help.

It was agreed that Mr. T would move in with his parents until treatment was satisfactorily underway. No court action was initiated. The family complied with the plan, which included individual sessions for all four parties, marital sessions, and family therapy. Four months after treatment began, Mr. T was allowed to return home. Treatment was successfully terminated one year after the reporting of the sexual abuse.

TYPE II CASES

Type II cases are those where the mother appears to be independent, nurturing, and protective of her children, but the father has many areas of problematic behavior and does not evidence guilt about the extensive sexual abuse in which he has been involved. In such cases, the general thrust of intervention is toward maintaining intact and treating the mother and children and excluding the perpetrator. Men who malfunction as just described not only are usually untreatable, but also tend to be unmanageable. They are unlikely to comply with a voluntary intervention plan and may well pose a threat to the mother and children (and possibly others) when these people go against their wishes. Legal intervention is necessary to remove these offenders from the home and prevent their harassment and abuse of the family. Arrest and criminal prosecution for the sexual abuse are appropriate, and restraining orders often are indicated when the perpetrator is in the community. If the perpetrator is incarcerated, as a rule, he will not learn how to function better. However, his absence from the family gives it a chance to change, and society is temporarily protected from the him.

In Type II cases the mother and children are then referred for treatment to deal with the sexual abuse. This may include individual, dyad, and group sessions as well as therapy for the mother and children as a unit. The mother may need concrete services, for example, day care and financial aid. The case that follows is a Type II case.

EXAMPLE 2:   The A's have two girls, 3½ and 4½. Mrs. A. married her
husband when she became pregnant by him at sixteen. They had gone
together for about a year. Before they were married, she said she thought
he was pretty nice except he used too many drugs and would then go
riding into people's yards on his motorcycle and scare the daylights out of
them. On one occasion before they were married, he beat her up, but she
was pregnant and felt she had no choice but to marry him. She knew that
he cheated on her after they got married but tried to overlook this because
she was pregnant. She also said she did not like sex with him anyway. He
was rough and it reminded her of her father who had sexually abused her
when she was a child.

Mr. A worked sporadically driving a truck. Mrs. A would have to
come to his job and get the money after he cashed his paycheck. Otherwise he would spend it on drugs and liquor or parts for his motorcycle.
Frequently Mrs. A had to borrow money from her family for food. She
asserted the only thing that was good about the marriage was the kids.
Mrs. A said they were so much fun.

Mrs. A had to go out of town for a family funeral and left the
children in her husband's care. When she returned the girls were very
upset. They said their father had invited a lady friend over and they had
"sniffed white powder." Then "he sucked her titties, then he put his
dinky in her mouth, and then he put it in her baby hole." He made them
watch. He then "put his dinky in our mouths and peed in our mouths."
Then he made the 4½-year-old "lick his poop hole." This child also said
her dad had made her do nasty things like that "lotsa times before."
When Mrs. A found out she took the children and went to her mother's.
She filed for a divorce, called protective services, and assisted in the
criminal prosecution of Mr. A.

At first when Mr. A was confronted, he denied any of the activities
the children described. Later, when the police questioned him, he said he
had not done anything to them, but had merely allowed them to watch
him and his girlfriend. He stated he did not want them to get the wrong
idea from their mother — that sex was not fun.

After many delays, Mr. A was successfully criminally prosecuted. In
the meantime individual treatment was provided for Mrs. A, therapy for
the girls together was undertaken, and sessions for mother and daughters
were initiated.

TYPE III CASES

In Type III cases, mothers are dependent, hostile or cold toward
their children, and unprotective. Fathers are much better functioning
than mothers, although they have sexually abused the children. The
mother is usually someone who does not form close relationships with
anyone including her spouse and her children and has marked unmet
dependency needs. The father may have gravitated toward the child

because his affective needs, and sometimes sexual needs, are not satisfied by his wife. He usually genuinely loves and cares for his children and feels guilty about the sexual abuse. He may seem overinvested in his children.

Intervention presents many dilemmas. Often the child's primary attachment is to the perpetrator, and the likelihood of the mother protecting the victim from him is not good. The initial intervention should involve working with the mother to mobilize and enhance her protective and appropriate responses and with the father on his sexually abusive behavior. At the same time work should be done with the marital pair to try to enable the couple, particularly the father, to get more gratification from that relationship. Such attempts should be time limited with careful reassessment at the end of six months. Frequently, a good approach is to go into the juvenile court to take jurisdiction of the victims and place them with a relative. This allows more liberal visitation than foster care and, if the mother does not change, a plan to allow long-term relative placement can flow smoothly from the initial placement. However, it is necesary to assess the relative carefully, because sexual abuse is often an extended family problem. The case below is fairly typical.

> EXAMPLE 3: Teresa and Larry, high school sweethearts, got married when she was four months pregnant. Teresa, who was very pretty, was described by Larry as having had a rough childhood. Her father was an alcoholic and beat Teresa and her mother. He also sexually abused Teresa. When Teresa was 15, her mother committed suicide. At first Teresa went to live with her grandmother, who was very religious, requiring Teresa to go to church five times a week. Teresa ran away and asked Larry's family to take her in. They did, and she stayed there until she was 17 and pregnant by Larry.
>
> Larry's parents got them an apartment and paid the rent until Larry finished high school. He worked in the afternoon in a butcher shop in order to support them. Teresa was a poor cook, so Larry and Teresa usually ate dinner at Larry's parents. Teresa gained seventy pounds while she was pregnant and was very upset by this. She began to call the baby a "curse." The baby was two weeks late and weighed 9 pounds. She was named Louise after Larry's mother and was a very beautiful baby. Teresa was quite upset because Louise got all the attention. Larry had to constantly reassure Teresa that he still loved her. Teresa gave much of the care of Louise to her mother-in-law while she concentrated on getting her figure back. However, Teresa also felt jealous because Louise was so fond of her grandmother. Teresa would often contradict her mother-in-law when she set limits for Louise. Larry was also very close to Louise and was the parent who got up with her in the night.

After Larry finished high school, he continued working in the butcher shop and within three years was its manager. His life centered around Louise and his work. Often when Larry came home, Teresa would give him full responsibility for Louise. She began to go out in the evenings leaving Larry to care for Louise. Initially she went to see her girlfriend, but then they began to go to bars and pick up men. On two occasions, Teresa left Larry and moved in with men she had met, but then asked to return when the relationships did not work out. Larry allowed her to return. During this period, Louise began sleeping in Larry and Teresa's bed. When Teresa was there, Louise would insist she sleep between them and neither parent resisted. Louise entered day care when she was four. The day care center became concerned about statements she was making about her daddy's "ding-dong." Protective services was called. Louise said she and her dad would "lie belly to belly" and he would put his "ding-dong" between her legs and "wiggle it around." Then he would "go wet on me." Louise said she told her mother, and her mother told her not to let him "put it in my mouth or my pussy." She also said she had told her grandmother, but her grandmother did not believe her.

When Larry was first confronted, he denied the sexual abuse. Teresa corroborated his story. However after Louise had been in foster care two weeks, Larry confessed to the protective services worker. Teresa got very angry at him and told him he should have "stonewalled." Larry said he confessed because he was afraid of "hurting his little girl," and he would do whatever was necessary to get her back. Larry received treatment, but Teresa did not attend regularly. Eventually she went off with another man, leaving the state. Louise was placed with her grandmother with instructions that Larry could have liberal visits with her but that he should not be left alone with her.

TYPE IV CASES

Cases falling into Type IV are those where the father malfunctions in many areas, evidences no guilt about the sexual abuse, and has been involved in extensive sexual abuse. The mother is dependent, cold toward the victim, and unprotective. When both parents are this seriously impaired, the prognosis for change is very, very poor. Children should be removed from the home and placed in what can be a permanent home. Parental rights should almost always be terminated. Treatment for the children is very likely to be necessary for a year or more, and at later developmental stages additional treatment may well be indicated. The new caretakers will also need to participate in treatment sessions. Criminal prosecution may be appropriate for the perpetrator—not because he will improve in prison, but because society will be protected while he is there. Treatment for the mother or father is very unlikely to be successful. The mother, after her children have been removed, may repeat the cycle—that is, she may have additional children whom she also places at risk, either with her sexually abusive spouse or someone else. The case example below is a dramatic illustration of a Type IV case.

EXAMPLE 4: Ralph, 25, lived with Debbie, 23. Ralph had one child, Lucy, of whom he gained custody when his wife, Cindy, 20, abandoned her. Lucy was three and a half. Ralph and Debbie had a six month old daughter, Sarah.

Ralph occasionally worked as a roofer and did not declare his income. His primary means of support was AFDC. Ralph had been using drugs since he was 12, and he got drunk every night. He beat up Debbie, he beat Lucy, he went out with other women, he cheated the welfare, he sold drugs to junior high school students, and he shoplifted.

Debbie had been brutally abused as a child by her mother. Her mother held her hands in the flame of a gas burner when her brother, three years her junior, for whom Debbie was responsible, stole a piece of gum from a drugstore. Debbie was the oldest child in the family and had to take care of the three younger children. When Debbie was 16 and her brother 13, she shot him and paralyzed him from the waist down. They had been having an incestuous affair and he had wanted to break it off because he had a new girlfriend. Debbie subsequently spent four months in a psychiatric hospital and then one year in a home for delinquents. Debbie reported she had started drinking at 8 and recalled going to school drunk in the seventh grade. At 18, Debbie almost died of alcoholism. She also used drugs and was psychotic some of the time.

Debbie had a series of liaisons with men who took sexual and other kinds of advantage of her. She could not extricate herself from these relationships; rather they woud terminate when the men got tired of her. She felt she could not give up Ralph because he was "the only man I've ever met who would give his name to my baby." However, she had also attempted to abort Sarah, and she described the child as having ruined her life. Moreover, she had placed Sarah in foster care for one month when Sarah was two months old because she was overwhelmed with the responsibility and was spanking Sarah.

Both Sarah and Lucy were sexually abused by Ralph. He insisted that Lucy watch him and Debbie have intercourse so she could learn to do it right. Debbie would wake Lucy up, get her out of bed, and disrobe her for these events. Ralph also attempted intercourse with Lucy. In addition, Ralph had Debbie undress Sarah, and he licked Sarah's vulva, saying he "wanted to taste a virgin," while he masturbated. Further, Lucy reported observing Ralph attempt intercourse with Sarah. When Debbie was asked how she felt about what Ralph had done to the girls, she said at first not much, but later when she thought about it, she was kind of mad. However, she said she couldn't stop him because his welfare check was bigger than hers. Both children were removed from the care of Debbie and Ralph and placed in a potentially adoptive foster home. Therapy was initiated for Lucy and the foster parents. Ralph admitted to the sexual abuse and was sentenced to five years in prison. Attempts were made to assist Debbie, but she shunned them.

D. Families That Don't Fit the Four Case Types

Unfortunately, reality is often more complex than the guidelines presented in the decision matrix (table 10.1). Three kinds of problems are likely to emerge when trying to fit a family into the matrix. In the first place, each of the paternal and maternal factors represents a continuum, and parental functioning is not necessarily at one end or the other. In addition, the factors do not always covary as described. Furthermore, the data necessary for the decision-making process may not be available.

In cases that cannot be classified with certainty, we suggest professionals first be sure the child is protected and then try treatment and carefully assess its impact. Time limits should be placed on how long therapy should be tried before decisions are made regarding disposition, and court intervention should be used to facilitate treatment goals.

The first problem—that the paternal and maternal factors are continua—has already been alluded to in the earlier descriptions of the factors. For example a father may feel neither extremely guilty nor guiltless about the sexual abuse; but may instead feel moderate guilt, or the guilty feelings may quickly pass. Similarly a mother is not necessarily either very loving or totally cold or hostile toward the victim. She may have positive nurturing feelings and some angry feelings as well. The example below is one where both parents fall somewhere in between the two ends of the continua.

> EXAMPLE 5:   The first reports that Mary Jane was being sexually abused came from her mother, Jean, when Mary Jane was 2½. This was a time of marital discord and the couple separated. Dave, the father, had been unemployed for a time and Jean had been working as a waitress. Dave was also drinking. They had been living with Jean's mother in her trailer because they had been evicted from their apartment. Dave moved in with his minister after the allegations were made. He was a vigorous advocate for Dave. The minister described Jean's family as "man haters" and "not good Christians." Dave moved out of the minister's house and in with a girlfriend who had a four-year-old daughter. However, after about four months Dave and Jean reconciled. Jean told protective services that she thought she had been wrong about the sexual abuse. By that time, Dave had obtained a job as a salesman and Jean quit work. She became pregnant by Dave and had a boy, Daniel.

When Mary Jane was 4½ and in day care, she was observed to masturbate excessively. Protective services was called and they interviewed Mary Jane. She told the worker that her father put his fingers inside her vagina and "sometimes gives me a kiss on those funny lips down there." She further stated that daddy goes to bed with mommy, but sometimes comes and gets in bed with her before it gets light in the morning. This is when he does the things. Her mom tells him not to when she finds him there.

Both Dave and Jean denied Mary Jane's allegations. Jean said that she was having trouble managing Mary Jane, that she always wanted her way and now she was making up stories.

Mary Jane was placed with her maternal great-aunt temporarily and individual treatment was initiated for Dave and Jean. Jean soon acknowledged that Mary Jane must have been telling the truth, noting her earlier suspicions. Dave continued to deny the sexual abuse.

In this case we find a father who is neither a model citizen nor totally dysfunctional. It is difficult to assess his guilt because of the absence of admission. The extent of sexual abuse appears moderate. With regard to the mother, she appears somewhat dependent upon the perpetrator, to have ambivalent feelings toward her daughter, and to have reacted both protectively and unprotectively at different times.

The second problem noted with the matrix is lack of covariance of parental factors. For instance a father who has engaged in extensive sexual abuse may, rather than discounting the behavior, feel more guilt than a man with a comparable superego but less abusive behavior. As mentioned earlier, the man who engages in extensive sexual abuse may be obsessional. This type of man may feel a great deal of guilt but still be unable to control his behavior. Further, some men who have many areas of appropriate functioning nevertheless have engaged in extensive sexual abuse. Again, this may be an obsessional pattern. Similarly, a mother may be quite independent of the perpetrator but nevertheless have very negative feelings toward the victim. Often she frankly does not care very much about what goes on within the family, as her interests lie outside. There are also mothers who care very much about their children but are very dependent upon their husbands. These women also are often battered, and stay in the abusive situation in the vain hope the spouse will change. They even may allow themselves to be abused as a way to protect the children. The example below illustrates lack of covariance.

EXAMPLE 6: The J's have four children, three girls — ages 10, 8 and 6 — and a boy, 2 — a mistake. Mrs. J is very involved in the church, to which she goes three times a week. Although she had wanted children, she finds them messy, whiny, sacrilegious and time-consuming. Her husband prefers their company to going to church and so he watches them while she attends. In fact, the couple spends little time together because he is at work and when he comes home she goes to church. This suits her fine because he gets sloppy and sentimental at times when they are together and he wants to cuddle on the couch. She does not have time for this silliness.

One night she came home and found him in the bed with the two older girls, and all three of them were naked. They had fallen asleep. When she questioned her husband about what was going on, he said that they had taken showers and forgotten to put their nightclothes on.

However, the eight-year-old said that they did this lots of times and daddy rubs their "pussies" and they rub his "peter." The ten-year-old said the eight-year-old was a liar. Mrs. J was ready to believe the ten-year-old, except that her husband had acted so guilty. Two days later, he confessed, and cried, and asked for help. She told him he needed to ask God for forgiveness, not her. If he did that, she would be satisfied, but she would never have sex with him again. She did not seek any help for the children nor for her husband and continued in her pattern of leaving him alone with the children. About two years later, the youngest daughter, then 8, told her teacher about a game they played with daddy's "peter." She also said her daddy puts his "peter" in her sister's "pussy almost every night." This led to protective services intervention. All four children were removed from the home and placed in temporary foster care. Mrs. J was humiliated because the foster mother was a member of her church. She and Mr. J were referred for treatment.

In this case, we see a mother who is cool toward her children and not protective, but nevertheless independent of the perpetrator. The perpetrator has a fair number of areas of appropriate functioning and feels guilty about the sexual abuse, but the sexual abuse is extensive.

The third problem encountered when trying to apply the matrix is the absence of all the pertinent information. Frequently, case decisions must be made on an emergency basis when the data are not all available. In addition, the family, even the victim, may not be candid. Thus the decisionmaker does not know the extent of the sexual abuse and may not be told about other family and individual dysfunction. Moreover, a mother may assert in the presence of the professional that she is not dependent upon her spouse but behave in quite a different manner out of the professional's view. In addition, a mother may be aware that her negative feelings toward the victim are not acceptable and may conceal them. The case example below illustrates some of these problems.

EXAMPLE 7: Jennie, age 7, first was referred to protective services because she was drawing pictures in school of men with penises. At that time, the worker talked to Jennie's mother and stepfather, querying why Jennie would draw such pictures and they could offer no explanation. The case was kept open and various services were provided, including someone to work with the couple on parenting. Both parents admitted they could control their children only with harsh discipline. Jennie saw a social worker at school every week in part because she was placed in an emotionally impaired classroom. After about nine months the case was closed.

A year after the first referral Jennie again began drawing pictures with penises on them. At that point she was seen by an expert in sexual abuse. Three, two-hour diagnostic sessions took place with Jennie, and the parents were seen a total of four hours. In Jennie's first diagnostic session she asserted her stepfather had physically abused her and said he did "something else terrible." This would happen when her father was working at home and only she was there. She admitted to seeing her father's penis but would not reveal the circumstances. She said she had told her mother about what was happening and her mother told her not to tell anyone else. She said she knew she would get a beating if she told. She cried bitterly as she related these things. At the end of the interview, Jennie was placed in temporary foster care. She cried when they took her into care, explaining how mad her mother would be.

The subsequent two interviews yielded no additional information and some recantation, with Jennie stating over and over again "nothing happened I tell you, nothing happened." When the parents were interviewed both admitted having discipline problems with Jennie but denied any sexual abuse. The father had a good work history. He was a self-made man, who had his own construction business. When work was slack during the winter, he worked on his own house and took courses at the local community college.

The mother reported that she was not a physically affectionate person and said she found Jennie very frustrating to handle. She stated that the family was functioning much better now that Jennie was in foster care because she had fought so much with her two younger brothers. She also described the children's father (her first husband) as a batterer who had very perverse sexual habits. She said when Jennie was four and visiting him for two weeks in Tennessee, something scary and sexual went on but she does not know what. She also stated that around that time, Jennie was fondled in the street by a stranger. She wondered if either of these incidents could have led Jennie to draw the pictures.

Jennie remained in foster care and was involved in treatment. The major treatment focus was trying to find out if Jennie had been sexually abused. Family therapy was also initiated.

The major problem in this case is not knowing with absolute certainty if Jennie was sexually abused. Jennie will not say and her parents deny it. We do know that the father evidences fairly good overall functioning and the mother has negative feelings toward Jennie. These findings prompted temporary placement of Jennie to assure her protection, and treatment in order to find out more about the allegations.

III. CONCLUSION

A review of the literature on sexual abuse reveals a lack of appreciation of the variability in cases, and the fact that different types of cases require different intervention approaches. This chapter has attempted to address this shortcoming by providing guidelines for case management of intrafamilial sexual abuse cases.

CHAPTER ELEVEN

Treatment of the Victim

I. INTRODUCTION

Frequently victims of sexual abuse require treatment in their own right. That is, family therapy or other forms of treatment may be employed to address the dynamics of the sexual abuse, but individual treatment for the victim may be needed to prepare her for family sessions or to attend to issues that are not addressed in other treatment contexts. Treatment of victims may be the only intervention indicated in cases of extrafamilial sexual abuse, but with intrafamilial sexual abuse, additional forms of treatment are required unless the child is out of the home, will not return, and there are no other potential victims in the home. Victim treatment may be very brief, consisting of only one or two sessions, or it may be extended, lasting several years.

In this chapter, criteria for deciding when individual treatment for the victim is needed will be presented, the use of surrogates to assist the therapist will be discussed, and seven treatment issues and techniques will be examined.

II. WHEN IS INDIVIDUAL TREATMENT NEEDED?

One should be cautious about automatically requiring individual therapy for the victim. Such intervention may be interpreted by the victim or others as indicating that the victim is the one who has the problem, particularly if attempts to engage the family or perpetrator in therapy have been unsuccessful. In addition, treatment can sometimes exacerbate the trauma by focusing on the abuse and making it more of an issue than it actually was. For example, suppose a four-year-old girl was fondled by a ten-year-old neighbor boy once, appropriately responded by resisting and telling a supportive adult, and did not evidence any trauma from the event. Extended treatment might alter her perception of the abuse to the point where she might begin to feel stigmatized and guilty. Finally, children should not be forced to go to treatment. If they are, then treatment becomes yet another form of coercion in the child's eyes. However, children can be urged to "try it and see" or, if this strategy is unsuccessful, they can be told that "the problem won't go away" and when they feel ready to work on it, they should seek help.

Nevertheless, there are certain indicators that individual treatment should be provided. One is when sexual abuse has been extensive. From the victim's viewpoint, extensive sexual abuse is defined in terms of duration, frequency, and intrusiveness of the sexual abuse—and number of perpetrators. Denise's experience, also discussed in chapter 6, was one of extensive sexual abuse and necessitated individual treatment.

> EXAMPLE 1:   Denise, 8, reported to her grandmother what her father and two male babysitters were doing. Her father had fondled her "pussy willow," had put buttery flavored Crisco around her anus and engaged in anal intercourse with her, and had engaged in genital intercourse with her, penetrating her from behind. Bill, who was her father's cousin and her babysitter, engaged in genital intercourse with Denise and made her fellate him. Denise said, "He made me swallow the white stuff." Jim, who babysat for Denise when Bill could not, also made Denise submit to genital intercourse and fellatio. She had told her mother and her mother did nothing.
>
> Denise was removed from her parents' care and parental rights were terminated. Denise was involved in play therapy for two years to deal with the sexual abuse, and work was done with her foster parents on child management.

In Denise's case, we do not know how long the sexual abuse went on, but probably for years, several times a week. Fortunately, Denise was in a supportive foster home and with treatment was able to make a remarkable recovery.

Treatment is also usually necessary if physical force has been used or the child has been physically harmed. The injury may be to the genitalia or to other parts of the body. Anal intercourse is particularly likely to produce physical trauma and therefore the need for treatment. Julia's case, also cited in chapter 5, is typical of this kind of bodily harm and accompanying psychological trauma.

> EXAMPLE 2:   Julia, 6 was sexually abused by her father who was divorced from her mother. One of the things he did was to put a child's toy in her vagina. She would return from visits with swollen and red genitalia. On one occasion she was bleeding from the vagina. She began having nightmares, wetting the bed, and wanting "to sleep with my mommy." She received treatment with her mother's participation.

Not only did Julia suffer repeated physical injury, but her case illustrates a third situation when the child needs treatment: when there is evident psychological distress. If the child has emotional symptoms such as withdrawal, anxiety, depression, fear, guilt, or anger, treatment should be provided. Additional behavioral indicators of emotional disturbance include sleep difficulties (nightmares, inability to go to sleep, sleepwalking), enuresis or encopresis, self-destructive behavior (drug and alcohol use, repeated accidents, and suicidal thoughts and attempts), acting-out behavior (fighting, stealing, running away, truanting), problems with school work, and difficulty in peer relationships. Janice, also discussed in chapter 6, is an example of a victim with such problems.

> EXAMPLE 3:   Janice 15, had been sexually abused by her mother's boyfriend beginning when she was about 6. The abuse included his watching, through a hole in the bathroom wall, while she went to the toilet or took a bath and requiring that she watch him, digital penetration, fellatio, and attempted genital intercourse. At 13, Janice began to drink and use drugs; she was sexually active; did poorly in school; and attempted suicide. Her behavior was very unpredictable; sometimes she was hostile and uncooperative with professionals, but other times she was quite civil.
>   Janice received individual treatment that focused upon the underlying causes of her behavior. Treatment went slowly because sometimes she would refuse to talk, but eventually she was able to deal with her feelings and her behavior improved markedly.

Janice is fairly typical of adolescents who have been victims of sexual abuse over a period of years. Often, naive professionals focus intervention on the acting out behaviors without any appreciation of the underlying cause.

Finally, treatment should also be provided if the child has a residue of inappropriate sexual behaviors. These might be excessive masturbation, sexual aggression, an unusual amount of sexual play with other children, and making sexual advances toward adults. These behaviors may be manifested at home and observed by foster or natural parents. Alternatively, they may be noted in day care or school settings, or other children may complain about being sexually accosted by the victim. In general, these behaviors are characteristic of younger victims. The case of Brenda and Wendy, discussed earlier in chapter 5, typifies this type of problem.

> EXAMPLE 4:   Brenda, 6, and Wendy, 4, had been sexually abused by their father but with their mother's collusion. In foster care, they would fondle each other in bed at night. Brenda would sit on the foster father's lap and try to unbutton his shirt and rub his chest. Wendy on several occasions followed the foster father into the bathroom, saying she wanted to watch his penis when he urinated. Both girls received therapy in which ap-

propriate interaction with other people was an important focus, and soon
the sexual behaviors all but disappeared.

Treatment in this case was crucial because the sexual behavior was
very difficult for the foster family to tolerate. Without treatment, the
foster family probably would have requested the children be moved.

III. SURROGATES IN TREATMENT OF THE CHILD

The role of parents (when they did not play a part in the abuse), foster
parents, or other important persons in the victims' lives may be central in
treatment. They may serve as "surrogate therapists." It is particularly
appropriate to use surrogates with children under the age of ten. There
are several rationales for doing this. First, the therapist will want persons
in the child's natural environment to respond therapeutically to the
child's concerns and needs. Second, very young children are not able to
form treatment alliances. Because of their developmental stage, their investment is in their caretakers and living situations, so attempts to treat
them outside the family context may have little impact. Third, many
children will not compliantly trot out their worries for the therapist, and
further trauma may be induced by the therapist's forcing them to deal
with the stressful material. Most children, particularly young ones, much
prefer to confide their fears in people whom they know and trust—their
parents, foster parents, or other caretakers. Further, they are likely to
raise concerns about abuse at awkward times for therapy: at bed time or
when they wake up with a bad dream in the middle of the night.

There is a final reason for inducting parents into a treatment role.
It is fairly common for them to be more traumatized by the sexual abuse
than the children. If nothing is done to calm the parents down and assist
them in responding supportively and appropriately to the child, they can
exacerbate the damage. Although this danger exists in all cases, inappropriate parental responses are particularly likely to occur when the
abuse arouses unresolved feelings, often related to the parents' own sexual abuse as children.

The surrogate therapist may play a minor or a major role. The
professional therapist's task is to acquaint the surrogate with the kinds of
worries and symptomatic behaviors the victim is likely to exhibit, and
coach the surrogate in how to respond in a helpful way. Sometimes this
training process is as simple as instructing the mother, "If the child
thinks she is responsible for her daddy being in jail, tell her she is not. He

broke the law. She did not break the law. She told the truth. He knew what he was doing is against the law." In other instances, the therapist can model how to handle the victim's concerns in sessions involving the child and surrogate. Alternatively, without the child present, the therapist may role play with the surrogate critical incidents and appropriate caretaker responses to these. The therapist then builds in feedback sessions so that the surrogate can recount instances when the child has brought up material and how this was handled. The example below typifies the appropriate use of a surrogate.

> EXAMPLE 5:   Belinda, 7 ½, had been placed with her maternal aunt after she and her two sisters were removed from their parents' custody because of physical abuse by the mother and physical and sexual abuse by the father. In therapy, Belinda was able to talk about the physical abuse but would become extremely upset at the mention of the sexual abuse and refused to acknowledge that it had happened. After two attempts to get Belinda to talk about the sexual abuse, the therapist decided a superior strategy was to make use of Belinda's maternal aunt as a surrogate therapist. The therapist met with the aunt and Belinda bi-weekly, spending a half hour with the aunt, addressing aspects of the sexual abuse Belinda had brought up with her and how she had dealt with them. The remainder of the time was spent with Belinda in play and gently approaching issues related to the sexual abuse. Eventually Belinda was able to bring up with the therapist the fears she had discussed with her aunt.

Thus, the use of surrogates can facilitate the treatment process, reduce trauma which might result from treatment, and provide the victim with a supportive person long after the end of treatment.

IV. ISSUES IN TREATMENT OF THE VICTIM

There are several interrelated concerns which are likely to emerge in treatment of the victim. Not all of the concerns may be present in a given case, and the intensity and pervasiveness of these issues will vary. They are: (a) loss of trust; (b) altered body image; (c) guilt feelings and feeling responsible; (d) anger; (e) depression and self-destructive behaviors; (f) understanding the meaning of the sexual abuse; and (g) strategies for self-protection. Each of these issues will be discussed separately, along with appropriate treatment techniques. However, in reality, the treatment issues are overlapping and techniques often will address more than one treatment issue.

A. Loss of Trust

The most fundamental trauma that can result from sexual abuse is damage to the child's ability to form trusting relationships, particularly with caretaking figures.

What has undermined this trust is exploitation by someone who should have been the child's protector, nurturer, and teacher. Often children do not understand what they are becoming involved in when the sexual abuse begins. As they come to comprehend the meaning of the sexual abuse, the impact is quite devastating. Trust is further undermined when the perpetrator—as is usually the case—involves the child in a conspiracy of silence. When the abuse does come to light, the perpetrator usually lies and attempts to get others to believe that the victim is lying. This array of manipulations from someone whom the child is supposed to trust is both bewildering and overwhelming.

This type of damage is not an outcome in all cases. However, the closer the relationship between victim and offender, the more likely the damage to the child's ability to trust. If the perpetrator is a father, but the child has a stepfather who behaves appropriately, the harm will be mediated. Similarly, if the father is sexually abusive but the mother is supportive, her response will lessen the damage to the child's ability to trust. It follows then that trauma is exacerbated when the perpetrator is a parent and the nonoffending parent does not support the victim. Examples of nonsupportive responses include situations where the mother, although not a perpetrator, has knowledge of the sexual abuse yet does not protect the child, where the victim tells the mother of the sexual abuse and she disbelieves the child, and where the mother chooses to side with the perpetrator rather than with the victim when the case comes to professional attention. In addition, when both caretakers sexually abuse the child or when the perpetrator is assisted by the other parent in the victimization, damage to the child's ability to trust is pervasive. Likewise, the trauma is compounded if there are multiple perpetrators. Finally, when other forms of maltreatment, misuse, and family dysfunction are also part of the child's experience, damage is increased (Conte 1985).

As a rule, victims who have experienced abuse by an adult of one sex, usually a man, will exhibit distrust of adults of that sex. When victimized by adults of both sexes, or if the nonoffending parent has not been supportive, there is pervasive damage to the victims' ability to invest in people, especially adults. Susan, who is also mentioned in chapter 1, is a dramatic example of loss of trust.

EXAMPLE 6: Susan, 13, was described as manipulative, as forming superficial relationships, and as being distrustful of men. Her psychiatric diagnosis at 13 was severe character disorder. There were reports to protective services about her mother's abuse and neglect of Susan and her younger brother beginning when Susan was four months old. Her mother was an assaultive and angry woman who resented Susan's interference with her adolescence. Susan was born when her mother was 17 and had just been discharged from girls' training school. When Susan was eight, her mother went to jail for two years on a conspiracy charge. The mother refused to turn state's evidence on her boyfriend who was stealing and cashing welfare checks. Susan and her brother went into foster care, but were returned to their mother's care upon her discharge. Several different men lived with Susan's mother and were abusive to the children.

When Susan was 10, her mother's old boyfriend, the check thief, got out of prison and came to live with them. He began sexually abusing Susan. When her mother was at work (she worked evenings as a nurse's aide) this man would make Susan come to bed with him. He engaged in a program of gradual genital penetration of Susan, complimenting Susan by telling her he could get his penis farther in her than in her mother. Susan told her mother about the sexual abuse at least six times over a three-year period. The mother's typical response was to make Susan confront the boyfriend with her assertions. He would then call Susan a liar and so would her mother. On one occasion, Susan's mother would not allow Susan to go to school, to church, or to her after-school activities until she retracted her assertions.

When the case came to the attention of protective services, the mother went to extreme lengths to persuade people that Susan was a liar. She acquired Susan's diary and letters to and from friends, which of course revealed Susan's private thoughts, doubts, and worries. Her mother read these aloud in court. She enlisted the support of school personnel to testify against Susan. She coerced Susan's brother, who had observed the sexual abuse, to testify that he had observed nothing.

This is a tragic example of how a victim's trust can be undermined, not only by the perpetrator but also by the mother who has turned against her child. Susan had significant problems in object relations and the ability to trust. However, these problems in forming relationships began earlier with the mother's abusive and neglectful treatment of the children.

Ameliorating loss of trust requires a range of interventions and cannot be accomplished solely through individual treatment of the victim. However, the general thrust of the interventions is to afford the child opportunities to form relationships and have interactions with people who can be trusted. The therapist should be one of these. Therefore, it is very important that the therapist be dependable, for example, by keeping appointments and promises, by supporting the child through the legal and other procedures, and by accepting the victim no matter how unacceptable her behavior may become. It is also important that the therapist be honest and straightforward with the child and encourage other professionals to be so. For example, in the effort to encourage the child to tell about the sexual abuse, there is the temptation to reassure the child that everything will be all right if she tells. Professionals should resist this temptation. Similarly, professionals may be very anxious for successful prosecution of the perpetrator in situations where the child does not want the perpetrator to go to jail. In most cases, the victim's testimony is necessary for a conviction, but professionals may be loath to inform the victim of the implications of her testimony because of fear the victim will refuse to talk on the stand. Difficult though it may be, it is essential that professionals be candid with the child. Otherwise, she will feel she has again been tricked by adults.

In addition, the therapist becomes for the child an adult who can be caring and even affectionate without becoming sexual. The relationship becomes a model for the child of appropriate primary relationships. Therefore, depending upon the age and the response of the child, the therapist will give pats on the head, hugs, and allow the child to sit on her lap, while being careful to keep the contact affectionate but not sensual. It is often therapeutic for the therapist to point out to the child that the kind of touch they are engaging in is "OK" but that other types of touch are not. (See section G for a further discussion of touch).

Another important role for the therapist is to assist other key people in the child's life in understanding the child's difficulty with trust and to aid them in being trustworthy adults. Often these people are surrogates employed in the treatment or foster parents. If the child is with the parents or is to return home, then parents need to receive therapy so that they can become trustworthy adults.

Foster parents and adoptive parents are often expected to provide an environment that compensates for the deficiencies of the one from which the child has been removed. However, children whose ability to trust is impaired because of sexual abuse may not be responsive to their attempts to nurture. Foster and even adoptive parents may become discouraged because they do not seem to be able to "make the difference" for the victim. Then they may stop trying to get close to the child or, worse still, ask that the victim be moved because they feel the victim doesn't like them; both of these responses further hamper the child's ability to trust adults. The therapist must sensitize the child's caretakers to the difficulties the victim is likely to have in responding to their attempts to be nurturing, assist them to be patient and keep trying, and interpret the victim's misbehavior as a defensive maneuver because of fear of getting close. The example of Candy, described below, illustrates how the therapist used herself and the victim's environment as contexts for helping Candy reestablish trust.

EXAMPLE 7:   Candy S, 5, had been sexually abused by her mother's boyfriend, George. Ms. S, a single parent, was reported to have a drinking problem by relatives, but she staunchly denied this. She also had a history of mental instability. Ms. S moved frequently from place to place, living with friends, relatives, and her boyfriend, George. When Candy and her mother had been living with George for about four months, she told her mother that George made her play with his wiener when Ms. S was passed out on the couch. Candy's mother was drunk at the time Candy told her, and she called Candy a dirty liar. However, the idea that George might have done this began to obsess Ms. S, and she had a nervous breakdown and was hospitalized. Candy went into foster care.

She kept the foster mother, Diane, at arm's length and was fearful of the foster father, Mark. Like many foster parents, Diane and Mark were distressed that Candy did not respond in kind to their attempts to show affection. The therapist explained to them how difficult it was for Candy to make an investment in a relationship with them because of her past experiences. The therapist was able to assist the foster parents to consistently reach out to Candy but also to tolerate her minimal responses to them. Eventually these efforts paid off, and about four months into the placement Candy began to show some affection. However, she also would become upset and angry if left with a babysitter or if Mark had to go away on business. The foster parents needed assurance to understand and tolerate this behavior, which reflected fear of losing them, too.

The therapist saw Candy on a weekly basis, beginning when she first was placed. Initially, she made it clear to Candy that she believed Candy when she reported she had been sexually abused by George. The therapist also told Candy she knew it was hard when people she was close to, like her mom, didn't believe her and when they went away. Candy nodded. The therapist told Candy that her foster parents believed her, too.

The therapist then asked Candy what she thought should happen to George. Candy said, "He ought to be taken into court." The therapist then asked what the court should do and Candy said, "Put him in jail." Candy was then told she would have to tell the judge what George had done for him to go to jail and was asked if she thought she could do that. Defiantly she said, "Yes!" The court process then was described to Candy.

In the third session the preparation for court was begun. Candy was told about all aspects of the process, including cross-examination, and the fact that her mother was being called as a witness for George's side. (On the stand, Candy's mother said Candy had mentioned sexual abuse to her, but she did not take it seriously because she was accustomed to Candy's lying.) Candy's feelings about the process were anticipated and articulated by the therapist.

It took a year before all of the court work was done, and the therapist remained involved throughout that time and after George was convicted. Candy remained in the same foster home and her foster parents began to express an interest in adopting her.

Candy's mother had had another child by a man whom she met in the mental hospital. She stopped visiting Candy and did not follow through on the contract she had made with the foster care worker, which specified what she had to do in order for Candy to be returned. The next stage of work for the therapist and Candy was to help her deal with termination of her mother's parental rights, which would represent another significant loss for Candy. Fortunately, however, she was forming good relationships with the foster parents and was verbalizing a wish to remain with them indefinitely.

Candy, like Susan, experienced significant undermining of trust as a result of the sexual abuse because her belief in the dependability of others and her environment was already quite fragile. Further, these are both cases where the child was dealing not only with betrayal by the perpetrator but also with lack of support by the mother. A key factor in success with Candy is that she had a therapist who continued to be involved and foster parents who eventually decided to adopt her. Intervention to address trust problems as severe as these takes a long time and is not always successful. In cases where the damage is not so pervasive, prognosis is much better.

B. Altered Body Image

Often children who have been sexually abused suffer an altered body image. They feel they are physically damaged, dirty, ruined, or no longer whole or perfect. They may develop a special abhorrence for their private parts. Sgroi et al. (1982) call this the "damaged goods syndrome." Victims are particularly likely to have feelings of being damaged when physical injury has resulted or when the sexual assault was forced. Victims may feel others can tell, merely by looking at them, that there is something wrong with them, that they are different. At times victims will treat their bodies in such a way that they do become damaged and dirty. Victims may overeat and become obese or undereat and become emaciated. Both patterns have the dual purpose of causing the victim to become "the freak she feels she is" and of making her less attractive to an abuser. Some victims fail to bathe, do not practice good hygiene, and dress in a sloppy or unattractive manner. The example of Gina is illustrative.

EXAMPLE 8:   Gina, 11 and black, was penetrated vaginally and anally by her 15-year-old brother. He was large for his age and a very aggressive and disturbed boy. Gina's mother would leave the two children at home alone together several times a week, despite Gina's protests, while she went to a bar. Gina's brother would beat her up and then rape her. Frequently Gina would have bruises as a result of his assaults. After two years, she told her aunt, who called protective services. Gina ended up living her aunt because of her mother's lack of cooperation with protective services. In treatment, Gina described her discomfort when going to her new school because she was sure everyone could tell by looking at her what her brother had done. She neglected her personal hygiene, avoiding baths, and particularly neglecting to wash her vaginal area. She acknowledged in treatment that she felt dirty and so she let herself be dirty.

With Gina, the feelings of being damaged were especially manifest when she entered a new environment where she felt people had not had her experience. Her new school was middle class and interracial, whereas her old school was in an urban ghetto and black. She acted out the feelings she had about her body, that it was tainted, by not washing.

For some children, the perception of themselves as damaged becomes a self-fulfilling prophecy. They come to behave as they see themselves, and others respond to them accordingly. Sometimes others, either peers or adults, find out about the sexual abuse and make derogatory remarks or accost them sexually. These reactions reinforce victims' feelings about their bodies.

Treatment of altered body image involves continued reassurance and support. The therapist tells the child in many different ways that she is intact. If there are physical injuries, the child should be told they will heal soon and that there will not be any permanent scars (assuming there will be none). Sometimes a physical exam that will document the absence of physical damage can be helpful (Sgroi et al. 1982).

Young children may express how damaged they feel in pictures or in play, and these media become opportunities for treatment. Patterns found in self-drawing may include the victim's depicting herself with legs apart (indicating vulnerability to sexual abuse) or with no arms or no hands (suggesting an inability to resist the encounters). She may also draw her private parts or other details of the genital area (suggesting a preoccupation with the sexual abuse), or depict herself as angry or sad.

The therapist can take a number of approaches using the drawings as a medium for treatment. The therapist may merely support the victim in drawing efforts, believing that the child will, in drawing and in the therapy as a whole, work through these feelings. Another more directive technique is to ask the child questions about the picture—for example, "Why doesn't the little boy (or "you," if the child has so identified the picture) have any arms?" or offer interpretations. "I think sometimes you feel like you have no arms because you couldn't stop Uncle George from hurting your fanny." The therapist might then talk to the child about what it feels like to be vulnerable or damaged and then move on to ask what it would take for her to feel safe and strong again. The discussion might resolve the child's feelings about her body, or it might lead to further intervention by the therapist in the child's environment. Frequently the results of the discussion and/or intervention emerge in later drawings.

An even more directive approach is for the therapist to control the endeavor by asking the victim to change the drawing, or the therapist may herself change the drawing to make the victim whole. This intervention might then lead to a discussion of why the child draws her damaged and what can be done to help the child feel good about her body. How directive the therapist chooses to be will depend upon her preference in approach, the particular child, and the specific play situation.

The example of Sandra below shows how drawings can be used as a medium for treatment.

> EXAMPLE 9: Sandra, age 5, whose self-drawing appears both in chapter 6, and as figure 11.1a, continually drew herself with her legs apart. When asked about this, she related it to a time that a picture of her genitalia was taken to be sold as child pornography. However, the therapist thought the picture also reflected a more general feeling of being accessible to men and having that part of her anatomy exposed to them. Sandra had been sexually abused by a number of men. After some months of therapy addressing issues of body image and other feelings, her self-pictures began to change so that she did not appear so vulnerable. (See Figure 11.1b).
>
> In Figure 11.1b, note that Sandra is smiling, she has a dog, FooFoo, and flowers are growing around her, all indications of better feelings about herself. She is also wearing rings on all her fingers. The therapist wore lots of rings and Sandra was identifying with her.

The therapist can work with children in similar ways through the medium of play. That is, the therapist can merely provide a supportive environment in which the child can work through her feelings, can structure the play by controlling the toys or rules of the play, or can become actively involved in the play so that certain interactions take place. In the example of Amy, the therapist took on quite an active role.

> EXAMPLE 10: Amy, 4, had been involved in a longstanding incestuous relationship with her father. She liked to play Barbie dolls and preferred

one whose hair had been all cut off (by another victim) and whose leg kept coming out of its socket. She named the doll Jennifer, a name she wished to change her own to, and said Jennifer was "all messed up." Jennifer would get "throwed down the stairs by her mom" which always made her leg come off, and was not allowed to go to school until her hair grew back in because it would embarrass her sisters too much.

The therapist took another Barbie doll who became a "lady doctor," and operated on Jennifer's leg. She also insisted that Jennifer wear a wig, which was included in the Barbie doll paraphernalia. In a later session, when again Amy was playing with Jennifer, the therapist asked Amy if Jennifer was kind of like Amy. Amy nodded, and when asked how Amy and Jennifer were alike, she said, "Nobody likes her." The therapist then asked Amy if she felt "all messed up" like Jennifer, and Amy said, "Sometimes." The therapist then reminded Amy of what the "lady doctor" had done for Jennifer and said that they were doing that for Amy in treatment. After that, Amy began to choose an intact Barbie doll whom she called Jennifer and gradually lost her preference for the doll that was "all messed up."

The intervention just described is one of many efforts to help Amy feel better about herself.

Another very important strategy for changing feelings of being damaged is assisting the child in developing or enhancing activities and areas of functioning where the child performs well, can feel whole, and can experience a sense of competence. Early in the treatment process, the therapist should attempt to identify the child's interests and strengths. The therapist should build upon these so that satisfying interactions and esteem-enhancing activities are developed and expanded to become a progressively larger part of the child's life, while the sexual abuse diminishes in importance. This process helps change the child's identity from that of a sexually abused child to, for example, that of a good swimmer, a good speller, or a good friend. If the child has no such areas of functioning to build upon, the therapist should create opportunities for their development. In the example to follow, this technique was employed with Sandra, mentioned earlier. Sandra had a lot of innate ability which made her a good candidate for this approach. This was fortunate because she had experienced serious and pervasive sexual abuse.

EXAMPLE II: Despite the experience of very traumatic sexual abuse, Sandra was quite intelligent and had a lot of athletic skill. She was started in day care and subsequently in kindergarten where she could have very different experiences. She did well and made a number of good friends. Further, she was enrolled in a gymnastics and a swimming class at the local Y, where she excelled. Not only did the athletic activity have a considerable impact on her identity, but it helped her to begin to feel good about her body.

FIGURE 11.1 Sandra, age 5, continually drew herself
with her legs apart (a).

A technique that can be employed instead of or in conjunction
with the one just described is as follows: The therapist and child get a
large piece of paper (we use newsprint) and entitle two columns "Things
I like about myself" and "Things I don't like about myself." The
therapist asks the child to list items first in the "like" column and then in
the "don't like" column. Each item is then discussed. The therapist can
also add items she likes or dislikes to the columns. As a rule the therapist
will try to add things to the "like" column. When appropriate, the
therapist will work with the child on the items in the "don't like" col-

Foo Foo

As she progressed in therapy she began to draw herself (b) with her legs together (see example 9).

umn. Sometimes these are items that are amenable to behavioral change. Sometimes they are areas where insight development or cognitive restructuring—that is, changing the way the child views an experience or trait—is more appropriate. The example of Gina cited below shows the use of the lists of "likes" and "dislikes." The reader will recall Gina being described earlier in this section (example 8).

EXAMPLE 12: The therapist worked with Gina, 11, over a period of several sessions to help her deal with her feelings of being damaged and dirty as a result of sexual abuse by her brother, 15, and with a generalized fear of men. In the third session, the therapist got Gina to make lists of the things she liked and disliked about herself. They were as follows:

LIKES
1. I am funny (I can make people laugh).
2. I am popular (I am member of the Magnificent 6)
3. I can cook brownies real good
4. I help my aunt out
5. I am smart (get A's and B's in school except for last week)
    To the "like" list, the therapist added two items:
6. Gina really cares about other people (her mom, her brother, her friends)
7. Gina always tries to make the best of a difficult situation

DISLIKES
1. My cousin Abdha (6 year old brat) (sometimes we get along good)
2. That I smell funky sometimes
3. That it's my fault that my brother is in reform school—He's mad at me.

After discussing each of the likes, Gina and the therapist worked on the dislikes. Abdha was the son of the aunt with whom Gina was living. He felt displaced by her move into the home. Capitalizing upon Gina's "caring for people" and her "ability to make the best of a difficult situation," the therapist began helping Gina understand things from Abdha's viewpoint. She pointed out to Gina that Abdha used to have his mom all to himself. Now he had to share. It was hard for Abdha to share his room, too, and his toys—especially his video games. Also, work was done to get Gina to do special things for Abdha so that he would see her presence as positive rather than negative.

As noted in example 8, Gina did not bathe regularly after the sexual abuse, and therefore, as she put it, "smelled funky." The therapist set up a schedule for regular bathing with Gina and her aunt. This went well, and after the problem was under control, Gina acknowledged that when she felt dirty she let herself become dirty. Now she was clean and she also felt better about her body. In working with Gina about her brother's institutionalization, the therapist pointed out that he had done the behavior, that is, raped her, that resulted in institutionalization. Further, if he didn't get some help, he would have continued to hurt her and probably would have hurt other kids.

The use of lists with Gina was quite successful. She had enough strengths and treatment had progressed far enough so that the list of "likes" was considerably longer than the list of "dislikes." Placing the two side by side enhanced Gina's feelings of self-worth. In addition efforts were made to work on the "dislikes" list. These intervention techniques are also useful in addressing guilt feelings which will be discussed below.

C. Guilt Feelings and Feeling Responsible

Specialists in the treatment of sexual abuse (e.g., Zaphiris 1978; Sgroi et al. 1982) identify guilt as one of the major reactions experienced by children who have been sexually abused. The guilt is many faceted. Some aspects are related to the child's altered body image, just discussed, but there are additional sources of guilt.

Often the strategies the perpetrator employs in co-opting the child are ones which make her feel responsible for the abuse. For example, he may tell the child that she was so seductive he couldn't resist her. Alternatively, the victim may refuse certain sexual acts, and the perpetrator may twist that refusal by stating the sexual acts he is engaging in are the ones the child likes.

Further, victims are frequently admonished not to tell by the perpetrator who says, "If you tell, I will go to jail," "I will never be able to see you again," "I will get in a lot of trouble with your mother [father, family]," "Your mother [my wife] will divorce me," "They will take you away from your family," or "People will think you're very bad because you did these things." Very frequently these consequences do come to pass when the child tells. Therefore, ironically, the child may feel at fault for the negative impact of the revelation upon the perpetrator, herself, or her family. The following case is an example of this type of guilt induction.

> EXAMPLE 13: Lucy, at 8, told her mother of a sexually abusive relationship with her paternal uncle which had gone on for about two years. Her mother believed her but her father doubted her story. This led to conflict between the extended families. The uncle steadfastly denied the abuse. In front of Lucy's family he admonished her severely for telling such a nasty story, stating that she must have done this because he wasn't bringing her candy like he used to. According to Lucy, privately, he told her that she had better change her story, that she was making lot of trouble for him in the family and destroying their nice relationship. If he went to jail, he would see to it she went to a home for disturbed children, and she would have to stay there until she was 16. Lucy stuck to her story, but as an adult still felt she was responsible for the fighting between her parents and their estrangement from the paternal extended family. No negative consequences ever accrued to her uncle, as far as she knows.

Thus, as a young adult, Lucy still bears the marks of her uncle's manipulations to make her feel responsible for the consequences of telling about the sexual abuse.

One of the most troubling sources of guilt the therapist has to address is that which arises from any physical pleasure associated with the sexual encounter. If force is used, there generally are no pleasurable sensations. Further, from the accounts of some victims, they "switch off" during the abuse so they are not aware of any physical sensations. However, for many children the approach is gentle or seductive, and there is physical pleasure associated with the sexual interaction, in some cases including erections and orgasm. Pleasure is particularly likely to occur with children who do not understand the meaning of the behavior. Later they come to discover that the sexual interaction which felt good was really very bad. Not only do children feel guilty because they enjoyed something that was bad, but they feel they must be bad since they liked it. Frequently, children have great difficulty acknowledging the pleasurable aspects of the sexual abuse.

In cases of father/daughter incest and other intrafamilial sexual abuse, the victim's burden of guilt involves more than what has already been described. The child is likely to experience guilt about upsetting the ordinary pattern of relations in the marriage by in effect replacing her mother and joining in a sexual relationship with her father. Guilt comes partly from having done a "bad thing" but also from the positive aspects of the relationship. Being close to father in a sexual way often brings with it his affection and preferential treatment. Further, sometimes there is hostility and competition between mother and daughter, and the incestuous relationship allows the daughter to best the mother in this competition. These experiences can be very satisfying at one level but will engender guilt at another. Lena's reaction to the sexually abusive relationship she had with her stepfather illustrates this.

EXAMPLE 14: Lena, 12, had been sexually involved with her stepfather for two years. The pattern of a special relationship with him started even before he married Lena's mother. She said she felt "close to" her stepfather. He would talk to her about the problems he was having with her mother. After the marriage, he complained that Lena's mother did not like sex. He persuaded Lena to come to bed with him. They would both be undressed and he would caress her body while she masturbated him. He told her that he "didn't want to do more to me because I should save myself for my husband."

In treatment, she admitted that sometimes she felt jealous of her mother when her mother and stepfather went out. On a number of occasions, she had "faked sick" to get them not to go out or to get them to return home early. She said the entire situation made her feel "real bad and sick in my stomach." On one occasion she took an overdose of aspirin.

The reader will recall the discussion of stepfather cases in chapter 3. This case reflects the dynamics caused by simultaneous courting of mother and daughter by the stepfather. This engendered a great deal of guilt for Lena.

Moreover, the role of the daughter in the intrafamilial triangle may bring with it an abnormal amount of power. The child can, by virtue of the secret she holds, manipulate other members of the family. If the incest is not known to her mother, she can manipulate her father, by demanding special favors or privileges of him. Sometimes, though, the father will bribe the victim and grant favors without the victim requesting them. If the sexual abuse is known within the family, the child can conceivably manipulate all family members in exchange for not telling anyone outside the family. This is rare, however. For children who have some superego functioning, this abnormal balance of power and manipulation makes them feel very guilty (see Zaphiris 1978).

Finally, as mentioned earlier, if the victim does tell, she experiences guilt because of what happens to the perpetrator. The situation is usually much more overwhelming when the perpetrator is part of the family. There may also be family disgrace and family financial ruin for which the victim must bear responsibility. The situation of Anne described below is a poignant example of such guilt feelings.

EXAMPLE 15:   Anne, 16, had been sexually abused by her father beginning at age seven or eight. Her family appeared to be a successful middle class family, her father being an executive in a large corporation and her mother a school psychologist. Anne had two sisters, one who was in college and the other, 13, who was at home.

Anne had been suicidal for some time. She described her earlier suicidal feelings as related to her feelings of pain, guilt, and worthlessness because of what her father was doing to her. Recently her desire to kill herself was a result of observing the consequences to her family of her having told about the sexual abuse. Anne said that she just could not live with it. Her father was going to jail. Her mother would have to work longer hours. Her little sister might be removed from the home. Her older sister would have to quit college because there wouldn't be enough money for her to go. Anne said that she could not bring herself to recant and live with herself. But she had already lost her family (they had turned against her), and she did not want to destroy them. The shame would be unbearable. She said she did not want to have that power over her family. The only way out was for her to kill herself. She thought everyone, including herself, would be better off if she were dead.

The case of Anne illustrates a commonly found result of the guilt feelings and altered body image; there are suicidal feelings and suicide attempts. These will be discussed in greater detail later in this chapter.

The major thrust for the therapist in addressing guilt feelings is to place the responsibility where it legitimately lies, with the perpetrator. The child did not sexually abuse the perpetrator; he sexually abused her and must accept total responsibility for the consequences. The example below is one described in chapter 3 and illustrates placing responsibility on the perpetrator.

> EXAMPLE 16:   Peggy, 14, and Joan, 12, had been sexually abused by their stepfather. After the preliminary hearing, where they had to testify with him facing them in the courtroom, they had very mixed feelings. Joan had been sodomized by him and was the first victim. She did not tell at the time, partly because her stepfather said he would go to jail if she did. After the preliminary hearing she said, ''Either I should have told right away or neither one of us should have told. If I'd told right away he would have gone to jail for only a little time. If neither one of us had told, he would not have to go to jail at all.'' Her mother took them to see a social worker because she was worried about the effect on them of the abuse and the court intervention.
>
> Treatment focused in large part on the fact that their stepfather was responsible for his own behavior. The success of the treatment is indicated by their comments after their stepfather got five concurrent sentences totaling 13 years. Peggy said, ''Well, if he didn't want to go to jail, he shouldn't have done it.'' Joan added, ''He even told me he would go to jail, so he knew what was coming.''
>
> About six months after incarceration, their stepfather wrote to them apologizing for what he had done and taking full responsibility. He was also transferred to a sex offender treatment program and was to get out in one and a half years.

Another part of a strategy for shifting the blame and guilt from the victim to the perpetrator is to point out that the perpetrator is an adult and knows the difference between right and wrong. In contrast, the victim is a child and, as a child, is taught to trust adults and follow their lead. Children learn right and wrong from adults. Adults do not learn this from children.

The therapist should be creative in developing methods for concretizing the shift of guilt from the child to others. With young children, this may be done with guided play, as in the example below.

> EXAMPLE 17:   Dorothy, 10, but developmentally delayed, had been sexually abused by her father, another man, and a 16-year-old boy. She initiated the scenario by wanting a girl anatomically explicit doll to be

Dorothy and a boy doll, John, the 16-year-old. She had the therapist "work Dorothy" and she John. John lured Dorothy into the woods and persuaded her to engage in sexual intercourse. At the end of the scene, the therapist asked Dorothy who did wrong and Dorothy said, "I did." The therapist then said, "Did you want to do that with John?" and Dorothy shook her head. Then Dorothy was asked if she knew it was wrong when John did it, and she said, "Sort of." As to whether John knew it was wrong, Dorothy asserted "Yes." The therapist asked who was bigger and who was stronger and Dorothy replied, "John." The therapist then said that John was the one who had done wrong; he knew he should not do it and he was bigger and stronger and could make Dorothy do it if she did not want to.

Dorothy then took adult male and female anatomically explicit dolls and had them engage in sexual intercourse and had the male doll suck the female doll's breasts. When asked who they were, she said, "My mommy and dad." She said they engaged in these sexual behaviors "all the time," and that she had observed them "lotsa times" and she thought sex was "gross." The therapist asked if their having sex all the time meant they did not take care of her very well. Dorothy replied, "Yes, they didn't even know John took me to the woods."

The therapist then emphasized that "parents are supposed to take care of kids and not let bad things happen to them." Dorothy then changed the scene and had the adult dolls hold the Dorothy doll between them and reprimand the John doll. This was the beginning of a shift for Dorothy from blaming herself for her victimization to seeing the offenders as guilty and her mother as being unprotective.

In the case just described, the child took the initiative and played out the material very directly. Frequently the victim will not be able to do this, and the therapist must take a more active role. The therapist might take a doll the child could identify with and say, "This little girl had a bad thing happen to her. What do you think that was?" The child may choose to describe her own situation or an incident different from the sexual abuse. If the therapist is creative, work can still be done on the issue of guilt when the scene depicted is not sexual in nature. For instance, suppose the child says, "A bad man stole my purse." The therapist might talk about how the theft was similar to and different from what happened to the victim; for example, something was stolen from the victim, too. In addition, the therapist might emphasize feelings both the doll and victim have.

Having children eight years and older write about their guilt feelings is another useful technique (Mayer 1983). The therapist might, with the child's help, make a list of reasons the child should not feel guilty or bad about the sexual abuse. The child might be given an assignment between sessions to think of one reason why the sexual abuse was not her fault.

A similar strategy, better suited to an older child, is to have the child write about her feelings regarding being sexually abused, and then discuss these with the therapist. The therapist can give the child assignments for between sessions, for example, to write in a diary or to write a paragraph. Such an exercise facilitates the child's thinking about feelings and gives the therapist something concrete to work from. The goal of the therapist will be to help the child come to understand that she is not to blame and should not feel guilty. Feelings other than guilt are likely to come up in these exercises and should also be dealt with in treatment.

Often children have special difficulty dealing with guilt associated with the pleasurable qualities of the sexual abuse. When children do not bring up these feelings, the therapist can acknowledge positive aspects, such as the sensations of physical pleasure, and help the child deal with them by to an extent normalizing these feelings. The therapist might say, "Part of what happened must have made you feel good. Lots of kids I've known feel that way." Or, "When you touch yourself there, it feels good. It usually feels good when other people touch you, too." This gives the child permission to talk about these feelings.

In a similar fashion, if the child cannot articulate other positive aspects of the sexual abuse, the therapist can affirm that it felt good to get affection from and have a special relationship with the perpetrator, and that such feelings are normal.

Addressing the child's guilt because of her competitive role with the mother, which is present in some cases, is a more delicate matter. Sometimes it is important to acknowledge the sources of that competition. Other times, it is best not to address the issue but rather to emphasize commonalities between mother and daughter, that they are both victims, at least during the early stages of treatment. (See also chapter 13.)

D. Anger

Anger is another common response of victims to sexual abuse. The focus of the anger may be the perpetrator, the mother or other caretaker who is viewed by the victim as unprotective, other siblings, both victims and nonvictims, extended family, depending upon their response, and/or professionals who have intervened. Sometimes the anger is fused with caring for the perpetrator or others who are its focus.

Sometimes the child is angry because she perceives she has been made to feel guilty.

The task of the therapist is to help the victim handle the anger so that it is constructive rather than destructive to the victim's functioning. The child has every right to be angry, and it is far more constructive and healthy for her to feel angry at those who have wronged her than to accept responsibility for adult transgressions. Early in treatment the thrust should be toward allowing the child to express those angry feelings. Only after this ventilation has taken place should the therapist begin to shift the focus in order to help the child resolve angry feelings.

There are many ways the child can be helped to express anger. With young children, especially when they are unable to express it directly the anger may be expressed in play. The therapist in such a situation not only encourages the child in this expression but also makes the connection for the child between the play and her experience.

A punching bag or a pillow can be used as targets for the physical expression of anger. The object can become the perpetrator. Children may also achieve some sense of mastery from this kind of exercise, since the object does not retaliate. Dolls, especially anatomically explicit ones, can also be used to represent people in the expression of anger. In addition, sometimes toy guns, knives, and soldiers can be helpful. In the example below, an anatomically explicit doll triggered the victim's anger.

> EXAMPLE 18: Jane, 4, who had been sexually abused by her father, brought her transitional object, a bear named Beatie, to treatment. She had Beatie jump up and down on and kick an anatomically explicit male doll in the head. After Beatie had knocked the doll down, she pulled the doll's penis out of his pants and twisted it. The therapist asked Jane why Beatie had hurt the male doll, and she replied, "Because of this," twisting the penis again. The therapist asked, "Who else has a penis?" and Jane said, "My dad." The therapist asked Jane if she wanted to hurt her dad like Beatie hurt the doll, and she said, "The next time I see him, I'm going to smash him." They went on to talk about why Jane wanted to smash her dad and she was told she had a right to be angry.

In this example, Beatie represents Jane, and the bear's name, which suggests aggression, is highly significant. The anatomically explicit doll is clearly her father.

Children can also be helped by role playing what they would like to say to the perpetrator (or the nonprotecting parent). The therapist can play the offending adult, a doll can be used, or merely a chair. (The empty chair is Gestalt terminology.) Sometimes the role play will be a prelude to an actual confrontation. If this is the case, the therapist can assist the child not only in her own statements but in generating responses to the adult's replies when confronted. If the child is actually going to confront the adult, the therapist or another supportive person should usually be present.

Another technique to facilitate expression of anger is to have the child write a letter to the offender detailing how it felt to have been, or feels to be, the victim. Sometimes the letter will be sent, but it may also be used in other ways. The victim may read it out loud to the therapist and the child's feelings can then be worked through. Or the letter may be read to the offending parent(s) or the family in treatment. In the latter situation, it might be read by the child or the therapist.

Sometimes a telephone call to the perpetrator, which the therapist plans with the child, can serve the function of expression of anger. We have also had several children who have made videotapes to be played for or sent to the perpetrator or family, in which the child ventilates her feelings. In Alice's case, the therapist used letter writing.

> EXAMPLE 19:   Alice, 10, was in foster care because her stepfather had sexually abused her and her mother had chosen to believe her stepfather. She was in individual treatment and the parents were in conjoint therapy. Little headway was being made in conjoint therapy because the couple continued to deny the sexual abuse. Alice was making good progress in treatment but was not having visits with her mother and stepfather because of fear they might put pressure on her to change her story. There was a trial pending in which she would have to testify.
>
> The therapist suggested Alice write them a letter since she could not see them. Alice said she did not know what to say in the letter because she wanted to tell them how upset she was about everything, including what they were doing now. The therapist said she thought that it was O.K. for Alice to write an upset letter because this was a special situation. Alice decided she wanted to write a letter only to her mom. She wrote:
>
>> Dear Mommy,
>> When you go to school, Don comes into my room and does nasties. He pulled down the covers and licked my bottom. I played like I was asleep but I wasn't. He did this plenty, even when Martha was there. You guys are being real stinkers and lying. You might not know you're lying, but Don does. He told me that if I said anything he would get in big trouble. Now *I'm* in trouble. I have to go to Anderson school. I don't like it. Plus I have to stay in the Sweats' house and call them mom and dad. Also I can't talk to you. I think Don should have to go to jail or to Russia where they lock up people like him. I am SAD and MAD. I hate him and think you should throw him out like you did before.
>>
>>   Alice, your daughter

Alice and the therapist decided that instead of sending the letter, the therapist should read it to the couple in the next session. This was done and subsequently the mother separated from the stepfather.

For Alice, this outcome was tremendously therapeutic. She saw her mother's separation as just and was very gratified that her mother had finally believed her.

While expression of anger is an important initial step, the therapist also wants the victim to come to some resolution of these feelings, so that they do not remain overwhelming. Sometimes resolution results from the mere expression of the feelings. Other times resolution occurs as the child comes to understand why the offender is a sexual abuser, why the mother was unable to protect, or why professionals felt they had to intervene. The nature of the insight will vary with the child's developmental stage.

Anger becomes dysfunctional when it is preoccupying the victim to such an extent that she cannot focus on other things, when it distorts the victim's perception of reality, and when it leads to angry acting-out behavior that precipitates social sanction. The example below is illustrative.

EXAMPLE 20:   Jane, 15, had been sexually abused by both her father and her stepfather. Her mother had divorced each of them when she discovered the abuse. However, Jane was totally dissatisfied with this solution, stating they ought to be either "put in jail or killed." Further, she was even angrier at her mother, whom she blamed for their behavior, stating her mother was "a whore and a tramp" for having been involved with those men and that authorities ought to take Jane and the three younger children away from her mother because she was unfit.

After the departure and divorce of her stepfather, Jane persisted in angry denunciations of him, her father, and her mother in the presence of people she hardly knew. She would not mind her mother and withdrew from appropriate participation in the family. She refused to eat food prepared by her mother, would no longer babysit for her younger siblings while her mother worked, physically assaulted her mother and willfully destroyed her mother's possessions. She would not get up in the morning and go to school, and when she was at school she involved herself in fights with other girls.

Jane's anger resulted in a distorted view of her mother and consuming hatred of her abusers. It was destructive of family life and devastating for her mother. It also was damaging to Jane because her resultant behavior isolated her from her family and caused her difficulties at school.

When anger takes on the manifestations just described, the therapist needs to help the victim see how painful, self-defeating, and self-destructive the patterns are. Adolescence is usually the peak time for this kind of angry acting-out, and some of this will resolve with time. But it is still important to help the victim deal constructively with the anger to avoid more serious trouble with consequences that will resolve with time.

E. Depression and Self-Destructive Behavior

Victims of sexual abuse may be depressed and self-destructive. Frequently these symptoms are manifest long before their underlying cause is known. Unfortunately, it is not uncommon for professionals to try to treat the depression and self-destructive behavior without an appreciation of why the victim has these problems. Depression and self-destructive behavior are very much related to treatment issues discussed thus far: victims' feelings of being damaged, their sense of guilt, and their anger. Depression may be masked by aggressive acting-out behavior. It may also manifest itself in the form of somatic complaints, for example, stomach aches and backaches. One child in our sample complained of a pain in her side which physicians diagnosed as psychosomatic. During treatment, she revealed the pain would come on when she thought about the sexual things.

Self-destructive behavior includes self-mutilation, drug and alcohol abuse, suicidal feelings, and suicide attempts. Self-mutilation may be on impulse or planned. For example, one adolescent victim in our sample impulsively scratched and tore the skin on her cheeks and forehead after her father fondled her as he was returning her to the psychiatric unit, where she had been hospitalized for depression and suicide attempts. An example of planned self-mutilation is a ten year old child who carved the tattoo "BAD" on her chest.

As already noted, another common form of self-destructive behavior is chemical dependency. Victims of sexual abuse will frequently become involved in alcohol and drug use during late latency and early adolescence. Some of them recognize the substance use as an effort to deal with their pain and depression and are in touch with its harmful effects. Others are less insightful and talk about the fun they have when they are high.

In addition, some victims engage in self-destructive behavior while high. One 15-year-old child in our sample twice fell out of a moving car while drunk. Both times she opened the car door and leaned out.

This victim also fell down a flight of stairs and broke an ankle while drunk.

Almost all of the adolescent victims in our sample have suicidal thoughts, the most direct expression of self-destructive wishes. Half of them have made suicide attempts, frequently multiple attempts. One 16-year-old victim made 16 attempts. However, even younger victims may consider suicide. A seven-year-old who had been sexually abused by her uncle, who was a police officer, openly expressed the wish to die. She inquired about how long it would take her to drown in the apartment complex swimming pool. She could not swim. A five-year-old victim stepped in front of an oncoming car in an attempt to kill herself. When questioned about her behavior, she said she thought she would "die quick and it wouldn't hurt too much."

The following is a characteristic example of a self-destructive adolescent victim.

> EXAMPLE 21: Shelly was 13 and for two years had been drinking, smoking pot, and taking a variety of pills. The substance abuse coincided with the onset of fondling by her stepfather. Before that time he had made sexual comments to her but had not touched her. Shelly got the drugs at school and would get high in the middle of the day and come home and go to bed. Thus, she was also truanting from school. She got a neighbor man, who was in his mid-20s and unemployed, to buy her alcohol. They drank together at his apartment. Shelly had plenty of money because her stepfather was paying her not to tell her mother about the sexual abuse.
>
> Shelly attempted suicide three times, each attempt following an incident of sexual abuse. One time she swallowed a whole bottle of cold capsules. Another time she took 21 Midol tablets. The third time she ingested a combination of street drugs, her mother's hypertension medication, and alcohol. On the first occasion, Shelly was sick and groggy for a day or so and vomited. Her parents did not know what was the matter with her. The second time, her five-year-old sister observed her taking the pills and told her parents. Shelly was taken to the doctor and given an emetic. On the third occasion, she was hospitalized and quite ill. The parents became aware of the third attempt because her mother noticed her medication was gone and Shelly was acting strangely.

In this case, the victim engaged in multiple self-destructive behaviors that appear to be directly related to the sexual abuse. Shelly's choice of a drinking partner ten years older than she is also significant. Her suicide attempts are progressively more lethal. The third time she ingested three different kinds of drugs and had to be hospitalized. The next attempt could be successful.

Methods for intervention where the victim manifests depression and self-destructive behavior include many of the techniques already cited. Thus, strategies which address the child's feelings about being damaged, guilt, and anger may also alleviate depression and reduce self-destructive behavior. For example, efforts to enhance and expand positive aspects of the child's life also can diminish depression. Likewise, as the child feels less guilty about the various aspects of her involvement in the sexual abuse, she is less likely to feel depressed and to behave self-destructively. Depression is often conceptualized as repressed anger, and anger may be turned against the self. If the child gains insight into these dynamics, then the sad feelings and self-punitive behavior may abate.

In some cases the therapist may face the dilemma of not being able to effect therapeutic change quickly enough to assure the child's safety. However depression and self-destructive behavior may decrease when the sexual abuse stops. Particular self-destructive acts, mutilations or suicide attempts, may be precipitated by specific incidents of sexual abuse, as in the case of Shelly. Alternatively, depression and self-destructive behavior may diminish when the victim is removed from the environment where the sexual abuse occurred. Relief from the sexual abuse and the family situation may lead to a decrease in symptomatic behavior. A change in environment may also lead to an absence of access to drugs and alcohol, as well as to friends who encourage the victim in self-destructive behavior.

The example below is one cited in chapter 6, and earlier in this chapter, and illustrates how environmental change can improve the victim's functioning.

EXAMPLE 22: Janice, 15, had been extensively sexually abused by her mother's living-together partner beginning when she was six. At 12, Janice began drinking and using drugs. She said she drank what would get her drunk the quickest because she did not like the taste. She used marijuana, cocaine, PCP, LSD, and Quaaludes. She also ran away from home six times in an effort to avoid the sexual abuse. She attempted suicide once when she feared the loss of love from her older sister, the family member to whom she was the closest. The other family members rejected her because of her acting out behavior. Janice also did poorly in school.

At 13, she told a teacher about the sexual abuse. There was a protective services investigation, but they did not believe Janice. Six months later she ran away, and when apprehended by the police told them of the sexual abuse. She was placed in foster care. While on a weekend visit home, her parents took her and the other children and moved to another state. Janice wrote to her foster mother telling her where they were. This led to an investigation of the family's present circumstances, and Janice was removed from her family and placed in a supportive and consistent foster home. Her mother, however, told the professionals that her daughter was an extremely disturbed liar who had given the family a lot of trouble. She requested Janice be put in a mental institution.

In foster care Janice did quite well. She attended school regularly and got B's and C's. She got along well with the foster parents and their adult daughter. She took two new arrivals in foster care, ages 10 and 11, under her wing. She did not drink or use drugs, but rather came home right after school to do her homework and her chores. There were no further instances of running away or suicide attempts.

In discussing her circumstances of being in foster care, being rejected by her family, and her mother pressuring the court to have her committed, she admitted that she did not like this but that it was a relief to be away from her mother's partner. She said she did not feel as down as she had at home. She said she did not crave drugs and alcohol and now regarded her use of them as stupid. She was very distressed by the possibility of institutionalization and said she missed her mother and sister. However, she said that no matter what happened, it wouldn't be for too long. In a little more than two years she would be 18 and could do what she wanted. She wanted to marry her boyfriend and have a baby.

In this case, while surely Janice is not free of problems, there was a remarkable transformation once the sexual abuse stopped and she was away from her family. Placement in a mental hospital would have been totally unwarranted.

With other children, the results from change of environment are not so positive. Feelings about the sexual abuse are more deep-seated and additional trauma occurs after discovery of the sexual abuse. A principal source of further stress may be the court process and particularly court testimony. It can be frightening, can make the victim depressed, and can lead to additional self-destructive and suicidal behavior.

Suicidal gestures often cause professionals to consider hospitalization, which itself presents dilemmas because it may exacerbate the victim's depression and lead the victim and others to think the child, not the perpetrator, is the one with the problem. A number of steps should be taken before hospitalization is sought. First, it is important for the therapist and others working with the victim to determine whether the behavior should be characterized as a gesture or an attempt. In general, gestures should not precipitate hospitalization. Second, alternatives to hospitalization that still allow close monitoring should be explored. For example, a foster mother who is around much of the time and who communicates well with the victim may be preferable. Third, the therapist should play an important role in prevention of suicide, regularly asking the victim about her feelings and being alert for despondency and suicidal thoughts. If a child has such thoughts, the therapist should inquire if she has a concrete plan. The lethality of the plan should be assessed. Such behaviors as giving away or selling possessions and personal revelations whose consequences would make living difficult should be looked upon with concern. When victims actually engage in gestures and attempts, their potential lethality must be evaluated. In general, suicidal behavior that occurs in isolated circumstances where discovery is unlikely is more worrisome, as are situations where the child uses multiple methods for killing herself.

Helping the child develop plans other than suicide for expressing frustration is a potentially useful strategy, as is making short-term contracts with the child not to attempt suicide — say not until the next therapy session. Alternatively, the therapist can contract with the child to call if she feels suicidal or before attempting suicide again. Sometimes it helps to reassure the child that this too shall pass, that the therapist has worked with other victims in similar circumstances who have overcome their feelings and problems. Introduction of the victim to another victim who has progressed through this stage or an adult survivor whose circumstances were comparable can be helpful in this regard. The example below illustrates both the use of contracting and employing a role model.

EXAMPLE 23: Tanya, 15, had made two suicide attempts before revealing sexual abuse by her mother's younger brother, George. George had first asked to see Tanya's pussy when she was 7 and he 15. Soon they were engaged in mutual fondling and then in oral copulation. While she suspected this was inappropriate behavior because of George's admonition not to tell her mother, she enjoyed the encounters and idolized George. When Tanya was 12, George had intercourse with her. Although this hurt, Tanya allowed it because George told her if she didn't like it, he could easily get a woman his age to do it with him. Because at that age Tanya understood the inappropriateness of the behavior, she began to feel progressively more guilty and depressed. She made her first suicide attempt at 13 by taking ten of her mother's thyroid pills. On another occasion she stole the family car and attempted to drive it off a bridge, but she only damaged a fender.

She told her mother when she was 15 about the sexual relationship she had with George. By that time he was married and had an infant. Tanya sometimes babysat for the child and George would come home when Tanya was babysitting for his son and they would have sex. When Tanya told her mother, she became hysterical. She said she had thought there was something suspicious in their relationship. She said she always had known her brother had problems. She immediately called George's wife, who did not believe Tanya's story. Tanya's mother then called her own mother, who arrived at the house full of accusations that Tanya had encouraged George. Tanya's mother called protective services. After talking to Tanya, the worker went to George's house and removed his son from his home. Tanya's father was told when he came home from work. He had to be restrained from going to George's house and killing him. That night, Tanya took an overdose of sleeping medication. She was hospitalized in the psychiatric wing of the local general hospital. Protective services referred her to their local therapist who specializes in treatment of sexual abuse. The therapist began seeing Tanya while she was still in the hospital. Tanya hated the hospital because there were ''a whole bunch of old people there,'' senile persons who were maintained in the hospital. She wanted desperately to leave. She cut her wrists in the bathtub while in the hospital. The therapist told her she couldn't leave the hospital as long as she was suicidal. Tanya then told the therapist she didn't want to kill herself anymore.

The therapist felt that the overdose of sleeping pills was a genuine attempt in a moment of desperation but thought the wrist-slitting was a gesture because the wound was quite superficial. Nevertheless, she was skeptical about Tanya's assertion that she no longer wished to commit suicide. Even so, arrangements were made for Tanya to go to a foster home, with a single foster mother who had herself been sexually abused by her older half-brother. It was felt that Tanya's home was too chaotic for her to return at the time. Tanya was initially seen by the therapist twice a week and the therapist contracted with Tanya each session not to kill herself before the next one. Tanya also talked a lot to the foster mother about her feelings. The only worrisome event while Tanya was in placement occurred when George called the foster home and spoke to Tanya, begging her to tell the police she had made it all up. Tanya went screaming out of the house, and it took her foster mother two hours to find her.

Tanya did tell the police she made it all up and refused to testify against George. He was therefore not criminally prosecuted. However, Tanya continued to talk about the sexual abuse and her feelings to the foster mother and the therapist. Eventually, Tanya's parents were brought into the treatment. She returned home after two months in care.

In this case the incest survivor who was used was a foster mother. The therapist's assessment was that Tanya was becoming more depressed because of the circumstances on the psychiatric wing, and the depression might increase the likelihood of her making additional suicidal gestures. The therapist also thought that if Tanya was in a therapeutic foster home away from the turmoil in her family, the likelihood of further suicide attempts would be diminished.

F. Understanding the Meaning of the Sexual Abuse

Another important goal in treatment of the child is helping her understand why the perpetrator did what he did and its significance. What is required in terms of explanation will vary according to the nature of the abuse and the child's developmental stage. Young children will have little or no knowledge of sex and sexual behavior. They will have questions about what the abuser was doing. Alternatively, they may be bewildered when adults other than the perpetrator find activities, which were a little strange but nevertheless pleasurable, abhorrent or at least cause for considerable questioning and concern. Somewhat older children may know about procreation but need some information to put the sexual abuse in context. Still others have knowledge of sex and the kinds of activities which cause sexual pleasure but are bewildered by the fact that an adult has been sexually attracted to a child.

The therapist, in trying to help the child understand the meaning of the abuse, attempts to balance several, often incompatible, goals. On the one hand, it is important to help the child understand why the sexual abuse is taboo. However, it is also necessary to mindful of the limitation of the child's developmental stage. For example, a three-year-old will have the barest knowledge of "how babies are made," much less the ability to comprehend the perversion of sexual abuse. She should be told merely that what the perpetrator did was wrong — that "daddies don't touch there." Older children, of course, should be given a more complete explanation, and as victims become older additional interpretation may be necessary. Finally, if possible, the therapist should try to keep separate the sexual abuse and normal sexuality. An incident of sexual abuse should not automatically precipitate a full-scale explanation of "the birds and the bees." If the child can avoid associating the sexual abuse with normal human sexuality, the ability to do so can reduce trauma at later developmental stages and potential negative effects on adult sexual functioning. The intervention with Joy illustrates how to explain the meaning of the sexual abuse to a young child and what will probably be required as explanations at later stages.

EXAMPLE 24:   Joy, at 3½, was sexually abused by her stepfather. He engaged in digital penetration of her anus and her vagina and told her he was "making brown sugar" and "making white sugar" when he did this.

At the same time, he masturbated himself with his other hand and wiped his penis off with her underwear after ejaculation. As far as the therapist could tell, Joy experienced neither pleasure nor pain from this intrusion. She delayed reporting the incident to her grandmother because her stepfather urged her not to tell, saying that the rest of the family would not understand.

The therapist, in explaining people's concerns about the abuse, said that "daddies are not supposed to put their fingers in little girls' privates. They are called privates because you can touch them in private but other people are not supposed to. Sometimes the doctor has to touch or look at them, and your mommy can put medicine on them if they get hurt or sore." Joy was also told that her daddy knew he was wrong to do this and that is why he told her not to tell. Joy's mother and grandmother were warned to be alert in later years for additional concerns about the meaning of the behavior. For example, the time might come when Joy would need to be told there is something wrong with her stepfather because he chose to be sexual with a child. When Joy becomes aware of the range of sexual behaviors, and if questions arise regarding her stepfather, then it may be necessary to tell her that this digital penetration was supposed to be sexually stimulating for both of them.

George was some years older than Joy and already knew abut procreation. His case is also discussed in chapter 6. The explanation to him took this into account.

EXAMPLE 25:   George was eight years old when his Cub Scout leader abused him, by attempting to engage in mutual fondling. In addition, he would pick George up and hug him at Scout meetings and talk in a funny high-pitched voice. George at first did not understand that he had been abused because he had no knowledge of homosexuality and did not equate the fondling with sexual behavior.

George was seen for only one session. The therapist explained to him that the Cub Scout leader liked boys instead of grown women and that his fondling and hugging was an expression of his preference. George made a face and said, "El creepo." The therapist then said that the Cub Scout leader was disturbed and that was why he preferred little boys. However, what the leader did was also against the law and he had done similar things to many other boys. Because of this, the leader was a threat to other boys and needed to be gotten off the street. George's testimony in a criminal prosecution would help to do this. George was happy to testify. He said he was "mad" about what happened to him.

George's parents, who were present during the treatment session, were told that George had a healthy attitude about what happened and did not need any more treatment at this time. However, they should be mindful of the possibility of future worries about the abuse. Specifically, they were apprised of the fact that many boys worry they will become homosexual after being sexually abused by a man.

Finally, here is an explanation to an adolescent, Lucille, who has full knowledge of sexual behavior.

EXAMPLE 26:   Lucille, 15, was coerced by her father to have sexual intercourse. He was a retired naval officer who had spent most of his time
prior to retirement away from home. When away he would get drunk and
go out and find a prostitute. His pattern of sexual abuse was similar. He
would get drunk and then would corner Lucille and insist on intercourse.
Lucille's parents did not get along well, and in fact both of them had
histories of alcoholism. Her mother had been in an automobile accident,
while intoxicated, and had many facial scars. In addition, she paid little attention to her appearance and did not enjoy sex.
        Lucille's response to the sexual abuse was, ''Why did he pick on
me?'' Lucille was told that something was wrong with her father because
he sexually abused his daughter. In addition, it was explained that part of
the problem was that he had been sexually abused as a child. Further, the
therapist pointed out that his pattern within the family was similar to the
one he had developed in the Navy. Lucille was also told how the marital
problems fit into the picture, in that many times men who sexually abuse
their children have sexual and other problems in their marriages.

Note that in the first two examples only brief treatment was needed, but the therapist shared with the victims' families anticipated later
treatment needs. With Lucille, longer-term treatment was needed both
because the sexual abuse had persisted longer and because Lucille ap-
preciated the violation of norms involved.

Furthermore, variability in individual values makes explaining sexual behavior
difficult. For example, some people do not believe oral-genital sex has
any place in normal sexual relations, while others believe that it has.
Some people regard homosexual behavior as perverse and others see it as
acceptable. It is important for the therapist to ascertain what the family
values are (or those of the substitute care taker) and take them into account in interpreting the sexual behavior to the child.

G. Strategies for Self-Protection

Finally, the therapist will be concerned about how to protect the
child from future vulnerability to sexual abuse. The need to deal with
protection arises from two sources: the propensity of some victims to
"relive the trauma," and fears the child may have about trusting adults
in the future.

Children who have been sexually abused frequently have been
socialized by the abuser to interact in a sexual way. If there has been a
positive aspect to the sexual abuse, the child may be prone to show affection in a sexual way. Even when the essence of the relationship has been
traumatic, the child may still be very much a risk for future sexual abuse

because she has no other way of interacting with men (or women, if the perpetrator was a woman) in her repertoire. One of the difficulties in this aspect of treatment is enabling children to protect themselves without inhibiting their ability to develop and maintain appropriate physically intimate relationships. There are several approaches which are useful in addressing issues of self-protection.

With young children the therapist may need to begin with teaching them what parts of the body are "their privates." This can be done with a little game in which the therapist on her own body shows the child which parts are private by crossing her arms over the parts and having the child imitate: the face, the chest, the lower abdomen and groin, and the buttocks (see figure 11.2). The person uses a kind of sweeping motion with the arms in doing this.[1] It can be an exercise which is repeated over several treatment sessions. An explanation about what "privates" are is also offered. It is likely to be something like, "Those are parts that you can touch in private (that's why they are called privates), but others do not touch. When you grow up (and fall in love, get married, etc.) you can let your partner touch your privates, but no adult should touch you there now."

In the example below, this exercise was used to good effect.

EXAMPLE 27:   Jody, 5, was sexually abused by her grandfather and a friend of his, and then six months later by a grocery store owner. The behavior consisted of fondling. In the first treatment session, the therapist taught Jody the exercise about the privates. At the beginning of each subsequent session, the therapist would ask Jody to repeat the exercise by saying, "Show me with your arms where your privates are." Jody would demonstrate where her privates were. The therapist would then ask Jody if anyone had tried to touch her privates during the intervening week and if so, how Jody had handled it.

At the fourth session, Jody asked if her mother, who usually stayed in the waiting room during Jody's treatment session, could come in. The therapist assented and Jody said to her mother, "Where's your privates?" Her mother dutifully went through the exercise. It turned out that Jody had taught the exercise not only to everyone in her family but also to several of her kindergarten classmates.

Another approach to self-protection is for the therapist to talk about touch, explaining the different types of touch and with whom the child should engage in them. The therapist states that shaking hands is a type of touch that is sometimes appropriate with strangers and with friends as well. Other types of touch feel good but are not appropriate with strangers, for instance, a hug, a kiss, or a pat on the head. Touch may also hurt, as when the child is spanked by a parent or hit by a peer in

FIGURE 11.2. With young children the therapist teaches them
which parts of the body are their "privates" by crossing her arms

a fight. There is also tickle touch. Finally, touch can be sexual, involving
the intimate parts.[2] Adults should not do sexual touching with children.
The child is then asked to give examples of her experience with these
various kinds of touch.

A related technique is to define good touch, bad touch, and tricky
touch. Good touch includes, for example, hugs and kisses from people
you are close to. Bad touch is when someone hurts you. Tricky touch
might feel good but later on gives you that "uh-oh" feeling; that is sexual touching.

The privates exercise and touch identification are important
techniques with young children who are confused or do not know which
their intimate parts are. Older children usually know which parts are
private.

The therapist's second task is to help the child identify what she
would do if someone who should not touch her privates does so. With
older children the intervention begins by identifying these protective
strategies. There are a number of approaches which can be taken. In
situations where the offender is not a household member, the victim
might be taught to emphatically say, "No, don't touch me," run away,

over the parts and having the child imitate the face, chest, lower abdomen, groin, and buttocks.

or go home and tell a caretaker. Where the situation is one in which the former perpetrator is close to the family, and there is fear that he may again abuse the child, it is useful to identify a specific person for the child to tell or call. Depending upon the circumstances of the case, this might be a mother, a teacher, a school counselor, a therapist, a child protection worker, or the police. The techniques for self protection just described are also employed in primary prevention programs. The following case demonstrates the successful building in of a self-protective response for an older child.

> EXAMPLE 28:   Terry, age 10, had been sexually abused by her step-father over a two-year period. He confessed to the sexual abuse and requested treatment. He remained at home and he and his wife were being seen by a therapist. Terry was seen by the court worker once a week, and was told at the beginning of treatment that if her father accosted her again she should tell the court worker. About six weeks into treatment, Terry said she was starting to get worried. The source of her worries was that she "could smell my father's smell in my room" so that she said she knew that he had been there. The court worker, rather than confronting the parents directly, talked first with their therapist and found the therapist

was not dealing with the sexual abuse in treatment and, in fact, had some doubts about whether it had occurred (despite the father's confession!). The court worker and therapist then met jointly with the couple, and the court worker confronted them about Terry's fears. The father admitted to "napping on Terry's bed" from time to time.

He was told that he was to stay out of Terry's room and if any other instances of sexual abuse occurred, he would be criminally prosecuted.

Thus, in this case the "warning system" worked so well that the supportive person was notified before anything actually occurred.

There are additional strategies which may be useful, particularly with older children. Assertiveness training, training in self defense, and being involved in support groups for victims are often the treatments of choice.

Unfortunately, the techniques just described to facilitate a self protection may not be sufficient in cases where the sexual abuse was of significant duration and where victims lack modes other than sexual ones for interacting with adults. These victims may learn the protective techniques but will still be vulnerable in the context of sexual abuse. Often the helplessness and compliance has been internalized, and they cannot use protective strategies when threatening situations arise.

DeYoung (1984) has an interesting interpretation of the phenomenon of multiple victimization. She reports on four young children who had a marked phobic response to initial sexual abuse, yet later were involved in other sexually abusive situations. She sees this as counterphobic behavior, that is, the children repeatedly involved themselves in the phobic situation in order to achieve mastery over it. We have also observed that children may get some gratification from the sexually abusive situation, and this compels their involvement even though at some level they do not wish it. Frequently this latter group of children is fairly disturbed and the sexual abuse is to a degree ego-syntonic. The reader will recall from the discussion in chapter 2 that almost one-fifth of children in our sample were victimized by more than one person. Many of these children were not able to develop good protective mechanisms.

In these types of cases the approach of the therapist must include the development of appropriate and compensatory intimate relationships so that the child no longer gravitates toward sexually abusive relationships. Examples of such appropriate relationships might be the child's relationship with the therapist, a successful referral to a Big Brother or Big Sister program, an improved relationship with a grandparent, or an altered parent-child interaction that is appropriate and nonsexual. The reader will recall building of such relationships was also described as a technique to be used with children whose trust has been undermined by the sexual abuse. In the case of Anna, also discussed in chapter 6, she was placed in a situation that provided the opportunity to develop such a relationship.

> EXAMPLE 29:   Anna, 10, had had a sexual relationship with her brother, who was four years older than she, for about five years, and also with her father. Anna was mildly retarded and came from a family environment where both parents were quite disturbed and there had been intractable neglect of four children. In foster care, she asked both her foster brother and a neighbor boy to have sex with her. Attempts to explain to her why she should not do this were unavailing, and the foster family was so distressed by Anna's behavior they asked that she be moved. The foster care worker located a new foster home where there were no other children and where the foster father, who was a school counselor, expressed an interest in working with Anna around her relationships with males. He was assisted in how to firmly but gently limit Anna's sexual behavior and how to engage her in appropriate, nonsexual activities.
>
> Anna's foster father became an alternate male role model who helped her to develop ways other than sexual for relating to men.

Interventions of the sort provided in this case also reduce the risk of adolescent prostitution and involvement in other exploitative relationships.

V. CONCLUSION

The vast majority of cases of child sexual abuse require some individual treatment of the child, either in her own right, or in conjunction with other modes of intervention. Further, there are treatment issues which are fairly universal: (1) the loss of trust; (2) altered body image; (3) guilt and feeling responsible for the abuse; (4) anger; (5) depression and self-destructive behavior; (6) the need to understand the meaning of the sexual behavior; and (7) self-protection.

The length of individual treatment will vary considerably, depending in part upon the amount of physical trauma, the degree of intimacy between victim and perpetrator, and the duration of the abuse. The sooner after discovery of the sexual abuse that treatment is instituted, the more efficacious it is likely to be. However, in many cases treatment will need to be provided intermittently; that is, there should be crisis intervention at the time of discovery, but at later developmental stages new issues may arise or old ones may resurface. If this happens, additional treatment needs to be offered. Future points in development which may reactivate concerns are the following: (1) when the child comes to fully understand the meaning of the sexual behavior; (2) when the child enters puberty; (3) when the child becomes sexually active; (4) when the victim marries; (5) when the victim has children; and (6) when those children reach the age at which sexual abuse began with the victim. Therefore, while treatment at the time of discovery of sexual abuse is essential in cases requiring individual therapy, it is often not sufficient. Addressing the sequelae of sexual abuse is an ongoing process, reaching far into the victim's future.

NOTES

1. This technique was first described to me by Bennie Stovall, then of the Special Family Problems Unit of Children's Aid Society, Detroit, Michigan.

2. The Illusion Theatre, a troupe from Hennepin County, Minnesota, does a mime show entitled "Touch" which incorporates these concepts.

CHAPTER TWELVE

An Overview of Treatment and Individual Treatment Issues

I. INTRODUCTION

Professionals are in the process of learning how to successfully treat sexual abuse. Factors which complicate the evaluation of treatment outcome are the following: there are a range of types of sexual abuse, a variety of relationships where there is risk for sexual abuse, and differing prognoses. Furthermore, professionals do not necessarily agree on what an appropriate course of treatment is. Unfortunately, in the field of sexual abuse at this time there is a tendency for professionals to make a strong ideological commitment to a particular treatment approach and to be unwilling to grant the possibility that other interventions have merit. This kind of inflexibility occurs in a context in which there has been hardly any evaluation of the effects of various interventions, the exceptions being the works of Kroth (1979) and Daro and Cohen (1984).

Therefore, what can be said about the appropriateness of different kinds of interventions is based upon clinical experience rather than evaluation research. Our discussion will draw upon our clinical experience, that of other professionals with whom we have contact, and the clinical literature. It will address selected treatment issues.

The focus will be upon the treatment of intrafamilial sexual abuse. Three chapters will be dedicated to this discussion. In this chapter some general guidelines for treatment will be presented, and individual treatment issues will be discussed. In chapter 13 dyadic treatment issues will be described. Chapter 14 will consist of a discussion of family and group treatment issues.

II GENERAL GUIDELINES FOR TREATMENT

In this section we shall discuss the historical background of incest treatment, the issue of confession, the use of outreach, the role of treatment teams, and the orchestration of treatment modalities.

A. Background to the Treatment Process

Historically, in cases of incest it was the practice to send the offender, usually the father, to treatment on the assumption that his treatment would cure the problem (Rush 1980). Sadly, most clinicians are aware of cases where the perpetrator was in individual treatment and continued or resumed the sexual abuse. Frequently in such cases, the perpetrator would refuse to admit to the sexual abuse or discounted its significance, and the focus of treatment would shift to other problems the perpetrator was more willing to address. The result was that no real changes took place in the perpetrator's sexual orientation and behavior. Because the therapist had no ongoing contact with the family, she would have no idea that sexual abuse was persisting.

The combination of experience with this very devastating treatment outcome and recognition that family factors play a role in most intrafamilial sexual abuse cases has resulted in a shift to family focused intervention. It is unfortunate that many professionals have made too complete a shift so that family factors are sometimes treated as the exclusive cause of sexual abuse. Thus, the central focus of treatment is on changing the family so the perpetrator does not "have to" sexually abuse a child anymore in order to get his needs met. This approach is unfortunate because it fails to appreciate that the prerequisite causes of sexual abuse are the existence of a person who is sexually attracted to children and who has the willingness to act upon these feelings.

Thus, often treatment consists, first, of addressing contributing causes, such as poor communication in the family, marital discord, the parental role assumed by the victim, and social isolation; and second, of setting up an "external superego" for the perpetrator. Because the perpetrator has weak internal controls for his behavior, mechanisms that result in external control may be constructed to reduce the risk of future sexual abuse. For example, the child may be assisted in developing a plan for what to do if the perpetrator again attempts sexual abuse. Such a plan usually involves the child telling a protective person immediately. Because the perpetrator is informed of how the victim will respond, the plan has a deterrent effect. If the deterrent is unsuccessful, the plan should lead to immediate reporting of the sexual abuse and its cessation.

Other "external superego" mechanisms include the wife informing the perpetrator she will divorce him if he again attempts sexual abuse or the court warning the perpetrator that any subsequent attempt will result in incarceration or loss of custody of the child. Some have even suggested (e.g., Boulder County Sexual Abuse Unit 1983) that the prospect of again being subjected to the intensive sexual abuse treatment also may serve as a deterrent. One of the disadvantages of "external superego" strategies is that they may be time limited. The court's supervision or probation period will eventually end, and maternal vigilance may flag over time.

It is understandable why treatment foci have shifted to the contributing factors and engineering external controls. Compared to trying to change the perpetrator's sexual orientation and superego functioning, the former treatment goals are relatively easily accomplished. To date it is unclear whether efforts to change sexual orientation have been successful (Groth and Birnbaum 1979; Rosen and Fracher 1983; Longo 1983; Tracy et al. 1983; Pithers et al. 1983; Groth et al. 1982; Carnes 1984). So far such treatment has been limited primarily to offenders whose problems have been sufficiently severe that they became involved in the criminal justice system, a population not representative of all sex offenders.

Intrafamilial sex offenders, who are the primary focus of the treatment material in this book, appear to have less intense sexual feelings toward children, these feelings may occur less frequently, and the perpetrator's primary sexual orientation is less likely to be toward children. Therefore, the intrafamilial perpetrator may be more treatable than the population of sex offenders involved with the criminal justice system. However, intrafamilial perpetrators in our sample indicate it is difficult for them to predict when they are going to experience sexual feelings toward children and whether they will act upon them. Therefore, a prudent approach is to inform them and their families that sexual abuse appears to be a chronic problem, similar to alcoholism. Knopp (1985) speaks of *control* rather than *cure* for sex offenders.

These cautionary remarks should not be interpreted as a condemnation of current treatment, but rather as a warning regarding its limitations. Further, therapists should try, to the extent they are able, to attend to and change the perpetrator's sexual feelings toward children.

B. The Issue of Confession

A question about which there continues to be controversy in sexual abuse treatment is the necessity and significance of the perpetrator's

confession in the treatment process. Some clinicians do not see admission
as essential to successful treatment because they think that the family can
be restructured to be safe for the victim without admission (Mayer 1983;
Stovall 1979; McPeek 1985). Others exclude from treatment perpetrators
who do not make a confession (Giarretto 1982; Gottleib 1983; Boulder
County Sexual Abuse Unit Staff 1983).

Our position lies somewhere between these two extremes. The
possibility of successful treatment is greatly enhanced by a full confession from the offender. While the family structure can be altered to
reduce the likelihood of reincidence without the perpetrator's confessing,
there will continue to be considerable risk. His admission is a prerequisite
to strengthening his superego by having him take responsibility for the
sexual abuse, show an appreciation for the harm he has done, and
develop empathy for the victim. Enhancing the perpetrator's superego is
at least as important a prevention measure as restructuring the family.

Furthermore, the absence of recurrence is only one index of successful treatment. Equally important are factors related to the victim's
functioning, such as her feelings about her body, her self-image, and her
sense of guilt and responsibility, as discussed in chapter 11. It is extremely difficult to fully address these issues without a paternal confession and
acceptance of responsibility for the sexual abuse. Therefore, only in rare
circumstances should treatment be regarded as successfully concluded
without the perpetrator's admission and acceptance of responsibility.

Nevertheless confession should not be a prerequisite for treatment. Full confession is likely to be a process and can result from successful treatment. When treatment is initiated, it is necessary only that
the offender be willing to participate, or alternatively that his presence be
guaranteed by court order or other means. Treatment of the offender
becomes diagnostic because the therapist will measure success in part by
the perpetrator's confession, acceptance of responsibility, and appreciation of the traumatic effect of his abuse on the victim and others. If,
after several sessions, the perpetrator has not begun to acknowledge the
sexual abuse, the therapist should inform him that she questions whether
he is treatable at all. When termination is a result of lack of treatability,
the child will need indefinite protection from the perpetrator.

C. The Use of Outreach

Engagement of sexually abusive families in treatment may require
persistence by those trying to offer help. One strategy that can be very

useful is outreach, in which the therapist goes to the family rather than the other way around. The therapist also calls the family to encourage them to come to treatment or to ascertain why they have missed sessions, and uses volunteers, usually members of sexually abusive families who have already made some progress in treatment and who extend themselves to families that have just been referred to treatment.

Although doing treatment in the client's home has been demonstrated to be effective with a range of client populations (Maybanks and Bryce 1979), it is often resisted by therapists for both legitimate and illegitimate reasons. However, programs that incorporate outreach have proven quite successful with low-functioning and resistant families that might otherwise not receive treatment (Lilliston 1985). Usually outreach is employed in the early stages of treatment to overcome initial resistance to therapy and to develop an alliance with the family. The therapist works toward getting the family to come to the office. In addition, in-home treatment is likely to be used for some aspects of the therapy—for example, family sessions—but is infeasible for others, group therapy for instance. Transportation or carfare may be provided to assure clients come to the groups.

As an example of outreach using volunteers, in one treatment program, therapists and department of social services staff ask for volunteers from their mothers' group to contact new mothers as they are referred and invite them to the group (Stankwitz 1985). Giarretto (1982 a and b) reports that in his program each incoming family is hooked up to a supportive family that has already been through the program. Thus a father is linked to a father, a mother to a mother, and a victim to a victim. The supportive family is intensively involved, several hours during the first two weeks after referral. He reports this effort leads to confession by the perpetrator 90 percent of the time. According to Giarretto, a formerly sexually abusive family is better equipped to confront a family coming into the system than are professionals, and the family that has already been through the program can overcome fear of the unknown and of the criminal system for the entering family (Giarretto 1982 a and b).

D. Treatment Teams

Collaboration among two or more therapists is optimal when treating sexually abusive families. One reason for multiple therapists is that a number of treatment modalities may be employed concurrently

with one family. For instance, several family members may require weekly individual sessions in addition to needing to participate in groups.
Alternately the therapist may be using dyadic and family modes of
therapy at the same time.

Secondly, two or more therapists increases the range of appropriate role models for the family. Ideally the team should include
both male and female members. In addition to providing the family with
both male and female role models, this flexibility takes into account the
fact that individuals within the family may find it easier to form an
alliance with a therapist of a particular sex. In dyadic, family, and some
kinds of group therapy it will be advisable to have male and female co-
therapists. They become an "appropriate couple." In addition the
therapists can alternate roles within the therapy context.

A third reason for more than one therapist relates to the emotional needs of the family members. Some sexually abusive families are
characterized by pervasive unmet dependency needs. Such families can
overwhelm a single worker with demands for nurturance and other types
of emotional gratification. The needs of individuals within the family
may be competing and incompatible, causing a single therapist to feel
torn in many directions. Further, the modes family members employ to
get their dependency needs met may vary and change over time. For example the therapist may be dealing simultaneously with provocative
behavior by one family member, withdrawal and depression by another,
and frantic telephone calls from yet another member. Although particular family members may exhibit dependency needs at different stages
in treatment, such a pattern of family behavior is more likely to be
characteristic earlier in therapy when the family is in crisis. It is essential
that the therapist try to respond fairly immediately to these demands in
order to engage individuals or maintain their involvement in treatment.
It is virtually impossible for one person to do this.

A fourth reason for having multiple therapists, also related to
family neediness, is therapist burnout. The intense involvement required
and demands for support can burn out the solo therapist. In addition,
the burden of decision-making and responsibility can exhaust an individual worker. For instance, she may have to decide to remove a child
against the wishes of parents and child, to pursue police involvement, to
terminate treatment because of success or lack of success, or to return a
child to the home. All of these are difficult decisions to make alone. In
cases of child sexual abuse shared decision-making not only can decrease
worker burnout, but can also enhance the probability appropriate decisions are made.

E. Orchestration of Treatment

In order to address the prerequisite causes of sexual abuse as well as the contributing factors, what is needed is a multimodal approach to the family. This usually involves a combination of individual, dyadic, family, and group therapy. However, just because a problem is defined, for example, as an individual issue, does not mean it can be addressed only within the context of individual treatment. It could be attended to in other treatment modalities. However, such a problem probably is more naturally dealt with in individual treatment

All cases will not require all four treatment modalities, and the sequencing and modalities needed will vary depending upon the case (as well as upon what treatment resources are available in the community). In general, however, it is useful to begin with individual treatment for the family members involved. This is so because the first task is to establish alliances with individual family members. Some are likely to be more committed to treatment than others. Perpetrators, for example, may be more frightened and less willing to change than victims. The therapist has to work harder and often spend more time with recalcitrant participants in order to attain a more or less equal level of commitment from all. Group treatment for victims, mothers, and fathers is usually employed throughout the intervention, although sometimes clients need to be prepared for participation in groups. Family therapy is seen as a primary modality in the final phase of treatment. Thus, a fairly common pattern for treatment of intrafamilial sexual abuse is to begin with individual treatment, which is then followed by dyadic and subsequently family therapy, while group therapy is employed throughout.

The offenders' sexual feelings toward children and their superego deficits are most properly addressed in individual and group treatment for perpetrators. However, the task of constructing "external superego" mechanisms belongs in dyadic, family, and group modalities. The primary arenas for addressing factors that contribute to the sexual abuse are dyadic, family, and group treatment, but some work on them can also be accomplished in individual treatment.

Before discussing individual, dyadic, family, and group treatment, it is useful to point out some of the general dynamics that contribute to intrafamilial sexual abuse and note how the therapist attempts to alter these in treatment. However, recall from chapter 4, where the dynamics of sexual abuse were discussed, that there are both prerequisite and contributing causes of sexual abuse, both of which must be addressed, and there is quite a lot of variability among sexually abusive families.

No single family will display all the possible contributing factors and indeed, in some families, few if any of the characteristic patterns will be noted. In the latter type of family, it is likely that the causative factors are to be found in the prerequisites.

However, the patterns that can play a contributing role and the therapist's general intervention for these are as follows. First, sometimes sexually abusive families are enmeshed families whose boundaries are impermeable to the outside world. Further, boundaries of family members and family subsystems are blurred. Thus, individuals turn inward to the family to get their needs met and isolate themselves from the external environment. Sexual difficulties may exist in the family. In addition, there is frequently a rift in the husband-wife relationship, the relationship between the mother and daughter (victim) may be distant or problematic, sometimes the daughter is a parental child, and the relationship between the victim and her father is abnormal (overly close, detached, or hostile, as well as being sexual). Finally, relationships among children, both victims and nonvictims, are sometimes fraught with difficulties.

Since these patterns can contribute to the sexual abuse, changing them can reduce the likelihood of future sexual abuse. The therapist will be involved in changing role relationships and role responsibilities, in establishing generational boundaries, in altering the affective quality of the relationships, and in making people closer to or more distant from one another or the family. The most important relationship to change appears to be that between the mother and the daughter.

In the discussion of treatment issues, techniques for restructuring the family, thereby addressing contributing causes, will be described, as well as techniques for addressing the prerequisite causes of sexual abuse.

III. INDIVIDUAL TREATMENT ISSUES

Three individual treatment issues, present in many cases of intrafamilial sexual abuse, will be discussed: self-esteem, independence, and sexuality. These are issues for all members of the family, although the discussion will center around mother and father (see chapter 11 for treatment of victims). As already noted, individual issues can be addressed using treatments other than individual therapy.

A. Self-Esteem

Perpetrators, victims, and mothers of victims in situations of intrafamilial sexual abuse are likely to suffer from low self-esteem, which is at once a prerequisite for involvement in the sexually abusive family; and a consequence of participation in the sexually abusive situation.

The offender's low self-esteem may originate from many sources. The literature describes many sexually abusive men as inadequate in their functioning external to the family, for example in the world of work (Tormes 1969; Lukianowicz 1978; Bagley 1965). Recall from chapter 2 that about half of our sample had employment difficulties. Further, it was noted in chapter 4 that loss of employment or physical injury can be contributing factors to sexual abuse. In addition, adolescent perpetrators often have poor self-image because they lack the social skills to relate to peers—including peers of the opposite sex—and gravitate toward children.

Mothers of victims are frequently described as inadequate women, because they do not work outside the home, cannot provide good care for their children, or suffer from physical illness. They often experience other kinds of problems which have an impact upon their self-esteem, such as being battered by their partners, having a substance abuse problem, or being afflicted by mental illness.

Similarly, victims may be particularly vulnerable to sexual abuse because they suffer from low self-esteem and certainly their victimization has a negative impact upon their self-image.

Possible dynamics for the role of the perpetrator's low self-esteem are the following. Since he feels inadequate and unworthy, he chooses a child as a sexual partner because she is less likely to rebuff or challenge him. In a sexual encounter with a child, he gains a sense of mastery and control because he is able to get the child to do his will, which could make him feel better and improve his self-esteem. But at the same time, if the perpetrator has any superego, engaging in sexual abuse is likely to make him feel like a bad person, which would of course have a negative impact upon his self-esteem. Thus, the problem of self-esteem is a cyclical one. Similar cyclical dynamics exist for the victim and the nonperpetrating parent.

Treatment of low self-esteem involves sensitizing the client—perpetrator, mother, or victim—to those aspects of their lives where they do function well. In addition, they are helped to engage in activities which have a positive effect on self-esteem and to develop mastery over the sexual abuse. In pursuing the first goal, the therapist must not only recognize and reinforce for example, the perpetrator's areas of positive functioning but also assist other family members to do this. Examples of interventions to improve self-esteem are numerous and such interventions are fairly straightforward. For instance, assisting an unemployed perpetrator to get a job may enhance his self-esteem. He will begin to feel good about himself because he again is able to support his family. (In addition, being employed reduces the time spent with the children and thereby decreases the risk of sexual abuse). Employment for the mother who is the nonperpetrating parent can have a similar positive effect on self-esteem. Parenting classes that increase either parent's childcaring competence can have a beneficial impact on self-esteem. Giving the adult the opportunity to teach or offer guidance to someone else can also be a very useful intervention. As noted earlier, in some sexual abuse treatment programs, adults and children who have already made progress may be connected to newcomers. Among other benefits, this strategy does a great deal to enhance self-esteem for old members who give support to new members. Another similar technique is to employ adolescent victims who are making progress in treatment as big sisters or big brothers for the younger victims.

B. Independence

Strategies that positively affect self-esteem can also be beneficial in addressing the second individual treatment issue, assisting individuals in becoming more independent of the family. For example, if the mother works she necessarily becomes less dependent upon the family, particularly upon the perpetrator, assuming he is the primary wage earner. Involving family members in such outside activities as clubs, hobbies, and recreational pursuits can also gain them outside supports and make them less dependent upon the family for the satisfaction of their needs. Frequently the perpetrator-father insists that family members be dependent upon him while at the same time he looks to the family as the place where all his needs are met. He may be quite tyrannical in these endeavors. He may not allow his wife to buy the groceries without his being present. He may ration the gas in her car to control her activities. He often restricts his daughter's extracurricular activities in the guise of making sure she does well in school. He gives her the "third degree" when she wants to go out on a date. He sees his family as his refuge from the cruel world. It is essential that he let go and allow family members their independence as well as free himself from exclusive dependence upon the family. The following case example (also mentioned in chapter 5) illustrates interventions that address the issues of self-esteem and independence.

> EXAMPLE 1: Mrs. S, 29, had four children, two by her husband and two by her boyfriend, Mr. B, who had sexually abused her six-year-old daughter, Laura.

Mrs. S described herself as the "dumb one" in her family. She had only a ninth-grade education. Her two sisters had graduated from high school and had good husbands. She appeared depressed and in need of dental work. She lived in a trailer in an isolated rural area and was dependent upon Mr. B for transportation. She did not have a driver's license and she had no car. Although initially she reacted very appropriately when she encountered Mr. B attempting intercourse with Laura by calling the police and throwing him out of the trailer, she changed her story to say that she had not actually seen anything because Mr. B's back was to her and Laura was in front of him. She did this in part because it became apparent to her how totally dependent she was upon him.

Her family lived in the adjacent county and were fairly supportive when they learned of the sexual abuse. They took Laura into their home and they accompanied Mrs. S to the court hearing.

The therapist decided to involve the extended family in her work with Mrs. S and her children and asked Mrs. S to invite her parents to a treatment session. The therapist facilitated the parents in offering emotional and practical support to Mrs. S. Her father offered to fix up an old car for her to drive and extended-family members took turns giving Mrs. S driving lessons. Within four months she had a driver's license and a car. She then could take the two younger children to day care, buy her groceries, and keep medical appointments. She was also able to attend a parenting class.

As these things happened, her statements regarding Mr. B in therapy began to change. She no longer denied the sexual abuse and admitted to the therapist that Mr. B drank up her rent money and would hit her when she tried to stop him. She said she was ending their relationship and vowed she would not take him back. At the end of treatment she was planning to go back to school and get a GED and was in the process of getting her teeth fixed.

In this case the combination of emotional and practical support from extended family and therapist enabled Mrs. S to free herself from dependence upon the perpetrator and to come to do things for herself. She then no longer had the need to deny the sexual abuse and Mr. B's mistreatment of her. As she became more self-reliant, she began to feel better about herself. An index that she no longer saw herself as "the dumb one" was her decision to obtain a GED. Another indicator that she valued herself more was her decision to get her teeth fixed.

Such interventions have several rationales. As mother and daughter gain self-esteem they become less vulnerable to exploitation, and as the perpetrator acquires a better self image, he will be less in need of a child to make him feel good and powerful, and more able to seek sexual gratification from a peer. Similarly, as family members are more independent of the family and the perpetrator, they will have options other than staying in a sexually abusive situation should the sexual abuse recur.

C. Sexuality

A central individual treatment issue is sexuality. This issue is also interactive, and therefore, must, in part be addressed in dyadic and sometimes family sessions. The substance of the sexuality treatment issue varies depending upon the family member: victim, mother, and perpetrator. As this issue for victims is discussed in chapter 11, we shall focus here on sexuality as a treatment issue for mothers and perpetrators.

1. *Sexuality Issues for Mothers.* Some mothers in sexually abusive families have sexual problems. These are of two types. Some mothers dislike or fear sex, have an aversion to certain types of sexual behavior, or avoid sex at certain times. Fear of pregnancy, illness, or rejection of the spouse can play a role in lack of sexual performance. Further, as noted in chapter 4, avoidance of sex may be related to being sexually victimized as a child.

When the mother is nonresponsive sexually, the risk that her partner will sexually abuse the children may increase. Moreover, as discussed in chapter 4, the mother's own sexual abuse as a child may play a role in her choice of a sexually abusive partner, may result in her placing her child at risk, or may lead to denial when sexual abuse is reported because it is too overwhelming for her to accept.

When these dynamics are diagnosed, the therapist must interpret them to the mother in a supportive way. In making these interpretations it is important not to imply that the mother is therefore responsible for the sexual abuse. Often blaming her can be avoided by reminding her that she did not sexually abuse her child even though her own experience or behavior may have played a part. The second thing that needs to be done, if the mother was a victim as a child, is to help her work through feelings about her own sexual abuse. Chances are good that she has not received treatment for her own trauma, and even if she has, the sexual abuse of her child(ren) is likely to reactivate feelings regarding her own sexual abuse. It will take several sessions for the mother to ventilate and resolve these feelings. Strategies for enhancing the mother's sexual availability and increasing her sexual satisfaction will be discussed in the next chapter.

Some mothers of victims have quite the opposite kind of sexual problem. Instead of avoidance of sexual contact, they may be quite active and promiscuous. This pattern may be an outcome of having been a victim herself, or it may have other origins. In some situations, sexual abuse of the children occurs because the woman's partner is angry about the promiscuity and looks to the child as an opportunity for expressing his anger as well as a source of emotional comfort. In other situations the child is sexually abused by one or more of the mother's partners. The opportunity exists for such victimization because the mother may not provide adequate supervision, and may in some instances use these partners as babysitters. At times both mother and daughter appear to be victims of sexual and other abuse. Furthermore, even though the mother is promiscuous, she may be frigid and not enjoy sex. The example below is illustrative of some of the dynamics of situations where the mother has sexual problems and intervention to address them.

> EXAMPLE 2: Mona, 27, brought her biracial daughter, Cherry, 6, to the child protection team asking that Cherry be stopped from telling lies and setting fires. As to the lies, Mona said that Cherry was saying that men were putting their "things" (penises) in her "pocketbook" (Cherry's word for vagina).
>
> Mona related a history of serious physical abuse by her own mother; she had seated Mona on a coal shovel and tried to put her in the fire when she wet her pants. Her mother died of cervical cancer when Mona was six. Her father remarried four years after the mother's death. Mona was disliked by her stepmother.
>
> For two years a neighbor called Granddad molested Mona and her older sister. He would offer to take them downtown, to the amusement park, or buy them candy and things in exchange for sexual favors. Then he would not deliver the bribes.
>
> At 18, Mona left her family and "began living in the streets," which, when pressed, she said meant she was working as a prostitute or masseuse and using drugs. In a bar one evening she met her future husband, Greg. He was 40 and she was 20. Greg was black and Mona was white. He was also obese and had high blood pressure. They both were using heroin and cocaine. Mona said she loved him a lot and he was like a father to her. He did not make many sexual demands upon her because of his physical ailments and drug use. She was able to stop prostituting because Greg made good money dealing in drugs. She had Cherry, and when Cherry was 2, Greg died of complications from drug use.
>
> Mona went back to being a masseuse and a prostitute. She would leave Cherry with men whom Mona said were babysitters and they would sexually abuse her. One of the abusers was Mona's pimp, Billy. He moved into the family, taking over all the finances, and also would whip Cherry severely with a switch. When Mona was out in the evenings working as a masseuse, Billy would babysit for Cherry. Soon Cherry began to complain Billy was putting his thing into her pocketbook. At that point Mona took Cherry to the child protective team for lying and firesetting.

After a careful assessment Mona was told that Cherry was not lying, that indeed she had been sexually abused by at least three men.
Because of Cherry's firesetting and her mother's nonprotectiveness,
Cherry was removed from the home and placed, with the mother's agreement, in residential care. Work was then done with Mona, in an attempt to
get her to see the effects of her own past sexual and physical abuse on her
lifestyle and to see that she could not provide a safe place for Cherry if she
continued in her current lifestyle. Mona was highly motivated to get
Cherry back. She viewed her as the one thing left from the good part of her
life, when her husband was still living.

Mona was helped to see the relationship between being used sexually as a child and allowing herself to be used sexually as an adult. The
connection was made for her between receiving money for sex as an adult
and the promised but not delivered bribes as a child—that is, in part prostitution was a way to finally get her due. She was also able to understand
how her childhood sexual abuse made her unable to find satisfaction in
sex. After three months of therapy, Mona was able to come into the session and say, "You know, I spend most of my time doing the one thing
that disgusts me. If I ever want to be happy, I have to find a real job."
Work was then begun in therapy relating her drug use to a need to blot out
her pain. Eventually work was done with Mona to help her see that just as
she allowed herself to be victimized, she also let Cherry be victimized. At
this point she was confronted very directly about the kind of people she
left Cherry with. She was told that she would never be able to provide a
safe home for Cherry if she continued in her current lifestyle.

About two months before Cherry's planned discharge from residential treatment into foster care, Mona moved out of Billy's house and in
with a girlfriend. She also stopped prostituting and massaging.

This case is a fairly dramatic illustration of the role that the
mother's sexual problems can play in sexual abuse. The mother had
moderately good insight capabilities and was fairly verbal despite her
lifestyle. At this point, her response to understanding the contribution
she made to her daughter's and her own abuse is avoidance of risky situations. She will need more assistance if she again seeks a partner.

A strategy we have employed with other women with less insight
than Mona is to encourage them to find out the sexual habits of men they
are attracted to so they can avoid situations in which children might be
sexually abused. This may involve discussions with past wives or girlfriends, talks with parents, and sometimes conversations with the
children of these men. Often these encounters are role played in treatment before the client actually attempts them.

2. *Sexuality Issues for Perpetrators.* The perpetrator's sexuality is
the central and most important treatment issue in sexual abuse, for it is
his sexual orientation toward children which is one of the two prere-

quisite causes of sexual abuse. Yet as already noted, changing someone's sexual orientation is a difficult therapeutic task. However, there are a number of techniques that can be employed to address the perpetrator's sexual feelings toward children. The development of insight, behavior modification, development of ways for coping with sexual feelings, generating alternative need-satisfying behaviors, and drugs will be discussed.

a. *Helping the Perpetrator Develop Insight.* With perpetrators who are willing to be candid and able to develop insight, a helpful approach may be assisting them to understand why they are sexually attracted to children. In some cases, insight leads to diminished sexual feelings toward children and a few perpetrators in our sample report the disappearance of such feelings. Even without these positive results, making feelings which may appear mysterious and even monstrous comprehensible to the perpetrator can be very helpful in assisting him to gain control over them.

Generally, a fruitful strategy for understanding sexual abuse is to begin by exploring the perpetrator's childhood, probing in the following areas: how the perpetrator was parented, how he came to know about sex, what he was told, and whether the perpetrator had any sexual experiences as a child. (The patterns one would expect to find are described in chapters 3, 4, and 7). It is particularly important to explore not merely what happened but how the perpetrator felt about it at the time and how he feels now. It is common to find gaps in childhood memory of persons who have been sexually abused, including perpetrators. Techniques such as continually refocusing on the time frame in question, hypnosis, and reading or listening to accounts of other victims may release childhood memories.

Issues related to current functioning are also important to explore in understanding why the sexual abuse happened, for example, marital relationship and job satisfaction, views about sexuality, and relationships with children. The example below is a case where the therapist helped the perpetrator understand why he had sexually abused his daughters.

EXAMPLE 3:   When Mr. D first came to treatment he said he had not sexually abused his daughters, Cindy, 16, and Laura, 11. He had admitted to allegations in the Juvenile Court only to avoid a nasty trial. The therapist, who had already seen both girls, told him that she had never heard of anybody admitting to such allegations unless he was guilty and further asserted she believed his daughters. Mr. D was told that there would be no benefit from treatment if he refused to admit the sexual abuse.

In the next session he confessed to much of the sexual abuse, but said he could not understand why he had done it, that it was totally uncharacteristic. He had always been a very upright person. The therapist said she would try to assist him to understand why he had sexually abused his daughters, and after understanding, help to prevent further sexual abuse. As support for how uncharacteristic sexual abuse was, Mr. D described being brought up very strictly to obey. He said he was hardly ever physically punished as a child. He could recall being beaten once, and that was on an occasion when he was six and had thrown a piece of paper under the porch. Further probing revealed that Mr. D was hardly ever physically punished because he was so terrified of his parents that he rarely disobeyed. He had observed his older brother being beaten numerous times. When his brother was 14 he had run away and gone to the police. When the police came to the house Mr. D was told to say that his brother got the marks from beating at his grandparent's house. Mr. D showed his own back to the police, which was free of marks.

Initially, Mr. D said he very much approved of his parents' childrearing techniques. They taught him how to control himself. However, when noting later how differently he raised his own children, he acknowledge how frightened he was all the time as a child and how guilty he had felt when he betrayed his brother.

Mr. D could not recall any instances when his parents showed affection, although he said his mother now acknowledges she had been too strict. Discussion revealed that today he feels awkward even when he has to show affection to his wife.

As additional illustration of how uncharacteristic sexual abuse was of him, Mr. D said sex was never discussed when he was a child. He found out about sex when he was 14 and his older brother was 17. At that time his brother had gotten a girl pregnant. He did not recall masturbating as a child but did remember his mother accusing him of playing with himself in bed at night and telling him it was evil to touch himself. At 18, when he joined the army, he began masturbating.

When the information described above had been revealed, the therapist made the following interpretation. She told Mr. D that his punitive and unaffectionate background made it difficult for him to show affection because he really had not learned how to be loving in a nonsexual way as a child. As an adolescent he learned about sex as a way of showing affection, and part of the reason he became sexual with his daughters was because he had little experience in showing affection in a nonsexual way. However, the fact that sex was shameful, forbidden, and fascinating when he was a child also played a role in the sexual abuse.

As Mr. D came to comprehend his sexual feelings toward his daughters as expressions of affection he was helped to show his feelings in more appropriate ways when he had supervised visits. One of the first things he said to his older daughter when visits were initiated was, "I love you." He had never told her this before.

This is an example of the beginning stages of assisting an offender to understand why he sexually abused his children. However, other inter-

pretive work had to be done, and insight development was not the only technique employed.

b. *Behavioral Techniques.* Behavior modification techniques have been employed for many years and with varying success, in attempts to eliminate deviant sexual responses and other undesired behaviors. For the child sexual abuser the method seeks to eliminate sexual arousal to children and substitute arousal to other more appropriate stimuli. A variety of techniques can be employed. However, the basic strategy is to pair deviant sexual responses with a negative stimulus. Sometimes the perpetrator is shown pictures of children and these are followed by an electrical shock or noxious odor. Other times the perpetrator is asked to imagine sexually stimulating scenes involving children and then delivered the negative stimulus; or the treatment involves having the perpetrator consider negative consequences of the sexual abuse, such as being arrested and taken to jail or his wife divorcing him. He is encouraged to imagine all the details of the consequences so that he can recreate the scenario vividly. He is then instructed to imagine the scenario when presented with a sexually arousing stimulus or when he becomes sexually aroused by the child (Abel et al. 1985; Knopp 1985).

The pairing of the child stimulus with the negative consequence is meant to decrease the arousal response to the child. In some interventions, the negative stimulus will be terminated when the perpetrator switches from a picture of a child to, for example, an adult woman. Some clinicians employ a device (a penile plethysmograph) which is attached to the penis and measures erectile response as a way of assessing sexual arousal (Greer and Stuart 1983; Laws and Osborn 1983; Pithers et al. 1983).

Other behavioral techniques may be employed to enhance sexual arousal to appropriate stimuli. For example, the perpetrator may be instructed to masturbate to fantasies of adult women or while observing pictures of adult women or adults having intercourse. Behavioral techniques are one of the few interventions where efforts have been made to assess effectiveness. In general, the findings are that merely attempting to reduce sexual arousal to inappropriate stimuli is not sufficient. Some reprogramming to develop a repertoire of alternative appropriate sexual behaviors greatly enhances success (Greer and Stuart 1983; Quinsey and Marshall 1983). Further, this type of treatment is successful only when the perpetrator is candid and cooperative. He must honestly report sexual feelings, must engage in many practice sessions, and must be willing to return for followup sessions if sexual responses to children recur, as reportedly they often do.

c. *Other Coping Mechanisms.* Another technique for dealing with the perpetrator's sexual feelings toward children is to teach him to note these when they are occurring and to handle them in ways other than becoming sexual with children. What will be described here has some relationship to behavioral approaches but is suited to a less sophisticated and less motivated client. It is, in a sense, the "cold shower technique." The therapist problem-solves with the perpetrator what he might do when sexual feelings arise toward children. Tactics could include leaving the room, going out for a walk, or telling somebody. The strategies that appear to be the most successful are those that involve an incompatible activity away from the child.

In some cases the perpetrator, rather than inadvertently finding himself in situations that arouse him sexually, engages in a series of actions that set the scene for sexual abuse. Perpetrators may have varying levels of conscious awareness that they are setting the stage for sexual abuse. In some cases, the perpetrator appears to be totally unaware that he is preparing for sexual abuse. In others, he recognizes the situation as one in which he is at risk for sexually abusing, but deludes himself that it will not happen this time. In still other cases, the perpetrator consciously sets the scene for sexual abuse.

The sequence of events may begin by the perpetrator's offering to babysit for the children, by his going to the park where children sometimes play, or by his staying up and drinking too much while his wife goes to bed. Other times the first event in the sequence is something that frustrates him or makes him feel angry, sometimes at his wife, and the next step allows him access to victims or reduces his inhibitions. In treatment the therapist explores with the perpetrator whether a chain of events leads to the sexual abuse. If such a pattern or patterns are discovered, then the therapist assists the perpetrator in recognizing the early events in the sequence and stopping the series at the beginning when the perpetrator will have greater ability to control his behavior than at the end of the chain of events. Often it is quite difficult to interrupt the sequence late in the chain because the perpetrator has diminished capacity (he is intoxicated) or no way of leaving the scene (he cannot leave the children unattended).

The example below is one of a noncustodial father who developed a pattern of behaviors that led to sexual abuse.

EXAMPLE 4:   Mr. W had two daughters, Janie, 7, and Kim, 3. He and his wife had been divorced one year. He was required by the court to visit his daughters at his mother's house because he had a drug and alcohol problem. Before this restriction on his visits, Mr. W had the children overnight at his house, and on one occasion he had gotten high and had Janie rub his penis.

The visits at Mr. W's mother's were supposed to be all day Sunday and Wednesday afternoons. However, Mr. W asked that they be changed to Saturday nights and Sunday because sometimes he had to work Wednesday afternoon. The court and Mrs. W agreed to this change in visitation. It was convenient for Mrs. W because she had a new boyfriend and liked to go out on Saturday night.

The first weekend of the new visitation schedule Mr. W kept the girls up quite late playing with them and letting them watch television. After he put them to bed, he asked his mother if it was all right if he slept on the couch rather than driving home in a bad storm. She assented. He did not attempt any sexual abuse that weekend.

The next visitation, Mr. W engaged in a similar pattern, and again it was late when he asked his mother if he could sleep on the couch. This time his mother objected because her fiance was there and had planned to sleep over. Mr. W suggested that his mother and her fiance might want to go to his apartment, and Mr. W would stay and watch the girls. His mother agreed to this. Mr. W smoked a joint and then got Janie up and engaged in interfemoral intercourse with her.

This was the beginning of a pattern of sexual abuse which involved Mr. W persuading his mother to leave him alone with the children, drinking or using drugs, and then sexually abusing one or the other daughter. After this had been going on for about three months, Janie tearfully begged her father on a Sunday morning to go back to being the old daddy. Her pleas distressed him, and furthermore, his ex-wife was becoming suspicious because the children were saying they did not like to visit their grandmother.

Mr. W vowed he would stop the sexual abuse. His first technique involved attempting to get himself too drunk to get out of bed. However, he vomited, felt better, and went into the bedroom and fondled Kim. Then he tried not drinking, but that was no more successful. His next effort was to tell his mother she should stay in her apartment that night because he might have to leave at five o'clock in the morning. About midnight she caught Mr. W in bed with Janie. Janie was whimpering as Mr. W made her masturbate him.

Mr. W's mother insisted he go to therapy and alerted the children's mother to the sexual abuse. In treatment, Mr. W was tearful and explained to the therapist that he had a compulsion to sexually abuse his daughters that was totally out of his control. He related his unsuccessful attempts to control his behavior. He appeared to divorce himself from any real responsibility by defining his behavior as being out of his control.

As part of the treatment, the therapist retraced the history of the visitation pattern. With questioning, she discovered that there had only been one Wednesday visit that Mr. W was forced to cancel because of work and that he could control his work hours sufficiently so that only rarely would he have to work on Wednesdays. As this was discussed in treatment, it appeared that Mr. W was not fully aware that his unavailability on Wednesdays was not real. The therapist also pointed out that being alone with the children at night was associated with sexual abuse, and whether Mr. W was aware of it or not, he had engineered this situation by staying too late to return to his house and by getting his mother to stay with her boyfriend. Finally, the therapist noted getting drunk and high were also associated with sexual abuse, although not necessary for it to occur.

It was suggested to Mr. W that he had made two unsuccessful attempts to control his sexually abusive behavior, drinking too much and not drinking, and one successful attempt, getting his mother to stay home. While the latter did not prevent the sexual abuse, it successfully interrupted the pattern because he was caught in the act. Therefore, his behavior was not at all out of his control. If he had interrupted the sequence earlier, before he was alone with his daughters at night, he would have been quite successful in controlling it. Moreover, if he examined the whole chain of events leading to the context of the sexual abuse, he should be able to see he played an active role in engineering it.

Mr. W's initial reaction to the therapist's interpretation was to see her as being unappreciative of his situation and having unrealistic expectations of his ability to control his behavior. The therapist continued to work with him, dealing with a range of issues, and also referred him to a substance abuse treatment program. Somewhat later in treatment, Mr. W spontaneously brought up his responsibility for switching the Wednesday visits to Saturday night. He said he now thought the therapist was probably right.

The therapist applauded Mr. W's insights and reinforced her earlier statements that the way for him to avoid sexually abusive situations was simply to interrupt at the early stages sequences of events that might result with him having unsupervised access to his children, and to recognize that he was prone to engineering such situations even though at a conscious level he might not be aware of the purposiveness of his behavior. About six months later, supervised visits were resumed, and some more work was done with Mr. W to identify situations where a series of events might lead to sexual abuse.

In the case of Mr. W, the therapist, by taking a careful history, could readily identify the chain of events leading to sexual abuse. Mr. W did not appear to be completely aware of his responsibility for setting the stage for the sexual abuse and certainly resisted this interpretation when it was first made. It is fairly common for clients to resist interpretations, and the therapist moved to other treatment issues with the expectation that she would later return to this one. The fact that Mr. W spontaneously returned to this and was so much more accepting of the interpretation speaks not only to his insight capabilities and the therapist's skill, but also to the fact that he was in a substance abuse treatment program which took a parallel approach to Mr. W's chemical dependency.

     d. *Alternative Need Satisfying Behaviors.* A third technique for dealing with sexual feelings is to channel them to more appropriate objects. As was noted in chapter 4, sometimes persons have sexual feelings toward children because of the absence of access to more appropriate sex objects. In addition, the reason sexual responses are elicited by a child rather than an adult may be because a child is a less threatening and more manageable love object.

     Earlier in this section, in the discussion of behavior modification, some behavioral techniques were cited for increasing sexual arousal to more appropriate sex objects. There is a range of additional strategies which are not strictly behavioral for redirecting sexual feelings. Those which involve enhancing the marital relationship will be discussed in the next chapter. The remainder are suitable for situations where there is no partner and do not really belong in a chapter focused on treatment of intrafamilial sexual abuse. Therefore, strategies will merely be mentioned rather than described in detail. They include affording the perpetrator access to contemporaries, usually of the opposite sex, by involving him in a range of activities, developing social skills through structured or unstructured social skills training and assertiveness training that prepares the individual for a range of previously frightening social situations. (Assertiveness training is also used to help the offender handle feelings of anger). Further, sometimes sex therapy with the use of surrogates is a helpful intervention.

     e. *Drugs.* Recently drugs which reduce sexual drive, principally Depo-Provera, have been employed with sex offenders. Their use is new and controversial (Groth et al. 1982; Quinsey and Marshall 1983; Berlin 1983). While some sex offenders are quite positive about their effects, some researchers point out that there is no evidence that sex offenders have greater than normal sexual drive (Quinsey and Marshall 1983). Further, clinicians argue that sexual abuse is a pseudosexual act and therefore reducing sexual drive does not guarantee there will not be sexual abuse. There also is concern about the drug's side effects which may be increased risk of cancer. In addition, it can be argued that allowing perpetrators to blame their sexually abusive behavior on their unusually high sexual drive gives them permission to avoid responsibility for their abusive behavior.

     A great deal of work still needs to be done before we understand the potential benefits and limitations of drug therapy. However, it is a very important treatment to explore because changing sexual orientation is so difficult by other available methods.

IV. CONCLUSION

This chapter has offered some general guidelines for treatment of sexual abuse and has focused on individual treatment issues and techniques. The therapist must remember there are prerequisite causes and contributing factors to sexual abuse. In addressing these issues, treatment needs to be multimodal, usually involving individual, dyadic, family, and group approaches. To date there is no evidence that any techniques completely "cure" the offender.

An important first stage of treatment is engagement using individual treatment. Three treatment issues were discussed: self-esteem, independence, and sexuality, as were treatment strategies to address these.

CHAPTER THIRTEEN

Treating Dyadic Relationships

I. INTRODUCTION

There are three dyadic relationships — mother-daughter, husband-wife, and father-daughter — which usually require intervention in intrafamilial sexual abuse. The treatment issues for each relationship will be discussed in this chapter, and techniques for addressing their problematic aspects will be described.

II. TREATMENT OF THE MOTHER-DAUGHTER DYAD

The quality of the mother-daughter relationship is not only an important prognostic indicator, but also crucial for assuring the victim's future safety and well-being. The goal of the therapy is to make the dyad strong and independent of the father, nurturing and supportive for the daughter, gratifying for the mother, and open in terms of its communications.

As noted in chapter 4, the nature of the mother-daughter relationship varies from case to case, but usually there are some difficulties. In some, mothers are hostile toward, blaming of, and competitive with their daughters. In others, the victim may display a lot of problematic behavior, whose origin, unbeknownst to the mother, is the sexual abuse. There is as a result much tension between the mother and daughter because of the daughter's behavior. In still others, the daughter does a lot of caretaking and is a parental child, and thus is competitive with the mother for her role, or there is role reversal between mother and daugher. Sometimes there is a lot of closeness and mutual caring, but the daughter does not tell the mother about the sexual abuse in order to avoid distressing her.

A variety of techniques are useful in changing the mother-daughter relationship. We will decribe four: sharing feelings, resolving conflicts, developing relationship-enhancing activities, and engineering a protective relationship.

A. Sharing Feelings

It is important that both mother and daughter share with one another their feelings about the sexual abuse. The following are common emotional reactions to sexual abuse. The mother is likely to feel guilt and remorse because of what happened to her daughter, but she may also be angry at the victim or bewildered because she allowed the sexual abuse or delayed in telling. She may also be distressed with the daughter because the consequences of telling have caused a dramatic upset in the family's life. The daughter may well harbor anger toward the mother as well as the perpetrator, and she may have experienced a sense of relief when telling; but she may also feel guilty and damaged because of what has happened to her.

The therapist needs to orchestrate the expression of these feelings carefully so that they enhance rather than undermine the mother-victim relationship. Frequently, it is a good idea to delay the mother's expression of her negative feelings until the therapist has had a chance to build mutual trust between the mother and daughter, or to allow the mother to express the feelings first in individual sessions. A strategy which is sometimes useful is to emphasize that both mother and daughter are victims; they both have been betrayed by the perpetrator. A method for doing this is to have them recount the family history and point out each instance of mistreatment. When the intention is to reunite the father with the family, this strategy must be used with some moderation, for example, by also pointing out positive aspects of his functioning, so that mother and daughter do not become too alienated from the father.

In many cases, a goal of this sharing of feelings is not only to reinforce the victimization of both mother and daughter, but also to recognize that their positions are different. The mother is an adult and the victim is a child. The mother chose the father as a partner; the child had no choice. Therefore, the mother must take some responsibility for what happened to her daughter. Often, the mother readily acknowledges her role, but in cases where she refuses, the therapist must assist her. This acknowledgment is a prerequisite for her becoming the child's protector, a treatment issue that will be discussed at the end of this section.

In the example below, also cited in chapter 5, the therapist facilitated the sharing of feelings between mother and daughter related to multiple victimization.

EXAMPLE 1:   By age 15, Terry had been sexually abused by her father, her stepfather, and one of her mother's boyfriends. Terry's mother, Shirlee, had married Terry's father, Lenard, when she was 13 and pregnant by him. Four more children were born in quick succession so that, at 18, Shirlee had five children, a husband who beat both her and four younger children, sexually abused Terry, rarely worked, had been hospitalized in the local mental institution twice, and had been incarcerated twice for burglary. He was also an arsonist. When Terry was five, Shirlee left Lenard and placed the four younger children in foster care. Shirlee divorced him and married George. Terry was returned to her mother, and Shirlee had two daughters by George. George was not as bad as Lenard, but he was a womanizer, immature, a drinker, and had trouble holding a steady job. Shirlee persuaded him to join the service in order to learn some work habits. He was sent to Germany. After his departure, Terry and Colleen, the oldest daughter by him, told Shirlee of a game he had invoved them in called "Pussy," which entailed fondling. At this time, Terry also told her mother about having to fellate her father in the car when he took her for visits. Shirlee divorced George and cut off visits with Lenard. Terry was ten at the time.

Shirlee started going out with Roy when Terry was fourteen. Terry told her mother she did not like Roy, but her mother continued to see him. What Terry did not tell her mother was that Roy was making sexual remarks to her. He told her that he thought she had nicer breasts than her mother and said that all she had to do was "say the word and he would bust my cherry for me." Terry babysat her younger sisters while her mother worked at a factory. Roy told her that he was going to "come around and see me while my mother was at work."

Terry became increasingly difficult for her mother to handle. She refused to get up for school. She came home late at night. She was disrespectful. She would have tantrums and break things. Eventually, Terry ran away. When she was found and reunited with her mother, Terry told about Roy's advances and vented a tremendous amount of hostility toward her mother, whom she called a whore and whom she blamed for all of the sexual abuse. Shirlee was overwhelmed and wept. She said she did not want Terry back because she did not feel she could handle her. However, she did get rid of Roy.

Terry was placed in foster care while the therapist worked with Terry and Shirlee to improve their relationship. In the first session, she asked each to share with her their experiences with Lenard, George, and Roy. In therapy, Terry revealed to her mother for the first time that her father had begun stroking her vulva and having her stroke his penis when she was four. Her mother was very distressed and asked Terry why she had not told her. Terry replied that her mother was always too busy when Terry wanted to talk. Shirlee acknowledged that she was overwhelmed by the responsibility of so many young children and that, in fact, she used

Terry to help her out rather than treating her like the child she was. She told Terry she was very sorry she had ignored her.

Shirlee described what it was like to be married to Lenard. He was totally unpredictable and would fly into a rage without any warning. She described a number of instances when he had beaten her because she had intervened to protect the children. Terry had no recollection of these events. Once, he had stolen the food money given to Shirlee by his mother and beat her with a baseball bat when she tried to get the money back. Shirlee said she was frightened of him and stated he had threatened to find them and kill the children if she left him.

Terry acknowledged that this must have been hard, but she then said she would never forgive her mother for giving away her sisters and brothers. Her mother described the event that precipitated her placing the four younger children in foster care. She and the four younger children were being driven to the store by Lenard. Jimmy, who was 1 ½, accidentally caught his fingers in the car door. He screamed and Lenard began yelling at him to shut up. Jimmy screamed louder. Eventually, he stopped the car, took off his belt, and beat all the children.

Later that day, when Lenard had gone out with some friends, Shirlee took the four younger children to Catholic Social Services and asked that they be placed. She thought her husband was less likely to find them and kill them if they were in foster care. Terry was at her paternal grandmother's. Her intention was to get a job and a place to live and then get the kids back. Unfortunately, she was unable to find a job that would allow her to get a large enough place for the family. She could not get AFDC, because she did not have the children and after two years her parental rights were terminated. She told Terry that she had no idea that her kids could be taken away from her permanently when she placed them.

This was new information for Terry, but then she brought up George. She said she was really mad at her mother because George had not gone to jail for what he had done to her and Colleen. Her mother responded that, when Colleen and Terry first told her about George, she really did not believe them. She could believe it of Leonard, but not of George. She wrote George a letter telling him of the allegations and asking for his explanation. However, after writing the letter, she changed her mind and determined not to give him the benefit of the doubt. She decided there was no way both girls could be lying. She initiated divorce proceedings. Terry said he ought to have gone to jail, not just divorced. Her mother said she was thinking of Colleen and Kim, the two younger children, and she knew they would not want their daddy to go to jail. Terry was not persuaded, but she seemed to understand her mother's reasoning.

Terry then took her mother to task for her relationship with Roy. Her mother said that Roy had been very helpful. He had protected the family when George came home on leave and wanted to resume his role in the family. Terry asserted that she had warned her mother about Roy. Her mother responded that Terry never liked any of her boyfriends and she had no idea what Roy was doing. She said she was sorry about all the things that had happened to the children.

This session was the first of several that were necessary to facilitate the mutual sharing of feelings. Terry was full of rage, a lot of which was focused upon her mother. Her mother, in turn, was quite depressed and overwhelmed. This mutual sharing eventually brought Terry and her mother closer together and facilitated Terry's return home.

B. Conflict Resolution

In improving the mother-daughter relationship, specific areas of dispute may need to be resolved. These may be disagreements about the victim's chores, dress, curfew, school attendance and performance, relationships with the opposite sex, and interactions with other family members, as well as objections the victim has to some of the mother's behavior. Often, these conflicts are only between the mother and daughter, because the perpetrator is a permissive parent who undermines the mother's authority. She then is polarized by his maneuvers into being even stricter. Since, in most cases, the mother will temporarily or permanently have sole responsibility for the children, resolution of mother-victim disputes is important. Techniques for developing parental consensus about child management will be discussed in the section on marital dyad treatment.

In dealing with mother-daughter conflicts, we suggest strategies effective in other child-management situations. Thus, problem-solving, communication, or behavior management techniques are quite useful. For example, the therapist facilitates the mother-daughter dyad in defining the problems and their ramifications, helps them generate possible solutions, involves them in choosing a solution to try, and assists in implementing a plan. The example that follows illustrates the use of conflict-resolution to reduce tension between mother and daughter.

EXAMPLE 2:   Jane, age 13, was sexually abused by her stepfather. Her mother, who initially did not believe her, eventually changed her mind and required the stepfather to leave the family. Jane also had a history of truancy from school. Jane's mother was struggling to raise two children on AFDC, a new experience for her, and Jane was continuing to cause her difficulties six months after the stepfather's departure.

Jane and her mother were involved in conjoint treatment. When the therapist asked about Jane's not getting up on time for school, she admitted she did not go to sleep when she was supposed to but read Judy

Blume books, using a flashlight under the blankets. She had started reading secretively in this manner when her stepfather was still at home, for two reasons. She had trouble sleeping because of her distress over the sexual abuse, and she had to read Judy Blume books in secret, since her stepfather disapproved of them. Jane continued to stay up at night reading after her stepfather's departure because she liked the cozy feeling of reading under the covers. She also was quite angry at her mother for bringing her stepfather into the household, for, in her eyes, preferring him to her, and for not believing her initially when she told about the sexual abuse.

At the point dyadic treatment began, Jane was ready to reduce the tension between herself and her mother, and was beginning to trust her mother again. She agreed that, if she went to sleep earlier, she could get up and go to school in the morning. The therapist's suggestion was that Jane go to bed at 8:00 rather than 9:00 so she could still read in bed. Her mother was to call up to her when it was 9:00 and time to turn off the light. Jane also asked for an alarm clock to use to wake her up instead of having her mother yell at her. The therapist bought this, as Jane's mother did not have the funds.

Another area of disagreement between Jane and her mother was Jane's desire to date. Her mother thought she should wait until she was 16 to date, but Jane already had a boyfriend at school. The therapist assisted Jane and her mother in negotiating an agreement which allowed Jane to go out with her boyfriend either Friday or Saturday night to a place approved by Jane's mother, if she had arrived at school on time the previous week. However, almost as soon as the agreement was made, Jane broke up with her boyfriend. Therefore, the plan was changed so that Jane could go out with friends.

Another problem that arose in the plan was that when Jane missed one morning of getting to school on time she had no incentive to get up on time the rest of the week. Therefore, the plan was changed so that, for every morning Jane got up and to school on time, she got to stay out 45 minutes on Friday or Saturday night.

This plan led to marked improvement in Jane's getting to school on time and removed school attendance and going out on weekends as sources of conflict between Jane and her mother.

This case illustrates problem-solving and behavioral intervention, addressing two conflict areas: going to school and going out on weekends. There were other areas which were addressed in a similar fashion.

C. Relationship-Enhancing Activities

Resolving conflicts as described above clears the way for more positive techniques for improving the mother-daughter relationship. By the time sexual abuse is revealed, the mother-daughter relationship may consist entirely of hostile, conflict-ridden encounters, especially when the victim is an adolescent. Mother and daughter may be involved in few experiences which are mutually enjoyable or beneficial. An important technique for the therapist is to foster positive activities. These can vary greatly; they could include the mother and daughter baking a cake together, going to the movies, the mother accompanying her daughter to her Girl Scout ceremony, or their visiting a relative they both respect. For these kinds of arrangements to be relationship-enhancing and not to become additional arenas of conflict, work in the two areas just described is necessary first.

The example below is illustrative, and is another from the case of Terry, cited earlier.

EXAMPLE 3: After tensions between Terry and her mother, Shirlee, had been resolved somewhat by sharing feelings, the therapist considered working on some of the conflicts between them. However, these had been resolved temporarily by her placement in foster care.

The therapist decided to use some relationship-enhancing activities while Terry remained in foster care. Terry had a lot of complaints about how her clothing fit. She felt her jeans were not tight enough. Shirlee could sew and was willing to teach Terry. While the therapist had some misgivings about Terry's tight clothes, she was sure Terry would alter them anyway and thought it would be better to involve her mother in the alterations. On the next visit home, Terry brought all her jeans that she wanted taken in. Her mother demonstrated on one pair and Terry, with her mother's help, sewed the others.

During the sewing lesson, Terry asked her mother how hard it would be to make a bikini. Ready-to-wear bathing suits which fit Terry in the bottom were too tight in the top. Their project for the next visit was a bathing suit. When time came for the visit to end, they hadn't finished. Terry and her mother asked if Terry could stay overnight to finish the suit. The visit was going so well that the foster care worker allowed this. In the morning, Terry go up and fixed breakfast for her two younger sisters so that her mother could sleep in. Shirlee took Terry back to foster care at noon when she had to go to work.

Their next project was a dress for the Junior Prom. A friend of Shirlee's gave them the material. At this time, visits were prolonged, so there was ample opportunity to complete the dress. Her mother sewed the difficult parts and Terry the easier parts.

Things were going so well between Terry and Shirlee that they both asked that Terry come home. Because Terry would have to switch schools for the last month of school and because she was finally in a pattern of good attendance and performance in school, the therapist thought it would be better for her to complete the school year in foster care. Further,

that would give the therapist the summer to work with Terry and Shirlee
without having to worry about Terry's school attendance.

In the example just described, the sewing activities designated for
visitation were valued by both mother and daughter, and enhanced their
relationship. They were something positive that could be built upon.
Thus, both Shirlee and Terry wanted to extend them, and Terry recipro-
cated for her mother's help by fixing breakfast for her sisters. This interaction had the additional advantage of placing Shirlee in a role where
she was competent and in charge.

D. Making the Mother the Protector

The fourth technique for improving the mother-daughter relationship is developing for the mother the role of protector of the
daughter. This intervention belongs, in part, in mother-daughter dyad
treatment. For it to be successful, there must be open communication
between the mother and daughter about issues related to the daughter's
safety, tension between them must have been reduced by conflict resolution, and their relationship must be strong enough for the daughter to
believe her mother will protect her.

The first step in the strategy is to identify situations where the
perpetrator had access to the victim. Although such information is
sometimes revealed by the perpetrator, the victim is a more reliable
source of data. For example, the sexual abuse may have occurred when
the perpetrator took the child on recreational outings or when the victim
and perpetrator were alone in the evenings. Second, the mother, the victim, and the therapist arrive at ways of reducing the offender's unsupervised access to the victim.

Third, a plan needs to be developed for what to do if the perpetrator again attempts sexual abuse. Chapter 11 described techniques for
assisting the victim if there is another attempt, but the mother must also
make a plan. Further, the victim needs to know what the mother's plan
will be. In most cases, the plan is also communicated to the perpetrator,
and as noted in chapter 12, it is hoped that the existence of such a plan
will act as an external superego for the perpetrator. In the example
below, also cited in chapters 4 and 8, protections were initiated during
the mother-daughter treatment:

EXAMPLE 4:   Lucy, 10, was her father's favorite child. He had an older
daughter, Patsy, 22, and sons, Todd, 19, and James, 15. Lucy was sexually abused by her father over a two-year period. This occurred after

school and in the evenings when her mother worked. By this time, Patsy was married and out of the home. Todd and James usually were out participating in school activities or involved with friends. The abuse was discovered when Patsy asked Lucy whether their father was doing anything sexual with her. Mr. A had attempted to sexually abuse Patsy and it precipitated her leaving the family. Mrs. A was extremely upset that Lucy had not told her. When she found out Patsy had also been sexually accosted, she was even more distressed. Initially, Lucy was placed with Patsy because their dad was still in the home. The boys and Lucy did not want him to leave, and financially it would have been very difficult for the family if he left.

The relationship between Lucy and her mother was basically a good one even though Lucy had become rather difficult to manage since the onset of the sexual abuse. Mrs. A felt keenly the loss of her daughter and resented not being the one to buy her new clothes and not being able to talk with her about what had happened.

As soon as it was feasible in treatment, dyadic sessions between mother and daughter were initiated; Patsy was involved in many of these as well. In addition, Lucy and her mother were allowed visits which involved relationship-enhancing activities, although in fact, these were a continuation of the normal patterns between Lucy and Mrs. A.

After about two months of living with Patsy, Lucy was begging to return home. In preparation, Mrs. A told Lucy numerous times in treatment that, if anything ever happened again, she should tell her. Mrs. A also made a plan to have weekly talks with Lucy to assess any occurrence of sexual abuse. These were a kind of continuation of the dyadic therapy sessions.

Mrs. A switched her working schedule to days so that her husband would not have unsupervised access to Lucy in the evenings. There was an hour in the morning, before Lucy had to be in school, when Mrs. A had to be at work. Mrs. A made arrangements to take Lucy to a friend's who lived near her school. After school, Lucy went to Patsy's and stayed until her mother came and picked her up.

In addition, Mrs. A let her husband know in no uncertain terms that if he did anything that was in violation of the treatment plan, or even was alone with Lucy, she would file for a divorce and take Lucy and go to her family in Florida.

While Lucy was told that further attempts by her father to sexually abuse her would mean she and her mother would have to leave, this aspect of the intervention plan was not emphasized because of concern that she might not tell in order to protect her father. Rather, the importance of not being alone with him and of telling her mother if anything happened were underscored.

The plan for protection in the A case involved the mother's reorganizing her schedule at considerable inconvenience to herself and

making it very clear to the father what the consequences of any transgression would be. Happily, the mother's commitment to protection and the essentially positive relationship she had with her daughter meant that she had decided without any urging by the therapist that Lucy's welfare was the first priority.

Finally, as part of enhancing the mother-daughter dyad, it should be noted that the process of seeing the mother and daughter together and involving them in a range of activities in and out of session reinforces for them their ongoing relationship. The relationship is being sanctioned by the therapist, and its separateness from the rest of the family is emphasized by virtue of the fact that they are seen in treatment without other family members.

III. TREATMENT OF THE FATHER-DAUGHTER DYAD

In cases where the family is to be reunited or where it remains intact, intervention to change the father-daughter relationship is essential. Even when there will be no reunification, some normalization of that relationship may be important to the victim's future development. Exactly when in the treatment process father-daughter sessions take place will vary a great deal. However, they generally begin after a fair amount of individual work has already been done and after dyadic work with the mother-daughter and husband-wife relationships is well underway. Often, treatment of the father-daughter relationship comes shortly before family reunification.

Treatment issues for the father-daughter dyad include those related to the sexual abuse itself as well as aspects of the relationship which may have contributed to or resulted from the sexual abuse. Common issues that fall into the former category are need for the victim to express her feelings about the sexual abuse to her father and to have him respond appropriately by taking responsibility for the sexual abuse. Regarding the latter, as noted in chapter 12, abnormalities usually exist in the father-daughter relationship. Moreover the discovery of the abuse usually further disrupts that relationship. It would be naive to expect that the father-daughter tie will ever be completely normal, but work can be done to improve it and to decrease the level of discomfort for both parties.

In this section, three treatment issues will be discussed: the need to share feelings, the father's taking responsibility for the sexual abuse, and making the father-daughter relationship more normal.

A. Sharing Feelings

Just as it is important for mother and daughter to share feelings about the sexual abuse, so it is also essential for father and daughter to do so. However, it is more imperative than in the case of the mother that the father's expression of feelings be controlled by the therapist. As noted in chapter 12, some perpetrators have hostile feelings toward their victims, blame them for the revelation of the sexual abuse, and sometimes hold them responsible for the abuse itself. The therapist needs to address these responses, if they exist, in individual or group treatment before any meetings between father and daughter. The perpetrator must come to empathize with, and demonstrate some level of care for, the victim, and appreciate that the victim is not responsible for the abuse and the consequences of its revelation. If the perpetrator does not come to feel this way about the sexual abuse, then reunification of the family is inadvisable. Getting the perpetrator to the point where he can see the situation from the child's viewpoint may not be possible merely using individual and group therapy. However, this may be facilitated by his hearing the victim's feelings, which can be accomplished by techniques described in chapter 11. The victim may, for example, write a letter or make a tape for the perpetrator, or the therapist may carefully orchestrate a dyadic session in which the child expresses her feelings. The therapist must not only rehearse with the child, but must also moderate the perpetrator's responses to the child's statements, as many of these fathers are highly manipulative and can take over a session.

Thus, a major goal of father-daughter dyad treatment is to allow the child to communicate her feelings of anger, betrayal, and pain in the hope that this will cause the father to express empathy and love for the victim. If the therapist thinks the father feels sorry for what he had done, he should be encouraged to apologize to the child.

B. Taking Responsibility

In addition to being able to say he is sorry and understand how much the child has suffered, the perpetrator must take responsibility for his abusive behavior. This process is often rehearsed in individual sessions. Simple statements the child will understand should be used. For example, statements in chapter 11 described for use by the therapist can be altered: "It's not your fault; it's my fault." "I sexually abused you. You didn't sexually abuse me." "I'm a grown-up; you're a kid. I knew it was wrong when I did it."

The father's empathy for the child and taking responsibility for the sexual abuse should moderate the child's guilt feelings, depression, and negative feelings toward the perpetrator and allow the opportunity for a more appropriate relationship between the father and daughter to develop. When these changes take place, the path is cleared for further steps to normalize the father-daughter relationship and to reunify the family. The example below illustrates both the process of work on the feelings of father and daughter, and the father's taking responsibility. It comes from the case of Mr. D, cited in chapter 12, and involves work with his older daughter, Cindy, 16.

EXAMPLE 5: Although Mr. D initially denied sexual abuse, by the second individual therapy session, he admitted to having done it. What followed were several sessions helping him understand why he had sexually abused his daughters, Cindy and Laura. When the therapist heard from Cindy that while on a supervised visit her father had told her he loved her, she decided to institute dyadic treatment between Cindy and her father. At that time, there had already been individual work with Laura and Mrs. D, and dyadic sessions with Mr. and Mrs. D. The therapist felt the relationship between Cindy and her father was better than that between Cindy and her mother and decided to precede mother-daughter treatment with father-daughter treatment.

Before the first father-daughter session, the therapist stressed to Mr. D that his was his opportunity to make amends to Cindy. Cindy had been alienated from the family because he had sexually abused her. She had been victimized for ten years, and now she was left out in the cold. Mr. D was reminded of his wife's negative feelings about Cindy and how bad this must make her feel. Just after her removal from home and before Mr. D admitted to the sexual abuse, Cindy had overdosed on aspirin. She had told the therapist that if she died the family would be happy. These statements were called to Mr. D's attention. Mr. D said he understood what it must be like for Cindy and he wanted an opportunity to apologize to her. He said he did not know how far he could go because he did not think his wife wanted Cindy back. The therapist said it was still important that he do what he could so Cindy did not feel like such an outcast.

When Cindy and her father were first in the room together, there was a long silence. Mr. D looked down at his hands and Cindy played with the zipper on her purse. Finally, Mr. D said, "I'm sorry," and Cindy replied, "Me, too.' Mr. D went on to say that he knew things had been very bad for her and that none of it was her fault. He could not change what had already happened but wanted things to be different in the future. Cindy said she was "really glad" they could finally talk about what happened. It had been hard because even Laura had told her a couple of times she should not have told, that she had ruined the family. Mr. D told her she had not ruined the family. He had. But now he was trying to help the family and he wanted to help her if he could. Cindy told him she still loved him and he said, ''Me, too.'' Mr. D told her again that he was sorry for what he had done. He asked if she would like to come home for a visit.

This session and later ones between Cindy and her father did a great deal to make them both feel better.

C. Restructuring the Father-Daughter Relationship

Sharing of feelings and the father's taking responsibility for the sexual abuse are prerequisites for further restructuring of this relationship. Prior to the discovery of the sexual abuse, it may be characterized by a variety of aberrant patterns. Sometimes there is little contact between father and daughter other than sexual contact. Other times, the relationship is characterized by a lot of contentious interaction which has its root in the anger the child feels because of the sexual abuse. In still other situations, the father is overinvolved with the daughter and is quite intrusive in her activities. Finally, there are cases where the father overinvolves the daughter in his activities, often using her as his confidante. Moreover, whatever the relationship has been prior to discovery, professional involvement usually abruptly cuts off that relationship, adding another dimension to treatment needs.

The therapist must restructure the father-daughter relationship so that they engage in appropriate activities together. What these will consist of will vary according to the child's developmental stage. However, activities are usually initially restricted to encounters that can be monitored by the therapist, the mother, other adults, or sometimes other children. For example, the father might participate in a school conference with the daughter, take her to a school play, take her roller skating in a public place with another father who is also taking his child skating, or assist her with her homework in the presence of the mother.

An issue that arises when the father-daughter activities are being reprogrammed is the physical expression of affection. As noted earlier, the verbal expression of affection is encouraged, and ideally there should be the possibility for expression of physical affection as well. However, there are several prerequisites for this. The child should desire it, and the father should want it—and he should be able to express physical affection without becoming sexually aroused. If these conditions exist, then the therapist sets rules for the expression of physical affection. The following guidelines can be useful. First, such affection should only be expressed in the presence of a third party. Second, embraces should be brief. Third, kisses should be on the cheek, forehead, or top of the head, not on the mouth or other parts of the body. Fourth, the expression of physical affection should not take place if either father or daughter is only partially clothed or nude. The therapist usually monitors initial expressions of physical affection during treatment.

In the case example below, reprogramming of the father-daughter relationship was initiated in preparation for the father's return to the family.

EXAMPLE 6:   This family consisted of Joyce L, 4, her parents, and an infant son, Johnny. Mr. L had a very intense investment in his daughter, Joyce. When he came home from work, he held her on his lap while he watched the news on television and had a drink. Sometimes, he played with her while Mrs. L prepared supper. He also insisted that he give Joyce baths and wash her, even though her mother felt Joyce was old enough to bathe herself.

Otherwise, Mrs. L had total responsibility for Joyce, although, when Mrs. L disciplined Joyce by sending her to her room, her father would often go and get her, telling her she did not have to remain there.

When Mr. L was bathing Joyce, he would often fondle her genitals. Further, after he had dried her, he sometimes would kiss her all over her body. This pattern evolved into his disrobing her and himself and rubbing up against her body. Later, he began interfemoral intercourse with her. Joyce told her mother that her daddy had a ''nose down there'' and the nose rubbed up against her and sometimes got between her legs.

Mrs. L called protective services. The worker interviewed Joyce and concluded she was being sexually abused by her father. Mr. L was ordered to leave the home. Mrs. L filed for divorce, but then had second thoughts. She had a new baby and needed her husband's support. In addition, Joyce frequently got upset and said, ''I miss my daddy.'' Joyce had no visitation with her father. Mr. L had admitted to the sexual abuse and had independently involved himself in treatment.

When Mrs. L began to consider the possibility of reconciliation, husband-wife treatment sessions were initiated and Mr. L was allowed to visit Joyce and Johnny. The child protection worker was quite concerned by Mr. L's behavior during the visits. He hugged Joyce and told her how much he loved her and missed her. He often would cry at the end of the visit because he was not going to be able to see Joyce for two whole weeks. Joyce would then become upset. Mr. L ignored Johnny.

When the protective services worker admonished Mr. L for his behavior, he said he had not seen his daughter for three months and missed her very much. The worker decided the visits were unhealthy and made a referral for Mr. L to the therapist who was working with Mrs. L and Joyce. The therapist interviewed Mr. L and concluded that he was making good progress in his individual therapy, but on the basis of the worker's observations, thought dyadic sessions were essential. The therapist's intention was to begin by having Mr. L tell Joyce the sexual abuse and its ramifications were his fault. She rehearsed with Mr. L how he should tell Joyce that his separation from the family was necessary because of his touching her and using his "nose" on her.

As Joyce entered the session, he gave her a full body embrace and kissed her on the mouth. He then attempted to get her on his lap so they could talk. Joyce struggled to get down and play with the toys while Mr. L told her he had dreamed about her the night before, and he was sorry for what he had done.

The therapist decided to forgo working on Mr. L's responsibility for the sexual abuse and instructed Mr. L to let Joyce get down and play. The therapist asked Joyce what she wanted to do and Joyce said she wished to paint. The therapist helped her put on a smock (she was wearing a new dress) and choose which paints to use, and asked her to explain what she was painting. The therapist sat near Joyce, but did not touch her and talked to her about her painting as well as about her activities during the past week. The therapist then had Mr. L do likewise, explaining to him that four-year-olds are really very active and interested in doing things. They usually resist sitting on people's laps for long periods of time. After about a half hour, the therapist suggested it was time for Joyce to leave so the therapist could talk to Mr. L. Joyce readily put away the paints and took off her smock, as she was used to this pattern when she came to see the therapist with her mother. Mr. L started to protest that he had not seen his little girl long enough, and he had not gotten a chance to tell her how he was feeling. The therapist said that was all for today; he would see Joyce again the next week. The therapist also said that, when he kissed Joyce good-bye, it should be on the cheek and that he should just hug her around the shoulders. While Mr. L was taken aback, he followed the therapist's instructions.

With Mr. L alone, the therapist discussed in greater detail appropriate interaction with a four-year-old. The therapist defined his embraces, kisses, and holding Joyce on his lap as inappropriate. She told Mr. L something that Joyce had already told the therapist in treatment: she did not like all the hugging and kissing; it made her feel "icky" just like the "bad touching" her daddy did. Appropriate physical contact with Joyce was defined for Mr. L.

In the discussion that followed, the therapist discovered that Mr. L had little knowledge of child development and not much of an idea of what might be appropriate activities to involve himself in with Joyce. The therapist described to Mr. L some of the things that she had found Joyce enjoyed and suggested to him ways of finding out what Joyce liked, instead of sitting with her on his lap.

In addition, the therapist told Mr. L it was unfair to Joyce that he burden her with his problems. He was treating her as though she were an adult and were responsible for his loneliness and his missing her. It was not her role to make him feel better. He said he did not realize he was doing that; he just wanted her to know that he loved her.

In this case, the father-daughter relationship was a major focus of the intervention. Although the interventions described may seem artificial and difficult to maintain, they nevertheless constitute the prototypes for later interactions between father and daughter, and they can increase in number and become a part of family interaction when the family is reunited. However, the father-daughter relationship will continue to require monitoring, initially by the therapist and subsequently by the mother.

IV. THE MARITAL-DYAD TREATMENT

If marital problems were not in evidence before the revelation of the sexual abuse, they will certainly develop when the wife discovers her husband has sexually abused her children. If a wife does not report some dissatisfaction with a man who has been sexual with her children, then she is unlikely to be able to protect the children in the future. Because marital difficulty has contibuted to or is an outcome of sexual abuse, marital treatment must occur at some point during the reconciliation of a sexually abusive family. Further, because blurred generational boundries are frequently found in families where there is sexual abuse, it is important to include treatment sessions that clearly define adults and separate from children and help the couple see themselves as a unit.

Many of the marital difficulties found in families where there is sexual abuse do not differ from those found in other problematic marriages. Therefore, techniques employed in other types of marital therapy are also appropriate for sexually abusive families. Marital treatment issues will be divided into five categories: (a) sharing feelings and accepting responsibility; (b) dealing with sexual dysfunction; (c) solving problems; (d) child management; and (e) creating opportunities for more positive interaction. Unique aspects of these treatment issues in sexually abusive families will be highlighted, treatment techniques will be briefly described, and case examples will be provided.

A. Sharing Feelings and Accepting Responsibility

Just as it is important in other dyads for feelings to be shared and for the offender to accept responsibility for the sexual abuse, so it is in the marital dyad. The wife is likely to feel a lot of anger toward her husband, a sense of betrayal not only of the victim but also of herself. She is likely to want to ask the perpetrator why he did this. She may also feel some guilt for not knowing, for not responding appropriately to what she did know, or for what she perceives as her role in causing the sexual abuse. The therapist should moderate any attempts she makes to accept blame for the sexual abuse as, at this point in treatment, it is important that the perpetrator accept responsibility for the sexual abuse.

The perpetrator, one hopes, will express feelings of remorse and guilt and will be concerned about the damage to both the child and his wife. The therapist may have to take the initiative in eliciting these responses from him. The perpetrator may also be angry at his wife for what he perceives as her lack of support or rejection that led him to sexually abuse the child, or he may even blame his victim. While such emotions must be shared and dealt with, again the therapist should see to it that the perpetrator does not shift blame to his wife or the victim, but rather accepts responsibility for his behavior. These are the common emotional reactions couples have; however, there are as many individual emotional reactions to being in a family where there is sexual abuse as there are individuals involved. The individual work that prepared the father to respond appropriately to the victim can also prepare him to respond appropriately to his wife's feelings and to take responsibility in sessions with her.

B. Dealing With Sexual Dysfunction

An issue in marital-dyad treatment in some sexually abusive families is sexual dysfunction. Two types can be differentiated in sexually abusive families: an aversion to sex, often by both husband and wife, that results from the discovery of the sexual abuse; and sexual problems that preceded the sexual abuse and may have contributed to it. In addition, discovery of the sexual abuse will usually exacerbate existing sexual problems in the marriage.

Aversion to sex when the sexual abuse becomes known is a fairly appropriate reaction for both the mother and the perpetrator, and should be allowed to run its course. Because of this need and because sexual problems cannot be addressed before other marital conflicts are resolved, treatment for sexual problems should come at a later stage of the treatment. For example, the sharing of feelings, the perpetrator's taking responsibility, and the resolving of parental conflicts ought to precede treatment of sexual dysfunction.

In addressing sexual issues, a good starting point is the work on sexuality already undertaken in individual sessions. Information and insights gained there should be shared in marital-dyad treatment. This may include a history of past sexual abuse, kept secret from the other partner, other sexual experiences or attitudes, and the role each partner's sexuality might have played in the sexual abuse. This sharing is likely to lead to a better understanding of the sexual problems that exist in the marriage. The precise nature of the sexual problems can vary a great deal. Sometimes, they can be resolved as other aspects of the relationship improve; at other times they are addressed by each party's better understanding the other's sexual background, and by improved communication regarding sexual needs and preferences; but there will also be cases when the couple needs to be referred to sex therapy for more extended work. The example below will be used both to illustrate the sharing of feelings and dealing with sexual difficulties.

> EXAMPLE 7: Mrs. T began avoiding sexual contact with her husband when she felt that he was not pulling his weight in the family. She worked full time while he worked only intermittently. She also feared another pregnancy. They already had three children from her first marriage—-Juanita, 10, Roy, 8, and Anita, 6—and one from his, Jason, 5. Mr. T also was ''not a good Christian'' in her eyes, and drank. She often became exasperated with him. He was sometimes contrite and other times resentful of her treatment.
>
> As Mrs. T withdrew from her husband, he cultivated a relationship with Juanita, who became his confidante and eventually his sex partner. After Mr. T had been having Juanita fellate him for about a year, she told her mother. Her mother was furious, declaring this was the last straw and threw Mr. T out. She called the police, who referred her to a sexual abuse treatment program. Individual treatment was begun with Mr. T; Mrs. T and Juanita received group therapy.
>
> After being in treatment two months, Mrs. T declared she wanted to give the marriage one last try, and Mr. T was grateful for having another chance. During their first marital session, Mrs. T gave full vent to her anger, telling her husband that he had done the worst possible thing to her, ''fucking my daughter.'' He was lucky he had left the home because she would have murdered him in his bed if he had stayed. Mr. T was very apologetic and remorseful. However, with the therapist's encouragement he was also able to share his frustration about the marriage. He felt he could never please his wife and his needs were not being met. He was always the bad guy and she the good guy. He told his wife how rejected he felt when she withheld sex from him. He knew that this did not justify his sexually abusing Juanita, but he thought it was part of the reason he had.
>
> Mrs. T admitted that she withheld sex from him, but said that at this point she could not imagine ever wanting sex again. He said he wasn't too

eager right now, either. The next several marital sessions focused on what could be done to make Mr. T have a more gratifying role in the marriage and on attempts to revive the positive aspects of their relationship. The situation was helped by the fact that Mr. T got a steady job transporting nursing home patients to and from medical and other appointments. He enjoyed this very much. He also began attending church regularly with his family.

The therapist then raised the question of the T's sexual relationship, which had already been addressed with each in individual treatment. Mrs. T said she understood how her sexual withdrawal had played a role in the sexual abuse. She also said she was feeling better about their having a sexual relationship in the future. Mr. T said he was glad of this. He admitted that he also played a part in their sexual problems because he had not made his needs known.

Mr. T was allowed to accompany Mrs. T and the children on a church retreat. This occasioned a successful sexual encounter for them and was the beginning of an improved sexual relationship. Eventually, Mr. T returned to the home.

This case illustrates both an aversion to sex resulting from revelation of the sexual abuse and deterioration in the sexual relationship. First, the couple is encouraged to voice their feelings and, as changes occur in the relationship, there is motivation by both adults to try to revive their sex life.

C. Solving Problems

If the marital relationship is to improve, disputes between the couple must be addressed. The therapist's goal is not to resolve all problems, but rather to set up mechanisms for problem-solving and to deal with problems of overriding concern at the time of marital-dyad treatment. In some families, difficulties in this area are alleviated to some extent as communication is improved through the sharing of feelings. In other cases, these disputes can be resolved by a fairly straightforward problem-solving approach. That is, problems between the couple are identified, possible solutions are generated, a solution is chosen, and it is then implemented under the guidance of the therapist.

However, often marital problems in a sexually abusive family are much more complex. It is not possible to explore all possible complexities, but one dimension of the marital relationship where problems frequently occur is the power relationship. In fact, many authors (e.g., Groth & Birnbaum 1979; Sgroi 1982; Burgess et. al 1978; and Rush 1980) regard sexual abuse as more an abuse of power than a sexual act.

The power dimension is often reflected in how decisions are made (or not made) between partners. Two patterns of power distribution have been noted by the author and other researchers (Stern and Meyer 1980) in families where there is sexual abuse. In some sexually abusive families, the perpetrator dominates the mother and controls the decisions, while in others the mother has more control and the perpetrator is a rather immature individual who, for a variety of reasons, may be dominated by his wife. The T case, just described, illustrates a mother-dominated decision structure. The reader will recall the C case described in chapter 4 as an extreme and untreatable example of domination by a perpetrator. Mr. C felt it was his right to kill his son as well as utterly control and physically and sexually abuse other family members. Perpetrator domination appears to be a more common pattern.

In perpetrator-dominated families, indivdual work with husband and wife that addresses the issue of independence should alter the power balance somewhat. As the wife feels less dependent upon the perpetrator, her power increases. The more willing she is to leave him if necessary, the less control he has over her. Further, the more the perpetrator is able to get his needs satisfied outside the family, the less compelled he feels to control family members and family functioning for his own gratification.

In the wife-dominated family, often individual work that focuses upon the issue of self-esteem, particularly the perpetrator's self-esteem, will enable him to take a more active role in family decisions.

However, in both wife-dominated and husband-dominated marriages, additional work must be done to establish more satisfying decision-making structures and to resolve specific disputes. A range of techniques can be employed by the therapist. However, only two will be briefly cited, as there is a whole literature of relevant marital therapy techniques (e.g. Thomas 1977; Stuart 1980; Steil 1983; Silverman 1972; Wolman and Strickner 1983; Paolino and McGrady 1978). The therapist may assist in establishing new processes for resolution of problems by mediating a particular conflict. As it is resolved, the therapist recapitulates the process, explicitly stating what rules were used to resolve the conflict and how they might be applied to future conflicts. Often, the couple is then asked to apply the rules to another conflict and report back to the therapist on the process and their progress.

In other families, it is useful to look at specific areas of family functioning and assist the couple in designating which should be primarily controlled by the husband, which should be primarily controlled by the wife, which require joint decision-making, and which areas children should have a say about. Families vary a great deal as to what proportion of decisions are made jointly, and what proportion with one adult having control, as well as in the extent to which children have a say. Typically, individuals in the family also vary in the extent to which they care about different aspects of family functioning, and this investment partially determines the amount of control they have over various areas.

In some sexually abusive families, the process of changing the power structure includes wresting some power from the victim who is a parental child in the family. While changes in the amount of control the victim has generally are initiated in couple sessions, such decisions need to be shared with the child in family sessions.

D. Child Management

Child-management issues are really a subcategory of marital problems. However, they will receive separate treatment because of their particular salience in sexually abusive families. The following are common patterns of parenting dysfunction. There may be disputes about how to handle the children, or alternatively parents may fail to control them. A lack of childrearing skills and ignorance about child development may be found. In some sexually abusive families, the child becomes one of the foci for parental disharmony. One parent is strict, while the other is lenient, and the child learns to manipulate the situation. The father may openly interdict the mother's attempts at discipline as in the L case cited earlier in this chapter. Where there are several children in the family, parents may have favorites, for example the mother preferring the boys and the father the girls. Another fairly common pattern is to find a father who is very rigid and a strict and sometimes abusive disciplinarian and a mother who is more humane and tries to soften the father's blows both literally and figuratively. In cases where there is an absence of parental control, often the victim fills the vacuum and becomes a parental child, as noted earlier.

A wide range of approaches to improving parenting skills have been developed (e.g. Graziano 1971; Patterson and Brodsky 1966; Gordon 1972). They vary in theoretical orientation. For example, some are behavioral, while others rely primarily on improved communication, and still others take a problem-solving approach. The way these approaches are imparted also varies: parenting classes, small-group experiential sessions, and child-management treatment provided by a therapist. The therapist should be guided in the choice of techniques by the nature of the child-management difficulties, the level of family functioning, and what approach appears compatible with family style. Because the types of child management problems in sexually abusive families do not differ markedly from those in other families, and because most therapists know techniques for addressing child management problems, specific technologies will not be described. The case example that follows illustrates therapeutic work to assist the couple in dispute resolution and disagreements about child management.

> EXAMPLE 8:   The E family consists of Mrs. E and Mr. E, Mrs. E's 14-year-old daughter Teresa by her first marriage, and two-year-old Joy, the E's daughter. From the time Teresa was 3 until she was 10, Mrs. E was a single parent. She was very lenient with Teresa and seemed indifferent when the school reported Teresa was absent too much. In third grade, Teresa missed 80 days of school.
>
> Mrs. E met Mr. E through a friend. He began to take her out and she felt her whole life was changing for the better. Mr. E took her to nice restaurants, he brought her flowers, and he bought clothes for Mrs. E and Teresa.
>
> After six months of courtship, the E's were married. Mrs. E described the early months of the marriage as wonderful. She no longer had to work. Prior to the marriage, she had worked cleaning house. She moved into a nice house that belonged to her husband. All she had to do was keep the house clean and have the meals on the table. If she wanted something, all she had to do was ask her husband and he would usually get it.
>
> She had only two complaints. First, Mr. E was very hard on Teresa. He thought she was a spoiled brat. Second, her husband often came home unexpectedly during the day and questioned her about her activities.
>
> Mrs. E felt that, after Joy was born, the marriage became very stifling. She was expected to take care of Joy all the time. She never went out without her and was not allowed to have babysitters. Mr. E could not understand why she had difficulty keeping a clean house, cooking, and caring for the baby. (She had been 34 when Joy was born and was quite exhausted after the birth.) Mr. E would ask her to account for herself at the end of the day. He bought her a car after Joy was born because she said it was hard to walk and use the bus with a baby. However, he filled the gas tank only every two weeks. He also would feel the car hood when he came home to see if it was warm, an indicator she had been out, and then would question her about where she had been.
>
> Mr. E also became increasingly punitive with Teresa. He beat her when her grades were not good and insisted she go to school when she said she did not feel well. She would call home after her stepfather had left for work, saying she was sick. Her mother would allow her to come home. These absences from school were concealed from Mr. E. However, on one occasion, he came home unexpectedly during the day and found Teresa there, supposedly ill, but babysitting for Joy while Mrs. E was out.

He was furious and went looking for his wife. He encountered her a block away from home returning in her car. When they got home, he accused her of cheating on him as well as conniving with Teresa to be truant from school and using her as a babysitter against his wishes. He would not allow Mrs. E to use the car for a whole month and grounded Teresa for a month. He went to school and found out what subjects Teresa was behind in. He made a schedule of work for her to do every day after school and checked it when he came home from work. Teresa's school performance and attendance improved markedly. However, she began to verbalize her hatred for her stepfather.

Shortly after these events, Teresa told her school principal about two instances of sexual abuse by her stepfather and protective services became involved. Teresa was initially removed from the house because her mother did not believe the sexual abuse had happened. However, before the case went to trial in juvenile court, Mr. E admitted to the sexual abuse and asked for help. Individual treatment for all three family members ensued and Teresa was placed in a group. At the recommendation of the therapist, Mrs. E was encouraged, over the objections of Mr. E, to initiate action against her first husband for child support. This was successful and Mrs. E received $8000 in back support as well as a monthly payment of $200.00.

Marital treatment was soon initiated, in part to deal with the disputes between Mr. and Mrs. E and problems over how to manage Teresa. In the marital treatment, the problems defined by Mrs. E were that she needed a babysitter sometimes, that she needed some help around the house, that her husband was too hard on Teresa, and that he was always checking up on her.

Mr. E said he thought the problems were that his wife had gone to the dogs. She was lazy, whereas she had a lot of energy when they first got married; she did not seem to like being a mother anymore. He saw himself as the only one in the family who was trying. He worked ten hours a day and did not complain, he bought the family everything it needed, and he tried to help his wife and stepdaughter so they could improve. All he got was grief.

The therapist helped the couple see the situation somewhat differently. Mr. E was trying to make all the decisions and control everything that went on in the family. When his wife disagreed with him she resorted to subterfuge, letting Teresa come home from school and allowing her to babysit for Joy. When Mr. E discovered these things, he became even more controlling, taking away what little freedom his wife had and grounding Teresa. Mr. E was able to see that, in fact, he was making all the decisions, but he felt that he was right and his wife was wrong. As proof of that, he pointed to Teresa. Mrs. E readily agreed that she had made mistakes with Teresa and that now she was going to school and doing better. But Mrs. E said Teresa was miserable and so was she. The therapist pointed out that having a baby at Mrs. E's age could sometimes be very tiring and that mothers need some time away from their children. The therapist also said that, while Mr. E might be right about Teresa, he was probably wrong in his decisions about his wife. The more he restricted her, the worse she performed in her household and childcare duties and the more depressed and overwhelmed she became.

The therapist asked Mr. E to try to think how he would feel if he had to account for his daily whereabouts, as his wife did, and had no say in family decisions and no money of his own.

Mr. E replied, "Well, now she does have money. Let her spend her money on a babysitter and a cleaning woman." Mrs. E said that was fine. That was just what she wanted to do.

Although Mr. E was not pleased, his wife made arrangements for a neighbor to come in three mornings each week and care for Joy and do some of the housework. Mrs. E used that time to go shopping and attend a class at the Y. She used her own money for gas for the car. Within a month, Mrs. E reported feeling much better. In the meantime, the therapist had suggested Mr. and Mrs. E each ask the other how their day had gone at the end of the day rather than having Mr. E check on his wife's whereabouts while she tried to conceal activities she thought he would not approve of. Mrs. E felt more positively about these changes than Mr. E, but he said the fact his wife was happier made his life easier.

Teresa remained in foster care. At the end of three months, the therapist felt it was time to plan for her return. The therapist suggested to the E's that, together, they needed to decide how they were going to handle Teresa when she returned home. Further, they should try to make this a joint decision process that might serve as a model for future decision-making.

Mrs. E wanted to pay Teresa $5 for each A out of her support payments. Mr. E felt that was not good enough. Teresa might not be able to think that far ahead and might skip school. Mr. E suggested they give Teresa money for going to school, doing her homework and obtaining good grades. Heretofore, Teresa had received no set allowance. She would ask her stepfather when she wanted money, and he would give it to her if he was in a good mood. Mr. E said he did not want Teresa's support payments used to pay for her school performance. He would pay and her support could be saved for her future.

The therapist suggested that the specifics of the plan be negotiated with Teresa present so that she had a part in its development and would feel that it was fair.

Family therapy was initiated and, soon, Teresa returned home. Mr. and Mrs.. E did not immediately have any other disputes to resolve using joint decision-making, but later on were able to make use of these new skills.

The case just described is one where the perpetrator dominated all family decisions, although he saw the arrangement as a reciprocal one.

The idea that his wife would want family life to be different was initially quite foreign to him. Yet he had sufficient sensitivity and investment in the family to understand his wife's viewpoint and to try to change.

E. Creating Opportunities for More Positive Interaction

As in the other dyadic relationships discussed, the therapist should try to provide opportunities for the marital couple to have positive experiences together. Often, in enmeshed sexually abusive families, the couple never does anything separate from the children. All activities are family activities. The couple is not an entity with needs and preferences separate from the family as a whole. Alternatively, in disorganized, chaotic, and strife-ridden sexually abusive families, positive interactions between husband and wife are rare and participation in activities which they both enjoy is nonexistent.

Interventions to facilitate these positive encounters need to take place after other issues have been addressed or else they will be counter productive. For example, feelings about sexual abuse must be partially resolved and some of the couple's problems addressed so that there is a reservoir of good faith between them. Encounters that are intended to be positive can quickly be sabotaged or become painful if things are still going badly between the couple. Activities need to be chosen carefully so that they are potentially mutually satisfying. Mr. J, a 61-year-old client who suffered from impotence as a result of alcoholism and the discovery of his sexually abusive behavior, determined to implement this kind of intervention after it was described by the therapist. On the way home from the therapy session, he persuaded his wife to stop at a motel with pornographic movies. He became quite excited and was able to perform sexually but she reported afterward feeling dirty and embarrassed. This was not a mutually-satisfying encounter.

Often, it is useful for couples to set aside a regular time, perhaps on a weekly basis, which is theirs alone. While sometimes involving themselves in activities with other couples is an appropriate use of this time, some opportunity for them to be alone together is important. An appropriate example of the use of this technique can be found below in the R case.

EXAMPLE 9:   The R's have six children and have been married fourteen years. The first baby came within a year of their marriage and they never had time to experience life as a couple. They had never taken a vacation without children. Mr. R worked a ten-hour day and Mrs. R worked as a substitute teacher and cared for the children. The couple's leisure time was taken up with church activities and taking the children to all their extracurricular activities.

Mr. R sexually abused their four-year-old daughter, Jennifer, at a time when he was very depressed and disillusioned about his life and he and his wife were fighting.

There was a lot of ventilation of feelings of anger, frustration, and remorse by both partners. During the course of couple treatment, they both professed their love for each other but also acknowledged their relationship had been strained for a long time because they had so many parental responsibilities.

After some problem-solving that gave Mr. R more responsibility for the children and Mrs. R less, they arranged a series of events for themselves without the children. They went out to dinner twice, leaving their 13-year-old to babysit. These encounters went reasonably well, although they both said they were awaiting an emergency call at the restaurant. Next, they both arranged to take their ten-year-old son to camp and spend the night at a resort on the way back. A church member babysat for the children while they were away. This was quite an enjoyable occasion, and they reported they did not worry about the children. Then, a four-day weekend was planned during a visit from the maternal grandparents.

The couple reported they were getting to know each other better and to feel like human beings, not just parents.

The family just described appears to be an enmeshed one, where the adults had no identity other than that of parents. Despite the sexual abuse and other problems the couple had been having, there was enough of a positive relationship that significant improvement was made by instituting positive activities for the couple.

V. CONCLUSION

In this chapter, issues in treatment of three dyadic relationships, the mother-daughter dyad, the father-daughter dyad, and the husband-wife dyad are discussed. A number of treatment issues are parallel in all three dyads. Feelings need to be shared and to some extent resolved. Similarly, all of the relationships need to be restructured so that they are experienced as more positive and are more appropriate. The dyadic work is essential and paves the way for further restructuring in family therapy.

CHAPTER FOURTEEN

Family Treatment
and the Use of Groups

I. INTRODUCTION

This chapter will cover the role of family therapy in treatment of intrafamilial sexual abuse and consider three treatment issues best addressed in family sessions: family communication problems, family knowledge and rules about sex, and family coalitions. A discussion of different types of group treatment will follow. Family groups, children's groups, mother's groups, and perpetrator groups will be included. Since more has been written about family and group interventions with sexually abusive families than about other types of treatment, there will be less elaboration of techniques, and modalities that are not reported in other literature will be emphasized.

II. FAMILY TREATMENT

As a rule, family therapy is the final phase of treatment in cases of intrafamilial sexual abuse. Some work in family sessions involves only the victim(s) and parents while other intervention must include the whole family. Family therapy offers both an opportunity to culminate work which was begun in individual and dyadic sessions and an occasion to address additional issues more appropriately dealt with in family sessions.

Examples of treatment issues whose final stages might be addressed in family therapy include the following: feelings about the sexual abuse; shifting of responsibility for the sexual abuse to the perpetrator; final resolution of disputes already taken up in dyadic sessions; and child management. These issues may be redefined in family sessions to address broader problems in family functioning. The three family treatment issues to be discussed in this section — communication patterns, rules and knowledge about sex, and family coalitions and subsystems — are new ones, yet they involve redefinition of issues already discussed.

A. Changing Communication Patterns by an Open Discussion of the Sexual Abuse

Family sessions are an important vehicle for changing pathological communication patterns that often characterize sexually abusive families, particularly the absence of information sharing and, as noted earlier, secretiveness. These patterns usually have their origins in the perpetrator's behavior around the sexual abuse. He admonishes the victim not to tell about the abuse. He offers bribes and other inducements for silence which themselves must be kept secret. The pattern of dissembling is also reflected in his relationship with his partner as well as in the victim's relationships with siblings and her mother. It is not uncommon to discover multiple victims who know nothing of one another's plight and to find that the sexual abuse has been successfully kept from the mother over a period of years.

In family therapy, the therapist must expose family secrets and open up communication among family members. Thus the sexual abuse must be thoroughly discussed in family sessions. In an effort to use this as an opportunity for the development of new communication patterns, the therapist can ask the involved parties, father, mother, and victim(s) to speak about what has happened. It is important for the therapist to resist both the wishes of the parents not to tell the nonvictimized children as well as anyone's attempt to minimize the sexual abuse. However, descriptions of the sexual abuse should take into account the varying developmental levels of family members so that it can be comprehended by all the children.

In the discussions of the sexual abuse, all parties, should be asked to express their feelings about what they are hearing and what has taken place. This is also a good time to establish for the family who is responsible for the sexual abuse by having the perpetrator accept blame and in some cases the mother accept some responsibility.

From this discussion logically follows an explication of what will happen if the perpetrator should ever attempt sexual abuse again. This includes describing how the victim(s) and mother should react immediately (e.g., how to resist, who to tell) as well as the outcomes for family integrity (e.g., the father must leave, the children go into care). The case example that follows illusrates family secrecy and covers an initial family session focused upon sharing information about sexual abuse.

> EXAMPLE 1: The T family is a reconstituted family with recurrent sexual abuse, in part because the therapists made no efforts to facilitate open communication about the sexual abuse.
>
> Johnny T and Tommy T were left with their mother when their parents were separated. When the boys were 3½ and 2½ they were removed from their mother's care for neglect and placed with their father. Mr. T noted the boys were fondling each other's genitals frequently and told them to stop because God wouldn't love them.
>
> He hired a babysitter, Diane, to look after the boys while he worked. Eventually Mr. T and Diane became lovers and then married. Diane had two daughters from a previous marriage, Angela, 6, and Maria, 3. Her first husband had assaulted her brutally. She finally left him after she passed out when he choked her.
>
> Diane was quite concerned about the T boys' sexual interaction and confronted Johnny. Johnny said it was okay to do this, that their mama did it to them, and they did it to her when they all slept together. Johnny was whisked off to the police station to tell his story. The police were persuaded by his statements and arrested his mother. She confessed to the sexual abuse and was incarcerated for one year. Neither the sexual abuse nor the incarceration was mentioned in the family. No one talked to Tommy, and the boys received no treatment at the time.
>
> When Angela was 10, she reported that her stepfather, Mr. T had fondled her genitals while he was left to care for the children. He also had asked her to suck his penis. There were at least two occasions of this sexual abuse. Angela told her mother who confronted Mr. T. He confessed, crying, and begged God for forgiveness. He went to therapy and at the therapist's recommendaiton left the home. The boys and Maria were told that their father was out of the home because the parents were not getting along. Angela was placed in a treatment group for latency-aged victims but her therapy was never discussed at home. Her mother also went to individual therapy. Angela stopped treatment when she and Maria went to spend the summer with their biological father in Texas.
>
> When they came home at the end of the summer, the whole family was reunited because Mr. T was allowed to move back home. However, he was never left alone with the girls.
>
> In the meantime Tommy and Johnny, now 5 and 6, again began to act out sexually. They were caught sucking each others' penises. Soon thereafter they were found engaging in sexual activities with Maria. Mrs. T then insisted that Johnny leave the home. She said he was the instigator. He was placed in a therapeutic foster home, and treatment was begun with him. However, soon Tommy began engaging in additional sexually provocative behaviors. He would fail to zip up his fly and he would let his

penis hang out. He and Maria were caught by Angela fondling each other's genitals. However, Angela did not tell.

One weekend when Johnny was allowed home, he, Tommy, and Maria were all caught naked in the bed, involved in sexual play. Mrs. T then demanded that Tommy be removed too. She said she could not handle him, and she was also afraid she would injure him if he remained in her care. Tommy was removed and also placed in a therapeutic foster home, but separate from Johnny.

At this point the whole family was also referred for assessment and treatment. Because all family members except Maria had already been involved in some treatment and because of the secrecy surrounding the sexual abuse, the therapist began with some family sessions that required sharing information and feelings about the various forms of sexual abuse. Mr. T was resistant to this but Mrs. T favored it, and the process of information sharing was initiated.

The therapist began by saying that a lot of people in this family had problems that caused them to do sexual things with other family members, and that it was time to talk about it. The therapist first asked Mr. T to tell what had happened between himself and Angela. After a long pause, he said he had touched her while they were watching TV under a blanket, that this was a big mistake, and it would not happen again. He was sorry for what he had done. The therapist then asked him to be a little clearer: where did he touch her? what part of his body did he use? and did he touch her outside or inside her clothing? He said he had put his hand inside her pants and touched her vulva. When asked how long this had gone on, he said about a minute. Angela said no it was longer than that, that it went from one commercial to the next. She also said she had asked him not to do it, and he didn't stop. Angela told the family she then told him she was going to tell her mama, and he begged her not to tell. The therapist then asked Mr. T if what Angela said was correct, and he nodded.

The therapist asked Mr. T if this was the only time or if there were other times. He said "I don't remember; I think it was the only time." As he said this Angela was shaking her head. The therapist asked Angela what she meant when she shook her head, and she said that was the last time, not the only time, that her stepdad had done it other times. The therapist asked Mr. T if he had done anything else and he shook his head. The therapist turned to Angela and asked her. She said he had tried to make her suck his penis but she wouldn't. The therapist turned to Mr. T and asked if this was correct, and he said "I guess so."

The therapist asked Tommy and Johnny what they thought about this. Johnny said, "Why did you do it, dad?" Tommy wanted to know if that was why his dad was out of the home for a year. When Mr. T responded yes, Tommy said "Then you're just like us. Does that mean we get to go back home pretty soon?" Johnny said, "I thought you and mom were just fighting." The therapist then asked Maria what she was thinking, and she said "You shouldn't of did that, dad. That's naughty." Mr. T looked sheepish.

The therapist then asked Johnny and Tommy if they could remember living with their other mom. They both said yes. The therapist asked what it was like when they were there, and Johnny said, "Well it was OK, but she used to leave us alone a lot." The therapist asked where they slept and Johnny said "In her bed." The therapist asked if they remembered any sexual things happening to them when they were with their mom, and Johnny said, "We used to suck pee pees." As to whose pee pees got sucked, Johnny said his and Tommy's. They also had to lick their mom's pee pee. The therapist asked Tommy if he could remember this, and he replied, "No, I was too little, but Johnny told me about it. Sometimes we suck each other's." Mrs. T gasped.

The therapist asked Angela if she knew about these things that happened with Tommy and Johnny's mom, and she shook her head. Angela was asked what she thought about this, and she wanted to know if their mom had to move out. The therapist said Tommy and Johnny had moved out and came to stay with their dad, but their mom was punished. Johnny asked how she was punished and was told his mom went to jail for a year. He said, "She got what she deserved. She didn't give us no food neither." Tommy said, "She was bad."

The therapist asked Maria what she thought about what happened to Tommy and Johnny, and she said it was bad for them but they did the same naughty things to her. The therapist said to Maria it must have been very upsetting. Maybe they learned to do those things from their mom. Maria said, "Maybe yes."

Angela wanted to know if Mr. T learned them from Tommy and Johnny's mother since she used to be married to him. The therapist asked Mr. T "what about that?" He said, "No, she didn't do those kinds of things when we were married." However, he then went on to talk about being physically assaulted by his father, being sexually victimized by his older sister and brother, and being made to watch his father have sex with his sister. The therapist said sometimes we learn to do something that is wrong, like having sex with kids. Kids are too young to have sex either with grownups or with each other.

The therapist said it was very important that everybody in the family know what had happened to other people in the family and talk about how it all made them feel. After a little more discussion of their feelings, the session was ended.

This particular session was given over to communication about the sexual abuse and the children's feelings about it. Parents were not at this point encouraged to talk about their feelings because the father had a tendency to try to make people feel sorry for him, and the mother was highly emotional. Mr. T was asked to talk about what he did first in order for him to take responsibility. Although he accepted some responsibility, he was not forthcoming in admitting what he had done. After this session, Angela revealed that her biological father had sexually abused her when she and Maria had spent the summer with him. Ther therapist felt the family session enabled Angela to talk about the abuse by her father.

Sharing information and feelings about the sexual abuse becomes a prototype for open communication about other issues. The therapist may give the family an assignment to discuss another family problem, for example concerns about the mother's physical illness or father's alcohol abuse, using newly developed communication skills. The family might begin this work between sessions, report back to the therapist, and complete work at the next family session. Alternatively, the therapist might instruct the family to institute regular communication sessions at home.

B. Family Knowledge and Rules About Sex

Another important area for work in some families has to do with sexuality and practices that may increase the risk of sexual stimulation and sexual abuse. First, sexuality frequently is not discussed in sexually abusive families. Therefore, it becomes a taboo subject which may hold much fascination. Further, lack of information means children have no way of differentiating sex from other interactions and do not recognize inappropriate sexual activity. As a consequence, they are vulnerable to sexual abuse. Victims who are seen in individual or group treatment usually will have received some sex education, but information needs to be imparted in the family context so that there is a common body of knowledge about appropriate and inappropriate behavior. An excellent strategy is to employ the victim(s) in the education process, allowing them the opportunity to share with the family group what the private areas of the body are and what is wrong about sex between an adult and a child.

Second, during treatment the therapist may uncover family practices that exacerbate the risk for sexual stimulation and abuse. These not only increase the likelihood of sexual abuse by the perpetrator but may also enhance the vulnerability of victims to damaging sexual play among themselves. Examples of such practices are many. The therapist may find inappropriate sleeping patterns, such as adults and children regularly sleeping together, older children of the opposite sex sleeping in the same bed or room, or children over 2 sleeping in the same room or bed with their parents so they have opportunities for observing their parents' sexual activity. There may be other such opportunities; for example a mother or father may have a number of sexual partners and allow the children to observe sex, parents may have sex with the door open, or parents may have intercourse during the day, leaving the children unsupervised. There may also be bathing practices which can be sexually stimulating, children taking baths or showers with adults, games in the bath which include a lot of body or genital contact, or parents' excessive involvement in washing or drying children's genitals. Sometimes toileting practices are worrisome, such as lack of privacy because there are no bathroom doors or door locks, or because children are in the bathroom during parental toileting. Finally, there may be inappropriate nudity or excessive bodily contact between parents and children.

The practices just noted are not necessarily pathological, although many might be regarded as inappropriate. However, in families where there is an adult who has a problem with sexual attraction to children and children who have been sexually stimulated prematurely, such activities provide ongoing opportunities for sexual misuse and serve as constant reminders of past sexual abuse.

The therapist's role is to identify these practices as inappropriate and help the family set new rules. It is important that everyone, including the children, understand the rationale for the new rules as well as what the rules are. It is also essential that the new rules be feasible — that is, that they do not so inordinately inconvenience the family that they become a source of resentment or are not followed.

C. Family Coalitions and Subsystems

Another issue that needs to be addressed in family treatment is total family structure. Often there are coalitions that play a role in or are a result of the sexual abuse, or increase the likelihood of future sexual abuse. Some of these patterns are described in chapter 12, specifically the estrangement between mother and victim(s) and husband and wife, the pathological relationship between perpetrator and victim, and the parental position of the victim. In addition, there are often rivalries among children, sometimes between victim and nonvictim but at other times between victims who have divergent reactions to the sexual abuse. There may also be other coalitions between parents and children.

Quite a lot of work on family structure is done in dyadic and in individual sessions, insofar as enhancing dyadic relationships and making family members more independent has an impact on family structure. However, changes in dyadic relationships and individual functioning must be solidified in family sessions in part by proclamations to the family of the changes which have occurred. These statements about changed relationships should be made the family members involved.

In addition, the therapist plays a key role by pointing out examples of change which are demonstrated within and outside family sessions. For example, removing victims from parental child role relationships and disbanding divisive coalitions that exist between parents and children can be furthered by the acknowledgement that these relationships have existed in the family and that they are not good for the individuals involved or the family. This change process can also be supported by the parents as a dyad communicating to the children agreements developed during marital sessions on child management and their intention to apply the rules equally to all children.

Animosities among children often are not addressed until family sessions are initiated. Such feelings will be partially dealt with by the sharing of feelings about the sexual abuse, described earlier. That is, open communication about what it is like to be in the victim role and what it is like to be in the nonvictim role in a sexually abusive family assists in reducing hostility between children. Furthermore techniques employed in resolving mother-victim conflict and marital conflict can be employed to alter the relationships in the family as a whole. Thus the therapist may assist in problem-solving around specific disputes, such as who wears whose clothing, who has responsibility for keeping the room clean, and so forth. Similarly programming mutually enjoyable activities for sibling groups or the family as a whole can be a useful therapeutic technique.

The example below illustrates work on typical coalitions in sexually abusive families and therapeutic attempts to legitimate changes being made using other treatment modalities.

EXAMPLE 2:   In the J. family, there were two victims, Sarah, 10, and Kim, 4. The Js also had a son, George, 8, who during the assessment of the family declared he had no knowledge of the sexual abuse. Mr. J was the father of Kim, and stepfather of George and Sarah. Mrs. J was very dependent upon him and frequently became overwhelmed by parental and household responsibilities and turned these over to Sarah. Sarah was bossy with her younger sister and brother, instructing them in how to clean up the house. Kim and George didn't like Sarah. On an occasion when George was kept after school for getting in a fight, Sarah showed up to discuss the problem with the principal and take George home. Sarah and her stepfather were abnormally close. Mrs. J was isolated from the rest of the family.

Part of treatment involved getting a homemaker to help Mrs. J improve her household management and parenting. This help was much needed by Mrs. J because at the time Mr. J was out of the home, and she was very overwhelmed. Aside from helping Mrs. J organize her cooking

and cleaning, the homemaker helped her set rules for the children and enforce them. It took several weeks for Mrs. J to be able to enforce the rules
without the homemaker being there.

In marital treatment, Mrs. J was encouraged to take an active role
in describing the rules she had set for the children and enlisting Mr. J's
support for enforcing the rules when he would return home.

Family sessions were held in preparation for Mr. J's reintegration
into the family and to work on family coalitions. The therapist began by
stating that things were going to be different when Mr. J returned because
the family was involved in changes that were going to make the family a
safe place for kids.

She then asked Mrs. J to describe how things had been in the past.
Mrs. J said she had let too many things go and had put too much responsibility on Sarah. She said that with the help of the homemaker and the
therapist she was learning how to be a better mother.

The therapist then asked Mr. J if he knew about the changes his
wife was trying to make. He said they had talked about these changes in a
couple of sessions, and he thought the new rules were good ones. He said
now all members of the family had their own bedtimes and had their own
chores. Mrs. J put a check by each child's name on a chart if they followed rules. Mr. J said he and his wife would be a team, but there would
be a lot of things he would not be able to do because he couldn't be alone
with the children. He hoped the homemaker could continue to come, at
least for a while.

The therapist asked Sarah how she liked the new rules. She said
sometimes she felt like she was being treated like a little kid, but she had
more time to be with her friends. The therapist said she was still a kid, and
that she had been like a grownup before, which meant she didn't have
time for her friends. Kim said it was easier having Mom or the homemaker
boss her than Sarah because Sarah got mad. The therapist pointed out
that it was really hard for Sarah to be the boss like a grownup.

In this case, the homemaker becomes a surrogate parent and
forms an alliance with the mother. Together they remove Sarah from a
parental child position and make her one of the children. The therapist
readies the mother to assume the role the homemaker has played. While
Sarah is resistant to her loss of power, she also sees advantages to her
new role. Sarah is becoming more attractive to Kim, thus moving them
closer to one another.

III. GROUP TREATMENT

In many respects group therapy is the intervention of choice in sexual
abuse, and a variety of types of groups are being employed by practi-

tioners providing service to sexually abusive families. Professionals have been heavily influenced by the pioneering work of Henry Giarretto, who heads the Child Sexual Abuse Treatment Project (CSATP) in Santa Clara County, California. The project provides training and technical assistance to those wishing to start CSATP programs. This model of intervention makes extensive use of support groups for offenders, mothers, and couples (Parents United), for victims (Daughters and Sons United), and survivors (Adults Molested as Children). See Giarretto (1982a) for a thorough discussion of this model.

This chapter will discuss family, marital, children's, mothers' and offenders' groups. Particular attention will be paid to composition of the groups and treatment issues the groups are best suited to address.

A. Family Groups

Two types of family groups are currently being employed in the treatment of sexual abuse. The first is multiple family therapy which is not widely used but holds much promise when employed in conjunction with other approaches. This type of intervention originally was used with families with members who were frequently hospitalized for mental illness (Laqueur 1972; Laqueur et al. 1964). One of the reasons for the attractiveness of multiple family therapy is its efficient use of resources. Two therapists can serve three to five families rather than a single family, although sessions are usually a little longer, lasting approximately two hours. As is the case with other types of group treatment, individuals help one another. However, there is a richness of therapeutic possibilities in multiple family therapy that is not present in other forms of group treatment. Not only can victims assist one another, and perpetrators and mothers confront one another, but whole families can help whole families or individuals within a family. A mother from one family might confront a father from another, saying, "You're reacting just like my husband did"; or parents from one family can nurture or set limits for children from another. A variety of therapeutic possibilities can also be structured by including families who are at different treatment stages and by composing groups of families with differing strengths and problems or various adaptations and reactions to the sexual abuse. A multiple family group might meet on a monthly basis and would be used in combination with other treatment modalities requiring more frequent client participation. Usually these groups are open-ended with changing memberships. Families might attend five to ten sessions.

Three issues that lend themselves quite well to multiple family therapy are full disclosure of the sexual abuse, the perpetrator taking responsibility for the victimization thereby relieving the victim of that burden, and strategies to prevent recurrence. Although having to talk about the abuse in such a large group would seem daunting for the victim, the presence of and encouragement from other victims can overcome the victim's fears. Likewise, pressure and support from other offenders can assist the target parent in taking responsibility for the sexual abuse. Finally, since all families are in the process of or have already developed a plan to prevent recurrence, they can share ideas for constructing such a plan.

Another kind of family group work is called family outings or family activities (Lilliston 1985). These family groups are larger than the therapy groups and might involve fifty or more people. An agency providing sexual abuse treatment sponsors monthly family projects such as trips to the zoo, visits to museums, picnics, and parties. Therapists and family members join together for these events, but no treatment actually takes place. The purposes of such group activities are several. They enhance the agency in the clients' eyes and can overcome hostility toward being court ordered into treatment. They provide an opportunity for clients to develop social supports. They help families learn how to do something that is fun, and expand families' repertoires of recreational activities. Finally, these events allow clients to see their therapists in another role, as human beings enjoying themselves.

B. Marital Groups

Groups composed of couples, in which one partner sexually abused a child or children, are beginning to be used in treatment of sexual abuse (Giarretto 1982a), and occasionally marital groups are used in situations when the perpetrator is someone other than a parent (Lilliston 1985). However, these groups are most commonly composed of perpetrating and nonperpetrating spouses who wish to remain together or to be reunited. Usually couples' groups are led by male and female cotherapists.

When selecting clients for these groups, it is a good idea to eliminate very dysfunctional couples, who, in the therapists' opinion, are unlikely to regain custody of their children if they remain together. If such partners are desirous of marital treatment, it is better to see them as a marital pair rather than as part of a couples' group. Thus a couples' group is composed of partners who have a good potential for regaining custody of their children.

Another issue in group composition is related to the distribution of power between partners. As noted in chapters 4 and 13 two patterns of dominance have been observed in sexually abusive families—father dominant and mother dominant. It is useful to include both types of couples when composing groups. Although neither pattern is a good role model, the presence of both affords each type of couple opportunities to see that there are alternative power distributions.

Marital groups hold considerable promise as a treatment modality in sexual abuse. Some of the issues discussed in marital-dyad treatment might also be handled in a couples' group, for example marital conflicts and decision-making. Like multiple family groups they provide an optimal environment for parents taking responsibility for the sexual abuse. Offenders will usually represent a range of positions regarding responsibility for the sexual abuse, thus providing numerous possibilities for confrontation and change. The context is also a supportive one for nonperpetrating spouses to gain insight into any contributing role they might have played in the abuse because of the presence of other women in similar situations. Another advantage of couples' groups is the opportunity they offer for collaboration on child management strategies, a common issue in sexually abusive families. Sharing of ideas, successes, and failures with other couples can be quite helpful. In some instances the therapists will take some group time to present didactic material on child development and child management because sexually abusive families lack this background information. Therapists can judiciously employ such material to moderate the overwhelming impact of other topics covered in couples' groups. Finally, such groups give the couple an important reference group. Not only does membership in the group define them as adults separate from their children, a boundary that needs to be reinforced in sexually abusive families, but it provides the marital pair a reference group of people who hope to maintain their marriage despite the sexual abuse. This can be vital because both husband and wife will be subject to multiple pressures to dissolve the marriage as well as self doubts about staying together.

C. Children's Groups

Children's groups are the most widely used form of group intervention in sexual abuse. These groups vary in their purposes and their composition. As to purpose, some groups are primarily educational, focusing, for example, on sex education or prevention of sexual abuse. Others are therapeutic, with the intent of allowing children to express and resolve feelings or to understand and change behavior. Some combine educational and therapeutic goals. Activities may be employed as a context for intervention or as a vehicle for release of tension built up by group discussion. Regardless of the specific purpose and activities of the group, a major benefit is helping the children to appreciate that they are not alone. Thus groups alleviate the pervasive personal isolation often experienced by child victims.

The limited number of victims requiring group treatment at a specific time may raise a question of group composition for some communities. An issue is whether to include victims of both intra and extrafamilial sexual abuse in the same group or to limit group membership to one or the other. The advisability of doing the former will depend upon the scope of the group. For example, groups that focus on what is wrong about sex between children and adults, how this activity makes children feel, and how to prevent it in the future can include both types of cases. If both intrafamilial and extrafamilial victims are involved, it is important to include a spectrum of cases, rather than only cases from the two ends of the continuum (stranger rape and biological father incest). Groups composed of different kinds of incest victims appear to be quite successful as long as the therapist is sensitive to the varying experiences of group members.

Sex and age of children are other major principles of group composition. As a rule groups should be same-sexed. However, with young children, four through six, both sexes may be included in the same group and sometimes both sexes will be included in a latency-aged group. In addition, if children have been sexually abused in the same context—for example, in the same day care center, by the same perpetrator, or in the same family—both boys and girls can be included in the same group.

Age is the other organizing factor for groups for children. As a rule children are divided into three age categories for group composition: adolescents, older latency (9-12), and younger latency (5-8). Groups for children falling into the three age categories will be briefly described. A discussion of three special types of children's groups, sibling groups, foster home groups, and groups for male victims, will follow.

1. *Adolescent groups.* Because adolescence spans several years and involves a range of developmental issues, the therapist needs to be sure the group members are all at about the same developmental stage. Further, since some adolescent victims are quite regressed while others are pseudomature, care needs to be exercised when composing groups.

Adolescent girls tend to react in two somewhat opposing ways to sexual abuse, either with aggressive acting-out behaviors or with self-destructive behaviors. It is very useful to include girls with both reactions in the same group. Not only do they balance one another (a group consisting entirely of angry acting-out adolescents can be quite unmanageable, while one of depressed, withdrawn, suicidal girls can be overwhelming), but the opportunity for victims to see other reactions can be enlightening. Thus depressed girls discover that it's "OK to be mad" while aggressive girls are helped to get in touch with their own depression, which is masked by angry acting out. While some activities are useful with adolescents, the main technique will be group discussion. Sexuality, dating, and the relationship of the sexual abuse to normal sexuality are particularly important issues for adolescent victims. In addition, victim treatment issues discussed in chapter 11 are relevant for group treatment as well.

2. *Late latency-aged groups.* Groups consisting of children in late latency usually combine discussion with group activities. Children of this age cannot tolerate sitting and talking for an hour, especially about a topic that is so emotionally laden as sexual abuse. Activities may be an integral part of the exploration of therapeutic material, such as drawing a picture of the perpetrator, putting it up on the wall, and describing the perpetrator to the group (Berliner and Ernst 1984), or there may be for the purpose of tension release, for example calisthenics. Some activities, like competitive and cooperative games, may provide contexts for dealing with some of the sequelae of sexual abuse, for instance poor peer relationships, cheating and lying, and low self-esteem.

Again the reader is referred to chapter 11, which describes in greater detail treatment issues and techniques for victims. See also Berliner and Ernst (1984) and Mayer (1983) for very helpful discussions of activities to be employed in preadolescent groups.

3. *Groups for early latency-aged children.* The goals for groups of children five to eight will be somewhat different from those with older children. The younger the children, the less developed their social skills and the more oriented they are to caretakers. Therefore, there will be fewer opportunities to utilize children to help one another. In addition, the younger the victims are, the less developed their language, and consequently there will be rather little discussion and more activities. Clinicians have used groups for young children, both victims and their siblings, as an opportunity for socialization (Lilliston 1985). In addition, such groups are useful for imparting information about preventing future sexual abuse and material describing what is wrong about sex between adults and children. Play therapy can be successfully conducted with small groups (three or four members) of young children. However,

in order to avoid situations of parallel play and digression into irrelevant activities, the number of play items available should be limited and co-therapists should be used.

4. *Sibling groups*. Siblings will form a natural group because they have shared experiences. Thus, they will possess a lot of potential for cohesion even though members are at different developmental stages.

The goals for sibling groups are somewhat different from those of the other children's groups discussed. One goal is to address blurred generational boundaries found in many sexually abusive families by treating the children as a group separate from their parents. If there is a parental child victim in the family, the therapist, through intervention in the sibling group, gives a clear message that the victim is also a child. A second goal in sibling groups may be to uncover hitherto hidden victims. A sibling group is a particularly supportive context for revealing victimization. A third, and perhaps the most important, goal of sibling groups is to address hostilities and divisive patterns among siblings. A phenomenon called "incest jealousy" is sometimes found in sexually abusive families. Nonvictims are envious of victims because of the special privileges (bribes) they may have been given to obtain their cooperation or silence. Similarly nonvictims may be angry because of the amount of control victims have had in the family or because of all the attention they received when the sexual abuse was discovered. On the other side, victims may be envious of nonvictims because they were not sexually assaulted and were not damaged in the way victims were. Feelings on both sides can be shared and worked through in sibling groups. The goal of the therapist is to create a strong, supportive, and cohesive unit of siblings who will be able to protect one another from future attempts at sexual abuse and sometimes provide opportunities for nurturing and intimacy not available from the parents. The latter goal is more easily pursued when the age range of siblings is broad.

5. *Foster home groups*. Many victims of sexual abuse are placed in foster care, and often one home will have several such children because relatively few foster parents are willing to take them. Groups composed of children placed in one home, their foster parent(s), and a therapist can be very effective. In addition to pursuing therapeutic goals mentioned for victims in individual and group treatment, foster home groups will have several others. First, foster care has great potential as a total therapeutic environment, but it will not become so automatically. Foster parents and victims must be assisted to make the home therapeutic. Treatment endeavors begun in the group with foster parents present can then be extended into the foster home.

Second, frequently an important issue is setting appropriate limits for physical interaction between adults and children. Victims may avoid interaction with adults of the same sex as the perpetrator including the foster parent, or they may engage in inappropriate interaction with such adults. For example, in one case treated by the author, two female victims, ages 4 and 5, "mooned" their foster father and would sit in the laps of male visitors, stroking them and calling them "my man." Ground rules can be set in the group about appropriate and inappropriate interaction with adults.

A related issue is sexual interaction among victims or between victims and other children in the foster home. This is a very volatile issue because of the feelings it arouses in foster parents. It requires not only making rules but also the institution of safeguards in the foster home to reduce the opportunity for such sexual interaction.

A third issue which can usefully be handled in foster home groups is that of varying reactions to sexual abuse and consequent placement. While such individual differences will be present in other groups, they may be more apparent in foster home situations because of the crisis caused for the child by placement. To mention a few of the possible reactions: some children will worry about their parents; others will be angry at them. Some will blame themselves for the victimization; others will blame the offender or their mother. Some will want to talk about the sexual abuse; others will not. Some will be relieved to be in foster care; others will long to go home.

Finally, a point that perhaps is evident by the inclusion of the foster parent(s) in the group: without support from a therapist, many foster parents could not cope with the stress of working with sexually abused children and would ask that they be removed. The following is a brief description of a foster home group.

> EXAMPLE 3: The group consisted of three female children, one male child, and their foster mother, all of whom had been sexually abused. Mrs. M, the foster mother, was 57 and widowed. She had an abiding desire to help victims of sexual abuse because of her own victimization as a child. One of the children in the group was Alisa, 13, who had been sexually abused by her mother's boyfriend. Her mother had been very unprotective and was an alcoholic. Alisa had a lot of anger toward men in general and her mother's boyfriend in particular. In addition, there was 10 year old Jennifer who wanted to return home. She had been sexually abused by her stepfather but had recanted when she was afraid he would go to jail. The two other children were Jean, 9, who had been sexually abused by her father while her mother looked on, and Jason, 8, who had been sexually abused by both his mother and father.
>
> The precipitating cause for the group was Mrs. M finding Jason and Jean involved in mutual fondling. Her immediate reaction was to blame Jason and ask that he be removed. Since Jason had been with Mrs.

M the longest and had prospered there, the therapist and the foster care worker thought it would be damaging for him to move. It was decided to constitute a group to deal with this issue and others.

After joining with the children and Mrs. M in a board game, the therapist addressed the group by saying that they were a foster family and all families had problems and needed some rules. Further, since all of them had been sexually abused, they had that as a common problem. Mrs. M took the lead by telling the children that she, herself, had been sexually abused and knew how bad that was. She had decided to be a foster parent to help kids have a better life, but especially to help kids who had been sexually abused. She added that she loved them all, and they were all special to her. However, she said she couldn't understand how anyone who hated being sexually abused could sexually abuse another child. Jason became agitated and began to climb up the bookcase. Alisa stopped him and put her arm around him.

The therapist said she wanted to remind them of some things they talked about in individual counseling, that it was OK to touch your own body anywhere, even the private parts, but not to touch other people, especially if others did not want to be touched. Jason then blurted Jean let him and she touched him too. She yelled back, "I did not! Liar!" The therapist said that lots of kids who had been sexually abused got confused about how to show others that they liked them. They did sexual touching instead of telling other people that they liked them or giving them a pat on the back or a hug. These were OK ways to let people know that they were cared for. The therapist asked Alisa to show Jason that she liked him. Alisa said OK and put her arm around Jason's shoulders again, giving him a squeeze and said "You know you're a pretty good kid, Jason. I kind of like having you for my foster brother." The therapist then asked Jennifer to show Mrs. M that she liked her. Jennifer hesitated and said, "I like it when you tuck me in at night. Then I feel safe." Turning to the therapist, Jennifer asked, "Was that right?" The therapist said it was just fine and then said to Jason and Jean, "Now it's your turn." Jason danced nervously around the room and then approached Jean, holding out his hand. They shook hands vigorously. The therapist started to clap and the others followed suit. The therapist then praised Jason and Jean saying they showed a way to be affectionate that she had not even thought of.

The rest of the session was used to develop some ground rules "to keep everybody safe." They included:

1. Each child sleeps in his/her own bed at night.
2. Each child goes to the toilet by him/herself and closes the door when in the bathroom.
3. Each child takes a shower by him/herself.
4. The children would wear a bathrobe if not in their rooms and not dressed.

In the two following sessions the children shared feelings about being at Mrs. M's and about their parents. The therapist required that each

child tell at least one good thing and one bad thing about being at home.
Thereafter the group met occasionally.

This group intervention appeared to be effective in stabilizing the
foster home and enhancing group cohesion among the children. This
type of intervention appears to have much potential for victims who are
placed in care.

6. *Groups for male victims.* Male victims represent 20 percent of
our clinical sample, and some authors think the proportion of males to
females is even higher (Knopp 1982; Porter 1986). They present special
treatment issues often more productively addressed in a group than in-
dividually. Because of their smaller numbers and the emphasis on female
victims in the media, boy victims may feel even more isolated than their
female counterparts (Porter 1986). Unfortunately, because they are a
minority of referred cases, it is often difficult to have enough victims at
approximately the same developmental stage to compose a group.
However an effective intervention choice can be to form a group of boys
who cover a wide age span to deal with issues unique to being a male victim and using other treatment modalities to address other problems.

Several treatment issues appear to be specific to male victims. The
first relates to disclosure. Often male victims have greater difficulty admitting sexual abuse than females. They more frequently deny in the face
of overwhelming evidence. Paradoxically, those who do admit may not
show overt evidence of distress when speaking about what happened.
Thus, the first task of the therapist may be to obtain full statements from
each group member about what he experienced. This may be easier in a
group than in individual treatment because the victim can see that he is
not alone. The second task is to help boys articulate and get in touch with
their feelings about what happened.

Difficulties male victims have in disclosing frequently
relate to a third treatment issue unique to male victims, the impact upon
the boy's sexual identity. Perpetrators are mostly male, meaning the
abuse experienced by males is likely to be homosexual. Many boys fear
they are "queer" because of the sexual abuse. In addition, male victims
seem to be more likely to experience victimization by multiple
perpetrators than girls. (Rogers and Terry 1984), which might reinforce
perceptions that there is something wrong with them. Furthermore, even
when victimized by a female, the abuse has a profound impact on their
sense of masculinity because of their powerlessness (Porter 1986).

The therapist uses the group to convey that the sexual abuse was
something that happened to them rather than something they initiated,
and that it need not have a lasting effect upon their sexual identity. Being
in the presence of other "normal boys" who also have been victimized

can facilitate conveying this point. Unfortunately a response of some male victims to the trauma is identification with the aggressor and victimizing of younger children, often male victims. When this occurs, removing the label of homosexual is much more difficult.

The reason boys have difficulty expressing their feelings about being victimized is related to male socialization. They are taught that men are tough and don't cry. However, the group usually is an excellent context to address this problem because there will be at least one victim who can share his feelings. The therapist's praise of this child frees other victims to react emotionally.

A fourth issue is putting the sexual abuse in the larger context of human sexuality. This task may be complex if victims cover a considerable age span and have varying levels of knowledge about sex. Sometimes a rather general statement such as "these men like little boys instead of grown women" and some discussion of which sexual behaviors were supposed to make the perpetrators feel good and which the victims feel good can address this matter.

A final issue is that boys are more likely to involve themselves in compensatory aggressive behavior, as a conduit for their anger and a context for being control, than girls. As already noted, they may become sexually abusive. They may also physically attack younger children or otherwise victimize them. Sometimes sadistic attacks on animals or destruction of property are reactions. Three strategies can be helpful. The first is to interpret their behavior. "I think you're mad at James, and that's OK. You have every right to be angry at him, but I think you're taking it out on your little brother, and that's not OK. Sometimes people do that when it's too scary to take it out on the person they're really mad at, or they do it to make themselves feel tough and nobody will be able to mistreat them again."

A second strategy is encouraging victims to talk about their anger and to physically take it out on dolls, often anatomically explicit ones, a punching bag, or other toys that facilitate the expression of aggression.

Third, the therapist tries to help them develop more appropriate situations for exerting control in the group and outside. Examples of the latter include having parents enroll children in physical activities such as karate or football, which make them feel less vulnerable and allow for the discharge of aggression (Rogers and Terry 1984).

D. Mothers' Groups

Mothers of victims who are nonperpetrating parents are often seen in a group. While some of these groups are time limited and have a consistent membership others are open-ended and have a changing composition. Often the therapist has little choice in composing mothers' groups because both the population and treatment resources are limited. However, it is usually inappropriate to include mothers who were actual participants in the sexual abuse with those who were not. The same advantage noted in the discussion of composition of marital groups of including persons from both wife-dominant and husband-dominant marriages applies to mothers' groups. It is also helpful to include women whose response to knowledge of the sexual abuse was protective as well as those whose response was not, and to involve mothers who have essentially appropriate relationships with their children as well as those who do not.

The goals of mothers' groups are several. They provide a source of mutual support, and often first names and phone numbers are exchanged to facilitate contact between group sessions. As with victims, mothers' involvement in groups reinforces that they are not alone. A related point is that the group may allow the mother to become more independent of the offender because it provides her a point of reference other than him and helps her see that there are other ways of living and coping than she has thus far experienced. Her participation in the group may help a mother decide that it is better for herself and her children to separate from the father, or it may assist her in setting goals for change in the marital relationship.

A second goal for the group is mutual sharing of past trauma, particularly experiences of being physically abused and neglected, emotionally maltreated, abandoned, placed with relatives, in foster care, or in an institution, and sexually abused. These kinds of trauma are frequent in the backgrounds of mothers of victims. While mothers may deal with past victimization in individual treatment, additional insight and support can be gained by sharing these experiences and feelings about them with others similarly traumatized.

A third treatment issue that can be productively dealt with in the group, and perhaps more so than in other treatment contexts, is mothers' reactions to being told of abuse. Reactions have several aspects. The first is related to accepting the truth of the revelation. While some mothers believe immediately, many do not. The group is an excellent context for the mother to work through this reaction and come to accept the reality of what has happened to her child. A disbelieving mother can be assisted by other mothers who had a similar initial reaction. A second aspect of the mother's reaction is guilt. Many mothers feel they should have known or blame themselves because their children did not confide in them earlier. Other mothers will have been told by their children but disbelieved them or will have ignored what now appear to have been obvious signs. For example, a mother might have come home unexpectedly in the middle of the day and found the husband in the bath with the child and with an erect penis. Yet the mother did not question this behavior at the time. When mothers chastise themselves they can receive the support of others who are or were in the same position. A third aspect of the mothers' reaction is anger. Both the perpetrator and the victim can be the focus of anger, as can the intervening authorities. While the anger can be addressed in individual and dyadic treatment, it may be more profitably handled with others in similar circumstances. Anger can be mediated in the group context so that it can be more appropriately expressed in encounters with the abuser and the child both within and outside treatment.

E. Perpetrators' Groups

Groups can also be useful for perpetrators of sexual abuse. There is some disagreement among professionals regarding how confrontive and structured offenders' groups should be. These differences are related to whether the groups are viewed primarily as treatment groups or as self-help groups. In general, clinicians who are providing service to both sexual abusers of children and rapists of adult women are more confrontive and controlling of group process (Loss and Ross 1983; Wolfe 1981; Knopp 1984); in contrast, those who focus primarily on intrafamilial sexual abuse are more supportive and less structured in their intervention (Giarretto 1982a). In the author's opinion, groups for offenders need to be more structured than those for mothers or victims. Otherwise the group members may take control and engage in nontherapeutic discussion. Examples include blaming others including their wives, the victim, their parents, or their life experience for the sexually abusive behavior, and describing their sexually abusive behavior in ways that excite them sexually. Moreover, for many sexual abusers, control is an issue that must be directly addressed in treatment. They have controlled their children by inducing them to become involved in sexual activity, and many are domineering within their families. It is important that the therapist not let the perpetrator control the therapy in the same way he controls people in his family. Sgroi (1982) makes the point, in arguing for coercive intervention of the courts, that sexual abuse is an abuse of power, and the only way to counteract that abuse is by having more power. A similar argument can be made about the need to firmly control the therapeutic process and make it clear to the perpetrator that he cannot manipulate treatment the way he does other situations.

As with mothers' groups, offenders' groups will vary regarding their length. Some are short-term, for example eight weeks, but usually programs that have short-term groups require men to enroll in subsequent groups (Giarretto 1982a; Boulder County 1983). Others are long-term, lasting two to three years, while still other groups are open-ended (Knopp 1984). Groups may be run by an individual group leader but are more likely to be led by co-therapists. Co-therapists may be two male professionals, male and female professional co-therapists, or a professional and a lay therapist who is a student or a former offender.

Many issues that were discussed in the sections on individual and dyadic treatment are also suitable for group treatment. However, there are three issues which groups are particularly useful in addressing. One is models for male and female behavior. As noted in chapter 3, many men who are sexual abusers may have rigid ideas of male and female roles. Not only do they believe men must be dominant, but they think that it is weak and effeminate to show emotions or to demonstrate affection. These values are likely to be held by men from both husband-dominant and wife-dominant marriages. One advantage of the group is that members will have had a range of experiences, perhaps including egalitarian relationships and ones where they were victimized, which can be productive in changing values of group members. In addition, having male and female co-therapists to model and convey information about more egalitarian relationships can be helpful. Sometimes material provided in the group is supplemented by reading assignments. Finally, often it is useful to bring in mothers and victims, usually not related to group members, to share their feelings about being dominated and victimized and talk about how they would like the relationships in their families to be (Groth and Birnbaum 1979). Thus, one way to begin to change perpetrators' perceptions about family roles is to help them develop some empathy for people who are victimized. Work done in the group on sex roles can then be continued in marital and perpetrator-victim dyad treatment.

A second issue that productively can be addressed in the group is the perpetrator taking responsibility for the sexual abuse. While this is an issue that must be dealt with in the father-daughter dyad and family therapy, often preliminary work must be done to get the father to acknowledge the full extent of the sexual abuse and to accept full responsibility for these acts. Groups of perpetrators often provide a uniquely conducive environment for this process because the group members will be acutely sensitive to manipulations, rationalization, and minimizations. With active group leadership, the group members can be used to confront each other when they engage in these maneuvers.

A final issue for which group work can be particularly helpful is in assisting perpetrators to identify the antecedent behavior patterns that culminate in sexually abusive behavior. As noted in chapter 12, where individual treatment for the father is discussed, one of the ways of helping offenders to stop sexually abusing children is to aid them in discovering chains of events that lead to sexual abuse. Preliminary work may be done in individual sessions but, often because group members will have similar patterns, their input may help refine knowledge about these antecedents. In addition the group can be a resource for generating ways to interrupt the chain of events leading to sexual abuse or to avoid situations where the men will be vulnerable to sexually abusing.

IV. CONCLUSION

This chapter has described the use of family and group treatment in intrafamilial sexual abuse. Three treatment issues that are usually best addressed in family therapy are discussed: improving patterns of family communication, family knowledge and rules about sex, and family coalitions. A variety of different group treatment modalities are described and treatment issues best suited to the modalities are taken up. The discussion covered family groups, marital groups, children's groups, mothers' groups, and perpetrators' groups.

CHAPTER FIFTEEN

Legal Interventions

Donald N. Duquette

I. INTRODUCTION

Legal interventions in child sexual abuse cases include those of law enforcement, child protective services, juvenile court, prosecuting attorney, and the criminal court. Because these agences are accustomed to operating in traditional and separate spheres, child sexual abuse cases present a special challenge. Far too often these several arms of the government which intervene in the life of a child and her family are uncoordinated and may even move at odds with one another. Legal interventions are more likely to be successful (as measured by gaining court jurisdiction or criminal convictions when sought, protecting the child from further abuse from the perpetrator, and avoiding system-inflicted trauma) where a comprehensive coordinated community policy about handling child sexual abuse cases is developed. Clearly spelling out the roles of each of the agencies and institutions and developing protocols which establish the responsibilities of the various actors increase the likelihood that whatever intervention is pursued is a well considered and coordinated one. A coordinated community plan requires the support of judges and lawyers and the development of new techniques for handling child sexual abuse cases in the legal system.

II. INVESTIGATION

The community intervention should not retraumatize the child or cause additional problems. "Above all, do no harm." Several techniques to improve and coordinate the investigation are gaining widespread acceptance. Joint interviews, recorded on videotape, coordinated among child protection, mental health, and court staff may reduce the number of times a child has to be interviewed. A person who needs to know the child's story can merely review the videotape.

The most common application of videotape technology in child sexual abuse cases is to capture the child's first formal statement. The investigative videotape is used strictly as an investigation tool in most communities. However, in some states where special statutes have been passed or hearsay rules have been relaxed, such tapes may possibly be presented at preliminary examination in both juvenile and criminal proceedings, in the juvenile court at trial, or even at the criminal trial as proof that the incidents occurred (American Bar Association House of Delegates May 1985; hereafter ABA 1985). Reasons for videotaping the child's first statement include:

a. The child's memory of the event is still vivid, so the recollection may be richer with detail.
b. In intrafamily incest cases family members often pressure children into changing their stories, thus weakening the strength of the legal case; videotaping the statement preserves the child's initial (and possibly more accurate) version of events.
c. Videotaping may help reduce the number of interviews children must give, thereby allowing them to get on with their lives and minimizing the prospect of testimony that is so well rehearsed that it loses credibility.
d. In states that permit hearsay evidence at the preliminary hearing or before the grand jury, the video could preclude the need for the child's live testimony at these proceedings.
e. Many communities which make extensive use of videotape depositions report a significant increase in the number of pleas entered in criminal and juvenile court actions. Once the accused and his attorney see the statement of the young victim and are able to assess her credibility they seem more amenable to settling the case without trial.

Who should take the child's statement depends upon arrangements made in each individual community. In some communities law enforcement officers are primarily responsible for the videotaped interviews, in others social workers, and in still others physicians or psychologists. The most important point is that the protocol for taking the child's statements, for processing the case, and for dealing with the child's and her family's emotional concerns be clearly agreed upon by the entire community.

Use play, anatomically explicit dolls, and drawings to facilitate the child's communication. Regardless of who interviews the child, the questioner should be skilled in interviewing children, as well as knowledgeable of rules of evidence. Play, anatomically explicit dolls, and drawings are some of the techniques which may facilitate the child's telling an accurate story. Some research suggests that leading questions may elicit answers that are less reliable than a narrative answer (Goodman 1984a). The questioning therefore must not suggest the answers, and the questioner should be careful not to create a climate in which the child feels she must give particular answers to satisfy the adult in control.

A medical examination from a physician well trained in this field is an increasingly valuable component of child sexual abuse investigation as technology becomes more and more sophisticated. Be cautious, however. Inasmuch as the technology of physical exams is changing rapidly, not every physician in a community will be able to perform the medical exam with the same level of skill.

III. PROTECTING THE CHILD

The first priority in child sexual abuse cases, as in all other child abuse cases, is to protect the child. The traditional response of removing the child from her home environment has probably been overused. She may be protected by less drastic means. Assess the strengths of the immediate family: *Who* can protect her within the nuclear family? Is there someone in the extended family or a close family friend? Although removal may be required in many cases, there are also many in which the victim can be protected without foster placement or movement from her school, family, and friends. The least restrictive (most family-like) setting is ideal and required by law for federal funding of foster placements (P.L. 96–272, Adoption Assistance and Child Welfare Act of 1980).

Consider orders keeping the child in her own home under certain terms and conditions calculated to protect her from future harm while disrupting her living environment as little as possible. Such orders may include requiring visits of caseworkers, nurses, and other helping professionals. Consider ordering the removal of the suspected perpetrator from the home. Many juvenile and family courts have the authority to do so if they have the will to exercise it (Arthur 1986).

IV. ROLE OF THE PROSECUTOR

The prosecuting attorney is a key figure in a community's response to child sexual abuse. His leadership can be instrumental in improving the way child witness/victims are handled. By eliciting the advice of physicians and mental health professionals the prosecutor can expand the options available in child sexual abuse cases and improve the overall conviction rate. Madison County (Huntsville), Alabama presents an excellent example of prosecutorial leadership in developing a model community approach to child sexual abuse (Cramer 1985). In 1981 newly elected district attorney Robert E. Cramer, Jr. initiated a team review system that brought together child protective services, assistant district attorneys and law enforcement personnel. With widespread community support, that program expanded by opening a specialized Child Advocacy Center in 1985 in which all contacts with the child by the professionals involved take place. The Child Advocacy Center is meant to be a consistent and safe place for the child. The staff making contact with the child and her family are likewise consistent from contact to contact. The first interviews of the child occur there, as do subsequent meetings with the assistant district attorney and therapists for the child and family. Reporting of child sexual abuse in the Huntsville area and successful prosecution of same increased dramatically between 1981 and 1985 (Cramer 1985).

The prosecutor or district attorney is elected to reflect the community values as to what offenses warrant criminal prosecution. He exercises a prosecutorial discretion over all cases presented to him, including cases of alleged child sexual abuse. Not all transgressions of the criminal law are presented to court, nor are all transgressions prosecuted to their fullest. The prosecutor has discretion in deciding which cases to bring to the courts and what charges to bring against a particular individual. Some prosecutors have developed deferred sentencing programs for various offenders — including perpetrators of child sexual abuse — and the prosecutor decides who should enter those programs. In most jurisdictions the prosecutor also makes recommendations on sentencing.

The prosecuting attorney is in a very important position for coordinating the various aspects of the government intervention in response to child sexual abuse. The efforts of a child protection agency and juvenile court to treat and reunify a family are nullified if a successful criminal prosecution leads to the father's being sentenced to many years in prison. Regardless of what decision is made on pursuing criminal prosecution, treatment, or some combination of court intervention and therapy, the actions of the two courts, juvenile and criminal, must be coordinated with one another and with the mental health services. The prosecuting attorney is in the best position to do this. Some counties have developed a single prosecution unit for family offenses which handles cases in criminal and civil courts. The American Bar Association (ABA) and the Attorney General's Task Force on Family Violence have recommended "vertical prosecution," in which the same prosecutor handles all proceedings arising from a case of child sexual assault whether brought in civil (family or juvenile) court, or in criminal court.

A multidisciplinary team can advise the prosecutor so that the exercise of his discretion is informed from many different perspectives. The American Bar Association has so recommended (ABA 1985). Such a team would advise the prosecutor on the family dynamics in an incest case, the likelihood of rehabilitation of the perpetrator, and the effects on the child and the rest of the family of a vigorous criminal prosecution. The final authority rests on the elected prosecutor, but the decision should be informed from the perspective of considerations other than how well the child will testify and how strong the legal case is. The strength of the legal case is one valid set of considerations—but not the only one.

For example in Erie, Pennsylvania, there exists a community policy or understanding that no criminal prosecution will take place without a conference among the protective services, law enforcement, and the prosecutor's staff (ABA National Legal Resource Center on Child Advocacy and Protection 1981; hereafter ABA 1981). In Madison, Wisconsin, an investigation is carried out in all cases and then a joint multidisciplinary conference is held. A juvenile court petition is filed in all cases of incest. In about 75 percent of the cases the defendant and the family agree to juvenile court jurisdiction and a treatment plan is ordered by the court. Criminal prosecution is deferred under the terms of a carefully drawn contract. If the contract is broken, which happens in 25 percent of the cases, the criminal prosecution is pursued (ABA 1981).

V. CRITERIA FOR DECIDING TO PURSUE CRIMINAL PROSECUTION

In some jurisdictions the decision to pursue criminal prosecution or not turns straightforwardly on the strength of the case. Can sexual abuse be proven? Can the child testify credibly enough? What other supportive and corroborative proofs are there? While these utilitarian considerations of proof are important and a criminal case will obviously not be successful without them, there are other factors which the prosecutor should consider—probably with the assistance of a multidisciplinary team as discussed above.

Consider the relationship of the perpetrator to the victim. What are the characteristics of the perpetrator and the likelihood of rehabilitation? Assess the trauma to the victim resulting from the prosecution: repeated interviews, possibly being placed out of her home, multiple court appearances and the ordeal of cross examination, two, three, or more times. The parents' marriage may be stressed, weakened, or even break up. The mother and father lose work time because of repeated court appearances, adding to the family stresses. The father may leave home or be incarcerated. The family loses his economic support, so that other funds, perhaps public assistance, must be obtained.

Incest and child abuse are against the law. These acts violate our social norms, mores, and values. Technically the offenders are subject to our criminal law and the harshest penalties available under the law. The purposes of the criminal law are: to punish and exact retribution; to protect society by keeping the offender from hurting others; to act as a deterrent to keep others who may contemplate such acts from doing so.

However, rehabilitation is also a goal of the criminal process. A prosecutor might consider the goals of the child protection system, and keep in mind the social values which compete with the punishment and retribution goals of the criminal law.

a. To preserve a stable and healthy home for our children to the greatest extent possible.
b. To *protect* the child victim from further trauma.
c. To stabilize families and to strengthen them.
d. To keep productive citizens working.
e. To rehabilitate offenders whenever possible.

VI. INNOVATIVE APPROACHES TO CRIMINAL PROSECUTION

The choice need not be a stark one between juvenile court (child protection) action or criminal prosecution — i.e., between rehabilitation and punishment. Alternatives are available which allow the community response to be modulated according to the needs of the specific case. Ordinarily such alternatives should be closely coordinated with whatever action is being pursued in the juvenile or family court.

Deferred prosecution provides a pretrial diversion alternative in which criminal proceedings are deferred conditional upon the defendant's performance. If he is successful, the criminal case is dismissed; if not, criminal prosecution is pursued. In some communities deferred prosecution is pursued in concert with juvenile court action (ABA 1981).

At least three considerations support the use of deferred prosecution and other pretrial diversions of *appropriate* offenders from the criminal process: (1) Deferred prosecution relieves congested court dockets and overcrowded prisons for dealing with cases that present a greater danger to the public. (2) Punishment for certain offenders is unlikely to deter future criminal behavior whereas counseling or treatment may help by addressing the real underlying problems. (3) A defendant may be more motivated to cooperate with diversion than counseling as a condition of probation because he wants to avoid a criminal record altogether, reduce public knowledge and embarrassment, and avoid incarceration. Further, deferred prosecution is a reasonably sure thing for a defendant who is offered that alternative. Probation and other postconviction alternatives to prison time depend upon the judge, who may be unwilling to grant such a sentence even in the face of the prosecutor's recommendation.

Diversion is not an end in itself, but a tool to facilitate personal changes in the offender and to protect the child. Nor is diversion the same as decriminalization of the offense. The prosecutor retains the power to press the criminal action should the defendant fail the conditions of the deferral. The defendant waives his right to a speedy trial as a condition of the deferred prosecution. In some communities a written confession is required and kept on file. In others the full investigation is completed and the evidence preserved for later use. If the deferred prosecution is successful, the defendant does not have a criminal record. On the other hand, if the defendant does not comply with the terms of the deferral agreement the criminal prosecution can proceed.

Certain persons are clearly not good candidates for diversion, since they may pose a danger to the same child or other children and may not be amenable to rehabilitation available in the community. Community support for such a program is critical. In one community the ABA reports that 70 percent of the cases in the program result in dismissal, with a 7 percent recidivism rate (ABA 1981).

Although deferred prosecution programs for child sexual abuse cases have considerable merit, they present some risks and a community should proceed with caution. The success of such programs will turn on the care and sophistication in screening and selecting appropriate defendants. Multidisciplinary advice to the prosecuting attorney is essential. Other communities have opted for other approaches out of concern that in a case in which a defendant fails in treatment many months after the initial action was brought, the case could be "cold" and evidence hard to reconstruct. The defendant sometimes persuades family members to retract their statements and not pursue the criminal prosecution.

Delayed sentencing presents another alternative. After entry of a conviction (usually based upon a plea) probation and counseling are pursued as alternatives to prison time. If the defendant is successful, the case is dismissed, if he fails, a formal sentence is entered. Probation may be formally ordered after conviction. If the defendant does not comply with the terms of probation it may be revoked and a different sentence, including prison time, may be entered.

VII. THE CHILD WITNESS

Child sexual abuse cases often result in children being required to give testimony in court. Widespread dissatisfaction exists with how children are dealt with in the justice system. Often they are retraumatized by their experience with the adversarial trial process. In recent years, nearly all states have contemplated or adopted legal reforms intended to ease the burden of the child witnesses.

Courts have greater latitude in protecting child witnesses in civil child protection proceedings than in the criminal process, where many procedural rights of defendants — such as confrontation and public trial — are constitutionally protected. Among the most common protections for child victim/witnesses a community can adopt are the following.

1. *Adopt the federal rule of evidence to presume competence of all witnesses, including children.* Recent psychological research does not support the common view that children are untrustworthy as witnesses (Goodman 1984a; ABA 1985). The legal requirement that a child undergo special questioning by the judge to determine whether she has sufficient intelligence and sense of obligation to tell the truth places another obstacle in the path of the child. The question of competence is easily confused with credibility. Twenty states have followed the federal rules of evidence (Federal Rule of Evidence 601) by presuming the competence of all persons to testify including children. The rule provides in part: "Every person is competent to be a witness except as otherwise provided in these rules ...." The Attorney General's Task Force on Family Violence urges that "Children, regardless of their age, should be presumed to be competent to testify in court. A child's testimony should be allowed into evidence with credibility being determined by the jury."

2. *Require prosecutors' offices to use multidisciplinary teams, carefully prepare children for testimony, and employ "vertical prosecution" where the same prosecutor handles a case from beginning to end.*

A multidisciplinary team consisting of the assistant prosecutor, police, child protective services, mental health professionals, and perhaps other support persons may be able to lessen the trauma of the legal process on children, improve their performance in the court process and achieve successful prosecutions more often. Team members would be specially trained and experienced in investigation, assessment, and prosecution of child sexual abuse cases. The team would utilize "vertical prosecution" in which a single prosecutor handles every stage of the legal proceedings in all courts, civil and criminal. A skilled interviewer might also conduct the initial interviews. The ABA and the Attorney General's Task Force on Family Violence have called for a coordinated team approach and for specialized training.

3. *Develop procedures to coordinate child protection, criminal, and other judicial proceedings in child sexual abuse matters.* In most states at least two level proceedings can be initiated in response to intrafamilial sexual abuse: a criminal proceeding and a civil child protection proceeding in juvenile or family court. Two proceedings, two judges, and two sets of prosecutors often double the stress on the child. The confusion of independent proceedings can result in inefficiencies and conflicting orders. Coordination between criminal and juvenile proceedings has already been instituted in several jurisdictions. In New Orleans, a single prosecutorial team is assigned to handle the criminal and juvenile cases while Madison, Wisconsin, initiated a formal policy of joint decision-making between juvenile and criminal prosecutors (ABA 1981). Des Moines, Iowa, and Orlando, Florida, courts utilize the guardian-ad-litem from the juvenile court to assist the child in criminal court. In Washington County, Vermont, juvenile and criminal proceedings are actually held in the same courtroom at the same time in front of the same judge (Whitcomb et al. 1985).

4. *Allow a support person for the child.* The strange and stressful surroundings and the unfamiliar persons encountered in the legal system can be overwhelming to a child. The unfamiliarity can reduce her ability to testify accurately and may even cause psychological harm. The presence of an emotionally supportive person for the child witness may alleviate these problems. A support person does not necessarily have to be a lawyer or an expert in child psychology. Anyone who makes the child more comfortable could be such a person including a parent, aunt or uncle, teacher, social worker, foster parent, or victim/witness advocate. Consistent with the recommendations of the ABA, many trial judges have used their discretion to permit support persons to help children cope with courtroom appearances (ABA 1985).

5. *Permit use of anatomically explicit dolls and drawings.*

Children often lack the appropriate "adult" sexual terminology to explain what happened to them. With skillful use of anatomically explicit dolls, a child can communicate exactly what physical contact the alleged offender had with her. Anatomically explicit dolls are generally acceptable demonstrative evidence in child abuse cases. A nonverbal or inarticulate child is often better able to explain a traumatic event if given the dolls and asked to show the court what happened using the dolls. The ABA recommends using such dolls and drawings to facilitate the child's testimony. A Texas appellate court recently quoted favorably from the transcript of a trial opinion where the child was permitted to use anatomically explicit dolls (*Alexander v. State,* 692 SW2d 563, 1985). The court ruled that the videotaped testimony of the four-year-old chief witness, made with the aid of anatomically explicit dolls, did not constitute the misuse of leading questions. The Michigan Court of Appeals in *In re Rinesmith* 144 Mich App 475 (1985) upheld the use of such dolls as an aid to a child's communication saying that "the dolls are a tool to permit children to communicate ideas which they are unable to express verbally because they are too young, or anxiety-ridden, or because they lack the vocabulary."

6. *Use a skilled interviewer for child witnesses when appropriate.* An interviewer with special training and experience in the legal and psychological aspects of questioning children may be best able to elicit accurate, reliable, and useful testimony from a child which would be videotaped for use by others in the process. Several countries, including Israel and Germany, require that only specially trained child psychologists interview child witnesses in sexual abuse cases (Goodman 1984b). Several communities have created a group of such interviewers, who may be law enforcement officers, social workers, or psychologists, and established whole programs to facilitate child witnesses (Whitcomb et al. 1985).

7. *Adopt speedy trial rules so that cases involving child witnesses will be expedited.* Besides being confusing for the child victim/witness, the legal system is often painfully slow in resolving cases where children are involved. The consequences of delay are exacerbated by a child's accelerated sense of time and the slowness often heightens the child's anxiety and sometimes leaves the door open for further victimization. If a trial involves a child victim as a witness the judge could expedite the case by carefully weighing each motion or request for continuance or delay against the knowledge that such a motion may have adverse effects on the child. Several states, including California, Colorado, and Wisconsin, have passed laws urging the expediting of trials involving child witnesses. The ABA, the National Conference of the Judiciary, and the Attorney

General's Task Force on Family Violence urge that other states take similar steps.

8. *Eliminate live testimony of a child at the preliminary examination or grand jury stage of criminal actions.* Since these hearings are a creature of statute and not of the constitution there is no federal constitutional right to confront witnesses as there is at trial. A child's testimony at such proceedings could be provided by videotape or through other reliable hearsay statements such as having a police officer or social worker recount what the child told them.

9. *Promote use of videotaped statements of a child at the investigation stage and as a substitute for the child's live testimony under certain conditions.* After making an allegation of sexual abuse for the first time, a child is often required to repeat her story many times to many different and unfamiliar adults. This repetition would tax the endurance and memory capacity of any adult, and even more so a child who has already been traumatized by sexual abuse. Videotape statements at both the investigation and litigation stages can eliminate the need for this repetition. At the investigation stage a statement would be taken from the child for use in all pretrial activities.

At least 16 states provide for the substitution of a videotape deposition of the child for the child's live testimony under certain circumstances (ABA 1985). Commonly the testimony is taken in a small, informal room in which the defendant observes the taking of testimony through a one-way mirror so that he can see and hear the child without being seen or heard by her. Questioning is either conducted by a court appointed expert or by the lawyers in traditional fashion.

10. *Create a specific hearsay exception for child victims of sexual assault.* Particularly in cases of child sexual abuse, the child's out-of-court statements may be the most compelling evidence in support of what actually has happened. The casual, innocent remarks of a child may be very reliable but are usually inadmissible because they do not fall within one of the available categories of hearsay exceptions. A number of authorities have recommended creation of a special hearsay exception for victims of child sexual abuse. The American Bar Association Guidelines for Fair Treatment of Child Witnesses recommend: "At pretrial hearings and in child protection proceedings the court in its discretion, if necessary to avoid the repeated appearance of a child witness, may allow the use of reliable hearsay" (ABA 1985).

Whitcomb et al. (1985) report that at least nine states have passed statutes which create a special exception to the hearsay rule for child sexual abuse victims. The state of Washington allows admission of a statement of a child under ten which is otherwise inadmissible if: the statement provides sufficient indicia of reliability *and* the child either testifies at the proceeding *or* the child is unavailable and there is corroborative evidence of the act (Washington Revised Code 9A.44.120).

11. *Move unnecessary persons out of courtroom and permit press and public and others to view proceedings on closed circuit TV.* A child who must testify in open court is often traumatized from the direct contact with the defendant and from the requirements of having to tell her story to a courtroom full of strangers. Closed circuit transmission of a child's live testimony may protect the child from psychological harm while at the same time safeguarding a defendant's confrontation right. Closed circuit television can broadcast the child's live testimony from a room near the courtroom into the courtroom where it is observed by the defendant, the press, and the public. Persons present in the room with the child would include the prosecuting attorney, the defense attorney, the camera person, a support person for the child and, perhaps, the judge and jury. The camera would be arranged so that all persons in the testimonial room would be visible in the monitors at all times. See the case *New Jersey v. Shepard,* 484 A2d 1330, New Jersey Superior Court, 1984 for an excellent discussion of the use of videotape and closed circuit television and for guidelines on the use and placement of cameras and monitors.

VIII. USE OF EXPERT WITNESSES

Expert witnesses may be used to describe the conceptual ability of children at certain ages and thus their ability to perceive and remember past events and articulate them accurately. An expert may be asked to testify as to the child's ability to understand certain questions put to them (Berliner et al. 1982). Increasingly, expert testimony is admitted to describe common characteristics of children who have been sexually abused. The testimony of an expert as to the child's credibility will ordinarily not be admitted. (See, for example, State v. Middleton 294 Oregon 427). Nor will testimony as to the traits of sexual abusers be admitted. (See, for example, In re Cheryl H. 153 California Appeals 3d 1098, 1984). Testimony as to the characteristics and traits exhibited by sexually abused children is commonly admitted, however. (See, for example, State v. Myers, 349 N.W.2d 606, Minnesota 1984; In re Rinesmith, 144 Mich App 475 [1985]; Berliner et al 1982). Experts are often able to put into perspective for a judge or jury the "child sexual abuse accommodation syndrome" (Summit 1983) including delays in reporting, frequent recantation by victims, and common behaviors of child victims after the trauma.

CONCLUSION

Mental health professionals can be important advocates for sexually abused children facing the legal system. Our society has not responded well to sexual abuse, and our efforts to intervene on behalf of children and to prosecute the offenders have often resulted in even greater trauma to victims than that caused by the original incidents. There are steps that can be taken within a community with the assistance of psychologists, psychiatrists, and social workers which will help judges and lawyers moderate the justice process so that it responds more sensitively to the legitimate special needs of children.

Medical Glossary

Compiled by Mary Steinberg

Acid Phosphatase: A phosphate enzyme active in acid medium; found in prostatic tissue and secretions.

Avulsion: A forcible tearing away of a part of structure.

Colposcope: An instrument originally designed for examination of the tissues of the cervix and vagina by means of a magnifying lens; now also being used to examine the external genitalia in sexual abuse evaluations.

Cribiform: Sieve-like.

Eccentric: Peripheral, off-center.

Edematous: Swollen.

Encopresis: Fecal incontinence not due to illness or organic defect.

Enuresis: Incontinence; involuntry urination.

Erythema: Redness.

Fiberoptic Vaginoscope: An instrument for examining the inner vagina; fiberoptic instruments transmit light by means of bundles of glass or plastic fibers.

Fimbriated: Having finger-like projections.

Focal Liponecrosis: Localized loss of fatty tissue.

Gardenerella Vaginalis: A gram-negative bacteria suspected to be associated with the infection "non-specific vaginitis."

Genital Herpes: Herpes simplex virus infection of the male or female genital region; may be herpes simplex type I or II.

Gluteal Muscles: Muscles of the buttocks.

Huffman-Graves speculum: A form of vaginal speculum.

Hymenal Orifice: The entrance to the vagina; the hymen is the fold of mucous membrane tissue which normally partially covers this entrance.

Hyper (or Hypo) Pigmentation: Increased (or decreased) coloring of the body.

Hyperkeratotic: Overgrowth of the horny layer of the skin; thickening of the skin.

Ischial Tuberosities: The prominent lower portion of the hip bone.

Killian nasal speculum: An instrument for examination of the inner nostrils.

KOH: Potassium hydroxide, a strong base chemical.

K-Y Jelly: A clear gel-like substance used for lubrication.

Labia Majora: The two folds of fatty tissue lying on either side of the vaginal opening and forming the lateral borders of the vulva.

Labial Adhesions: A fibrous band holding together the otherwise separated labia minora.

Lithotomy Position: The dorsosacral position; lying on back with legs elevated and thighs abducted and externally rotated.

405

Mons Pubis: The pubic eminence; the prominent tissue overlying the pubic bone.

Mucosal Tissue: Tissue having the nature of or resembling mucus.

Neovascularization: The process of new vessel growth.

Otoscope: A device for examining the ear.

Pederson Bi-Valved Speculum: A form of two-valved vaginal speculum.

Perianal: Occurring around the anus.

Perineum: The external region between the vulva and anus in a female or between the scrotum and anus in a male.

Periurethral: Occurring around the urethra.

Petechiae: Small purplish hemorrhagic spots on the skin or mucous membranes.

Pharyngitis: Inflammation of the throat.

Posterior Fourchette: The tense band of mucous membrane at the posterior commissure of the vagina, connecting the posterior ends of the labia minora.

Pubococcygeal Muscles: The musculature of the pelvic area; these muscles help support the lower abdominal contents and resist increases in intra-abdominal pressure.

Punctate: Having pinpoint holes or depressions.

Sacrum: The base of the vertebral column (spine); it forms the posterior boundary of the pelvis.

Septate: Having a dividing wall.

Speculum: An instrument for exposing the interior of a passage or cavity of the body.

Symphysis Pubis: The junction of the pubic bones on midline in the front; the bony eminence under the pubic hair.

Synechiae: Any adhesion of parts.

Tanner Stages: A maturational classification system identifying the various stages of sexual development in both males and females, based on the appearance of the axillary hair, pubic hair, and breast tissue.

Toluidine Blue: An aniline dye, indigo color, picked up by cellular nuclei.

Transection: A division by cutting transversely, a cross-section.

Trichomonas Vaginalis: A flagellated parasitic protozoa primarily transmitted by sexual contact, causing vaginitis in females, and urethritis and/or prostatitis in males.

Trichotillomania: The unnatural impulse to pull out one's own hair.

Urethra: The canal for the discharge of urine, extending from the bladder to the outside.

Urogenital Chlamydia: Chlamydial infection of the male or female urinary or genital tract. Chlamydia are obligate intracellular organisms.

Vaginal Introitus: The opening to the vagina.

Vaginismus: Painful spasm of the vagina.

Venereal Warts: Moist reddish elevations on the genitals, cervix, or anus; due to or propagated by sexual contact. Also called condyloma accuminata or verruca accuminata.

Vulva: The external genitalia of a female.

Vulvoganitis: Inflammation of the vulva and vagina.

Wood's Lamp: An ultraviolet light source used to detect fluorescent materials.

References

Abel, G. G., J. V. Becker, J. Cunningham-Rathner, J. Rouleau, M. Kaplan, and J. Reich. 1985. *The Treatment of the Child Molester (A Manual)*.

Abel, G. G., J. V. Becker, N. Murphy, and B. Flanagan. 1981. Identifying Dangerous Child Molesters. In R.B. Stuart, ed. *Violent Behavior: Social Learning Approaches to Prediction, Management, and Treatment*. New York: Brunner/Mazel.

Abel, G. G., M. Mittelman, J. V. Becker. in press. "Sex Offenders: Results of Assessment and Recommendation for Treatment." In H. H. Ben-Aron, S.I. Hucker, and C. D. Webster, eds. *Clinical Criminology: Assessment and Treatment of Criminal Behavior*.

Adoption Assistance and Child Welfare Act of 1980, P.L. 96-272, 42 U.S.C. 627.

Altcheck, A. 1981. "Vulvovaginitis, Vulvar Skin Disease and Pelvic Inflammatory Disease." *Pediatric Clinics of North America* 28(2):397-432.

American Academy of Dermatology Task Force on Pediatric Dermatology. 1984. Genital Warts and Sexual Abuse in Children. *Journal of American Academy of Dermatology* 11:529-530.

American Bar Association National Legal Resource Center on Child Advocacy and Protection. 1981. *Innovations in Prosecution of Child Sexual Abuse Cases*. Washington, D.C.: American Bar Association.

American Bar Association—Criminal Justice Section. 1985. "Recommendations Regarding Guidelines for the Fair Treatment of Child Witnesses in Cases Where Child Abuse is Alleged." Passed by ABA House of Delegates, May 16.

American Humane Association. 1982. *National Analysis of Official Child Neglect and Abuse Reporting 1980*. Denver: American Humane Association.

American Humane Association. 1984. *Highlights of Official Child Neglect and Abuse Reporting 1982*. Denver: American Humane Association.

Andrews, Mary and Robert Boger. eds. 1980. *Michigan Family Sourcebook*. Lansing: College of Human Ecology, Michigan State University.

Arthur, L. G. 1986. "Child Sexual Abuse: Improving the System's Response" in *Juvenile and Family Court Journal*. 37(2):24.

Attorney General's Task Force on Family Violence. 1984. *Final Report* (Sept.), vol. 77.

Awad, Geary. 1976. "A Single-Case Study: Father and Son Incest—a Case Report. "*Journal of Nervous and Mental Disorders* 162(2):135-139.

Bagley, Christopher. 1969. "Incest Behavior and the Incest Taboo." *Social Problems* 16:505-519.

Becker, J. V., J. Cunningham-Rathner, and M. Kaplan. n.d. *Adolescent Sexual Offenders: Demographics, Criminal and Sexual Histories, and Recommendations for Reducing Future Offenses.* New York: New York State Psychiatric Institute, unpublished paper.

Becker, J. V., J. Cunningham-Rathner, and M. Kaplan. 1985. *The Adolescent Sexual Perpetrator,* paper given at the National Conference on Child Abuse and Neglect, Chicago.

Becker, J.V., J. Cunningham-Rathner, and R. Karoussi. In press. "Characteristics of Adolescent Incest Sexual Perpetrators: Preliminary Findings." *Journal of Family Violence.*

Bender, L. and A. Blau. 1952. "The Reaction of Children to Sexual Relations with Adults." *American Journal of Orthopsychiatry,* 22:825-837.

Benoist, Irving. 1977. "Incest: A Selective Review of the Literature." In Carlson and Riebel (1977).

Berlin, Fred. 1983. "Sex Offenders: A Biomedical Perspective and A Status Report on Biomedical Treatment." In Greer and Stuart (1983).

Berliner, Lucy. 1985. "Men Who Molest." On *ABC Frontline,* April 16.

Berliner, Lucy, L. C. Blick, and Josephine Bulkley. 1982. "Expert Testimony on the Dynamics of Intra-family Child Sexual Abuse and Principles of Child Development." In Bulkley, ed. *Child Sexual Abuse and the Law,* p. 166. Washington, D.C.: ABA National Legal Resource Center for Child Advocacy and Protection.

Berliner, Lucy, and Elise Ernst. 1984. "Group Work With PreAdolescent Sexual Assault Victims." In Stuart and Greer (1984).

Biddle, Bruce, and Edwin Thomas. 1966. *Role Theory: Concepts and Practice.* New York: Wiley.

Borgman, Robert. 1984. "Problems of Sexually Abused Girls and Their Treatment." *Social Casework* 182-186.

Boulder County Protective Services, Sexual Abuse Treatment Unit. 1983. Personal Communication, Boulder, Colorado.

Brooks, Barbara. 1982. "Familial Influences in Father-Daughter Incest." *Journal of Psychological Treatment and Evaluation* 4:117-124.

Bulkley, Josephine, ed. 1982. *Child Sexual Abuse and the Law.* Washington, D.C., American Bar Association: National Legal Resource Center for Child Advocacy and Protection.

Burgess, A., N. Groth, L. Holmstrom, and S. Sgroi. 1978. *Sexual Assault of Children and Adolescents.* Lexington, Mass.: Lexington Books.

Cantwell, H. B. 1983. "Vaginal Inspection as it Relates to Child Sexual Abuse in Girls Under Thirteen." *Child Abuse and Neglect* 7:171-176.

Carlson, N. and J. Riebel, eds. 1977. *Treatment of Family Sexual Abuse.* Minneapolis: University of Minnesota: Dept. of Family Practice and Community Health.

Carlson, N. and Riebel, J. 1978. *Family Sexual Abuse: A Resource Manual for Human Services Professionals.* Minneapolis: University of Minnesota Dept. of Family Practice and Community Health.

Carnes, Patrick. 1984. *The Sexual Addiction.* Minneapolis: CompCare Publications.

Cleveland, Dianne. 1986. *Incest: The Story of Three Women*. Lexington, Mass.: Lexington Books.

Committee on Early Childhood Adoption and Dependent Care. 1983. "Gonorrhea in Prepubertal Children." *Pediatrics* 71(4):553.

Concise Oxford Dictionary. 1964. 5th edition, Oxford, England: Clarendon Press.

Conte, Jon. 1985. "The Impact of Child Sexual Abuse." Paper presented at the National Association of Social Workers. Professional Symposium, Chicago. November.

Conte, Jon, and David Shore. 1982. *Social Work and Child Sexual Abuse*. New York: Haworth Press.

Cowell, C. 1981. "The Gynecologic Examination of Infants, Children and Adolescents." *Pediatric Clinics of North America* 28(2):247-266.

Cramer, Robert E. Jr. 1985. The District Attorney as a Mobilizer in a Community Approach to Child Sexual Abuse. *University of Miami Law Review,* November 40:1.

Daro, Deborah and Anne Cohen. 1984. *A Decade of Child Maltreatment and Evaluation Efforts; What We Have Learned*. Paper given at the Second Conference for Family Violence Researchers. Durham, New Hampshire, August.

DeFrancis, Vincent. 1971. *Protecting the Child Victim of Sexual Assault*. Denver: American Humane Association.

DeVine, Raylene. 1980. "Incest: A Review of the Literature." *Sexual Abuse of Children: Selected Readings*. Washington, D.C.: United States Government Printing Office, DHHS Pub # (OHDS) 78-30161.

DeYoung, Mary. 1984. "Counterphobic Behavior in Multiply Molested Children." *Child Welfare* 63(4):333-339.

DeYoung, Mary, 1985. Personal Communication. Grand Rapids, Michigan.

Dietz, Christine and John Craft. 1980. "Family Dynamics of Incest: A New Perspective." *Social Casework* 61:602-609.

Ellerstein, N.S. ed. 1981. *Child Abuse and Neglect: A Medical Reference*. New York: Wiley.

Faller, Kathleen Coulborn and Lucy Bauman. 1980. "Child Abuse and Substance Abuse." *Interdisciplinary Training Module*. Ann Arbor: University of Michigan IPCAN.

Faller, Kathleen Coulborn. 1986. Personal Communication. Ann Arbor.

Finkelhor, David. 1979. *Sexually Victimized Children*. New York: The Free Press.

Finkelhor, David. 1984. *Child Sexual Abuse: New Theory and Research,* New York: The Free Press.

Finkelhor, David et al. 1986. *Sourcebook on Child Sexual Abuse*. Beverly Hills: Sage Publishers.

Flugel, J. C. 1926. *The Psychoanalytic Study of the Family*. London: L. & V. Woolf.

Gagnon, J. H. 1965. "Sexuality and Sexual Learning in the Child." *Psychiatry* 28(3):212-228.

Giarretto, Henry. 1982a. *Integrated Treatment of Child Sexual Abuse: A Treat-*

ment and Training Manual. Palo Alto, Calif.: Science & Behavior Books.

Giarretto, Henry. 1982b. Workshop. *First National Conference on Sexual Victimization of Children,* Washington, D.C.

Goff, Gerald and David Demetrol. 1983. Personal Communication, Ann Arbor, Michigan.

Goodman, Gail. 1984. "The Child Witness." *Journal of Social Isues* (Fall) 40:2.

Goodman, Gail. 1984. "Children's Testimony in Historical Perspective." *Journal of Social Issues* (Fall) 40:9.

Goodwin, Jean. n.d. "Persecution and Gradiosity in Incest Fathers." unpublished manuscript.

Goodwin, Jean. 1982. *Sexual Abuse: Incest Victims and Their Families.* Boston: John Wright.

Goodwin, Jean. 1984. Personal Communication, Denver, Colorado.

Goodwin, Jean, Lawrence Cormier and John Owen. 1983. "Grandfather-Granddaughter Incest: A Trigenerational View." *Child Abuse & Neglect, the International Journal* 7:163-170.

Goodwin, Jean, Doris Sahd, and Richard Rada. 1982. "False Accusations and False Denials of Incest: Clinical Myths and Clinical Realities." In Goodwin (1982).

Goodwin, Jean, Doris Sahd, and Richard Rada. 1980. "Incest Hoax." In Holder (1980).

Gordon, Thomas. 1972. *Parent Effectiveness Training.* New York: Peter A. Wyden.

Gottlieb, Bruce. 1983. *Personal Communication,* Denver, Colorado.

Gottlieb, Bruce. 1980. "Incest: Therapeutic Intervention in a Unique Form of Sexual Abuse." In Warner (1980).

Graziano, Anthony. 1971. *Behavior Therapy With Children.* Chicago: Aldine/Atherton.

Greenberg, Nahman. 1978. "Traumatic Characteristics of Childhood Sexual Abuse." Paper presented at the International Congress on Child Abuse and Neglect. London, September.

Greer, J. and I. Stuart, eds. 1983. *The Sexual Aggressor.* New York: Van Nostrand-Reinhold.

Groth, A.N. 1977. "The Adolescent Sex Offender and His Prey." *International Journal of Offender Therapy and Comparative Criminology* 21(3):249-254.

Groth, A.N. and J. Birnbaum. 1979. *Men Who Rape.* New York: Plenum Press.

Groth, A.N., W.H. Hobson, and T.S. Gary. 1982. "The Child Molester: Clinical Observations." In Conte and Shore (1982).

Gutheil, T. and N. Avery. 1977. "Multiple Overt Incest as a Defense Against Family Loss" *Family Process,* pp. 105-116.

Guttmacher, M. S. 1951. *Sex Offenses.* New York: Norton.

Hammerschlag, M. et al. 1985. "Nonspecific Vaginitis Following Sexual Abuse." *Pediatrics* 75(6):1028-1031.

Heckman, Randall (Probate Judge of Kent County, Michigan). 1986. Personal Communication, Ann Arbor.

Henderson, D. James. 1972. "Incest: A Synthesis of the Data." *Canadian Psychiatric Association Journal* 17:299-313.

Herman, Judith. 1981. *Father-Daughter Incest*. Cambridge: Harvard University Press.

Herman, Judith and Lisa Hirschman. 1980. "Father-Daughter Incest." *Sexual Abuse of Children: Selected Readings*. Washington, DC: Government Printing Office Pub. #(OHDS) 78-30161.

Holder, Wayne, ed. 1980. *Sexual Abuse of Children: Implications for Treatment*. Englewood, Colorado: American Humane Association.

In re Cherl H. 153 Cal. App. 3d 1098, 200 Cal. Rptr 789 (2d Dist. 1984)

In re Rinesmith, 144 Mich App 475 (1985).

Janzen, Curtis. 1979. "Models of Assessing Treatment/Intervention Impact," Conference Workshop. Sexual Victimization of Children: Trauma, Trial, and Treatment, Washington, D.C.

Jason, Janine, S. Williams, A. Burton, and R. Rochat. 1982. "Epidemiologic Differences Between Sexual and Physical Child Abuse." *Journal of the American Medical Association* 247(24):3344-3348.

Jiles, Darrel. 1980. "Problems in the Assessment of Sexual Abuse Referrals." In Holder (1980).

Jones, David. 1985. "False Reports of Sexual Abuse: Do Children Lie?" Paper presented at the Seventh National Conference on Child Abuse and Neglect, Chicago, November.

Jones, David and Mary McQuiston. 1985. *Interviewing the Sexually Abused Child*. Denver, Colorado: The C. Henry Kempe National Center for the Prevention and Treatment of Child Abuse and Neglect.

Justice, B. and R. Justice, 1979. *The Broken Taboo*. New York: Human Sciences Press.

Kadushin, Alfred. 1980. *Child Welfare Services* (3d ed.). New York: MacMillan.

Kaufman, I., A. Peck, and C. Taguri. 1954. "The Family Constellation of Overt Incestuous Relations Between Father and Daughter." *American Journal of Orthopsychiatry* 24:266-279.

Kempe, C. Henry. 1977. "Sexual Abuse: Another Hidden Pediatric Problem." C. Anderson Aldrich Lecture, American Academy of Pediatrics Annual Meeting, New York.

Kempe, C. Henry. 1978. "Sexual Abuse: Another Hidden Pediatric Problem." *Pediatrics* 62(3):382-389.

Kempe, Ruth and C. Henry Kempe. 1984. *The Common Secret*. New York: W. H. Freeman.

Knopp, Fay Honey. 1982. *Remedial Intervention in Adolescent Sex Offenses: Nine Program Descriptions*. Syracuse: The Safer Society Press.

Knopp, Fay Honey. 1985. *Retraining Adult Sex Offenders: Methods and Models*. Syracuse: The Safer Society Press.

Kroth, Jerome. 1979. *Child Sexual Abuse*. Springfield, Indiana: Charles Thomas.

Laqueur, Peter. 1972. "Mechanisms of Change in Multiple Family Therapy. In Clifford Sager and H. Singer-Kaplan eds. *Progress in Group and Family Therapy*. New York: Brunner/Mazel, Publishers, 400-415.

Laqueur, Peter et. al. 1964. "Multiple Family Therapy." In J. H. Masserman, ed. *Current Psychiatric Therapies,* vol. 4. New York: Grune and Stratton.

Lauber, A. A. et al. 1982. "Use of Toluidine Blue for Documentation of Traumatic Intercourse." *Obstetrics and Gynecology* 60(5):644-648.

Laws, D. R. and Candice Osborn. 1983. "How To Build and Operate a Behavioral Laboratory To Evaluate and Treat Sexual Deviance." In Greer, and Stuart (1983).

Leaman, Karen. 1980. "Sexual Abuse: The Reactions of Child and Family." In *Sexual Abuse of Children: Selected Readings.* Washington, D.C.: DHSS Pub. #(OHDS) 78-30161.

Levine, M. 1981. "The Schoolchild with Encopresis." *Pediatrics in Review,* 2(9): 285-290.

Lilliston, Cecilia. 1985. Discussion of the Sexual Abuse Treatment Program at Children's Center, Detroit.

Lloyd, David. 1982. "The Corroboration of Sexual Victimization of Children." In Josephine Bulkley, ed. *Child Sexual Abuse and the Law.* Washington, D.C.: American Bar Association.

Longo, Robert. 1983. "Administering a Comprehensive Sexual Aggressive Treatment Program in a Maximum Security Setting." In Greer and Stuart (1983).

Loss, P. and J.E. Ross. 1983. "Juvenile and Adult Sex Offenders: Treatment Strategies for Offenders in Nonresidential Programs." Workshop sponsored by the Tompkins Co. Sexual Abuse Task Force. Utica, New York, December.

Lukianowicz, N. 1978. "Incest." In Carlson and Riebel (1978).

Lustig, N., J. Dressler, S. Spellman, and T. Murray. 1965. *Incest: A Family Group Survival Pattern.* Los Angeles, Neuropsychiatric Institute: UCLA.

McCarty, Loretta. 1981. "Investigation of Incest: Opportunity To Motivate Families To Seek Help." *Child Welfare* 60(10):679-689.

McDonald, J. M. 1971. *Rape: Offenders and Their Victims.* Springfield, Illinois: Charles Thomas.

McHugh, M. 1985. "Sexual Abuse: Detection and Assessment." *Missing/ Abused* 1(2):3-11.

McMillan, J.A. 1985. "Chlamydia: Unspected, Undiagnosed, Untreated." *Contemporary Pediatrics* (December), pp. 14-28.

McPeek, Phillip. 1985. *Personal Communication,* Detroit.

Machotka, P., F. Pittman, and K. Flomanhaft. 1967. "Incest As A Family Affair." *Family Process* (March) 6(1)98-116.

Masson, Jeffrey. 1984. *The Assault on Truth.* New York: Farrar, Straus, and Giroux.

Masters, William and Virginia Johnson. 1970. *Human Sexual Inadequacy.* Boston: Little, Brown.

May, John. 1978. "Recognizing Intrafamily Sexual Abuse." In Carlson and Riebel (1978).

Maybanks, Sheila and Marvin Bryce, eds. 1979. *Homebased Services for Children and Families.* Springfield, Ill.: Charles Thomas.

Mayer, Adele. 1983. *Incest.* Holmes Beach, Florida: Learning Publications.

Mayer, Adele. 1985. *Sexual Abuse.* Holmes Beach, Florida: Learning Publications.

Meiselman, Karen. 1978. *Incest.* San Francisco: Jossey Bass.

Michigan Protective Services Management Information System Data. 1980–1984. Lansing, Michigan.

Molnar, G. and P. Cameron. 1975. "Incest Syndromes: Observations in a General Hospital Psychiatric Unit." *Canadian Psychiatric Association Journal* 20(5):373-377.

More, N., et al. 1983. "Tags and Bands of the Female External Genitalia in the Newborn Infant." *Clinical Pediatrics* 22(2):122-124.

Nakashima, I. and G. Zakus. 1977. "Incest: Review and Clinical Experience." *Pediatrics* 60(5):696-701.

National Committee for the Prevention of Child Abuse. 1985. *The State of The Child Abuse Problem.* Working Paper 008 (February). Chicago: National Committee for the Prevention of Child Abuse.

National Study of the Incidence of Severity of Child Abuse and Neglect: Executive Summary. 1981. Washington, D.C.: DHHS Pub. #(OHDS) 81-30329.

O'Brien, Michael. 1986. Treatment Programs for Adolescent Sex Offenders. Workshop for the Statewide Advisory Board for Sexual Abuse Programs, Lansing, Michigan.

O'Carroll, Tom. 1980. *Paedophilia: The Radical Case.* London: Peter Owen Limited.

O'Connor, P. and W. Oliver. 1985. "Group A B-hemolytic Streptoccal Vulvovaginitis: A Recurring Problem." *Pediatric Emergency Care* 1(2):94-95.

Paolino, Thomas and Barbara McCrady. 1978. *Marriage and Marital Therapy.* New York: Brunner/Mazel Publishers.

Patterson, G. R. and G. Brodsky. 1966. "A Behavior Modification Programme for a Child with Multiple Problem Behaviors." *Journal of Child Psychology and Psychiatry* 7:277-295.

Paul, D. 1975. The Medical Examination in Sexual Offices. *Med. Sci. Law,* 15:154.

Pierce, Robert and Lois Pierce. 1984. "Race as a Factor in Child Sexual Abuse." Paper given at the *National Conference for Family Violence Researchers,* Durham, N.H.

Pithers, W., J. Marques, C. Gibat, and A. Marlatt. 1983. "Relapse Prevention With Sexual Aggressives: A Self-Control Model of Treatment and Maintenance of Change." In Greer and Stuart (1983).

Pomeroy, C., C. Flax, and C. Wheeler. 1982. *Taking a Sex History.* New York: The Free Press.

Porter, Eugene. 1986. *Treating the Young Male Victim of Sexual Assault.* Syracuse: Safer Society Press.

Quinsey, V. and W. L. Marshall. 1983. "Procedures For Reducing Inappropriate Sexual Arousal: An Evaluation Review." In Greer and Stuart (1983).

Riemer, S. 1940. "A Research Note on Incest." *American Journal of Sociology* 45:554-556.

Roberts, R.E., L. Abrams, and J.R. Finch. 1973. "Delinquent Sexual Behavior Among Adolescents." *Medical Aspects of Human Sexuality* 7(1):162-183.

Rogers, Carl and Tremine Terry. 1984. "Clinical Intervention with Boy Victims of Sexual Abuse." In Stuart and Greer (1984).

Rosen, Raymond and Jeffrey Fracher. 1983. "Tension-Reduction Training in the Treatment of Compulsive Sex Offenders." In Greer and Stuart (1983).

Rush, Florence. 1980. *The Best-Kept Secret*. Englewood Cliffs, N.J.: Prentice-Hall.

Russell, Diana. 1983. "The Incidence and Prevalence of Intrafamilial and Extra-familial Sexual Abuse of Female Children." *Child Abuse and Neglect, The International Journal* 7:133-146.

Russell, Diana. 1986. *The Secret Trauma: Incest in the Lives of Girls and Women*. New York: Basic Books.

Sahd, Doris. 1980. "Psychological Assessment of Sexually Abusing Families and Treatment Implications." In Holder (1980).

Sarles, Richard. 1975. "Incest." *Pediatric Clinics of North America* 22:3.

Scherner, P. 1959. *Rural Criminal Sexuality*. Paris: Masson.

Sgroi, Suzanne. 1982. *Handbook of Clinical Intervention in Child Sexual Abuse*. Lexington, Massachusetts: Lexington Books.

Sheurer, Susan. 1980. Personal Communication, Lansing, Mich.

Silverman, Hirsch. 1972. *Marital Therapy*. Springfield, Illinois: Charles C. Thomas.

Sonden, T. 1936. "Incest Crimes in Sweden and Their Causes." *Acta Psychiatrica et Neurologica* 2:379-401.

Spencer, Joyce. 1978. "Father-Daughter Incest: A Clinical View From the Corrections Field." *Child Welfare* 57(9):581-590.

Stankwitz, Linda. 1985. Personal Communications. Ann Arbor, November.

State v. Middleton 294 Or. 427, 657 P.2d 1215 (1985).

State v. Myers, 349 N.W. 2d 606 (Minn. 1984).

Steil, Janice. 1983. "Marriage: An Unequal Partnership." In Wolman and Stricker (1983).

Stember, Clara Jo. 1980. "Art Therapy: A New Use in the Diagnosis and Treatment of Sexually Abused Children." In *Sexual Abuse of Children: Selected readings*. Washington D.C., Government Printing Office, Publication #(OHDS) 78-30161.

Stern, Maddi-Jane and Linda Meyer. 1980. "Family and Couple Interaction Patterns in Cases of Father/Daughter Incest." In *Sexual Abuse of Children: Selected Readings*. Washington, DC: Government Printing Office, Pub. #(OHDS) 78-30161.

Stovall, Bennie. 1979. Personal Communication. Detroit.

Stuart, Irving and JoAnne Greer, eds. 1984. *Victims of Sexual Aggression: Treatment of Children, Women, and Men*. New York Van Nostrand Reinhold.

Stuart, Richard B. 1980. *Helping Couples Change*. New York: Guilford Press.

Summit, Roland and JoAnn Kryso. 1978. "Sexual Abuse of Children: A Clinical Spectrum." *American Journal of Orthopsychiatry* 48(2):237.

Summit, Roland C. 1983. "The Child Sexual Abuse Accommodation Syndrome." *Child Abuse and Neglect: The International Journal* 7:177.

Teixeira, W.R. 1981. "Hymenal Colposcopic Examination in Sexual Offences." *American Journal of Forensic Medicine and Pathology.*" 2(3):209-215.

"The Scott County Case: How It Grew; Why it Died." (May 26, 1985). *Minneapolis Star Tribune*.

Thomas, Edwin. 1977. *Marital Communication and Decision Making*. New York: The Free Press.

Tormes, Yvonne M. 1969. *Child Victims of Incest*. Englewood, Colorado: American Humane Association.

Tracy, F., H. Donnelly, L. Morgenbesser, and O. McDonald. 1983. "Program Evaluation: Recidivism Research Involving Sex Offenders." In Greer and Stuart (1983).

University of Minnesota Department of Family Practice and Community Health. 1978. *Treatment of Family Sexual Abuse*. Workshop, Minneapolis.

Walters, David. 1975. *Physical and Sexual Abuse of Children: Causes and Treatment*. Bloomington: Indiana University Press.

Warner, C.C., ed. 1980. *Rape and Sexual Assault: Management and Intervention*. Germantown, Md.: Aspen Publications.

Weinberg, S. K. 1955. *Incest Behavior*. New York: Citadel Press.

Weiner, Irving B. 1964. "On Incest: A Survey." *Excerpta Criminologica*, 4:37.

Whitcomb, D., E. R. Shapiro, and L. D. Stellwagen. 1985. *When the Victim is a Child: Issues for Judges and Prosecutors*. U.S. Department of Justice, National Institute of Justice, August.

Wolfe, R. 1981. "Northwest Treatment Associates: An Outpatient Approach to the Treatment of Sex Offenders." *TSA News*, August 19.

Wolman, Benjamin and George Stricker, eds. 1983. *Handbook of Family and Marital Therapy*. New York: Plenum Press.

Woodling, B., J. Evans, and M. Bradbury. 1977. "Sexual Assault: Rape and Molestation." *Clinical Obstetrics and Gynecology* 20(3):509-530.

Woodling, B. and A. Heger. 1986. "The Use of the Colposcope in Diagnosis of Sexual Abuse in the Pediatric Age Group." *Child Abuse and Neglect, The International Journal* 10:111-114.

Woodling, B. and K. Kossoris. 1981. "Sexual Misuse: Rape, Molestation and Incest." *Pediatric Clinics of North America* 28(2):481-500.

Yates, A., L. Beutler, and M. Crago. 1985. "Drawings By Child Victims of Incest." *Child Abuse and Neglect, The International Journal*. 9(2):183-190.

Yorukoglu, A. and J. Kemph. 1966. "Children Not Severely Damaged by Incest With a Parent." *Journal of the American Academy of Child Psychiatry* 5:111-124.

Zaphiris, Alexander. 1978. *Incest: The Family With Two Known Victims*. Englewood, Colorado: American Humane Association.

Index

Page references in *italics* refer to illustrations.

Abdominal pain, 247
Abrasions, 250; of the mouth and genitals, 257
Absence of appropriate sexual partner, 34, 64, 66, 69, 213-14, 341
Abuse: combination of types of, 16, 33; physical, 268, 363 (*see also* Violence, intrafamilial); sexual (*see* Child sexual abuse; Sexual abuse; of substances, (*see* Substance abuse)
Acceptance: of responsibility by perpetrator, 223, 353-55, 359, 370, 379, 390 (*see also* Confession); of sexual role by victim, 113-15
Access to victim, perpetrator's, 195, 226, 350
Accident-prone abuse survivor, 283, 307
Acid phosphatase, 249, 405
Acquaintances, child sexual abuse by, 58-60
Activities: criminal (*see* Criminal activity); esteem-enhancing, 293; for late latency-aged groups, 382; relationship-enhancing, 348-50, 352, 367-68
Adhesions, labial, 259, 405
Admission, *see* Confession
Adolescent groups, treatment in, 381-82
Adolescent perpetrator, 24, 31, 71-76
Adolescent victims, 22; emotional reaction of, 174-75, 306, 307; establishing
Anger: mother's, 344, 359; perpetrator's,

interviewer's relationship with, 157-58; groups for, 381-82
Adoption Assistance and Child Welfare Act of *1980,* 394
Adults Molested as Children, 378
Affect, perpetrator's, toward children, 41-42, 196
Affection, physical, appropriate behavior sexualized, 51, 90, 355-58
Age differential between perpetrator and victim, 61, 71, 210-11
Age of onset, victim's, 26, 51, 61, 69
Aggressive behavior, sexual abuse survivor's, 29, 283, 387; sexual, 283
Alcohol, *see* Substance abuse
Alexander v. State (Texas), 401
Allegation of sexual abuse, 119-22; child's contextual narrative of, 173-76; mother's belief in, 226; validation of, 122-34, 166-68
Alliances, therapeutic: with dual therapists, 326; with perpetrator, 192; young children unable to form, 284
Allies, children's, 136-37
American Bar Association, 393, 395, 396, 400, 401-2; Guidelines for Fair Treatment of Child Witnesses, 402
Anal intercourse, 14-15, 27, 150, 258, 261, 282
Anal penetration, 14-15, 27, 150; forced, 253, 256, *258,* 282. *See also* Anal intercourse
Analingus, 13
17, 64, 96-97, 341; professional's, 7, 9;

417